Mormonism in Transition

Mormonism in Transition

A HISTORY OF
THE LATTER-DAY SAINTS,
1890–1930

Thomas G. Alexander

University of Illinois Press

Urbana and Chicago

Library of Congress Cataloging in Publishing Data

Alexander, Thomas G.
  Mormonism in transition.

  Bibliography: p.
  Includes index.
    1. Church of Jesus Christ of Latter-Day Saints—
History. 2. Mormon Church—History. I. Title.
BX8611.A465 1986   288.3′09   84-22164
ISBN 0-252-01185-6 (alk. paper)

For Brooke, Brenda, Tracy, Mark, and Paul
from a loving father

Contents

Preface

When I undertook this work two problems quickly became evident. First, unlike most of Latter-day Saint history in the nineteenth century, there was no narrative base from which to begin. The last chapters of B. H. Roberts's *Comprehensive History of the Church* were sketchy at best. Some additional detail was supplied by James Allen and Glen Leonard in *The Story of the Latter-day Saints* (Salt Lake City, 1976) and by James Allen and Richard Cowan in *Mormonism in the Twentieth Century* (Provo, Utah, 1964), but the scope of much of the history was unavailable. Secondly, I was faced with a mass of primary sources which could not possibly be summarized and integrated into a single volume. Diaries, minutes, and letters abound from this period from both official and unofficial sources.

Since both problems could not be solved in one moderate-sized volume, the writing involved compromises and selection. In the first place, I believed it was important to provide a basis for further research and study on the history of the church during the early twentieth century. For that reason, I have sacrificed detail in order to provide an insight into general trends, accomplishments, and problems. Secondly, I believed it was necessary, while not neglecting traditional political and administrative history, to provide insights into the social and intellectual life of the Latter-day Saints. How did they take their faith into the world, and what role did their church affiliation and beliefs play in shaping the views of that world? I conceived this problem broadly to include popular and formal culture as well as books and articles by which church members focused on the relationship between their faith and developments in the nation at the time.

Since some of the terminology in the volume will undoubtedly be unfamiliar to many non-Mormons, or "Gentiles," to use late nineteenth- and early twentieth-century parlance, I thought it important to provide some explanation.

Though virtually all males over twelve years of age hold the priesthood, authority in the Church of Jesus Christ of Latter-day Saints is exercised according to an hierarchical structure. The highest officials are general authorities, a term used to designate the principal presiding officers of the church. Below them are the stakes, regional organizations roughly equivalent to a diocese. The lowest local organizations are called wards, roughly equivalent to congregations or parishes.

The chief presiding officers of the church are the First Presidency, consisting of three high priests—a president and two counselors—sustained as Prophets, Seers, and Revelators. The president of the church is the only person authorized to exercise all priesthood authority, or "keys," at any time.

Next in authority is the Council (or Quorum) of Twelve Apostles. This body consists of twelve high priests, the most senior of whom is sustained as president of the quorum. They counsel with the First Presidency and exercise administrative and spiritual authority under the First Presidency's direction. Since the time of Brigham Young, the president of the quorum has succeeded to the presidency of the church on the death of the incumbent president.

The proper form of address for members of the First Presidency is "president," and for members of the Council of the Twelve, "elder."

Next in authority below the Twelve in the period between 1890 and 1930 was the First Council of the Seventy, consisting of seven presidents. They are called especially to preside over missionary work and over the Seventies Quorums of the church and to carry out other administrative responsibility under the direction of the Twelve.

Several others are considered general authorities as well. These include the Presiding Bishopric, consisting of a bishop and two counselors who supervise the temporal affairs of the church, under the direction of the First Presidency. In addition the patriarch to the church, or Presiding Patriarch, supervises the work of patriarchs throughout the church who give special blessings or personal revelations to church members.

The public business of the church is conducted in semiannual general conferences, held in April and October, and at what were in the early twentieth century quarterly stake conferences, held four times a year. At the general conferences members vote on (or vote to "sustain" in church terminology) proposed new general authorities, questions of general church policy, and new revelations. In addition, they are instructed by the general authorities or others designated to address the sessions. At the stake conferences, visited in the early twentieth century by two general authorities, members listened to counsel from church leaders and considered stake business.

All local authorities are lay members with occupations outside the ministry. The stakes are led by a stake presidency (a president and two counselors), who are advised by a stake high council of twelve or more high priests. A bishop with two counselors presides over the ward.

The priesthood is separated into higher (Melchizedek) and lower (Aaronic) divisions, each containing three offices. The offices in the Melchizedek Priesthood are elder, seventy, and high priest. They are not theoretically organized in ascending order, since the office of seventy is a calling for those engaged in missionary work and men are not generally ordained high priests unless they are called to serve in an administrative capacity. This is, however, not always the case, since older elders who have served faithfully, but have not been administrators, will often be ordained high priests. The Aaronic Priesthood offices of deacon, teacher, and priest are listed in ascending order, since each receives more authority to exercise temporal functions within the church.

The auxiliary organizations (Relief Society, Young Ladies [now Young Womens'] and Young Men's Mutual Improvement Associations, Primary Association, and Sunday School) are presided over by a general presidency or superintendency consisting of a president (or superintendent) and two counselors and a general board. The same administrative organization is replicated on the stake and ward level, except that the board on the ward level consists of the teachers in the organization.

In the completion of any work of this scope one is beholden to a large number of people and institutions for various types of assistance. A number of graduate students including Howard A. Christy, Harvard Heath, Jessie Embry, John Bluth, Steve Christiansen, Sharon Smith, and Jerry Lee assisted in research on the project. Howard Christy prepared the notes for an earlier version of the manuscript. Deanne Whitmore, Cindy Callahan, and Natalie Ethington helped with proofreading and typing, and final typing was done by the College of Family, Home, and Social Sciences Faculty Support Center under Marilyn Webb's direction. Lori Warren, Jennifer Dean, and Natalie Ethington helped with liaison with the Support Center. Natalie Ethington prepared the index. William Slaughter assisted with photographs. Leonard Arrington, Davis Bitton, Maureen Ursenbach Beecher, George D. Smith and Klaus Hansen have read versions of the manuscript and provided valuable suggestions for improvement. Jan Shipps and Lowell C. Bennion provided suggestions on an early version, and James Allen read and commented on parts of the work. All of them have provided valuable suggestions, but none is responsible for the final outcome.

The principal manuscript sources were located in the Archives of the Church of Jesus Christ of Latter-day Saints, the Manuscript Department of the Harold B. Lee Library at Brigham Young University, the Western Americana Collection in the Marriott Library at the University of Utah, and the library of the Utah State Historical Society. I appreciate the cooperation and help I received from the staffs of those depositories particularly.

My thanks also to Brigham Young University, especially Dean Martin B. Hickman and the College of Family, Home, and Social Sciences; the Charles Redd Center for Western Studies; and the Research Division for financial support for the research and typing of the project. I received two fellowships from the Historical Department of the Church of Jesus Christ of Latter-day Saints which provided time for research. Lowell Durham of Deseret Book Company provided considerable encouragement for the project, and Elizabeth Dulany and Cynthia Mitchell of University of Illinois Press have been most helpful.

Chapter 13 was previously published in *Dialogue: A Journal of Mormon Thought* and is reproduced here by permission.

Mormonism in Transition

1

The 1890s and the Challenge to the Mormon World View

IN AUGUST AND SEPTEMBER 1890 Wilford Woodruff, prophet, seer, and revelator, and president of the Church of Jesus Christ of Latter-day Saints undertook a psychic and physical journey which marked the end of one phase of Mormon history and ushered in the transition to a second. By 1930 that transition had largely been completed, and as the Mormons celebrated the centennial of their founding, they faced new and different problems. President Woodruff presumably did not know the full extent of the changes which would take place in the next forty years, but by late September he did understand that for the preservation of the Kingdom of God, for which he had worked since 1833, he had to make a number of necessary, if distasteful, decisions.[1]

Woodruff's travels took him through the principal settlements of the Mormon domain.[2] In a journey of 2,400 miles, he traveled through Wyoming, Colorado, Arizona, and New Mexico. Returning to Utah, he visited the Hawaiian colony at Iosepa in Skull Valley, and on September 3 he left for San Francisco. Meeting there with Isaac Trumbo and other California business and political leaders over a two-week period, he reviewed the difficulties which the church had experienced through the previous years and the future prospects for the Mormon people.[3]

Having gathered all the information he could on the problems before him from firsthand visits with the Mormon people and conversations with political leaders interested in Latter-day Saints, he prepared to make a decision. On September 21 he returned to Salt Lake City. On the twenty-fourth he met with his advisors, and by September 25 he knew that he had "arrived at a point in the history of my life as President of the Church of Jesus Christ of Latter-day Saints where I am in the necessity of acting for the Temporal Salvation of the Church." Pressure from the federal government and others had made the current patterns of action untenable, and "after praying to the Lord the feeling inspired by his spirit" he issued what has come to be called the Manifesto, in which he indicated his intention to give up the continued practice of plural marriage and to urge other church members to do the same.[4]

The change Wilford Woodruff inaugurated was a response to his own religious experiences and to pressure from forces outside the Mormon community. Since its early years, the LDS church and people had been subjected to legal and extra-legal persecution. Driven from Missouri and Illinois, they had seen Joseph Smith and his brother Hyrum murdered by Hancock County citizens. Woodruff's predecessor, John Taylor, who had witnessed the murders, had died in Kaysville, a small town north of Salt Lake City, while hiding from United States marshals bent on taking him to trial for practicing plural marriage.[5]

After moving to Utah, the Latter-day Saints had built a community which conjoined church and state, politics, the economy, and society into one whole. In that respect, it was much like the sort of community found in the definitions of Martin Buber and Robert Redfield, since virtually all aspects of life were shared within the group.[6] The Protestant majority in the United States responded with a series of laws, court tests, and political activities designed to break the back of the Mormon community and reshape it in the image of the remainder of the United States. These culminated in the passage of the Edmunds (1882) and Edmunds-Tucker (1887) acts, which disfranchised all polygamists, took control of Utah's Mormon-dominated public school system, abolished the territorial militia, disfranchised Utah women, provided for imprisonment of those practicing plural marriage, and confiscated virtually all the church's property. They insisted that the Latter-day Saints conform to the norms of Victorian America, which allowed religious influence to be exercised on moral questions but generally interdicted extensive church interference—at least by religions considered deviant—in political and economic matters.[7]

These changes did not come easily. An integrated community with its union of church, state, and society was long engrained in Latter-day Saint traditions. It could not be transformed without creating considerable disruption. Where were the Saints to find their fixed points in this moving world? By adopting a program-oriented approach? By concentrating on religion, narrowly defined? By stressing the family instead of community? By emphasizing missionary work? Forced by an unfriendly society to substantially modify the Mormon community, how did the church adjust? As the church members sought to redefine their political role, solve economic difficulties, and alter marriage practices, what were the problems? Opportunities? Strains?

This wrenching was compounded by financial distress of oppressive magnitude caused by the Edmunds-Tucker Act, which confiscated most church properties, and by debts contracted in an effort to continue the expansion of the kingdom and to save members from the effects of the depression of the 1890s. Tithing receipts declined from an average of more than $500,000 a year in the 1880s to approximately $350,000 per year in 1890. As early as 1893, the church began borrowing from stake presidents to try to finance its operations. This became only a stopgap measure, however; by mid-1898 the church stood $2.3 million in debt, principally to bankers outside of Utah.[8]

The situation became intolerable by late 1898, and President Lorenzo Snow moved in two ways to promote the church's solvency. First, to refund the debt, the church issued $1.5 million in 6-percent bonds to replace many short-term loans. The move seemed fiscally sound. Revenues from tithes were estimated at just under $1 million per year at the time, and the value of church property was estimated at $4 to $6 million. The income of the church was increasing at a rate of about 10 percent per year. The bonds were to be retired by pledging $80,000 from tithing revenues—including $30,000 for interest—annually.[9] Second, following in the footsteps of President Woodruff in the late 1880s, President Snow decided to abandon church control of a number of business undertakings, especially in mining and railroad ventures. Woodruff had reversed himself and invested in other enterprises during the depression. Snow shifted again. In December 1899 the Council of the Twelve and other church financial advisors decided to let their claims lapse to the Sterling mining property in Nevada. The loss was more than $300,000 but thought necessary because the property had been unproductive. The Twelve also authorized Heber J. Grant to wind up affairs of the Utah Loan and Trust Company of Ogden, also at a considerable loss.[10]

These efforts to promote increased financial stability had their spiritual side as well. In May 1899 Lorenzo Snow and a large party of general authorities went to St. George, where he promised the Saints that if they would pay their tithing—a full tenth of their incomes—the Lord would "open the windows of heaven" and bless them. On the way home he witnessed to his associates that the Lord had given him a revelation. He admonished them, under covenant, to obey the law of tithing. On June 12 and again on July 2, 1899, in special meetings President Snow and other general authorities emphasized the need for church members to pay a tenth. Brigham Young, Jr., a member of the Council of the Twelve, recorded in his journal that "the spirit of the Lord testified that all this was His mind."[11]

In line with this reemphasis, the Council of the Twelve sought out bishops and stake presidents who were not contributing and "labor[ed] with them kindly . . . help[ed] them to recover lost ground." By 1900 Elder Anthon H. Lund, who said that he once thought that there was a great deal of formality in preaching the word, learned that there was also a great deal of power in it; the preaching had increased tithes from $800,000 to $1.3 million in just one year.[12]

This new emphasis on tithing was for the Latter-day Saints another evidence of the changes in their community since the early years. An early revelation, usually referred to as the Law of Consecration and Stewardship, had required the Saints to consecrate all their property to the Lord, and then to manage properties under a stewardship arrangement. Tithing was a second-best accommodation, "suited to the needs and conditions of the Saints." Even though convinced that the law of tithing was necessary, Brigham Young, Jr., hoped to see the restoration of the Law of Consecration and Stewardship among the Saints. Shortly after Wilford Woodruff's death, Elder Young had a private conversation with Lorenzo Snow in which he expressed his hope that the president would provide for the establishment of consecration preparatory to the redemption of Zion. As late as May 1900 Elder Young contemplated suggesting to the Twelve the necessity of their taking the lead in establishing the United Order, the Utah version of Consecration and Stewardship. President Snow emphasized instead the need to pay tithing to redeem Zion. Thus, the new circumstances in which the members lived required a new revelation of God's will and an abandonment of previous practices.[13]

The changes which undermined the church's financial stability were reflected in politics as well. Although the Woodruff Manifesto, which announced the intention to end plural marriage, presaged eventual political accommodation, it did not at first mean full acceptance of the pluralistic political system characteristic of the United States as a whole. The Manifesto was issued on September 25, 1890; on October 5 the First Presidency met with the Twelve in the Gardo House, a large Victorian mansion constructed for the president of the church, and urged the reelection of John T. Caine, the Mormon-led People's party candidate, as territorial delegate.[14]

By May 1891, however, it had become clear that political solidarity within the church had contributed to the church's difficulties by promoting gentile opposition. In a meeting at the same Gardo House, George Q. Cannon counseled the leadership of the party to disband and to join the organized national parties. Shortly thereafter, Franklin S. Richards, church attorney and People's party chairman, called the leaders together and dissolved the party.[15]

The attempted shift away from a closed community created enormous tension. Almost immediately the spectre of a new set of Mormon-gentile parties appeared, since most Mormons flocked into the Democratic party whereas most non-Mormons were Republican. Cannon counseled against this division, and two of the senior members of the Twelve—Francis M. Lyman and John Henry Smith—together with Joseph F. Smith of the First Presidency became active in support of the Republican party. Because of the power of the GOP in national politics, increased Mormon membership in the Republican party became an important prerequisite to achieving statehood. Thus prominent church leaders who were also Republicans began to move among congregations and individuals calling upon the faithful to follow their file leaders and join the GOP. This created the needed division, but also upset both Mormons and Gentiles.[16]

In abandoning time-honored precepts and practices church leaders seemed inconsistent. In an interview published in the *Salt Lake Times*, June 23, 1891, President Woodruff said that the church would not claim "the right to control the political action of the members of our body." But in private conversation with Brigham Young, Jr., he said that though he was cautious about influencing "his brethren in [political] . . . matters" he was willing to do so "when prompted by others in whom he has the utmost confidence."[17]

Several other factors aided the efforts to promote the Republican party among church members—the Republican position on the tariff, the economic collapse during the Democratic administration of the 1890s, and the need for Republican support if Utah were to achieve statehood. After statehood came in 1896, emergence of the Republican party as the national majority party provided a further motivation for GOP support. This became easier because of the important role played in the mountain West by the mining industry, sheep raising, and beet sugar production. In fact, Democrats were hard pressed to justify the repeal of the Sherman Silver Purchase Act and the inauguration of the Wilson Gorman Tariff, the combined effect of which seemed to have forced the fall in the price of silver, raw wool, and sugar beets. The crippling of Utah home industries—many of which the church had promoted—in the depression of the 1890s hurt the Democratic party.[18]

If the emphasis on governmental paternalism helped the GOP, emphasis on individualism hurt the Democrats in the tightly knit Mormon community. Perhaps the best examples of that injury are the cases of Moses Thatcher of the Council of the Twelve and Brigham H. Roberts of the First Council of the Seventy. At the time of the division into two parties, several of the Twelve, led by Moses Thatcher, proposed that no member of the First Presidency, Council of Twelve, or First Council of the Seventy engage in partisan political activity. Thatcher favored this policy because he opposed a union of church and state. Since Thatcher's views were not generally accepted, he found himself increasingly isolated from the other general authorities not only in his political views but also because of his religious feelings, which did not reflect the consensus of the general authorities.[19]

In light of the views of the majority of the general authorities opposing any rule which prohibited church leaders from participating in politics, Thatcher together with Roberts and Charles W. Penrose, a prominent lay member later called to the Twelve, began to work actively for the Democratic party. This, however, did not sit well with some others because church leaders were attempting to balance Utah's political complexion by having high-ranking authorities recruit for the Republicans. In the fall of 1892 and early 1893 these activities in behalf of the Democrats brought the three under censure by the First Presidency and Twelve, and all were forced to acknowledge their errors and agree to live in harmony. In a speech at the dedication of the Salt Lake Temple in the midst of this dissension, President Woodruff "referred to recent divisions in opinions among the Apostles, and other leading Quorums of the Priesthood, mainly on political matters; and stated that the brethren had sought forgiveness by fasting and prayer; and had been assured of the Lord's continued acceptance."[20]

The harmony of the Salt Lake Temple dedication was short lived, however, and by November 1893 Roberts and Thatcher were "taking exception to" the influence of certain brethren. They complained that

Francis M. Lyman and John Henry Smith of the Council of the Twelve and others were "interfering with the agency of members of the Church" by "going around trying to get Democrats to become Republicans or getting Democrats to vote for certain Republicans." In the political battle which led to statehood, Roberts became a candidate for Congress and Thatcher seemed the front runner for one of the senatorial seats. As the election campaign progressed, in a special priesthood meeting on October 7, 1895, Joseph F. Smith intimated that both candidates had acted wrongly by not consulting ecclesiastical superiors before running. This position seemed to both Roberts and Thatcher to be inconsistent with American political practice and, in addition, to represent the introduction of a new element into ecclesiastical discipline. The new paradigm, they assumed, would allow complete freedom—including freedom from ecclesiastical permission to participate in politics.[21]

By early November 1895 the First Presidency had become increasingly uneasy. The prospects of an open disagreement which might endanger Utah's chances for statehood led President Woodruff to counsel restraint until after Utah entered the Union. In a sense, the church found itself between Scylla and Charybdis. If no ecclesiastical influence had been used to recruit Republicans, it is highly likely not only that the old Mormon-Gentile political alignments would have returned in the form of national parties but that the Republicans would have refused to support the movement for Utah statehood. On the other hand, the use of active church influence to recruit for the Republican party alienated Democrats who had to suffer what they considered unwarranted political insults in the name of ecclesiastical discipline.[22]

The Democratic party lost most offices in the elections in the fall of 1895, but the matter did not rest. Roberts and Thatcher viewed the Republican victory as a temporary setback, and in the interests of political balance both vowed to become candidates again in 1896. But this conflicted with the goal of not running general authorities for major offices. As general conference of April 1896 approached, the First Presidency, the Twelve, and the First Council of the Seventy discussed the matter earnestly. Roberts was questioned on his course and "made a statement justifying himself." Despite his "stubborn disposition" in a series of meetings, on March 26, 1896, Roberts gave full satisfaction and was retained as a seventies president. Elder Thatcher, in the meantime, refused to accept the so-called Political Manifesto which

held that no church officer might run for political office without securing the approval of his ecclesiastical superior, was dropped from the
Twelve, and saved his church membership only by recanting.[23]

In retrospect, the problems which led to the Political Manifesto were
an inevitable clash of two rights. The American political system had
traditionally resisted invasion by ecclesiastical authority. In the view of
Thatcher and Roberts, that tradition protected their political rights and
the church should not interfere. On the other hand, from the time of
Joseph Smith on, the church had found it necessary, in the interest of
survival, to maintain harmony in the community. Church leaders recognized that general authorities should not seek political office, except
in approved circumstances, and that the desired political balance
could be achieved only by giving some edge to the Republicans.

In August 1898 the First Presidency and a group of leading general
authorities agreed that there would be no interference with political
affairs. President Woodruff urged members of the council to remain
true to political divisions and to issues in the political process. Nevertheless, in mid-August 1898 Alfred W. McCune, a marginally active
Mormon who had made a fortune in mining ventures in British Columbia and Montana, asked Heber J. Grant, one of the Twelve Apostles, for assistance in the race for the United States Senate. Grant discussed the matter with Joseph F. Smith and John Henry Smith, and
both admitted that they "did not know of any Democrat they would
sooner see" in the Senate than McCune. While Grant worked for Mc-
Cune, two other apostles, Anthon H. Lund and Francis M. Lyman,
campaigned for Lyman's son-in-law, William H. King. In addition, a
large group of legislators supported James H. Moyle, and a number of
general authorities including President Woodruff supported George Q.
Cannon of the First Presidency. In the subsequent election—senators
at that time were elected by the legislature—the legislators deadlocked.
No senator was elected.[24]

John Henry Smith best summed up the problem when he said that,
given the deadlock over McCune's candidacy, a grave question had
arisen over how to use the political influence of the church for the
good of the people. The central question was not whether the church
would use its political influence but rather under what conditions that
influence should be used.[25] Protestations by Wilford Woodruff and
others announcing the general principle that the church did not interfere with political matters did not alter the fact that the force of cir-

cumstances often brought church leaders to a position where they felt it necessary to exercise influence for what they conceived to be the good of the community. The major problem for them was to exercise good judgment on the prudent and effective use of influence.

The attempt of the church leadership to define its role in politics was further complicated by the events following the 1898 election, in which Brigham H. Roberts was elected congressman from Utah. Carried into Congress in the Democratic landslide of 1898, Roberts, an avowed polygamist and a brilliant and charismatic orator, faced stiff opposition from the people of the United States and also from the Republican majority in the House of Representatives. Petitions against Roberts containing seven million signatures, principally from Evangelical Protestant religious organizations and women's clubs, flooded into Washington. In Utah, a number of Gentile Democrats, led by A. Theodore Schroeder, a Salt Lake lawyer later known, ironically, for his work in support of civil liberties, turned against Roberts.[26] Roberts was excluded from Congress, and another Mormon Democrat, William H. King, took his place in a special election in the spring of 1900. Nevertheless, the scars left by Roberts's expulsion and the other events of the 1900s continued to afflict the Democrats and the church for some time.

In addition to political and economic consequences, the changes of the 1890s had their social effects as well. Roberts had undoubtedly been excluded not because he was a Mormon but rather because he was a polygamist. President Woodruff recognized the sensitivity of the plural marriage issue, and in private conversation and in sworn testimony he insisted that the Manifesto had been a revelation of God's will.[27]

The Manifesto, however, did not change church doctrine, and the response of church members to the new revelation was much like their response to the change in the church's political stance. Like church control of politics, the principle and practice of plural marriage was firmly engrained in the Mormon community, and its alteration even by revelation was difficult. When church members spoke of celestial marriage or read Doctrine and Covenants Section 132, they thought of plurality of wives, not as Latter-day Saints do today, merely of marriage for time and eternity.[28] Under those conditions, and in light of a long history of commitment to "the principle," some members tended to believe that plural marriage was necessary for salvation and exaltation.

These feelings were evident, for instance, in the thought and actions of Elder Marriner W. Merrill, member of the Twelve. On the day of the Manifesto, he wrote that it was the only way to "retain the possession of our Temples and continue the ordinance work for the living and dead." In March 1891, however, he performed a plural marriage for his son Charles E. Merrill and Chloe Hendricks in his capacity as apostle and president of the Logan Temple. A few months after the marriage, he attended quarterly conference with presidents Woodruff, Cannon, and Smith and heard them teach "the people . . . that not only plural marriages had ceased in the church but that Brethren should not live with their plural families hereafter, but observe strictly the law of the land. . . ." Nevertheless, Merrill and at least seven other apostles, some members of the First Presidency, and many church members could not believe that the Lord actually required this. Clearly, considerable time would elapse before all Latter-day Saints would abandon their traditional support of plural marriage.[29]

The uninformed observer could easily view the public protestations coupled with the private continuation of the practice and performance of plural marriage in Mexico, the United States, and Canada as evidence of duplicity on the part of church leaders.[30] In fact, however, any practice once engrained so positively in the public sentiment is difficult to end. Thus, the Mormons' ambivalence about plural marriage, like the other struggles of the 1890s, is indicative of the tension any sensitive person will undoubtedly experience when faced with conflicting loyalties and principles. These were not just personal moral dilemmas. Since these acts were illegal, some people took advantage of lingering sentiments to prosecute those who continued to live with plural wives. Yet the men could hardly abandon their wives. And it was not reasonable to expect them to refrain from having children: some husbands and wives viewed childlessness as contrary to the law of God.[31]

In response to this renewed attack on polygamy, President Snow published an article in the *Deseret News* on January 8, 1900, announcing that the church fully accepted the Woodruff Manifesto, would not sanction new plural marriages, and would discipline members of the church who disobeyed the law of the land. Three days later, the Twelve and the First Presidency sustained, though with some opposition, President Snow's position. Still, a number of church officials continued to act contrary to President Snow's public statement. To try to maintain discipline President Snow found it necessary to be adamant. In response to one request for permission to take a plural wife his answer was "positively and absolutely no." When A. F. McDonald, a leader of the Saints in Mexico, brought a letter to President Snow in which a Mexican member asked him to perform a plural marriage, President Snow's reply was that "no sealings could be performed in Mexico" any more than in the United States.[32]

The statistical evidence also indicates that the number of those in old plural marriages was on the decline. A study made for the First Presidency in 1899 indicated that in 1890 there had been 2,451 polygamists in the United States. By 1899 there were only 1,543 remaining. Of the original number sixty-three had left the United States, ninety-five had been divorced, and 750 had died. The total is somewhat misleading, however, since the number of new polygamous marriages and those living outside the United States is not added to it.[33]

If problems like plural marriage continued to cause considerable difficulty within the church by 1900, some issues were more easily settled. One of these was the question of pacifism, which was resolved essentially during the Spanish American War.[34] At the outbreak of the war, some of the Twelve, including Brigham Young, Jr., took the view that Mormons were not justified in joining the conflict. To Elder Young, this was a foreign war, undeclared by God and thus not within the province of Latter-day Saints. This view was not shared by many of the other general authorities, however, and was particularly opposed by Joseph F. Smith and George Q. Cannon of the First Presidency. Following a discussion by the First Presidency and the Twelve, Elder Young was obliged to surrender his views, and the position of the First Presidency that loyalty to the nation was a necessary corollary of active church membership was made clear. With that loyalty came the obligation to serve in the armed forces if called upon to do so.

On the surface, this seemed like a small point for American citizens, but its implications for the doctrine of the Kingdom of God were enormous. Though Utah did not secede during the Civil War, for instance, the attitude of the general authorities was essentially millennial: they expected the Civil War to usher in the calamities predicted before the Second Coming. Mormons were not encouraged to join the armed services, and the only unit recruited in Utah was a small militia contingent used to guard the overland mail route for a few weeks. By 1898, however, with some abatement in the feeling of the immediacy of the millennium, participation in national policies presupposed loyalty to the government rather than simply tolerance of its existence. And for most Latter-day Saints, it was much easier to shift political loyalties to the United States government and accept military service in defense of that government than to give up a long engrained practice like plural marriage.

In a real sense, the Latter-day Saints faced problems similar to those suggested by Thomas S. Kuhn in his discussion of the history of science. Kuhn suggests that when one paradigm or means of understanding and interpreting evidence from the physical world fails to answer questions thought most important, a scientist or group of scientists will suggest a new formulation that supplies the answers.[35] Conditions during the period of the 1890s constituted for the Latter-day Saints a challenge to the paradigm under which they had operated at least since 1847. The previous paradigm necessitated the integration of religion, politics, society, and the economy into a single non-pluralistic community and adopted polygamy as a means of solving the traditional problem of the marriage relationship. This was simply unacceptable to Victorian America, so in the 1890s the Mormons began groping for a new paradigm that would save essential characteristics of their religious tradition, provide sufficient political stability to preserve the interests of the church, and allow them to live in peace with other Americans. Unlike the scientific revolutions about which Kuhn has written, the changes did not involve the adoption of a completely new world view. They did, however, require the abandonment or change of much that Mormons had considered essential before, including plural marriage, a church-controlled political party, and church domination of the public schools. The changes also required a revised definition of obligations that often involved reaching back into the Mormon past to reemphasize certain doctrines or practices that had been relatively dormant, such as the Word of Wisdom, a set of health regulations requiring abstinence from tea, coffee, liquor, and tobacco, and increased genealogical and temple work that drew faithful members into contemplation of their ancestors and into sacred space on a regular basis. It also brought about the adoption of a number of features of contemporary American society such as extensive recreational and athletic activities for young people within a church setting, and modern accounting and auditing procedures. But no solution could save all of the old paradigm. As Kuhn pointed out: "No paradigm ever solves all the problems it defines and since no two paradigms leave all the same problems unsolved, paradigm debates always involve the question: Which problems is it more significant to have solved?"[36] The following chapters try to explain those things that were solved and those that were not.

Since the changes which took place after 1890 involved some wrenching in the Mormon community, the Saints faced a problem Peter L. Berger has called "world maintenance." Specifically, the church leaders and members had to ensure "continuing consensus concerning the most important features of the social world."[37] Mormons faced the difficulty of legitimizing the changes which were taking place. Hardest were probably the attitudes on politics and marriage. For that reason, the following chapters consider those problems first. Though not too difficult to solve, the problem of business relations and adapting to the market economy posed a considerable public relations problem. Internal revitalization and administrative reorganization created some difficulty. Reconciling the cooperative attitudes of the nineteenth century with increased individualism in the twentieth required some internal accommodation. Organizing an educational system to replace the domination of the public schools brought about some innovations, some of which were adopted from contemporary American society. Somewhat less difficult was the change in dietary regulations. Some of the doctrinal redefinitions were extremely difficult, and others were easily accepted by the church members. Some things such as missionary work required little, if any, change.

2

The Search for
a Pluralistic Political System,
1900–1911

EVEN THOUGH FEW THINGS caused the LDS church as much difficulty during the nineteenth century as single party politics, the attempt to create a two-party system became a source of strain within the Mormon community and between Mormons and Gentiles. These problems developed in part from the attempt of some Mormon leaders to reward friends and punish enemies of the church. Thomas Kearns, for instance, fit into both categories at different times. The church and the nation also had to determine whether a prince in God's kingdom had to remain a second-class citizen in Caesar's. The B. H. Roberts case, mentioned in the last chapter, and the Reed Smoot case to be considered below fall into that category. In part, also, these problems developed because of differing perceptions of the degree to which the church had lived up to the tacit agreements made at Utah statehood. Such problems as new and continued plural marriage, church influence in politics, and church control of social and economic life fell into this category. In the period from 1900 to 1911 political differences within the church and in the relationship between Mormons and Gentiles provided too much strain for the new pluralistic system to hold.

Nevertheless, some progress was made. One success came in the Senate seating of Reed Smoot and the assurance of relatively equal protection of the law for all Mormons. Another was the development of sufficient bipartisan and nonsectarian cooperation to wipe the last successful vestiges of the anti-Mormon political party—the American party—from the Utah scene. Perhaps most important, however, was the manner in which church leaders reexamined the question of what responsibilities active citizenship in the United States dictated in regard to previous questions like plural marriage and the nature and obligations of subjects of the Kingdom of God.

Undoubtedly the central event in Mormon politics during the first decade of the twentieth century was the attempt of Apostle-Senator Reed Smoot to retain his seat in the United States Senate. The questions raised in the case prompted a full-scale investigation of Mormonism's current affairs and raised issues covering the full spectrum of American political practice: What was the proper role of a religious organization in American politics? Can a public official carry loyalties to leadership roles in both a church and the state? To what degree is a religious organization justified in supporting or opposing various candidates or in taking positions on issues of public policy? Are a church organization and machine politics compatible? How do political leaders respond to the influence and power of a religious organization?

The story of the Reed Smoot investigation begins in 1900 with Smoot's call to the Council of the Twelve and the growth of a business relationship with Thomas Kearns.[1] At the same time, discussion ensued on the upcoming senatorial election. Several members of the Council of Twelve thought it best not to send an apostle. Smoot himself consulted with William McKinley and other national leaders who advised against electing an apostle. After careful consideration, the church leadership decided against Smoot's candidacy in December 1900.[2]

On January 2, 1901, Kearns announced his candidacy, and on January 3 a majority of the First Presidency and Twelve thought that Kearns ought to serve since they now thought he could do most for the state. Nevertheless, Kearns was known to be a rude, uneducated man, and, as the cultured Anthon H. Lund put it: "what a man to send east! It will be a bitter pill for many to swallow." Lorenzo Snow said that he favored Kearns, "but laid no obligation on any one to work for him." Kearns was, however, a likely choice since he had demonstrated a willingness to work with the church leaders in both political and business matters. After a victory over William S. McCornick in the Republican caucus, Kearns won the legislative ballot.[3]

Even though leaders in the highest councils had supported Kearns, some Mormons and Gentiles were upset with his election. The *Salt Lake Tribune*, for instance, charged church influence in a bargain on the polygamy question, and Mormon businessman George M. Cannon, a nephew of George Q. Cannon, complained that President Snow had told him (Cannon) earlier that he had no objections to Cannon's candidacy.[4] In this connection, he had undoubtedly assumed, following the old paradigm, that permission to run was tantamount to church support.

Both the 1901 and 1903 senatorial elections revealed an important consideration in church politics. In practice it generally made little difference whether or not the First Presidency officially authorized a campaign on behalf of a particular candidate. What mattered, rather, was the perception of the church membership on the question. Such a perception seemed almost invariably to have had the effect of dividing the electorate both inside and outside the church and of promoting bitterness. Some church members, upon hearing a rumor that a candidate was the preference of some general authority, perceived it as a religious obligation to vote for that candidate whether his views corresponded to their interests or not. This was certainly more the case when a prominent churchman was running for office or when a member of the general authorities actively supported a particular candidate, as Lorenzo Snow did in 1901.

A similar situation occurred in the 1903 Utah senatorial election when Smoot received permission and announced his candidacy. As early as January 1902 a number of the general authorities actively supported Smoot. Though letters which passed between Smoot and Kearns in February and March 1902 indicate an understanding that Kearns would support Smoot, Kearns had some misgivings about the idea of an apostle-senator. Kearns thought that the Roosevelt administration would veto Smoot's candidacy and that Congress would refuse to seat him. Questions about the candidacy surfaced from such diverse sources as the *Salt Lake Tribune*, *Goodwin's Weekly*, the *Salt Lake Herald*, and the Salt Lake Ministerial Association.[5]

Smoot was linked to Kearns in the public mind, and his victory in the state convention was seen as the success of the Kearns-Smoot faction over the George Sutherland–Joseph Howell bloc. Nevertheless, by early January 1903 Thomas Kearns openly opposed Smoot's election. Kearns appealed fruitlessly to John Henry Smith to join "in knocking Reed Smoot out." Conferences between Kearns and Theodore Roosevelt led to the president's announced opposition to the apostle.[6]

In the meantime Reed Smoot had built local support. Though Joseph F. Smith denied that the church had "interfered" in politics, on November 14 members of the First Presidency discussed Smoot's candidacy and were generally favorable. John R. Winder, counselor in the

First Presidency and a Democrat, was reported as "eager" to have Smoot in the Senate. By November 21 Joseph Howell, newly elected to Congress, announced that he favored Smoot's candidacy. On December 19 the Reverend Alfred H. Henry of the Methodist church defended Smoot's position, and on January 2, 1903, a large group of Provo Gentiles indicated support for Smoot.[7]

Given the electoral shift toward the Republican party after 1900 and the generally conceded view that Smoot's election was popular with the majority, some of the methods used by Republican Mormons to intimidate Democratic Mormons seem gratuitous. Examples include pressure on the hypersensitive Frank J. Cannon, son of the late George Q. Cannon and state Democratic party chairman, and on the proud and loyal James H. Moyle, a Democratic party leader and stake high councilman. Neither of these, however, made a public protestation at the time, though both commented in retrospect.[8]

Although neither Cannon nor Moyle wished to deny the apostle his rightfully won seat, after Smoot's election a group of Salt Lake City businessmen, lawyers, and ministers sent a formal protest, thereby beginning what may have been the longest and most thorough investigation of any religious body in the history of the United States. Led by E. B. Critchlow, a prominent Salt Lake City lawyer, the group included W. M. Paden, pastor of the First Presbyterian Church of Salt Lake City; P. L. Williams, general counsel of the Oregon Short Line Railroad; E. W. Wilson, cashier of the Commercial National Bank; Charles C. Goodwin, for twenty years editor of the *Salt Lake Tribune*; W. A. Nelden, president of a wholesale drug company; Clarence T. Brown, pastor of the Congregational church; Ezra Thompson, mining investor and former mayor of Salt Lake City; J. J. Corum, a Salt Lake City real estate agent; George R. Hancock, a mining superintendent; W. Mont Ferry, a mining investor; J. L. Leilich, superintendent of Utah missions of the Methodist Episcopal church; Harry C. Hill, a businessman; C. E. Allen, general manager of the United States Mining Company; George M. Scott, businessman and former mayor; S. H. Lewis, master in chancery for the U.S. court; H. G. McMillan, entrepreneur and mining investor; and Abiel Leonard, bishop of the Protestant Episcopal church diocese of Utah. The leaders in the group were Critchlow, who actually wrote the protest, and Paden, who researched the information in it.[9]

Though the issues became somewhat clouded as the hearings proceeded, the first page of the protest spelled out the central complaint. The Senate should not seat Smoot, the protestors said, because he was "one of a self-perpetuating body of fifteen men, who constitute the ruling authorities of the Church of Jesus Christ of Latter-day Saints, or 'Mormon' Church, claim supreme authority, divinely sanctioned, to shape the belief and control the conduct of those under them in all matters whatsoever, civil and religious, temporal and spiritual, and who thus, uniting in themselves authority in church and state, do so exercise the same as to inculcate and encourage a belief in polygamy and polygamous cohabitation." The protesters then went on to spell out the evidence for their case in what constituted the first twenty-five pages of the official proceedings. They charged Smoot with "no offense recognizable by law." Nor, they said, "do we seek to put him in jeopardy of his liberty or his property." What they claimed, however, was that any obligation he might take to defend the Constitution "must be as threads of tow [flax] compared with covenants which bind his intellect, his will, and his affections" to the church. Nevertheless, the protesters emphasized that they did not question the right of any lay member of the church to serve in Congress. Their concern was merely over a general authority holding such a position. One of the protesters, the Reverend Mr. Leilich, charged that Smoot was a polygamist. This charge was never seriously considered by the Senate.[10]

In response to the petition, the Senate appointed a committee of nine Republicans and five Democrats to investigate Smoot and to recommend further action to the Senate. The case was not finally resolved until 1907, but in the meantime, Smoot, unlike Roberts, was allowed to take his seat. Though the membership changed over time Republicans on the original committee were Julius C. Burrows of Michigan, chairman; George F. Hoar of Massachusetts; Louis E. McComas of Maryland; Joseph B. Foraker of Ohio; Chauncy M. Depew of New York; Albert J. Beveridge of Indiana; William P. Dillingham of Vermont; Albert J. Hopkins of Illinois; and Philander C. Knox of Pennsylvania. Democratic members were Edmund W. Pettus of Alabama; Fred T. Dubois of Idaho; Joseph W. Bailey of Texas; Lee S. Overman of North Carolina; and James P. Clarke of Arkansas. Chief council for the committee was Robert W. Tayler, former congressman from Ohio, who had been B. H. Roberts's chief nemesis.

The Senate received other petitions in the case. Senator Burrows estimated that petitions opposing Smoot may have contained as many as four million signatures. Protests poured in from various groups throughout the nation, particularly patriotic, Evangelical Protestant, and women's groups. Newspapers and other organs of public opinion lined up both for and against Smoot.[11]

Leilich's patently false charges, apparently researched by Charles M. Owen, a Salt Lake City attorney and anti-Mormon crusader, helped rally support behind the apostle-senator. As early as February 28, 1903, Anthon H. Lund realized that "this charge of Leilich is proving a boomerang." It seems to have hurt Smoot among women's groups and Evangelical missionary organizations, two groups already generally opposed to him, but to have helped him among those groups supporting civil liberties. Even the Methodist church, embarrassed by Leilich's charge, transferred him from Utah to Scranton, Pennsylvania. The Utah Ministerial Association and the other protestors also hastened to disassociate themselves from the allegations.[12]

As the new session of Congress approached in late 1903, the First Presidency of the church and Smoot recognized the seriousness of his position and began to undertake thorough preparations. In early November, the First Presidency assigned Franklin S. Richards, the church's attorney, to help research the case. Presentation to the committee was left to A. S. Worthington, "a constitutional lawyer of national repute, familiar with legislative procedure and the rules and precedents governing the qualifications and elections of senators." Waldemar Van Cott of Salt Lake City joined him as cocounsel.[13]

Smoot believed that much from the church's distant past would be revived and that the committee would try to disfranchise all Mormons.[14] However, a careful reading of the proceedings of the Senate committee shows that the committee was concerned with recent church practice and belief, not with the distant past or with the politics of lay members.

In answering the charges, Smoot and his attorneys tried to limit the scope of the hearings. He said that only two conditions could legally bar him from holding his Senate seat—first, that he, himself, was violating the law by practicing polygamy, and, second, that he was bound by some oath or obligation inconsistent with the oath required by the Constitution. He denied both charges. The leaders of the church, he said, claim no authority, "either divinely sanctioned or otherwise, to shape the belief or control the conduct of those under them in all or any matters, civil or temporal." He said, however, "that the First Presi-

dency of . . . [the church] is vested with supreme authority in all
things spiritual and in all things temporal, so far as temporal things
pertain to the affairs of . . . [the church], and not otherwise." Van Cott
indicated that in "the Mormon Church there are men who are wise
and men who are very unwise"; this, however, was irrelevant. The
committee, he argued, could not prove that Smoot was breaking the
law or that he approved of law breaking simply because some of his
coreligionists did.[15]

Perhaps most crucial to Smoot's defense was the position taken by
Worthington on the day the hearings opened. In response to a question
raised by Senator Hoar, Worthington denied that Smoot's religious beliefs ought to be raised at all. Whether he believed in counterfeiting or
burning witches or anything else, Worthington argued, was irrelevant.
Anyone can believe "all they please, and the State never interferes with
them. It has no right to interfere with them. It protects their belief. It
does not make any difference what they believe." The protestors, he
pointed out, had accused Smoot of no illegal act. Proof of such an act,
he argued, was necessary for expulsion. Smoot's abstract belief in the
rightness of polygamy was not at issue. What the committee had to
prove was nothing less than "criminal conspiracy to violate the laws of
the State and the ordinance of agreement under which Utah was admitted into the Union." Beyond this, he argued, since Smoot did not
become a member of the church's governing body until 1900, evidence
relating to the period before that time was irrelevant.[16]

The most damaging revelations in the hearings seem to have been
those of the continued practice of polygamy among church members
and political, economic, and social "interference" by church officials.
Some of these bear emphasizing here. Joseph F. Smith's testimony on
a number of points immediately raised these questions. He admitted
that he had cohabited with all five of his wives since the Manifesto and
that he had continued to do so. He denied that any new plural marriages had been approved by the church since the Manifesto. He said
that he had received no revelations since becoming church president
but agreed that he was the one individual on earth entitled to receive
them.[17]

Some journalists thought Smith's testimony showed lack of faith on
the part of the Mormon people with the government of the United
States; some branded Mormon leaders as insincere and untruthful.
Even Senator Hoar, who supported Smoot, thought the church lead-

ership's attitude ambiguous. Why was Moses Thatcher disciplined for being out of harmony when "President Smith is out of harmony with this accepted revelation to the church [The Woodruff Manifesto] . . . and is sustained?" To counter this feeling, Senator Smoot wanted an announcement at the April conference that President Smith was in obedience to the law and that he counseled others to obey as well.[18]

Smoot passed on the views of Senator Hoar to President Smith, who responded that as far as he was concerned he had "never broken a law of God to my knowledge in my life." He said that he did not testify that he had. He had, as far as he knew broken "but one law of my country, and that law is against my conscience and against good morals, so far as I am concerned. This is the law against living with my family whom I took before the law was enacted." He said also that his case was different from the Thatcher case since Thatcher had transgressed a law of the church.[19]

President Smith defended his testimony to various church members. On the question of new plural marriages, President Smith told Smoot the same thing he had told the Senate committee: he "did not believe that any such marriages had taken place, and certainly had not [received] the sanction of the Presidency of the Church." In addition, he insisted on the truthfulness of his testimony on both polygamous cohabitation and continuous revelation. In spite of what the amnesty proclamations and hearings before the master in chancery in the 1890s had indicated, he said that the deal with the federal government was that those already living in plural marriage might continue to do so. No new marriages, he said, had taken place with the consent of the First Presidency. In addition, he said, his statement on continuous relevations was correct. He had received no personal revelations since becoming president of the church. His guidance for directing the church had come through impressions of the spirit.[20]

Undoubtedly, the greatest national attention focused on the question of cohabitation and plural marriage. On November 4, 1903, in a speech before the student body of the University of Utah, Heber J. Grant declared that he would give $150 to the university's alumni fund—$50 for himself and $50 for each of his two wives. After the applause and laughter which followed, he said, "Yes, I have two wives and the only reason I haven't got another is because the government won't let me." Elder Grant had already been called as president of the European Mission, and he and his family left shortly after that.[21] The remark, which the national press reported, caused such an uproar that Smoot found that "the whole criticism is laid at the door of the church and myself." As Smoot put it, "The American people will not make a distinction between unlawful cohabitation and polygamy." He had already tried to explain the difference to some rather sophisticated senators, but they had not understood. Nevertheless, there were Gentiles in Utah who understood and who agreed that the community generally accepted the old plural marriages, while many who may have understood thought the distinction irrelevant.[22]

Beyond this, some church leaders feared that some newly contracted plural marriages, authorized or not, would prove embarrassing. Anthon H. Lund wrote that his "mind is much agitated on account of the Smoot trial. I fear that there are more cases of late plural marriages than has been believed by us. There seems to be rumors of such all over."[23] Throughout the hearings, church leaders testified they were ignorant of new plural marriages, but their credibility was impaired because at least four key apostles charged with new polygamy did not appear. Two of them, Marriner W. Merrill and George Teasdale, were too ill during most of the period to travel. The two apostles whose testimony was most sought, John W. Taylor and Matthias F. Cowley, were relatively vigorous, but they successfully avoided subpoenas. Chairman Burrows asked President Smith to use his influence to secure the appearance of the two men. Insisting that this was a political and not an ecclesiastical matter, President Smith refused to require their attendance. He asked them to appear, but they refused to do so voluntarily. Burrows was angry, but, in retrospect, it appears that Smith took the only consistent position he could. Had he exercised ecclesiastic power to force them to appear before the Senate committee, he would, in effect, have been admitting that the protesters were right and that the church did exercise secular power in all matters.[24]

Another question of considerable importance in the Smoot case was the use of church influence in politics. It seems impossible from the perspective of the 1980s to argue that church leaders and thus "the church" were not involved in political affairs. The only question open today is the degree of the involvement and whether it was crucial in elections and other political decisions. In the first decade of the twentieth century, however, the question was asked much differently. Some of the Senate committee took the view that since church doctrine vests supreme authority in the head of the church, who receives revelation for the church, Smoot and other church members were bound to obey and accept church dictation whether spiritual or temporal.[25]

Some of the testimony in the hearings tended to bear out the contention that members were not only pressured on voting and other political decisions but that official action was taken against some who failed to follow the church's direction. Former federal judge Orlando Powers, for instance, cited the case of two men who were disciplined by local authorities in Salt Lake City for opposing Smoot's election. One was released from his position as a teacher in Sunday School on the ground that the member should not have criticized a general authority. In another instance, during a municipal election in 1897 in Salt Lake City a member was disfellowshipped for refusing to distribute literature for a candidate whom the bishop favored. Since 1892, however, Powers said, there had been a decline in open political influence.[26]

Both on the stand and in personal correspondence, Joseph F. Smith denied that the church used its influence in political affairs. He said he had nothing to do with Reed Smoot's election and also insisted that Smoot would not necessarily have been removed from the apostleship had he run for the Senate without asking permission. He was also convinced that the majority of the Mormon voters were Democrats and that most of them had probably opposed Smoot. In an editorial in the *Improvement Era*, Joseph F. Smith said that the church "is not in politics" and the Mormons "individually are free to vote as they please."[27]

Some church leaders thought that the church's position was equivocal. B. H. Roberts, for instance, attributed the condition in Utah not to church dictation but to the political ignorance of the Utah citizens who had grown up without national political parties. Charles Penrose pointed out that he was a Democrat but that the newspaper he edited, the *Deseret News*, was independent and that it supported or opposed issues, not parties.[28]

Even some of the Gentiles who testified in the hearings believed that charges of church political influence were considerably overrated. J. W. N. Whitecotton averred that the *Deseret News* was neutral in its political leanings, and Amasa S. Condon pointed out that the division of state and local offices was about equal between Mormons and Gentiles in spite of the fact that Mormons made up two-thirds of the state's population.[29]

Another question of particular importance relating to political matters was that of the conflict between national loyalty and loyalty to the church. In this case, however, the evidence was contradictory. B. H. Roberts said that "you would have to rely upon the patriotism and the judgment of the individual concerned" if the two loyalties were in conflict. Smoot took the view that if the law of the church and the law of the land conflicted, the law of the land prevailed, but he also said that if he found the two in irreconcilable conflict he might leave the country.[30]

When the evidence was in, the minority of committee members who supported Smoot took the view that though church political control had been a reality in the period from 1847 to 1890, an interregnum period had followed to 1900 and that the church had generally divorced itself from politics since 1900.[31]

On June 6, 1906, after the hearings had ended, the Burrows Committee voted seven to five for expulsion. Two Republicans, Burrows and Jonathan Dolliver, who had since been appointed, joined the five Democrats against Smoot. Five Republicans—Foraker, Knox, Dillingham, Hopkins, and Beveridge—supported Smoot. In 1907 in the vote in the full Senate Smoot received the support of thirty-nine Republicans and three Democrats—a clear majority. A crucial influence was that of President Roosevelt, who, after a private meeting with Smoot, threw his personal support behind the Utahn.[32]

Church leaders were jubilant over the outcome. Anthon H. Lund considered it "a great victory for right over prejudice," and George F. Richards wrote that the church was "vindicated at last. The Devil suffers defeat, Zion prospers." Joseph F. Smith congratulated Smoot and asked him to thank Senators Foraker, Knox, Dillingham, Hopkins, and Beveridge and President Roosevelt for their work and kindness.[33]

The effort to assist Smoot and to defend the church was bipartisan and multireligious. In January 1907, as the whole affair wound to a close, the First Presidency appointed Orson F. Whitney, Brigham H. Roberts, David O. McKay, James E. Talmage, Nephi L. Morris, LeGrand Young, Franklin S. Richards, and Richard W. Young, five Democrats and three Republicans, to write a defense of the church's position for the April 1907 conference. George Sutherland, a non-Mormon of LDS heritage, gave an eloquent speech defending Smoot before the Senate, and Senator Philander Knox of Pennsylvania braved the opposition of women's groups to defend the senator.[34]

The bipartisan nature of the victory had been long forgotten by 1911, however, and lasting credit has since gone to the Republicans.

On August 30, 1911, for instance, Susa Young Gates held a gathering of "those who worked in Washington for upholding our rights." All present were prominent Republicans, including Senator Smoot and Representative Howell, together with Presidents Smith and Lund. In September and November 1911, as well, Smoot worked unsuccessfully with the First Presidency to try to get them to remove Democrats LeGrand Young and Franklin S. Richards as the church's attorneys and employ the Republican firm of Stewart, Morris, and Bowman because he "thought it was about time that some law firm outside of our Democratic enemies ought to be recognized by the Church" in its employment of legal counsel.[35]

In retrospect, two factors seem to have been crucial. One was the perception of Republicans that, in spite of protestations to the contrary, the church probably did have some political influence which could be of advantage to them. The second was that Smoot himself was undoubtedly guilty of no illegal acts. Smoot's biographer, Milton R. Merrill, has argued that the hearings were an attack on Smoot personally and not on the church, but the view needs qualification. The hearings also attacked the secular power of the church's leadership. Had the hearings confined themselves to Smoot's own activities and to the practices of the church's hierarchy since Smoot became an apostle in 1900, Merrill's view would be well founded. The hearings constituted, however, a wide-ranging investigation of virtually every aspect of church activities since the Manifesto of 1890.[36]

On balance, the overall effect of the hearings on the church was mixed. The revelations of the hearings, particularly those of political and economic influence and new plural marriage, were to return over and over again to plague the church. The agitation for a constitutional amendment prohibiting polygamy was evidence of this. More serious was the development in Utah of a new anti-Mormon political party. The immediate cause of this new campaign was Joseph F. Smith's testimony in early March 1904. Apparently the active role in organizing the group was taken by Parley L. Williams, a Salt Lake City attorney. Somewhat belatedly, Senator Thomas Kearns and his supporters took an active part as the breach between him and the church widened.[37]

A battle ensued between Smoot and Kearns for control of the Republican party. Smoot gained the support of George Sutherland and other friendly Gentiles, and Kearns held some Mormon Republicans like Governor Heber M. Wells. Smoot, the First Presidency, and a number

of supporters like James H. Anderson and Edward H. Callister agreed
to support John C. Cutler for governor in 1904. Smoot showed his
early strength by securing the election of Anderson as state chairman.
In the convention, Cutler won the nomination over Wells, an indication of Smoot's strength.[38]

Smoot then consolidated his position as Utah's political czar by as-
sembling a political machine which dominated the state's politics until
1916. Generally called the Federal Bunch because most prominent
functionaries held federal appointments, the machine consisted of
Mormons and friendly Gentiles. The local machine leader was Edward H. Callister, who had served on the Salt Lake City Council and
was active in the Utah Woolgrowers Association and the National
Livestock Association. Elected chairman of the state Republican party
in 1900, he became internal revenue collector for Utah, a position he
held for twelve years. William Spry, confirmed as United States marshal for Utah, later served two terms as governor. James H. Anderson,
another state party chairman, became United States marshal after
Spry. James Clove was postmaster in Provo, and William Glasmann,
owner of the *Ogden Standard*, became postmaster in Ogden. Hiram E.
Booth was United States district attorney for Utah, and C. E. Loose, a
wealthy mining man and supporter of Smoot from Provo, was not a
public office holder.[39] Because of his membership in the Twelve, Smoot
also linked the Federal Bunch to the general authorities, particularly
Joseph F. Smith.

Smoot's success and Kearns's increasing isolation from political
power led the mining magnate to announce an open break with the
LDS church and to enter politics in opposition. With the defection of
Kearns's newspaper, the *Salt Lake Tribune*, no Republican paper in
Salt Lake City was friendly to the church, and the principal Democratic newspaper, the *Salt Lake Herald*, owned by Senator William A.
Clark, was also anti-Mormon. The Presidency agreed to provide financial support for a new paper, which began operation in February 1906
as the *Intermountain-Republican*.[40] In August 1909, on Callister's recommendation, the *Intermountain-Republican*, with funds secured
principally from Daniel C. Jackling and the LDS church, acquired
ownership of the *Salt Lake Herald*. The papers were merged under the
name *Herald-Republican*, and the church and Smoot owned the controlling interest. The church remained a silent partner in the association, with Smoot, Loose, Callister, and Anderson representing its inter-

est on the board of directors. Actual operation of the paper rested with Callister and Anderson, and in 1913, after his removal by the Wilson administration as collector of internal revenue for the state of Utah, Callister became general manager.[41]

Meanwhile, on September 7, 1904, a group of about 100 Gentiles gathered at the Auerbach Building to organize a new political party aimed at the LDS church. This time, Joseph Lippman, Kearns's campaign manager, attended, and Kearns threw his support behind the new American party. On September 30 Frank J. Cannon, now estranged from the church, announced himself a supporter of the American party, and after the November elections, Kearns took him on as editor of the *Tribune*.[42]

Far from being simply an arm of Kearns's political ambition, however, the American party consisted of at least two influences: Gentiles working against continued unlawful cohabitation and church influence in politics, and Kearns supporters who had lost in an interfactional dispute within the Republican party and whose resentment was political. Though both groups opposed the LDS church, they did so from differing motives—the one from a sincere opposition to church policy and the other out of political opportunism because of defeat in an intraparty battle.

Shortly after the election, Smoot met with the First Presidency to tell them of his feelings about the 1905 senatorial contest. He said that he favored George Sutherland, but the First Presidency counseled him not to take an active part in the senatorial fight. Smoot ignored the counsel and worked for Sutherland. The overwhelming Republican victory in the elections of 1904 led to Sutherland's election over William H. King by a fifty-seven to six majority. Even E. B. Critchlow, who had written the protest against Reed Smoot, said that the "Church leaders are entitled to what little credit can be figured out for them" in permitting the people of the state to send Sutherland to the Senate.[43]

An embittered and disappointed Kearns now openly attacked the church. On February 28, 1905, Kearns took to the Senate floor to sing his swan song and denounce the church authorities. Admitting he had won his seat in part because of Lorenzo Snow's support, he called upon the Senate to serve notice on the LDS church that it must live within the law. Frank Cannon published editorials entitled "An Address to the Earthly King of the Kingdom of God" and "An Analysis of the Church," attacking the church and Joseph F. Smith. He was excommunicated on March 14, 1905, and for some years thereafter, he alternated his time between editing the *Tribune* and delivering anti-Mormon lectures.[44]

Though the American party seemed a fearsome challenge at the time, it can be seen in part as the last gasp of the nineteenth-century political system. The participating Gentiles were not willing to acknowledge that, if the Mormons were to accept a pluralistic political system, so must they. All citizens—including ecclesiastical leaders—whether Mormons or non-Mormons, must be free to influence the outcome of the political process to their advantage. In the final analysis, the introduction of the progressive reform of commission government in Salt Lake City, based upon nonpartisan political selection, defeated the American party. But this took eight years.

The problems of establishing a pluralistic political system and of determining the role of church leaders in politics were apparent in the senatorial campaign of 1908–9. A number of prominent Republicans and church leaders thought that Smoot ought to step down now that he had been vindicated. On February 21, 1908, more than 100 well-known Republicans at the Wilson Hotel in Salt Lake City recorded themselves as opposing Smoot's renomination as senator from Utah.[45]

Joseph F. Smith, however, was adamant in his view that Smoot ought to remain in the Senate. As he and Charles W. Nibley were returning from a visit to Europe before the election, the two stood on deck talking about the politics, and Nibley suggested that it would be wise and prudent for Smoot not to run. Joseph F. Smith listened to Nibley, "but with some impatience. Finally, bringing his fist down on the railing between us he stated in these emphatic terms: 'If I have ever had the inspiration of the spirit of the Lord given to me forcefully and clearly it has been on this one point concerning Reed Smoot, and that is, instead of his being retired, he should be continued in the United States Senate.'" Nibley withdrew his opposition. As late as December 1907, however, evidence indicated that such apostles and counselors in the First Presidency as John R. Winder, Francis M. Lyman, John Henry Smith, George Albert Smith, and Charles W. Nibley opposed the strife which Smoot's candidacy aroused. Smoot himself even considered returning to the Senate, but giving up the apostleship.[46]

Recognizing the challenge of both Democrats and Americans, Smoot insisted that the First Presidency and Twelve fully support him. To Callister he lamented that President Smith and his close associates "agree upon a plan, and then parties to the agreement leave the meeting and work absolutely contrary to the plan adopted." The Republican party could not carry the state if "a number of the Twelve and the First Presidents of the Seventies travel through the State in opposition to it and also with the *Deseret News* every week or so claiming the church is out of politics and that President Smith has no desires or wishes in the matter." In essence, as Milton Merrill has pointed out, Smoot was repudiating the statements about the church being out of politics which had formed such an important part of the testimony before the Senate committee.[47]

For his part, President Smith seemed to see the welfare of the church involved in Republican success. Democratic Mormons like Brigham H. Roberts, on the other hand, believed that a pluralistic political system necessitated an active loyal opposition. On March 30, 1908, Roberts published an open letter to Richard R. Lyman, a Democrat and son of Apostle Francis M. Lyman, expressing his opposition to Smoot. He said that Smoot's reelection would rekindle animosity against the church and that there were many others who could fill the position. Even though he had once run for Congress himself, he was now convinced that high church officials ought not to run for public office because of the bitterness against the church and anti-Mormonism it engendered. Smoot's reelection, he said, would cause another setback for the church.[48] Roberts's letter occasioned considerable comment from members of the First Presidency and Twelve. Some Democrats like Heber J. Grant thought it uncalled for and believed it would aid the church's enemies. Roberts stood his ground, however, even to the extent of restating his position in a conference speech on October 6, 1908. In the closing talk of the conference, however, President Smith, without mentioning names, said some good words for Smoot. He "thanked God that this state of Utah is, and has been represented in the halls of Congress by honest men, men after God's own heart, men who love their own people, and who are just and impartial and true to all the citizens of our state."[49]

Though a number of Mormon Democrats probably supported the Republican ticket in 1908 in order to avoid an American party victory, some were obviously not comfortable in the role of temporary Republicans. On June 9, 1908, Heber J. Grant attended a reception given by Jacob F. and Susa Young Gates in honor of Reed Smoot. Grant thought it was "a mistake for Brother and Sister Gates to invite me, seeing I am a Democrat, to a meeting in honor of a Republican Senator." Particularly annoyed at the detailed account of the reception in the newspapers, he was afraid that it would "cause unfavorable comments by our enemies." Grant and John R. Winder of the First Presidency attempted to bring about a Republican-Democratic fusion, at least in Salt Lake County, where American party influence seemed greatest, but by early October this seemed impossible.[50] As the anti-Mormon charges of the American party flew, many Democrats seemed persuaded that the only way to save the church was to vote for the Republican party. By late October even Heber J. Grant was not embarrassed to be found in a Republican party rally in the Thatcher Opera House in Logan. Richard W. Young, a Democratic stake president, indicated to Elder Grant that he intended to vote the Republican ticket at least on the county level in order to avoid an American party victory, and John R. Winder was somewhat embarrassed when, because of a malfunction of a voting machine, it became public knowledge that he had voted for the Republicans.[51]

The attacks on the church by the American party and the response of the church leadership left the Republican party in good condition and the Democratic party in shambles. To try to salvage something from the campaign, William H. King, James H. Moyle, and Brigham H. Roberts interceded with Jesse Knight, a prominent Provo businessman, to run for governor. Knight, well known throughout the state as an active churchman and Democrat, accepted, somewhat against his better judgment. Smoot, Callister, Anderson, and Hull came to see the First Presidency to remonstrate against Knight's candidacy. They said that this would "solidify the Democratic Party and then the Americans will have a sure victory." Whether or not the church leadership convinced him he ought to withdraw, as charged by the *Salt Lake Tribune*, Knight left the campaign and his son J. William Knight took his place.[52]

The real battle for the governorship took place within the Republican party. Early indications were that some of the general authorities favored Cutler's reelection. By late June fear of the possibility of an American party victory, the desire of members of the Federal Bunch— Loose, Callister, and others—to run William Spry, and the belief that Cutler could not carry Cache, Weber, or Salt Lake counties led to second thoughts. Spry was nominated.[53]

When the votes were counted, the Republican party had won by a landslide. The Utah Democrats failed to carry a single county "and elected only two members of the state house of representatives and two or three unimportant and scattered county officers, whose election was chiefly due to personal popularity, or charitable sympathy." Smoot was reelected by a sixty-one to two vote of the 1909 legislature.[54]

Upset by the results, Democrats loyal to the church, among them J. William Knight and James H. Moyle, denounced the interference in politics. To rub salt in Democratic wounds, the Council of the Twelve and the First Council of the Seventy called B. H. Roberts before them again on January 6, 1909, accusing him of questioning the good faith and honesty of the First Presidency and the general authorities in his earlier letter. The consensus of the council was that Roberts ought to have taken "this grievance to his brethren." The matter was put aside, however, and was not revived, although Roberts was in and out of favor again and again for his active support of the Democratic party and his opposition to Apostle-Senator Smoot.[55]

In retrospect, opposition to the American party clearly required a Republican attempt to court Democrats and to select candidates suitable to both Mormons and Gentiles. Contrary to currently popular myths, the Democratic party contained a much higher percentage of Mormons than the Republicans did, and from the GOP ranks the American party made most of its recruits. Some leaders who might otherwise have supported John C. Cutler regretfully sacrificed his second term in part because of potential American party power. The fear of an American party victory was destructive to the Democratic party, since church leaders, fearing that Utah might return to the nineteenth-century polarization of its political system along religious lines, supported the Republicans. An easy way out would have been to allow Reed Smoot to resign his Senate seat, but that would have been a tacit acceptance of the American party proposition that church leaders were unacceptable in public life. In effect, the attempt to defeat the American party involved an effort to recruit Democrats who were not antichurch. When William Spry boasted that he would get "two Mormon Democrats to vote the Republican ticket" for every Republican he lost to the American party, he probably understated his case.[56]

In 1908 the Republican party seemed invincible, and Reed Smoot's position in the state and national parties improved. Whether in interceding to secure the release of detained Mormon immigrants, or squiring President William Howard Taft on his visits to Utah in 1909 and 1911, Smoot occupied the limelight.

As early as 1909, however, some cracks began to appear in the political machine which Smoot had put together. These were widened by the battle over statewide prohibition, which both Joseph F. Smith and Reed Smoot tried to avoid. Both feared that support of liquor control would drive Gentiles from the Republican party and bring about renewed support for parties drawn on religious lines. This same fear seems to have prompted William Spry to veto a local option liquor control bill which the legislature passed in 1909. Within the Republican party there appeared a group, headed by stake president Nephi Morris and calling themselves prohibition Republicans, who resisted the efforts of the Federal Bunch to downplay the prohibition issue. In the Democratic party, where the Mormons predominated, there seemed little problem on the issue and prominent Democrats, among them Heber J. Grant and Brigham H. Roberts, led in supporting liquor control. Thus church leaders in the beginning exhibited no consensus on the liquor control question. The two church newspapers reflected this ambivalence. The *Deseret News*, under Janne Sjodahl, campaigned for state-wide prohibition, while the *Herald-Republican* fought against it.[57]

In Idaho as well as in Utah, serious conflicts developed between Mormons and Gentiles over the level of church influence in politics. Although Fred T. Dubois and the Republican party had been largely responsible for disfranchisement of Mormons, Dubois changed his views and supported Utah statehood. After the McKinley-Bryan election of 1896, Dubois switched to the Democratic party and as general church and local Mormon leaders tried to recruit Mormons to the GOP, the Idaho senator moved into opposition. William Budge, president of the Bear Lake Stake, began active recruiting; conference assignments were arranged so Republican general authorities like Matthias F. Cowley and John Henry Smith could work for the GOP; and Ben E. Rich was allowed to return on leave from the Southern States Mission to campaign.[58]

The controversy continued to escalate. B. H. Roberts, Charles W. Penrose, and James E. Hart, a Montpelier Democrat, worked to counter the Republican efforts, but they were largely unsuccessful. Controversy developed within the Republican party between Rich and Judge Alfred Budge over Budge's candidacy for the state judiciary in opposition to Rich's brother. A representative of the Idaho State Democratic Central Committee called on the First Presidency in 1902, trying to get the church to keep Utah general authorities out of Idaho politics, but to no avail. In 1906 the Democratic party expelled all Mormons from their ranks, and increased Republican strength in the state led to the victory of William E. Borah over Dubois.[59]

By 1907 many Idaho Democrats recognized that attacks on the church had proved counterproductive. In April, Ada County Democrats repudiated Dubois and announced the exclusion of religion from partisan consideration. The crowning defeat for Dubois's hopes came during the trial of Alfred Budge, who had been elected judge of the state's fifth judicial district. Under the Idaho constitution, anyone practicing or teaching celestial (a synonym for plural) marriage was automatically disfranchised, and Dubois's supporters had challenged Budge's election, charging that, as a Mormon, he believed in celestial marriage even though he did not practice polygamy. In countering Dubois's efforts, a church committee (Anthon H. Lund, Franklin S. Richards, Brigham H. Roberts, and Orson F. Whitney) pointed out that even though much of the church's literature used the term "celestial marriage," the principle ought to be called "marriage for eternity." Thus, the church and Budge could deny believing in celestial marriage, which meant polygamy in the Idaho constitution anyway. The committee's report was confirmed by the First Presidency, and the Idaho Supreme Court, in sustaining Budge, agreed with this interpretation. Budge and other Mormons were not to be disfranchised unless they continued to live in plural marriage.[60]

By 1911 the problems in Idaho had passed, though to the disadvantage of Democrats, and the church was beginning to define its new role and to fit into the mainstream of American politics. Since members belonged to the two major parties, the church had moved in the direction of taking a political stance similar to that of most other religious groups. That is, the Latter-day Saints became more like a pressure group dealing in what they perceived to be the best interest of the community but declining to operate an exclusive political system. In the 1911 election many were able to support a nonpartisan slate in an attempt to promote better government in Salt Lake City. It is significant that this effort was quite unlike the single party system of the nineteenth century, since businessmen, Evangelical Protestants, and others supported the new commission form of government. In Idaho, the Democratic party learned that anti-Mormon politics could not work as long as church members could exercise the franchise, and they were forced to abandon the antichurch stance.

Nevertheless, the church members had a long way to go to understand and support a truly pluralistic political system. Continued official support for Reed Smoot and the Federal Bunch political machine rankled many and served as a divisive force within the church. The prohibition question had surfaced as an important issue, and the increasing pressure for reform of the political and economic system which Progressive politicians were promoting was to provide continued challenges into the next two decades.

3

The Politics of Change
and Reconciliation,
1912–30

SINCE ITS MOVE TO UTAH, the LDS church has passed through five
periods in its relationship to politics.[1] During the period from 1847 to
about 1891, the church unquestionably dominated the Utah scene.
Church-sponsored candidates regularly overwhelmed Gentiles in their
attempts to secure political office, and no real national parties existed.
Between 1891 and the end of World War I church leaders recognized
the need to divide into national parties and generally favored the Republicans. Most conspicuous by their pro-Republican activities were
President Joseph F. Smith and Elders Reed Smoot, John Henry Smith,
and Francis M. Lyman. At first the rationale for this activity was the
overwhelming number of Mormons in the Democratic party. Later,
however, habitual pro-Republicanism became the hallmark of the
early twentieth-century Mormon leadership.

In the period between World War I and the early years of the Great
Depression this situation changed. Church leaders became less partisan in their political activities, and even though the Republican party
tended to control the state legislature, it would be inaccurate to say
that church leaders favored the Republican party. Moreover, when
they entered the political scene it was generally for moral rather than
partisan reasons. In the period from the mid-1930s to the late 1950s,
however, church leaders again swung into the Republican party camp.
Heber J. Grant turned against the Democratic party, and J. Reuben
Clark penned editorials opposing the New Deal.[2] Active church support for candidates—generally Republican—was not uncommon.
From the late fifties to the early eighties, however, though most general church leaders have been avowedly Republican, they still entered
politics generally to support or oppose measures they considered moral
issues. Open support of or opposition to particular candidates has been
difficult to find.

Nevertheless, if the last seven years of Joseph F. Smith's administration reveal anything, it is that the church could never be completely out of politics. First, general authorities were both religious and community leaders who associated with various groups taking positions on political questions. Second, they exhibited conflicting political preferences which, like other citizens, they expressed openly, as Joseph F. Smith did in 1912, 1914, and 1916. Such open endorsements, unaccompanied by any obvious compelling moral issue, as Anthon H. Lund recognized, were bound to alienate some members and to attract others. Third, the fear of alienating Gentiles was an important consideration which undoubtedly helped dictate the stance which Republican church leaders took on the prohibition question. Finally, and most importantly, the church membership viewed the First Presidency and the Twelve as prophets who were inspired on all moral and social questions. Religion, whether among Catholics, Protestants, Jews, Moslems, or Mormons, has often set itself up as an arbiter of values.

Most Mormon leaders were conservatives. Some like Joseph F. Smith made it abundantly clear that they were personally fearful of change, particularly change that might tear the current social and political fabric. The attempt to preserve the status quo brought President Smith into open opposition to both the Democratic and Progressive parties and to much progressive reform.[3] He spoke on occasion of tilting slightly in favor of the party in power. Nevertheless, when the Democratic party gained control of the national government during the Wilson administration (1913–1920) and the state government during the Bamberger administration (1917–1920), he remained a loyal Republican.

Even the demise of the American party in 1911 did not diminish partisan activity on the part of church leaders. In March 1912 Joseph F. Smith and Reed Smoot threw their support behind William Howard Taft for president. Nevertheless, church members in places as diverse as the Big Horn Basin of Wyoming and the Snake River Valley of Idaho worked for Theodore Roosevelt's nomination.[4]

Three political parties entered the 1912 contest in Utah as well as in the nation. The Republicans renominated William Spry for governor on a moderately progressive platform, and the Democrats ran John F. Tolton on a set of somewhat more progressive planks. In July, after Roosevelt supporters bolted the Republican party, Mormons and Gentiles met in Provo to name delegates to the state Progressive party convention. Roosevelt himself spoke at the convention on September 13 in Ogden, where Nephi L. Morris, Salt Lake Stake president and businessman, was nominated for the governorship, and Stephen H. Love, traffic manager for Zion's Cooperative Mercantile Institution (ZCMI), was nominated for Congress. Made up in part of prohibitionist Republicans like Nephi L. Morris, the Progressive party also included Republican leaders who were opposed to domination by the Federal Bunch and who believed the Republican party not creative enough in dealing with problems caused by modernization.[5]

President Smith outlined his essentially conservative and pro-Republican views in a statement endorsing Taft which he published in the October 1912 *Improvement Era*. Taft had, he said, "met the just needs of the people and the economic demands of the country with steadfastness and wisdom." He supported Taft's Mexican policy and urged that the charges that Taft was "a tool for the 'Interests,' which means, doubtless, that he unduly favors 'big business,' or trusts," was without foundation. He had, rather, "done as much to regulate the trusts as was ever done by any other incumbent of the presidential chair, and he has done it legally."[6]

The editorial endorsement caused an immediate furor. Orlando Powers, chairman of the state Democratic party, resigned in disgust. He said that he had carried on a fight against ecclesiastical politics for twenty-eight years and had thought that the death of the American party had ended it. Some church members like Henry C. Lund, son of Anthon H. Lund of the First Presidency, were upset because they thought that with the demise of the anti-Mormon party, the Democrats would have a fair chance in 1912. On the heels of the furor raised by the endorsement, Janne Sjodahl, editor of the *Deseret News*, ran an interview with Joseph F. Smith, who defended his right to speak his views but claimed that the church had no candidates and that no one was authorized to speak for the church on party questions.[7]

The immediate result of this endorsement of Taft and conservative Republicanism was twofold. First, committees from the Democratic and Progressive parties began to discuss fusion. This was impossible so close to the 1912 election but was accomplished, in part, in time for the 1914 campaign.[8] The second effect was the attempt of Democrats to map out a place in the church for those who disagreed with President Smith's views. On October 5, 1912, Brigham H. Roberts tried this as part of his general conference talk. He said that all church members ought to agree on essential gospel principles. On other matters, such as civil government, they might differ. In conclusion, the Seventies president insisted, "there is no ground for serious division among us in respect of what is truth, and justice, and righteousness, and morality in all things, and in all relations." Political matters, Roberts said, were "non-essentials" where "one man's judgment may be as good as another's."[9]

Joseph F. Smith responded to Roberts's views. He said that though much of what had been said was true, he did not want to confine church members since they "may individually go unto God in faith and prayer, and find out what should guide and direct their human judgment and wisdom. . . . I would rather that they should seek God for a counselor and guide, than to follow the wild harangues of political leaders."[10]

The interpretation of the meaning of President Smith's speech was quite different among various general authorities. Anthon H. Lund thought that the president had basically agreed with Roberts, but considered it the privilege of Latter-day Saints to take counsel on any matter they pleased. Smoot, however, thought that "Pres. Smith referred to . . . [Roberts's talk] and then punctured it completely." In addition, Smoot believed that on the next day "[Charles W.] Penrose completely answered Roberts," and "[James E.] Talmage gave Roberts a rap also." "It is generally conceded," Smoot wrote, "that Roberts was sat upon for his speech yesterday morning. People [were] well satisfied but some of the Democrats were displeased." For Smoot, "Democrats" and "people" were two different species.[11]

In an attempt to pour oil on troubled waters, Elder David O. McKay, of the Quorum of the Twelve, gave an interview to the *Ogden Standard* insisting that "Church doctrine accords every man and woman his free agency and that right shall not be abridged." Presidents Smith and Penrose, he explained, "firmly believe in the representative form of government, while Elder Roberts is more Democratic and he believes that the people should more directly voice their political sentiments." He said that he did not think "the talks were made for political effect, and yet I think rather unfortunate that the subject was brought up at this time, on the eve of a political campaign."[12]

In retrospect, President Smith's endorsement of Taft probably had a slight, but indecisive, effect on the outcome of the election. The

Herald-Republican and the *Salt Lake Tribune* both defended Taft, as President Smith had done, on the basis of his moderate progressivism. Those second echelon church leaders, anti-Federal Bunch progressives, and others who organized the Progressive party thought him not progressive enough and considered the Federal Bunch in the same light. Taft's great popularity seems to have derived from his support of the protective tariff, which benefited Utah industry. In addition, Woodrow Wilson, the Democratic candidate, was not well known in Utah, and the only major newspaper supporting Roosevelt was the *Ogden Standard*, edited by William Glasmann, a gentile Republican who had been friendly to the church and to Reed Smoot but who thought Taft too conservative.[13]

Nevertheless, the final vote offered little long-range comfort to the Federal Bunch. Though Taft carried all counties in the state except Uinta and Weber, which Roosevelt won, and Cache, Grand, San Juan, Utah, and Washington, which went for Wilson, the combined popular vote for Wilson and Roosevelt exceeded Taft's total by nearly 19,000 votes or about 17 percent. Even the combined votes for Wilson and Socialist candidate Eugene Debs exceeded Taft's total. Votes for the other offices were similar, and though the Republicans carried the state by a plurality, a coalition of progressive forces could spell doom for the Federal Bunch in Utah politics.[14]

The Federal Bunch itself began to show internal signs of stress. A rift developed between William Spry and E. H. Callister. Spry, who was a much more able politician than John Cutler, had built his own political organization, and only the loyalty of the governor and the political boss to Smoot held the organization together in 1912 and 1914. The rift widened as the *Herald-Republican* attacked the Spry administration.[15]

Even though the role of this rift in the Republican party became increasingly significant, the most difficult problem in understanding politics during the teens is in dealing with the multitude of charges and countercharges, assertions and denials, of church political influence. Church leaders continued to insist that the church, as such, was not involved in politics. General authorities were, however, politically active. Reed Smoot, for his part, thought that as soon as others believed that "the church has no power with its people, the old time conditions will be but a zephyr compared with the storm that will sweep about our befuddled heads." He was convinced, in other words, that other influences would fill the vacuum caused by a lack of church political power.[16]

In an address to the world in 1907, church leaders renounced any claim to political dictation, but reserved the right of the church to defend itself. The major problem came in the assessment of individual members as to when the church was threatened and when problems were simply matters for personal judgment. The continual problems which B. H. Roberts encountered during his opposition to Reed Smoot and the Federal Bunch are a case in point. It is difficult to see how the defeat of Smoot or the success of other factions within the Republican party could have harmed the church, yet some church leaders sensed danger to the institution.

It also seems unlikely that the church needed vigorous partisanship to defend itself after 1911. By then the people of Utah had killed the American party and the Dubois faction had lost power in Idaho. With them went the spectre of anti-Mormon victory from the political scene. Nevertheless, Joseph F. Smith endorsed Taft in a church publication, and some church leaders, like George F. Richards, continued to insist on the need for sustaining the authorities "in temporal, political and religious matters." The church leaders, he argued, "have responsibility and act unselfishly; those who oppose them are usually promoted by selfish motives."[17]

By the 1914 election, progressive issues had taken their toll on support for the Republican party in general and Reed Smoot's Federal Bunch in particular. Smoot supported railroad rate regulation and natural resource conservation, but maintained a conservative image on such matters as direct democracy. Above all, he and Joseph F. Smith continued to fear rapid change. As early as March 1913 Joseph F. Smith had urged the senator to run again the following year, and on October 9 Smoot announced his candidacy. The ensuing 1914 election was probably the hardest Smoot faced until 1932 and was also extremely divisive as church leaders brought ecclesiastical pressure to bear for Smoot and in opposition to his opponent, James H. Moyle, also a faithful church member.[18]

Almost immediately, businessmen and politicians began to divide. Progressive party leaders decided their only chance to defeat Smoot was fusion with the Democrats. Early in March 1914 Fred J. Kiesel, a Gentile from Ogden, announced that he was leaving the Democratic party and joining the Republicans. Joseph F. Smith wrote him complimenting him on his decision. James H. Moyle, on the other hand, said that Kiesel was simply stating a fact which had already been accomplished, since he had long since left the Democrats. William Glassmann, a Progressive in 1912, rejoined the Republicans and announced his support of Smoot.[19]

Though some church leaders thought Smoot's opposition to prohibition would hurt his chances, the Republicans in and outside the church used effective strategy to secure the senator's reelection. In an attempt to woo Progressives from the Democrats, Smoot pushed the candidacy of former Progressive C. E. Loose for state Republican chairman.[20]

Beyond this, Francis M. Lyman applied ecclesiastical pressure on Progressive gubernatorial candidate and stake president Nephi L. Morris, urging him to back Smoot or remain politically inactive. Morris resented this and previous church pressure designed to get him to vote for church-sponsored candidates. He had voted for Thomas Kearns because an apostle had asked him to do so, in spite of the fact that he considered Kearns "a bag of gold and an ignorant ass." During other elections, he and other stake presidents had agreed to counsel members to vote the Republican ticket in order to elect Reed Smoot. The First Presidency had called him to work for state-wide prohibition, though he was not at first particularly interested in the problem; then Smoot got the First Presidency to back down, and Morris had been subjected to the abuse of the *Herald-Republican* for his efforts. In 1911 rumors had been circulated that he was out of harmony. Now, having endured personal abuse because he had attempted to follow the church leadership, he was asked to renounce his affiliation with the party that had run him for governor in 1912. It is perhaps an indication of his devotion that he agreed not to take part in the 1914 campaign. The Democratic-Progressive coalition found that many faithful Mormons wishing to appear in harmony with the church remained silent during the election.[21]

The election was extremely close, but the results indicate the extent of Smoot's staying power and of the crucial role of church influence in a tight election. Running on the Democratic-Progressive ticket, Moyle carried Beaver, Cache, Emery, Juab, Millard, Salt Lake, Sanpete, and Uintah counties. He lost in the other counties including Weber, which Theodore Roosevelt had carried for the Progressive party in 1912. The Republican party lost twenty-two seats in the legislature, control of the state House of Representatives, and the seat in the Second Congressional District, but Smoot defeated Moyle by just over 3,000 votes or slightly less than 3 percent of the total.[22]

In spite of Smoot's victory, by 1916 a rift in the Federal Bunch seemed irreparable. The dispute between Callister and Spry flared into the open, in part over Spry's unwillingness to support statewide prohibition. The Progressive element in the Republican party became dissatisfied, in addition, over the failure of the legislature to ratify the amendment for direct election of senators, to inaugurate regulation of public utilities, and to revise the state's regressive tax system.[23] Both Smoot and Smith worked to try to keep the Federal Bunch together and to maintain its control of the Republican party. Though both Callister and Spry wanted to run for governor, Smoot and Smith favored Edward E. Jenkins, who had not been involved in the interparty feuds. Callister pulled out of the race in June and threw his support to Jenkins. Thereafter, a number of church leaders attacked Spry, principally because of his veto of a statewide prohibition bill in 1915. He complained to the First Presidency, but they denied instigating the attacks.[24]

Disagreement within the ranks of the church Republicans was apparent. Presiding Bishop Charles W. Nibley told Joseph F. Smith and Anthon H. Lund that he thought Nephi Morris would be the strongest candidate. He had, after all, followed instructions in 1914 not to oppose Smoot, and Nibley believed he would have a loyal following. In addition, some prohibition-sensitive church leaders like David O. McKay supported Morris.[25]

By mid-summer the Republican party in Utah was floundering. Spry, with a considerable following among Gentiles, had effectively split the Federal Bunch's power base. Morris controlled the votes of the Progressives as well as of some church leaders. Beyond this, Morris was the second choice of a number of Mormon Republicans such as Anthon H. Lund, who recognized his strong following. The prohibition issue and control of the Salt Lake County delegation helped Morris. In the state convention the former progressive beat Spry by one vote.[26] Spry's defeat was the crowning blow to the Federal Bunch machine. Henceforth, Reed Smoot was largely on his own, without the active support of the organization he had so carefully built.[27]

In 1916, the Democratic party did not suffer the disability of an antagonistic church leadership. Heber J. Grant, for instance, worked actively within the party to nominate a gubernatorial candidate favoring prohibition. Simon Bamberger won the nomination. A Jewish businessman born in Darmstadt, Germany, Bamberger had come to the United States and amassed a fortune through mining and railroad ventures. Friendly to the church, he had worked with the Mormon majority in Salt Lake City as a member of the school board and as a state legislator, earning a reputation as a progressive. The senatorial nominee of the Democratic party was William H. King, a prominent church layman and former congressman. The Democrats nominated stake president Milton H. Welling for Congress.[28]

The platforms of the two parties were very similar and almost equally progressive. They both called for prohibition; a public utilities commission; the initiative, referendum, and recall; and workmen's compensation. Morris, however, led a badly divided Republican party. Callister said that he could hardly find a gentile Republican who would support Morris, and many Mormons would not vote for him.[29]

The candidates fought hard, but the Republican split was unbreachable. Bamberger, King, and Welling all won, and the Democrats ran up majorities in both houses of the state legislature. In addition, Woodrow Wilson carried Utah, defeating Charles Evans Hughes, whom Smoot had supported for the nomination.[30]

Joseph F. Smith, exhibiting his Republican partisanship, considered the outcome of the election "from the standpoint of wisdom and true statesmanship, . . . a huge blunder." On the day of the election, he was certain that the Democrats would lose since he believed Roberts, King, and others had hurt the party's cause by their persistent attacks on the Republicans. He was upset because William H. King, whom he considered a "pretentious, pedantic, two-faced democratic infidel," had defeated George Sutherland, whom he thought to be "consistent, capable, and friendly."[31]

Heber J. Grant, however, was pleased with the outcome. He met with Milton H. Welling at the Bear River Stake conference on November 17, 1917, and discussed the stake president's release prior to his departure for Washington. On December 8, 1916, Grant attended a Democratic party victory rally at the Newhouse Hotel in Salt Lake City. After the meeting, he lobbied for the appointment of Rulon S. Wells as state insurance commissioner.[32]

Bamberger followed a conciliatory policy toward the Mormon community. Heber J. Grant's work paid off, and in March 1917 the governor nominated Wells as insurance commissioner. In addition, Bamberger asked Republican Anthon H. Lund to pray at his inaugural. As his first official act after the inauguration, Bamberger appointed B. H. Roberts to the State Board of Equalization.[33]

Democratic control of both the state and national administrations further eroded the Federal Bunch's power base. The Wilson administration offered James H. Moyle, Democratic national committeeman from Utah, the position of first assistant secretary of the Treasury in September 1917, which he accepted. This gave Moyle the highest rank in the executive branch of government held to that time by a Utahn and brought considerable prestige both to him and to the LDS church. Heber J. Grant called on Moyle shortly after the appointment, congratulated him, prayed the Lord to bless him, and told him he considered it a distinct honor to the church since it was the first appointment of any importance that had come to a Mormon since statehood. In October 1917 William Gibbs McAdoo, President Wilson's son-in-law and secretary of the Treasury, spoke in the Salt Lake Theatre congratulating Moyle and the Mormon people. Moreover, Wilson appointed Isaac Blair Evans, Heber J. Grant's son-in-law, as United States attorney for Utah.[34]

These matters of domestic politics were interesting and vital to members of the church, but after 1914 the church members became increasingly concerned with World War I. Before the United States entered the war, Utah had sustained a strong peace movement. Prominent church leaders had led the peace organization and the predominant sentiment in the church seems to have been pacifistic. In an editorial in the *Improvement Era* in September 1914, shortly after the war began in Europe, Joseph F. Smith said that the war had been caused by "those professing Christian rulers 'who draw near to me with their lips, but their hearts are far from me.'" The war, he said, shows the fallacy of "the doctrine of peace by armed forces." The only way to peace, he stressed, "is the adoption of the Gospel of Jesus Christ."[35]

The First Presidency also stood as a moral force for peace. The church leadership, following the lead of President Wilson, called for prayers for peace on Sunday, October 4, 1914. President Smith himself acknowledged that defense was permissible against unlawful assaults but said that he favored a peaceful response. In the October 1915 general conference, Francis M. Lyman gave a strong address expressing admiration for Wilson's peace policy, sincerity, and courage. In the February 1917 *Improvement Era*, Fred L. W. Bennett published an article supporting the right of conscientious objection. War, he said, was degrading, wicked, and demoralizing, and the Saints ought to resist it.[36]

In spite of the gospel, conflicts between national groups developed in the LDS community. German-American Saints found themselves to be objects of considerable prejudice, and some were arrested because they criticized the United States government's pro-Allied policy. In meetings throughout the church, John M. Whitaker tried to get them to exercise caution in their utterances. Nevertheless, in the April 1917 general conference, only a few days before the United States entered the war, Joseph F. Smith cautioned the Saints to be tolerant, since there were no nationalities in the church.[37]

On April 26, 1917, the governor of Utah established the State Council of Defense for Utah, and local councils were organized in various counties. Under the leadership of L. H. Farnsworth, state chairman, the council promoted an active Americanism program. Supposed German influences, including teaching the German language in church schools, were suppressed.[38]

Preparations for war involved the mobilization of National Guard units and various training programs which affected many of the young men of the church. In May 1916, after Wilson's preparedness program had brought about the federalization of the National Guard, Utah was asked to furnish 1,600 men for service. Differences of opinion existed about volunteering or waiting for the draft, and members ordinarily did as they wished.[39]

The experience of Latter-day Saints in the armed services was quite mixed. Missionaries, as full-time ministers, were exempt from military service. Three Mormons—B. H. Roberts, Calvin F. Smith (a son of Joseph F.), and Herbert B. Maw (later a professor at the University of Utah and governor of Utah)—served as chaplains. The highest ranking officer was Brigadier General Richard W. Young, commander of the 145th Field Artillery, a federalized unit of the Utah National Guard. Latter-day Saints served in the Canadian and British armies as well, and some of their coreligionists fought for the Central Powers. More than twenty Maoris from the church agricultural college served in the New Zealand army.[40]

Church members were heavily involved in compassionate service, promoting food production, and providing temporary employees. Most

important was the work of the Relief Society. Its service supported the
Red Cross. At first, the Red Cross did not want to cooperate with the
Relief Society, calling it a sectarian organization. Joseph F. Smith
opined that the real reason for the unwillingness to cooperate was that
the Red Cross was, in fact, anti-Mormon like the YMCA, which Protestant denominations had used as a vehicle for promoting disaffection
among Mormon youth. Eventually the Red Cross administration recognized that cooperation with the Relief Society would be absolutely
necessary in Mormon-dominated towns. After some negotiation with
the western states regional director, the Relief Society sent Amy Brown
Lyman and Clarissa S. Williams to meetings in Denver. These joint
efforts led to the organization of more than 1,000 local Relief Society
units constituted as Red Cross auxiliaries. The Relief Society sponsored home canning demonstrations, classes in making bandages and
knitting, prizes for food production, and pledges for food conservation.
In England and on the Catawba Indian Reservation Relief Society sisters made mufflers, shirts, and other clothes for soldiers. Relief Society
sisters in Provo published a cookbook using foods recommended by
the U.S. Food Commission. The Relief Society continued its grain storage program until Herbert Hoover secured the wheat for the Food
Commission.[41]

In a similar way, other church auxiliaries cooperated in the war
effort. Mormon children from Mexico gave more than 75,000 hand-
made articles to the Red Cross. Young women prepared an index of
those who could take such wartime jobs as bookkeepers and nurses.
Boy Scouts volunteered for the Boy's Army, where they raised crops
and helped build ships.[42]

Heber J. Grant headed the Liberty Loan drive in Utah and was appointed a member of the Liberty Loan General Executive Committee
for the Twelfth Federal Reserve District. Contributions came from a
large number of church businesses, auxiliaries, and schools. In the
five Liberty and Victory Loan drives Utah, with a stipulated quota of
sightly more than $61 million, purchased $72.5 million in bonds and
nearly $80 million in stamps.[43]

In the Senate, Reed Smoot demonstrated a mixture of national patriotism and concern for Utah's interests. He supported the war effort
itself, voting for the declaration of war and most war measures except
the Espionage Act, a massive invasion of personal liberties, which the
federal government used principally to suppress radical groups in the

United States during and after the war. Turning to the pork barrel as well, he attempted, with some success, to secure federal largess for Utah.[44] In explaining his views, Smoot published an article in the *Forum* in which he argued that though some partisanship in wartime was necessary, partisanship on war considerations was unfortunate. He pointed out that the Senate Finance Committee had submitted no minority reports since the war began. He mentioned that individual Republicans had dissented on pieces of legislation and that vigorous discussion which involved some partisanship was necessary. On the other hand, he accused Wilson, whom he detested, of being an intense partisan.[45]

The intense activity on the part of Mormons in support of the war effort helped in changing the national image of the church. In January 1918 Heber J. Grant spoke at a dinner for the Twelfth Federal Reserve District Liberty Loan Committee. Recognizing this as an opportunity to create a favorable image, he talked for six and one-half minutes on Mormon history and three minutes on the bond drive.[46] The national recognition which the Mormons received from Wilson, Hoover, Mc-Adoo, and others undoubtedly helped the church, as did Utah's over-subscription to the Liberty Loan drives. Church attitudes on most secular matters were already quite conventional and middle class. Support of business, adherence to the two-party system, and opposition to radicalism were all generally shared attitudes.

Adherence to the two-party system was so strong that church leaders opposed not only Socialists and Bolshevists, but also independent agrarian organizations like the Nonpartisan League. During the latter part of the war, as the league began organizing in the northern Great Plains states, it also moved to Idaho. The First Presidency was particularly anxious about this movement and was upset when members of the priesthood quorums of the Fremont Stake around Rexburg began to express an interest in the organization. In a letter to stake leaders, the First Presidency said they feared fragmentation and felt that two parties were enough. They were particularly fearful that the league might "gain the balance of power" in elections.[47]

Although the church had come a long way in political matters under Joseph F. Smith, it had not evolved into a truly pluralistic political community. Probably because of the heritage of party unity from the nineteenth century and the need to recruit church members into the Republican party to achieve balance in the 1890s, as late as the teens

church members seemed unable to differentiate between political action necessary to protect the church's interests and political partisanship designed to use church influence to promote particular candidates or issues.

Such partisanship had at least two results. The first, and probably
least serious, was the public injection of the church-state issue into
political discourse. Such public discussion is to be expected because,
as citizens, church members and leaders were entitled to express their
views on political questions. The pronouncements of a prominent
church leader of support for or opposition to a particular candidate
or measure were undoubtedly unsettling to some, but a similar announcement from a powerful newspaper or from a business leader
with an equally large following would probably have been at least as
unsettling. More serious was the disruption of the internal harmony or
sense of community within the organization. In this connection, three
incidents come readily to mind. They were Joseph F. Smith's endorsement of the Republican party in 1912, ecclesiastical pressure on Nephi
Morris and other progressives in 1914, and opposition to the Nonpartisan League in 1918. In each case, official channels (a church
magazine, pressure from an apostle, and instructions from the First
Presidency to a stake president) were used to apply pressure on
church members to follow a prescribed course of action. The disruption of internal harmony was most evident in the events surrounding
the responses of B. H. Roberts to the 1912 announcement and of
Nephi L. Morris to the 1914 pressure. In each case, the harmony of
the organization was weakened as a result of what appears in retrospect to have been an unnecessary expression of political partisanship
rather than action necessary to protect the interests of the church.

On November 19, 1918, Joseph F. Smith died, and on November 23
Heber J. Grant was sustained as president of the LDS church. Grant's
call to the presidency of the church marked the beginning of the third
period of LDS political history. During the 1920s, the church leadership continued to support some candidates for public office, but they
generally did so because of particular moral issues connected with the
campaigns rather than out of political partisanship. There were some
exceptions, particularly in the case of Reed Smoot. By the late 1920s,
however, Grant refused to express himself either in public or even in
private to his own family for fear he might be accused of church interference in politics.

Some members sensed a change in the direction of political plural-ism had taken place. In the view of James H. Moyle, "Until [J. Reuben] Clark there was no Church interference in politics in [Heber J.] Grant's administration, because [Anthony W.] Ivins was the one man who would not stand for that."[48] In fact, the presently available evidence in-dicates that though the church leadership was generally reluctant to enter into politics and removed itself from some of the political involve-ment of previous years, church leaders had strong convictions and often expressed them, particularly when candidates were perceived as tainted by some moral fault. A principal difference, as Moyle perceived it, was that in the 1920s a partisan Democrat, Anthony W. Ivins, oc-cupied a position of power and authority in the First Presidency. Previ-ously, though John R. Winder and Charles W. Penrose, also Democrats, had served in the First Presidency, the political stance of the church was dominated by the strong will of President Joseph F. Smith and, until 1916, by the political machine built by Reed Smoot.

Ivins's views on the previous support for the Republican party are evident in a rather caustic entry in his diary in 1930 about the *Herald-Republican*, in which the church had been the majority stockholder. In 1919, he wrote, the church had sold its interest in the Republican party paper to Charles W. Nibley for an unsecured note of $80,000. Nibley paid the note in 1925 with 1,000 shares of Nibley-Stoddard lumber stock, which by 1930 had no value. The church, Ivins pointed out, had invested $544,000 in the *Herald-Republican* and all it had to show was some worthless lumber stock. In Ivins's view, the church support of the Republican party had had precisely the same value and had been a waste of church funds.[49]

Part of the background of the withdrawal from active partisanship during the 1920s involved a realignment of the Republican party which took place in the late teens. By 1916 Reed Smoot's Federal Bunch had lost its effectiveness in part because of intramachine squabbling over policies of the Spry administration and in part be-cause of the fight over prohibition. Charles Morris, who had belonged to the Federal Bunch faction led by Edward H. Callister and James H. Anderson, began his advance to power. Following World War I, Morris allied himself with Ernest Bamberger and Edward (Ned) Callister, E. H.'s son. Prominent in the organization were also George Odell and Clarence Bamberger, Odell's son-in-law and Ernest's brother, and George Wilson, political boss and purveyor of Republican patronage in

Salt Lake County. These men headed the Sevens, semisecret and ritu-
alistic interlocking groups of seven people that replaced the Federal
Bunch as the controlling organization of the party. Reed Smoot himself
pulled away from the manipulation of party politics to assume the status of elder statesman, using his power and patronage to assist friends
like William Spry, who was appointed commissioner of the General
Land Office, and the party in general rather than to control the
organization.[50]

After Heber J. Grant became church president in 1918, Smoot and
the Republicans began to face a new style of church administration.
President Grant willingly allowed a greater degree of diversity in the
open political discourse of church leaders than had Joseph F. Smith.
As a result, Ivins, Stephen L Richards, B. H. Roberts, Charles W. Penrose, and others became active in Democratic politics without fearing
official censure such as B. H. Roberts had received under Joseph F.
Smith.

In the League of Nations controversy, for instance, the tables were
turned and Heber J. Grant's moderating influence, rather than the
good will of various members of the Council of the Twelve, preserved
Reed Smoot from censure. Briefly, a number of the general authorities
were upset with Senator Smoot's antileague stand. In part, the differences developed over scriptural interpretation and the feelings about
the millennium. President Grant and a number of members of the
Twelve like Orson F. Whitney, Anthony W. Ivins, Stephen L Richards,
George F. Richards, Richard R. Lyman, and James E. Talmage saw the
league as a means of spreading Christianity throughout the world.
Richards said that the league was inspired of God, and Talmage addressed a congregation in the Tabernacle calling upon members of the
church to support Wilson and "his inspired work."[51]

With Smoot, however, were several of the Twelve together with the
church's presiding bishop. Bishop Charles W. Nibley thought Talmage's address "mere rot." Smoot said that the scriptures proved that
war and pestilence would continue until the Savior brought peace.[52]
Opposition to the league in the Twelve came from David O. McKay,
Rudger Clawson, and Joseph Fielding Smith.

Many members of the church and of the Twelve were convinced
that Smoot and Nibley, who were most vocal, were out of harmony, and
Smoot was afraid that his chances for reelection in 1920 would be
hurt. Stephen L Richards and Anthony W. Ivins were particularly ve-

hement in objecting to Smoot's opposition to the league "against the decision of the Council," and particularly his use of church scriptures to support his position.[53]

Members of the Twelve questioned Smoot's public position on the matter, and Anthony W. Ivins was particularly outraged that the Church-owned *Herald-Republican* should be attacking him (Ivins) on the league question. Smoot defended his right to act openly "as my judgment dictates, and in conformity to my oath of office." The question recurred again during 1920 with Anthony W. Ivins and others attacking Smoot for being out of harmony with the Twelve and First Presidency on the league. Technically, Smoot said in defense, Ivins was wrong, since he favored the league covenant without amendments, but with reservations proposed by Senator Henry Cabot Lodge of Massachusetts.[54]

Heber J. Grant, while favoring the league, played a moderating role in the dispute. Charting the conciliatory political course he was to follow during much of the twenties, he said that Smoot was not far from the council's position. He was sorry that the feeling had got abroad that Smoot was out of harmony, and particularly that the scriptures had entered the debate.[55]

By late October as the political campaign progressed, word was leaked that the First Presidency and Twelve had changed its position to support Smoot's views. On October 21 and 23, Grant met with Smoot, James E. Talmage, Richard R. Lyman, and Stephen L Richards. After some discussion, Smoot agreed to correct the false impression in a speech he was to give in Ogden. In spite of pressure from Charles W. Penrose and others, however, Smoot got President Grant's permission to make the denial in such an offhand way that it was unsatisfactory to many of the Twelve. In part, at least, the League of Nations controversy eventually led to the sale of the *Herald-Republican* because of partisan attacks by a church-owned newspaper on general authorities.[56]

In spite of Smoot's opposition to the league, he was definitely Heber J. Grant's candidate for the Senate in 1920. Grant's support of Smoot clearly upset a number of church members who were active Democrats. James H. Moyle, at the time assistant secretary of the Treasury and a friend of long standing, wrote President Grant pointing to Smoot's anti-Progressive record and opposition to the league. In reply, President Grant admitted that he had opposed Smoot in 1908 because of

Smoot's opposition to prohibition, but said that he had quietly supported Smoot in 1914 (when he ran against Moyle) and now supported him again because he looked upon Smoot "as one of the most practical, levelheaded businessmen in the United States Senate." He agreed that Smoot "may not have possessed as much constructive and progressive ability as some senators in Democratic measures with which I would be in hearty accord, nevertheless I recognize his great ability and the need of just such a man in the Senate at the present time." In response to a letter, he said that though he considered Milton Welling, a former congressman and stake president, a good man, Welling did not have Smoot's eighteen years of experience.[57]

As might be expected in this new era of relatively open politics, Grant allowed considerable latitude to church leaders in their active support of various political candidates. Stephen L Richards, Charles W. Penrose, Anthony W. Ivins, and Grant himself took active parts in the unsuccessful campaign of Democratic candidate Thomas N. Taylor for the governorship. The victor, Republican Charles R. Mabey, like Taylor, was an active church member.[58]

Grant did object, however, to the interjection of epithets directed against persons into the campaign. As Moyle opened attacks on Smoot, Grant began to defend Smoot and condemn Moyle. Late in the campaign, B. H. Roberts, whom the Democrats could always count on for colorful campaigning, attacked Smoot, and Grant denounced Roberts in private for his attacks.[59] In this new era of openness, Roberts was not brought before the Twelve as he had been during his opposition to Smoot in 1908, and the Republican victories in 1920 could hardly be said to have been church inspired or dictated.

As the 1920s progressed, it became clear that Heber J. Grant's political activities were based more on his feelings about the need for equity and morality than on party preferences. One of his initial hopes in 1922, for instance, was that a non-Mormon would be elected senator. At first he favored William H. Wattis, general manager of Utah-Idaho Sugar Company. At the same time, he opposed the candidacy of J. Reuben Clark, a man whom he also admired, because he thought the non-Mormons were entitled to one of the senatorial seats. One non-Mormon whom Grant did not want elected, however, was Ernest Bamberger, whom he considered an unsavory machine politician. Grant nevertheless insisted that the *Deseret News* remain neutral in the preconvention fight.[60]

The nominees of the two parties were Ernest Bamberger and incumbent Democrat William H. King. Besides President Grant, J. Reuben Clark and several other prominent Mormon Republicans expressed concern about Bamberger because of their opposition to boss rule and the Sevens, and Grant was "annoyed" when Charles W. Nibley, Reed Smoot, and other pro-Bamberger church leaders manipulated his—Grant's—public appearances to make it appear that he supported Bamberger.[61]

The refusal of the church leadership to support the Republican party in the 1922 election shocked Reed Smoot. On October 12 he attended a meeting of the First Presidency and the Twelve. President Grant criticised Ernest Bamberger, and Anthony W. Ivins complained of the cost to the church of the *Herald-Republican*. Smoot, who "thought it best to say nothing," felt a sense of personal injury when President Grant presided at rallies in Salt Lake City and Provo at which William Jennings Bryan spoke, and again at a Salt Lake rally addressed by William Gibbs McAdoo.[62]

The First Presidency issued a formal statement denying official church involvement in politics. Such statements had been issued before, and Smoot might well have expected continued support for the Republicans. But this did not happen. Among other things, the statement said that the church supported no particular candidates and that any opinions on political races were simply the personal views of those giving them. Nevertheless, the statement read, the church felt free "to use its influence in the promotion of good legislation, honest administration of government and matters calculated to benefit the state and its people and we likewise duly feel under obligation to exert its influence against introduction into our political organization of practices and methods which we regard as inimical to the free exercise of American rights and principles."[63]

As the senatorial campaign progressed, church leaders tried to separate their personal views from official policy. Heber J. Grant's position on the campaign was clear to all. He gave little open support to William H. King, but on the other hand, he refused to be drawn into appearing to favor Bamberger. He let it be known privately that he was much opposed to Bamberger's candidacy.

In two Salt Lake County sheriff's races President Grant supported particular candidates. In both cases, however, the support came because friends associated with organizations like the Social Welfare and

Betterment League of Salt Lake City presented evidence which led him to believe that the incumbents were not enforcing prohibition and other vice laws. In 1922 he supported Benjamin Harries, a nonpartisan candidate also supported by the Salt Lake Ministerial Association, and in 1930 he favored Grant Young, the Democratic candidate. In both cases, partisans of the opponents were upset. In the 1922 campaign Grant publically endorsed Harries. In 1930, however, a majority of the Twelve and First Presidency "talked him out of such an action."[64]

Grant's actions in the 1930 sheriff's race mirrored his posture in the 1928 senatorial election. Much as he detested Ernest Bamberger, he refused to allow himself to be pulled into the campaign. Reed Smoot, B. H. Roberts, and other Democratic and Republican partisans openly campaigned, but Grant refused to denounce Bamberger even at home with his own family.[65]

Two events which followed the 1922 election may indicate the results of the partisanship even when there seemed to be some moral justification for the action. On March 29, 1923, Republican C. Frank Emery, the former Salt Lake County sheriff, called Reed Smoot. He expressed sorrow at the action taken by "President Grant in the last election" and told Smoot that the whole affair had adversely affected his children. It had, he said, "shaken their faith in the church." Smoot was quite saddened by the impact on his friends, but he failed to see the corollary that Democratic Latter-day Saints and their children might have been hurt in the same way by the partisanship exhibited by the church leadership during the previous thirty years and during the period from the mid-1930s to the early 1950s.[66] The second event was the attempt to revive the American party in 1923 in response to the activities of the church in the 1922 senatorial campaign and of certain members of the Council of the Twelve in lobbying with the state legislature for cigarette prohibition during the 1923 legislative session. The new party, promoted by Ernest Bamberger and the Sevens, was called variously the Party of Freedom or League of Liberty, and finally named the American party in honor of its predecessor. It ran a full slate of candidates for the Salt Lake City Commission in 1923. The slate was defeated and the party killed largely because of its inability to pin the label of church candidate on C. Clarence Neslen, the incumbent mayor.[67]

In 1926 Reed Smoot's candidacy for the Senate again received President Grant's personal endorsement, but there is little evidence of active campaign work on the part of the church leader through official church channels. Smoot's support of the high protective tariff and porkbarrel legislation for Utah and his national prominence helped him immensely with the citizens of the state. Salt Lake City attorney-businessman Ashby Snow had little chance against the apostle-senator, and the Republican congressmen, Don Colton and Elmer Leatherwood, were also handily reelected.[68]

By the 1920s the standards for church involvement in politics had changed considerably. Unlike Joseph F. Smith, Heber J. Grant looked at political matters principally from a moralistic or tenure perspective. Republican, Democratic, or Independent persuasion mattered less to him than did his perception of the morality or experience of the candidate. This feeling explains both his support for Harries and Young and his opposition to Bamberger and Al Smith. He disliked Al Smith, probably because of his general image of favoring repeal of prohibition, but did not rebuke those within the church who supported Smith. He supported Smoot because of the senator's experience.

For the first time since the church divided itself along the partisan political lines in the 1890s, actively committed Democrats won positions of power. Anthony W. Ivins, particularly, was every bit as partisan on the Democratic side as Reed Smoot and Joseph F. Smith on the Republican, and his influence acted as a counterweight to Smoot's within church councils. Except when he could find a moral question like prohibition or machine politics, however, Ivins's principal contribution was to add balance rather than to drive the church into the Democratic column. If one excludes those questions which were perceived as moral, James H. Moyle's perception of official nonpartisanship during the 1920s is essentially accurate.

In general, between 1919 and 1930 the influence of the LDS church in Utah politics was grossly overrated. In retrospect, church leadership tended to reflect political opinion rather than to serve as the driving force behind opinion formation.

From the 1890s through the death of Joseph F. Smith in 1918, church leadership was active in its official support of the Republican party. The motivation for this support seems to have varied from avid pro-Republicanism to a desire to balance the two parties. In pursuit of those goals, Joseph F. Smith, in particular, sustained an active Republican political machine in the Federal Bunch and the *Herald-Republican*. Smith was also anxious not to antagonize Gentile Republicans. For that reason, he tried to ride two horses at once on the growing issue of prohibition. But prohibition did not divide on Mormon/non-Mormon lines. The antiliquor movement had widespread support throughout Utah and the whole nation, not only from Mormons but from Gentiles—particularly Evangelical Protestants. This widespread support led to the shattering of the Utah Republican party in 1916 and the election of a Democratic governor, senator, two congressmen, and a majority in both houses of the legislature. The Republicans did return to power in 1920, but the whole nation went Republican in 1920, and, statistically, Utah was less Republican than the average state. In fact, Utah is generally listed during the period from 1896 through 1970 as a swing state in which the winning candidates for the offices of governor, senator, and representative generally won by less than 55 percent of the vote.

The evidence is that in the four decades after the Manifesto the church leadership, whatever their motivation may have been, were reasonably successful in secularizing Utah politics. In the nineteenth century, the Mormon ideal had been a unitary, rather than pluralistic, community. The events following the Manifesto moved the church in the latter direction. By the 1920s Heber J. Grant and other church leaders were constantly concerned about the possible backlash that might follow active preference for one party or candidate. Even the attempts to generate support for nonpartisan candidates like Ben Harries or good government candidates like Grant Young caused considerable internal dissension even in the church's highest councils.

By the 1920s church political activity had become non-partisan. Moral considerations rather than political partisanship became the basis for church involvement. Moreover, the LDS church had ceased to wield decisive political influence in the determination of political candidates. Republican leaders like Reed Smoot were undoubtedly disturbed by this change, but at least by the late twenties, Heber J. Grant seems to have recognized the morass into which the church moved each time it tried to influence the course of political events. Only on those occasions when there seemed to be an important moral principle involved was he willing to try. Even then, assuming public opinion generally supported the move, the church risked a backlash which could undermine the internal harmony necessary to build the kingdom. When public opinion was decidedly against the church, such action revealed the vulnerability of the Lord's world dealing in Caesar's in this new pluralistic age.

On balance, it seems probable that most difficulty, dissension, and discord caused by apparent church involvement in politics came when church members or leaders saw an opportunity to gain points for their views by making others believe that the church had taken an official position on a particular cause or candidate. This tended to produce disharmony and on occasion drove otherwise faithful members from activity or out of the church completely, because church members, ordinarily able to separate the secular from the religious, had difficulty doing so when the two were combined in an area of political disagreement. Under those circumstances, the harmony and fellowship necessary to work together in building the kingdom quickly disappeared. Heber J. Grant and many of the church leaders seem to have recognized this in the 1920s, but by the mid-1930s they seem to have returned to the patterns characteristic of Joseph F. Smith's administration.

4

Recurrent Encounters with Plural Marriage

PERHAPS THE MOST important social and political consequences of the B. H. Roberts and Reed Smoot cases resulted from the resurrection of the question of continued plural marriage in the Mormon community. Among politicians, church involvement in affairs of state and economic and social control may have been most important, but the rank and file of Americans, and other nationals as well, saw the continuation of plural marriage as a betrayal deserving heavy punishment. Most Christians in the Western tradition could not understand how any enlightened human being could believe in or engage in a practice which they considered degrading to women at best and barbaric at worst.[1]

Mormons found the transition from the practice of plural marriage to the norms of Victorian America enormously painful. As many as a fifth of the inhabitants of most Mormon towns lived in plural families; most leaders—both general and local—had plural wives; and a whole generation of Latter-day Saints had grown up believing that plurality was not only wholesome and beneficial but ordained of God. Indeed, most church members probably interpreted Section 132 of the Doctrine and Covenants as requiring plural marriage for eternal exaltation. Generally, the terms "new and everlasting covenant" of marriage, "celestial marriage," and plural marriage were thought to be equivalent. At the time of the Smoot hearings and in connection with the Budge case relating to Idaho disfranchisement, church leaders were called upon to re-examine this question and to clarify their beliefs.[2]

Practices and beliefs once adhered to and continued over a long period of time take on a life of their own. The protests which came from some members after blacks were admitted to the priesthood in 1978 suggests not only the depth with which beliefs can be held, but the division which can take place between the more liberal or progressive elements in the church willing to accept change and conservatives or fundamentalists who find continuity in clinging to the old ways.[3]

Certainly the apparent divergence of public pronouncement and private practice was a difficult problem both for members and non-members. Perhaps the clearest announcement of the public position of the First Presidency following the Manifesto was the 1891 statement of President Woodruff before Judge Charles F. Loofbourow, appointed master in chancery to determine the future status of church property. At that time President Woodruff said that "the manifesto was intended to apply to the church everywhere in every nation and country. We are giving no liberty to enter the polygamous relations anywhere." Some Latter-day Saints, including a number of general authorities, interpreted this statement as "policy," not doctrine; as "expediency," not binding practice; as a temporary concession to the government for immediate legal purposes, and not as a directive. Ecclesiastical leaders who could not believe that the Lord would ask them to give up a principle for which they had contended so long reinforced this view.[4]

Nevertheless, at various times members of the church leadership reaffirmed President Woodruff's resolve. In a meeting of the Presidency and the Twelve in April 1901, some apostles raised the question of the possibility of new plural marriage outside the United States. President Lorenzo Snow said that such marriages were not permissible, and President Joseph F. Smith agreed. President Snow went as far as to say that God had removed from the president of the church the privilege of granting permission to perform plural marriages, and since the Prophet was the only one who could give such permission, it could not be granted.[5]

Some question exists as to the legal condition of plural marriages outside the United States at that time. Although polygamy was generally illegal under Mexican law, Heber J. Grant said that President Porfirio Diaz had granted permission for plural marriages. However, such marriages were illegal in Canada after 1890, if not before. In that year the Canadian Parliament had passed the Thompson bill, which defined polygamy as a crime punishable by fine and imprisonment. Somewhat earlier stake president Charles O. Card had assured Canadian authorities that the Saints were not practicing plural marriage in Canada.[6]

Nevertheless, it is clear today that plural marriages were contracted after the Manifesto. Two apostles eventually lost their positions as a result of the continuation of the practice, and later testimony has demonstrated that while some leaders such as John Henry Smith, Reed Smoot, Francis M. Lyman, and George F. Richards were adamantly opposed to polygamous marriages after 1904 if not before, some new marriages had the support of members of the church's hierarchy. Before that time, some church leaders opposed new plural marriages in public while encouraging selected members to enter into new unions in private. In part because of this, the evidence with respect to presidents Woodruff, Snow, and Smith is contradictory, and a number of general authorities like Abraham O. Woodruff and Matthias F. Cowley insisted that the church leadership including President Smith approved such marriages. On the other hand, President Smith performed no plural marriages himself, but rather performed a proxy temple sealing for the deceased David H. Cannon and the living Lillian Hamlin in 1896.[7]

Publicity generated by the Roberts case rekindled national curiosity and outrage over the practice, and it became a matter of national concern and discussion. National periodicals and Protestant journals such as *World's Work*, *Harper's*, *Arena*, and *Missionary Review of the World* published articles arguing that plural marriage had actually been expanding from 1891 to 1903. President Joseph Smith III, representing the Reorganized Church of Jesus Christ of Latter Day Saints, and Charles W. Penrose and Joseph F. Smith exchanged views in the *Arena*. Perhaps the most favorable article published by a non-Mormon was Richard Ely's April 1903 article in *Harper's*, which argued that, far from being a sign of lust, polygamy necessitated a commitment to frugality. Ray Stannard Baker pointed out that "there are still Mormons, as a citizen of Salt Lake City graphically put it, 'who can take a car going in any direction and get home.'" Charles Spahr in the *Outlook Magazine*, generally impressed by the people of Utah, was somewhat negative on polygamy, though he pointed out that the better classes, not the dregs of society, generally practiced it.[8]

Currently available evidence indicates that, while the number of new plural marriages was small in the LDS community as a whole, there was actually an increase from the late nineties until the time of the Smoot investigation. Moreover, a substantial proportion—perhaps as high as 15 percent—of stake and ward leaders had entered new polygamy, often at the urging of a church leader. Joseph Eckersley of

Wayne County reported that he had heard rumors that Abraham O. Woodruff had authorized secret marriages in Mexico and Arizona. Eckersley himself was set apart as second counselor in the stake presidency in November 1903, and Matthias F. Cowley told him that "it was not the policy of Prest. Joseph F. Smith to censure any man for entering the order of plural marriage since the days of the Manifesto, provided he acted wisely and done so with the sanction and by the authority of the proper authority." In meetings of the First Presidency and the Twelve during September and October 1903, at least John W. Taylor and Marriner W. Merrill were still urging that some plural marriages ought to be solemnized to keep the institution alive.[9]

Such discussion in a theoretical sense within the Twelve and clandestine efforts of some persons to promote plural marriage could be tolerated only until it became apparent that they caused irreparable harm to the church. The election of Reed Smoot and the subsequent protest, incorporating as it did the charge that the church in general and its leadership in particular encouraged lawlessness through new plural marriages, provided the catalyst for action on the matter.

The managers for those challenging Smoot's seating included Robert W. Tayler, who had led the opposition to B. H. Roberts's admission to the House of Representatives. The committee published extracts from the constitution and statutes of Utah, which prohibited not only new plural marriages but also any continued polygamous cohabitation. After the protests and answers had been entered into the record, Joseph F. Smith was called to testify on March 3, 1904. President Smith said that, with tacit federal and public approval, citizens of Utah who had entered into plural marriage prior to the Manifesto were permitted to continue to live in those relationships. He admitted that he was continuing his own marriages in accordance with this understanding. Tayler then proceeded to the consideration of new plural marriages. President Smith testified that "there has not any man, with the consent or knowledge or approval of the Church, ever married a plural wife since the Manifesto." During the course of the discussion, the question of the actual number of plural marriages arose. Joseph F. Smith stated that about 4,000 men had been in polygamy, about 2 percent of the church population. He also pointed out that plural marriage had declined and that half of the Twelve and both his counselors were monogamists. Fred T. Dubois, senator from Idaho and one of those protesting Smoot's seating, pointed out that Smith's total membership figures included children, who could not have been polygamists, and that as many as 23 percent of the Mormon population of Utah over age eighteen may have been involved in polygamy.[10]

Following the Smoot hearings, efforts by non-Mormons to prosecute polygamists and those continuing to live in plural marriage increased. The *Salt Lake Tribune*, for a long time neutral in regard to the church, opened an attack early in 1904 through a series of articles aimed at the practice of polygamy. The Women's Christian Temperance Union announced in October 1904 that it would not rest until polygamy was made a crime throughout the United States. In January 1905, the Women's Interdenominational Council announced that it had established a fund to track down polygamists. Investigations, which led in some cases to convictions, were opened in Arizona, New Mexico, Hawaii, and Canada.[11]

By the April Conference of 1904 the Twelve and the First Presidency discussed the wisdom of making a statement to pacify the country. Anthon H. Lund, with his usual perceptive insights, favored the statement as a means of letting the Saints themselves know the status of plural marriage in the church. He pointed out that many who were following the Smoot proceedings were beginning to doubt the sincerity of church leaders. Abraham O. Woodruff, a holdout on the issue, said he was very much opposed to anything against a principle "which had given him birth and which would tend to obliterate it."[12]

In spite of this sentiment, the consensus of the First Presidency and the Twelve was that a statement was necessary, and one was drafted. At the closing session of the general conference on April 6, 1904, Joseph F. Smith read the declaration, which stated that no plural marriages had been "solemnized with the sanction, consent or knowledge of the Church," and announced that "all such marriages are prohibited, and if any officer or member of the Church shall assume to solemnize or enter into any such marriage he will be deemed in transgression against the Church and will be liable to be dealt with . . . and excommunicated therefrom." Francis M. Lyman, president of the Council of the Twelve, moved the adoption of the statement as policy of the church and those voting in conference approved the resolution unanimously.[13]

Shortly before this declaration, called the Second Manifesto, was issued, Reed Smoot summed up the feelings of some of the Twelve. He observed in a letter to Jesse N. Smith that not all members of the church had "lived strictly to our agreements with the government and this lack of sincerity on our part goes farther to condemn us in the eyes of the public men of the nation than the mere fact of a few new polygamous cases or a polygamist before the Manifesto living in a state of unlawful cohabitation. . . . We must," he wrote, "be honest with ourselves, with our fellow-men, and with our God."[14]

After the adoption of the Second Manifesto, the Twelve began to take measures to enforce it. On May 3 Francis M. Lyman wrote John W. Taylor that he was advising each member of the council that the rule in regard to plural marriages "will be strictly enforced against each and every person who shall be found guilty of offense against that rule." Thereafter, circular letters were sent to various church officials stating the same policy. The Twelve pursued the matter quite vigorously. Letters were sent on June 3 and 9 to Anthony W. Ivins, leader of the Mormon colony at Colonia Juarez, Mexico, inquiring about a member who had gone to Juarez within the last two years to marry a plural wife. Ivins was asked to investigate and, in addition, "to put your foot on it, giving the parties to understand that President Woodruff's Manifesto is in effect, and that therefore such marriages cannot be performed with our sanction and approval." In the quarterly meeting of the Twelve in July 1904, the apostles agreed that no one should utter among the Saints sentiments contrary to the pledges of the president of the church. As a safeguard against the abuse of the sealing privilege, the First Presidency annulled the previously granted freedom of apostles to seal couples "for time and eternity" in Canada, Arizona, and Mexico, where there were no temples.[15]

Sentiment grew that some of those of the Twelve who had approved or participated in new plural marriages since the Manifesto should be disciplined. After a consideration, John W. Taylor and Matthias F. Cowley were not sustained at the October 1904 conference nor at the succeeding two general conferences. Their resignations were requested by and presented to the council on October 28, 1905, but not accepted at that time. Some general authorities were disturbed at the removal of the two, but many considered it a necessary sacrifice.[16] The resignations were asked for and received both for the relief of the church and because Taylor and Cowley had proved defiant against the position taken by the Presidency and the Twelve following the Second Manifesto. In many ways, the two apostles' positions were like those of Moses Thatcher and B. H. Roberts in the 1890s. As long as no definite rule had been adopted, each member of the Twelve and First Presidency could do as he wanted on the question. However, the Second Manifesto of April 6, 1904, had the same effect on Cowley and Taylor as the Political Manifesto had had on Roberts and Thatcher. President Smith clearly was saddened by the need to chasten these two men with whom he had served for many years. They had, however, "unwisely brought trouble both upon themselves and the Church. And the enemy is after them fiercely. I scarcely see," he wrote, "how they can escape most serious consequences."[17]

Some Latter-day Saints expressed disappointment or anger at the resolve to stop new plural marriages, but after 1904 President Smith and associates were adamant. Those teaching and practicing plural marriage since the Manifesto must be dealt with.[18] The illness and subsequent deaths of three members of the Twelve, Abraham O. Woodruff, Marriner W. Merrill, and George Teasdale, may have saved them from censure for continued defiance of the Second Manifesto.

At the quarterly meeting of the Twelve during April conference 1906, a decision was made to present the previously obtained resignations of the still-recalcitrant elders Taylor and Cowley to the conference. At the same time, the First Presidency and Twelve sustained George F. Richards to fill the vacancy caused by the death of Marriner W. Merrill and Orson F. Whitney and David O. McKay to fill Taylor's and Cowley's positions. The names of the three new apostles were presented at conference on April 8, 1906, but the council members registered considerable sadness over the resignations of Taylor and Cowley. Taylor left for Canada, and Cowley, remaining in the United States, was instructed that he might "bear testimony," but he was forbidden to accept invitations to preach.[19]

Repudiation of the principle of new plural marriage, however, could not spare President Smith and others from further humiliation. Indictments were issued against Heber J. Grant, Joseph F. Smith, and others, largely on the investigations of Charles M. Owen. The charge against President Smith grew out of the birth on May 21, 1906, of Royal G. Smith to Mary T. Schwartz Smith. In Europe at the time, Joseph F. Smith was arrested on September 30, 1906, following his return, on a charge of illegal cohabitation, and released on his own recognizance. Under considerable pressure, the case was brought to trial, and on November 23, 1906, Joseph F. Smith pled guilty and was fined $300.[20]

As revelations and charges of new plural marriage appeared, efforts at enforcement of the 1904 ban continued, and in 1909 the general authorities began an investigation which was to have long-range consequences. On July 14, 1909, the First Presidency called a committee consisting of Francis M. Lyman, John Henry Smith, and Heber J. Grant to look into alleged new plural marriages. The committee was charged with dealing "summarily" with those found guilty. Other apostles were asked to help. Several persons—patriarchs, stake presidents, mission presidents, and others—were asked to testify. Some were dropped from their church positions. One person who had been under consideration for appointment to the First Council of the Seventy was passed over because "he had married plural wives since the Manifesto and his appointment would bring trouble on the church sure." At a special meeting of the First Presidency and the Twelve with thirty-eight of the Church's sixty-two stake presidents, held February 8, 1910, President Smith reiterated that the church must keep its pledge to the federal government. "No one has the authority to solemnize plural marriages," President Smith said, adding that if marriages were performed, he would be held responsible. There was some dissension in the meeting, but President Smith stood firm. Stake presidents were to take the lead in disciplining those who had violated church rules. To make the matter perfectly clear to its members, the church began to announce excommunications for plural marriage in the pages of the *Deseret News*. A circular letter of October 5, 1910, instructed bishops to try new polygamists for their membership.[21]

The task of the Lyman Committee proved extremely difficult. On July 7, 1909, Carl A. Badger and Louise A. Badger called on Heber J. Grant with the news that their sister Bessie had recently married into plurality with one of Elder Grant's former European missionaries. In general the pattern of this case was similar to that of subsequent cases which came before the committee. Those called to testify were generally local church leaders. Most professed a lapse of memory, or dissembled on the witness stand, or refused to testify. Some took the position, undoubtedly because of statements made to them previously by authorities like Woodruff, Merrill, Taylor, or Cowley, that they were justified in taking new plural wives, "provided they could get them properly," by which they seemed to have meant that they could gain approval of an apostle, a stake patriarch, or someone they recognized as an authority and could keep the matter beyond the notice of the church's enemies. In those cases where sufficient evidence could be gathered to prove a marriage after 1904, excommunication often resulted.[22]

In some cases, local church leaders were asked to take jurisdiction. Understandably, it was sometimes difficult to get the stake presidents and bishops to act.[23] Since most of those entering plural marriages were the leaders in the church and the community, they were also generally close personal and ecclesiastical associates of the local authorities. Ordinarily, a high degree of trust, cooperative spirit, and brotherly love had developed, and local leaders were torn between their loyalty to members who had served long and well and their obligation to sustain the church Presidency and the Twelve. Often, considerable exhortation and counsel was necessary to secure action. Undoubtedly, the example of the Lyman Committee on the general church level helped to encourage local officials, but prosecution was no easy matter.

On November 15, 1910, Reed Smoot met with the First Presidency and Elder Lyman prior to returning to Washington. The discussion centered on new polygamy, and Smoot wanted a statement for President Taft making clear the church's position. The agreement, confirmed again by the First Presidency, was that those who had married after 1904 would be disciplined. Those cases between the Woodruff Manifesto of 1890 and 1904 would be "dealt with according to circumstances." If the parties had been "drawn into [new marriages] by Apostles they would not be excommunicated" but would be released from any position in the church where members were liable to be asked to vote for them. Though not strictly adhered to, enforcement generally followed this pattern.[24]

In spite of evidence that plural marriage was on the decline after 1904, attacks continued. Indeed, the revelations of the Smoot investigation and information of new plural marriage opened what amounted to a national magazine campaign against the church and its leadership. In May 1907 Senator Julius Burrows published an article in the nationally circulated *Independent*, charging new plural marriages and duplicity on the part of the church. Similar articles followed in 1908, and the intensity increased during 1910, when Harvey O'Higgins wrote an article in *Collier's* on new polygamy in Utah. Articles by Richard Barry appeared in the September, October, and November 1910 numbers of *Pearsons*, and in December 1910 ex-communicant

Frank J. Cannon began an eight-issue exposé in collaboration with O'Higgins, published first in *Everybody's* magazine and eventually issued in book form.[25]

Some of the articles were obviously poorly conceived and hastily written attacks. One of the best researched of the articles was that by Burton J. Hendrick, published in *McClure's* for February 1911. Hendrick spent more than a month and a half in Salt Lake City, visited the general conference, and talked with Anthon H. Lund, John Henry Smith, and Ben E. Rich about the new polygamy cases. Anthon H. Lund's fears after consulting with Hendrick that "with the poor showing which we are making on these cases that we will be represented in a bad light" were fully confirmed. Hendrick drew a picture of "a great secret society" in which "all members of the church are oath-bound under the most frightful penalties, not to reveal these [temple] mysteries." He wrote of a largely inaccessible rural society, suspicious of outsiders and sustained by duplicity. Though his article painted Mormonism in a thoroughly bad light, he showed the results of his research in an understanding of some of the finer distinctions of Mormon theology.[26]

In many ways, the most outrageous of the articles were Alfred Henry Lewis's "Viper" series. Unlike Hendrick's, Lewis's articles were poorly researched, showing an abysmal ignorance of Mormon theology and history. As an example, Lewis wrote that the church had developed from Joseph Smith's fraud, perpetrated, Lewis said, with the assistance of two fictitious "stenographic angels, Thummim and Urim," who were "detailed from on high" to assist Joseph Smith in "convenient" trances to render "the [golden] plates into English." The remainder of church history, he wrote, was filled with murder and terror which held the faithful and Gentiles alike in submission.[27]

Perhaps the major problem in this entire literary attack on Mormon society was a failure to understand the cement which held the Mormon ecclesiastical polity together. Stories of Danites, blood atonement, and temple mysteries notwithstanding, members remained loyal to the church because of shared testimonies of the gospel. In some cases, as is clearly evident in politics, members changed their views because of pressure from church leaders, but in the final analysis they did so voluntarily since the church had no power to attack their lives or property. Members who lost their testimonies could and did leave the church.

Thus, the Gentile residents in many towns and cities included apos-
tates who were unwilling to subordinate themselves to the authority of
the church leadership.[28]

In addition, church leaders were willing to tolerate a great deal of
latitude and disagreement as long as there was a basic "harmony" and
sense of purpose in building the kingdom. Far from being vindictive or
ruthless, the church leadership tended to be lenient with wayward
members who were basically in harmony with the church and its
doctrines. Defiance and insubordination, however, would not be accepted.[29] Beyond this, the church responded to unavoidable outside
pressure, such as that of the Smoot investigation. Many of those who
were excommunicated or disfellowshipped could probably have saved
their church membership had they not clung so tenaciously to a dis-
credited principle in opposition to contemporary prophetic dicta.

By early 1911 the magazine articles and books attacking the church
had brought about "the renewal of the discussion" of the "new polygamy cases." Reed Smoot, more politically sensitive than many other
leaders, "insisted that the only way the Church can clear itself is to
handle every new case of polygamy and remove from any position in
the Church those who entered." Merely because the church "has not
approved or sanctioned the marriages" did not mean that the nation
would not hold the church leaders "responsible for them." Smoot realized, of course, that church leaders were afraid that by offending
church members "if wholesale action is taken" they might breach the
harmony which held the organization together. Smoot himself thought
that "non action will have a worse effect, especially upon the young
people."[30]

The Council of the Twelve excommunicated Elder Taylor on March 28,
1911, and disfellowshipped Cowley two months later. The arguments
which Taylor and Cowley produced at their trials for the continued
practice and for their actions in promoting and protecting plural marriage were similar to those surfacing at other similar trials. Taylor, for
instance, believed that a revelation to his father, John Taylor, provided
all the authority necessary for members to continue, on their own, to
enter into and perform such marriages. He and others were thus extremely belligerent when the church judicial system began to deal
with them. Matthias F. Cowley believed that they had the approval of
the church leadership to continue to perform and enter into the marriages. In the effort to protect the church, in addition, Cowley and

Laying the capstone of the Salt Lake Temple, April 6, 1892.

The First Presidency of the LDS Church, 1894. Left to right: First Counselor George Q. Cannon (1827–1901), President Wilford Woodruff (1807–98), Second Counselor Joseph F. Smith (1838–1918).

The First Presidency and Council of the Twelve, 1900. Center, left to right: First Counselor George Q. Cannon, President Lorenzo Snow (1814–1901), Second Counselor Joseph F. Smith. Council of the Twelve (by seniority): clockwise from upper center left: Brigham Young, Jr. (1836–1903), Francis M. Lyman (1840–1916), John Henry Smith (1848–1911), George Teasdale (1831–1907), Heber J. Grant (1856–1945), John W. Taylor (1858–1916), Marriner W. Merrill (1832–1906), Anthon H. Lund (1844–1921), Matthias F. Cowley (1858–1940), Abraham Owen Woodruff (1872–1904), Rudger Clawson (1857–1943), Reed Smoot (1862–1941).

The First Presidency of the LDS Church, 1905. Left to right: First Counselor John R. Winder (1821–1910), President Joseph F. Smith (1838–1918), Second Counselor Anthon H. Lund (1844–1921).

The First Presidency of the LDS Church, 1910. Left to right: First Counselor Anthon H. Lund, President Joseph F. Smith, Second Counselor John Henry Smith.

The First Presidency of the LDS Church, 1920. Left to right: Second Counselor Charles W. Penrose (1832–1925), President Heber J. Grant (1856–1945), First Counselor Anthon H. Lund (1844–1921).

The First Presidency of the LDS Church, 1929. Left to right: President Heber J. Grant, Second Counselor Charles W. Nibley (1849–1931) (Presiding Bishop, 1907–25), First Counselor Anthony W. Ivins (1852–1934).

Reed Smoot (1862–1941), member of the Council of the Twelve (1900–41) and conservative Republican senator from Utah (1903–33).

Brigham H. Roberts (1857–1933), member of the First Council of the Seventy (1888–1933), leading theologian, progressive Democrat, and chaplain during World War I.

Stephen L Richards (1879–1959),
member of the Council of the Twelve
(1917–51), and leader in the development of social services in the LDS
Church.

Nephi L. Morris (1870–1943), Salt
Lake Stake president and Progressive
(1912) and Republican (1916) party
gubernatorial candidate.

John W. Taylor (1858–1916), member of the Council of the Twelve (1884–1905). Excommunicated (1911) for promoting polygamy after the Second Manifesto (1904), reinstated posthumously.

Matthias F. Cowley (1858–1940), member of the Council of the Twelve (1897–1905). Disfellowshipped (1911) for promoting polygamy after the Second Manifesto (1904), reinstated 1936.

others said that they were justified in lying in order to prevent embarrassment or punishment for doing "that which is right."[31]

As might be expected, antichurch activity continued. In February 1913 the Senate, over President Taft's veto, passed an immigration bill which prohibited believers in polygamy from entering the country. Reed Smoot received a telegram from Joseph F. Smith asking him to sustain the veto, but he wired the president that he could not and that if the present bill were "defeated a more radical one would be passed by next Congress." The old proposal for a constitutional amendment against polygamy was revived, and some of Smoot's friends thought he ought to support it in the Senate.[32]

The problems which the Latter-day Saints faced in dealing with the new plural marriages were similar to those which members of any organization might confront in the wake of rapid change. Any body will include people uncomfortable with change and insistent upon the old ways of doing things. In a religious organization this is particularly serious since the beliefs of the people are often tied to particular behavior. In this case those fundamentalists who insisted on entering new plural marriages were fearful that their salvation would be jeopardized should they fail to adhere to the principle. The realities of modern life, however, made such practices impossible, and conservatives like Joseph F. Smith, Heber J. Grant, and Reed Smoot were more anxious to have the church become accepted and continue to grow than to adhere to a way of life which had become outmoded.

In sociological terms, these events constituted a crisis in world maintenance. Even though the church was a voluntary organization in the nineteenth century, it was such a closed community in Utah and parts of Idaho, Arizona, Mexico, and Canada that the organization could be used to maintain what Peter Berger has called a "plausibility structure" or internal regulatory mechanism for the world view including political, social, and economic unity. By the twentieth century such a community was impossible, and as the church leaders found themselves unable to maintain all aspects of the world view of the nineteenth century, members learned that they could reject counsel and find some support among others in the church out of harmony with the Second Manifesto. Many simply refused to accept the new paradigm which rejected plural marriage as necessary for salvation. Some were punished, but others remained in the church clandestinely despite the efforts to ferret them out.[33]

Nevertheless, as the exhortations, circular letters, personal counsel, and church trials originating with the general authorities had the desired effect, those continuing to preach and practice new plural marriage were increasingly isolated from the church community. New local and general church leadership replaced the older generation of members committed to a perpetuation of the Principle, and by the 1920s some church members began to dread the discussion of plural marriage, which they considered an embarrassing blot on an otherwise glorious history.

By the 1920s conditions had obviously changed. While speaking to a group of temple workers in March 1921, President Grant denounced those "breaking the laws of God and Man . . . [who entered] into what they claimed to be plural marriage to obey the law of God. I laid it down very plainly," he wrote, "that it was to gratify animal passions instead of to fulfill the law of God." In 1924 the First Presidency assigned James E. Talmage to encourage the stakes to take action against dissidents. Joseph W. Musser, a high councilman from Salt Lake, and others were dealt with by the church in spite of the allegation that the church was casting out the best blood by cutting off those who entered into plural marriage. President Grant considered Musser's statements "impudent."[34]

These efforts to eradicate the celebration of new plural marriages and to discipline those who entered into them after 1904 reveal a great deal about the attitudes of church members on a number of important questions. In the first place, it seems evident that members detected, during at least the five years after 1904, a seeming conflict in church doctrine and practice. On the one hand, many believed that plural marriage was essential to the New and Everlasting Covenant. On the other, they bore testimony that God authorized the church president as prophet, seer, and revelator to reveal changes in church doctrine and practice. Instead of meeting this problem head on, which would probably have created additional conflict, they reinterpreted the meaning of the terms. Largely through the efforts of James E. Talmage, the leading theologian in the church at the time, the general authorities reaffirmed the need for eternal marriage but excluded the necessity of plural marriage from the requirements for exaltation. A second conflict which they faced was that between the need to preserve the church and its teachings pure and undefiled and the need to preserve the church organization itself to provide ordinances of salvation to its members and to spread the gospel abroad. Some thought the price of abandoning plural marriage and disciplining members who entered it too high, but most considered it little enough in view of the obvious benefits which accrued from a closer harmony to the general attitudes of early twentieth-century America.

The Second Manifesto of 1904 was an extremely important benchmark in resolving both of these conflicts. Prior to that time, members continued to receive support for the belief that the denials of new plural marriage were for the public consumption, and that for the initiated a different rule of "beating the devil at his own game" obtained. This produced a sort of dissonance difficult to maintain in a voluntary organization which required not only the good will of its adherents but of the larger society for its continued existence and prosperity. The Second Manifesto and its enforcement removed that dissonance and, in addition, isolated those within the organization who insisted upon perpetuating the duplicity which had previously existed. The organization itself was undoubtedly strengthened as a result.

5

The Temporal Kingdom

THOUGH THE TRANSITION in business affairs did not cause as much difficulty for the church as did politics or plural marriage, it nevertheless evoked considerable adverse publicity during the early twentieth century. Church involvement in business had a long tradition. In large part, businesses in which the church had an interest were either begun in the nineteenth century or were designed to promote local economic development. Church leaders had engaged in such diverse enterprises as a bank at Kirtland, Ohio; a manufacturing society at Nauvoo, Illinois; and merchandising in Utah. Cooperation with Gentile businessmen began as early as Brigham Young's grading contracts for the construction of the transcontinental railroad, and in the late 1880s Mormon and Gentile businessmen cooperated quite extensively, in many cases acquiring corporations which had been wholly or principally church owned before. During the depression of the 1890s, the church worked with both Mormon and Gentile businessmen in financing a number of development projects such as power, mining, and salt companies.[1]

In the nineteenth century, the church could handle its involvement in a large number of business enterprises through its internal community structure. Although Gentiles and dissident Mormons opposed the economic domination, faithful church members accepted such activity as part of their world view. Since the Mormon community encompassed politics, business, and social relations, the church leadership could require members as a matter of religious duty to trade at cooperative stores or to sell out to ZCMI.[2]

Victorian America, however, produced two trends into which the church had to fit. In the first place, monopolistic and nationally integrated business organizations rose in many industries in place of the earlier generally fragmented and localized enterprises. The first of these were railroads like the Union Pacific, which the church had helped to build. The second trend was the coordinate antimonopoly and business regulatory movements which produced the Interstate Commerce Act in 1887 and the Sherman Anti-Trust Act in 1890 together with a number of other acts and Supreme Court decisions affirming the legitimacy of governmental regulation of monopoly and business.[3]

Moreover, while the norms of American society did allow religious organizations to support business enterprise, they did not generally sanction economic domination as pervasive as that found in Utah. In a pluralistic society, church members had to be free to patronize or not to patronize a church business and churches were expected to use restraint in their exercise of economic power so private businesses were not unduly harmed.[4]

In practice the adoption of the world view that sanctioned economic pluralism began much earlier than the changes in politics and the practice of plural marriage. As early as 1882 the First Presidency announced the end of the Gentile boycott and the opening of retailing and manufacturing to private enterprise. As late as the 1890s local church leaders in some areas applied sanctions against members engaging in certain businesses in competition with LDS enterprises. In general, however, after 1900 church members were urged to patronize local firms, but neither the sort of official pressure applied in the political realm to support church-approved candidates nor the clandestine support of new plural marriage by particular authorities was evident in economic activity. At times, and especially after the beginning of the Grant administration, the church leaders became so sensitive about potential competition with private business that they adopted practices that hurt their own enterprises rather than offend church members in competing businesses. At the turn of the twentieth century, however, the erroneous perception of church support for monopoly was so pervasive that it dominated public thought about business in Utah.

Accusations that church leaders cooperated with monopolistic enterprises and made enormous profits led to attacks on church business dealings. These attacks rose in intensity during the Reed Smoot hearings and reached a peak in muckraking assaults from 1910 through 1912. After 1913 the attacks declined. During the teens and the First World War, in fact, the church received some favorable publicity, in part as a backlash against the muckrakers. During the 1920s fusillades declined as church-owned businesses suffered financial reverses. By then, too, the church's image had improved, and it began to receive considerable favorable publicity in the national press.[5]

Typical of the charges during the first decade of the twentieth century was the comment of the Reverend Joseph Cook. "Standing on Brigham Street in Salt Lake City, and gazing at the famous Eagle Gate, with its figure of an eagle perched upon a beehive," he thought he saw "a fit emblem—rapacity preying upon industry." In answer to such criticism and particularly to the attacks of muckrakers like Alfred Henry Lewis, Frank J. Cannon, and Burton J. Hendrick, Joseph F. Smith published an *Improvement Era* article in April 1912. The church, he said, had always tried to "help establish home industries and to aid in setting certain business enterprises on their feet," in order to provide employment and "to develop the material resources of the country, that the people and the land may prosper." Those purposes accomplished, the church had generally withdrawn, "holding in most cases only a very little financial interest in the enterprises." In his view, spiritual and temporal salvation complemented each other, and the church promoted both.[6]

The evidence that the American writer Julian Street in 1914 and the British journalist Randolph Churchill in 1915 found in Salt Lake City confirmed President Smith's view that the church was not the dominant force in Utah's economy. Of fourteen banks Street found in Salt Lake City, nine were controlled by non-Mormons. Of five department stores, four were non-Mormon. Gentiles owned four-fifths of the best residential property. All "skyscrapers" in Salt Lake City except one were owned by Gentiles. The Mormon leaders were largely businessmen, Street pointed out, but they did not dominate the business community. Every businessman with whom he talked asked him to set the record straight, and one Gentile said to "tell people that we raise something out here besides Mormons and hell!"[7]

This is not to say that church leaders were anti-business. A perusal of the interests listed in the diaries of church leaders reveals broad business connections throughout Utah and the West.[8] And though many observers complained about church involvement in business, there seemed to be little objection when the church assisted in unprofitable irrigation projects. Between 1900 and 1924 the church leadership invested in projects in a number of places including Arizona, Utah, and Idaho.[9]

The *Deseret News*, currently a church-controlled business, was in private hands during the 1890s. In early November 1898 President Lorenzo Snow proposed repurchasing the paper and calling Charles W. Penrose as editor to provide a daily organ for news and information. A discussion among the First Presidency and the Twelve ensued and a number of the Republican apostles opposed, since Penrose was an ardent Democrat. John Henry Smith proposed instead the inauguration of a weekly religious newspaper. He offered to buy the *Deseret News* and run it as a Republican party organ. Francis M. Lyman thought that if Penrose were editor, it would be thought the paper was Democratic. He said that President Snow ought to be the editor. But most of the Twelve favored the church purchase proposal, and President Snow hired Penrose as editor and Horace G. Whitney as business manager. Some Republicans in the church, like *Woman's Exponent* editor Emmeline B. Wells, were disturbed by Penrose's call, but, as she put it, they had to "take things philosophically or we could not survive." Penrose continued until 1907 when he was called as president of the European Mission, and Janne M. Sjodahl became editor.[10]

The paper's fortunes fluctuated. Under Penrose's and Whitney's supervision, the paper began making money. By the late teens, however, competition from the city's three other dailies had cut into its circulation, causing considerable financial difficulty. In 1924 Brigham F. Grant, a successful manager of LDS hospital, was appointed business manager in the hope that the paper's losses could be reduced.[11] The appointment caused immediate positive response in the business community. By the late 1920s Grant had put the paper on a relatively sound financial footing. After the depression began in 1929, however, the *News* began to run behind, and only a church subsidy kept it afloat. In 1954 the *Deseret News* and *Tribune*, which also experienced financial distress, formed the Newspaper Agency Corporation to handle the printing, advertising, and circulation of both papers.[12]

Perhaps the most disappointing and misunderstood financial venture of the church during this period was the Salt Lake Theatre. In January 1900 the church leadership purchased the theatre, which was losing money but which they valued as an important cultural alternative to cheap and often vulgar vaudeville shows. By 1914 vaudeville and the motion picture had cut deeply into the clientele for serious drama. The theatre drifted deeper into financial difficulty, and the management began to try to increase its patronage by offering some artistically inferior but popular plays borrowed from the Winter Garden in New York City. Nevertheless, the theatre continued to lose money.[13]

Problems in the 1920s made it impossible for the church to continue to subsidize the theatre. In August 1921 the management came under pressure from the Salt Lake City government to undertake extensive and costly renovations. By the late twenties, the theatre had succumbed to financial pressure and was under contract with a New York booking company to take all plays it dictated. President Grant expressed some disgust at the type of plays presented, but realized the theatre management had little choice.[14]

Shortly thereafter, Maude May Babcock of the University of Utah appealed for the church to foster the dramatic arts more than they had in the recent past. She told the president that the Salt Lake Theatre could succeed with local companies as it had in the nineteenth century. President Grant, who had lived through the financial stress caused by trying to compete with vaudeville and motion pictures, told her that he had "grave doubts" about such success. Babcock suggested as an alternative that the church turn the theatre over to LDS High School. This was out of the question, since the high school was being phased out at the time.[15]

By January 1928 the theatre had fallen into even more critical financial condition. Now, given the church's own financial distress, it could not "afford to go on having a loss of $100,000 capital and losing money in addition." Moreover, the quality of its presentations had deteriorated. In March 1928 the Mountain States Telephone Company offered $200,000 for the theatre property. President Grant discussed the matter with business associates and the Twelve. A long debate ensued, and after several members objected to its sale and wanted to save the theatre, President Grant agreed that if enough patrons would provide a subsidy they would not sell. He offered to contribute several thousand of his own money for the purpose, but none of the other brethren offered to help, so the church sold the property. On October 20, 1928, the theatre gave its final performance.[16]

After the closing, President Grant talked with the manager of the Santa Monica Playhouse. The Californian said that unless the community had enough "civic pride" to maintain legitimate theatre, movies would soon have the field to themselves. President Grant, who had spent a lifetime as a patron of the arts, thought that it was "remarkable to me how the taste of the public has degenerated for good plays. In my boyhood days vaudeville or anything of a character that was not up-lifting stood no show in the community, but that day seems to have passed." It is clear also that he was not speaking simply of moralistic or didactic plays. His tastes ran principally in the classical and realistic tradition. In commenting on one play, for instance, he said that he hoped it would be a success because "it was true to life." Part of it, he said, "would not do for Sunday school children," but that was no bar to its performance.[17]

Though financial stringency dictated the sale of many of the church's assets, the sales themselves and the consequences of those sales often presented ethical and legal difficulties for the church and its leaders. Perhaps the best example of this was the relationship of the church with Henry O. Havemeyer's monopolistic American Sugar Refining Company.

Discussions began in November 1901 between Havemeyer's representatives and church officials with a view to the purchase of half the assets of the Utah Sugar Company. At first some of the church leaders, such as Anthon H. Lund, were opposed to the undertaking. Elder Lund believed that it would be best to build and expand with home capital. Havemeyer pressed the church, however, by threatening to open a competing company. At a meeting on November 23, 1901, the directors agreed to negotiate and they sold a half interest. In 1907 an agreement between the Utah Sugar Company, the Idaho Sugar Company, and the Western Idaho Sugar Company created the Utah-Idaho Sugar Company (U and I), also part of the sugar trust but with church leaders as principal directors.[18]

Increasingly, the church leaders began to see that what had been thought of as a necessity in 1901 had become antithetical to the interests of the community. In 1903 the Amalgamated Sugar Company under Charles W. Nibley and David Eccles began planning the construction of a sugar factory at Lewiston in Cache Valley. Havemeyer's representatives complained because they considered this breaking the agreement to allow the trust to control the market. Lund, however, thought that a more important question with which church leaders had to wrestle was what would happen "if the people should get an idea that President Smith would hinder our people from starting industries for fear of the Trust." Nevertheless, in an apparent attempt to placate American Sugar, Nibley allowed the trust to buy a share in the factory.[19]

Upset with Nibley's actions, David Eccles complained to Joseph F. Smith. President Smith recognized the trap in which both the church and the people of Utah had fallen. He concluded, however, that acceding to the wishes of the sugar trust was, paradoxically, the only way that church members could have any control. He was convinced that to resist would place the church in "the unenviable position of discriminating against our people in the north end of Cache and prolonging a most disastrous conflict between yourselves [Amalgamated] and them [the sugar trust]."[20]

The church's cooperation with the sugar trust combined with Reed Smoot's position on the Senate Finance Committee, which wrote tariff legislation, caused considerable adverse criticism. The central issues were spelled out in an article by Judson Welliver in *Hampton's Magazine*. According to Welliver, the tariff, which Smoot supported, added two cents to the price of every pound of sugar consumed by the American people, a cost of $100 to $125 million per year. He attributed the protariff votes of Republican senators from Utah, Idaho, Wyoming, Oregon, and Nevada to the influence of the church. In May 1909 Senator Alexander S. Clay of Georgia went as far as to claim that Joseph F. Smith had himself fixed sugar beet prices in return for $20,000.[21]

That the church leaders had supported subsidies and high tariffs for sugar was true. That they controlled the votes of senators of six states or that Joseph F. Smith could himself fix the price of sugar was fantasy. Nevertheless, the charges were serious enough that Congress investigated sugar prices and price fixing policy. Church leaders appeared at least twice to testify on tariff and sugar related matters. In April 1910 Joseph F. Smith went to Pueblo, Colorado, under summons to appear as a witness. Again in June 1911 both Joseph F. Smith and Charles W. Nibley appeared before the Hardwick Committee then investigating the sugar trust.[22]

Church leaders thought the stability of sugar prices and subsidies through tariff important. In an article in the *Independent*, Reed Smoot argued that such subsidies were necessary to keep "people employed, and at a wage rate sufficient to allow them to live in accordance with the standard established in the particular country in which they reside." The American standard of living, highest in the world, could only be maintained, Smoot insisted, by a tariff that would allow industry to maintain its present wage scale.[23]

Smoot's concerns went far beyond the sugar business and included other industries of importance to Utah and the mountain West. From his seat on the Senate Finance Committee, he was "in a position to protect the interests of our sugar, our wool, our cattle, our hides, and our lead, and in fact every industry that brings wealth to our state."[24] In 1913, when the Democratic party took power in Congress and opposed subsidies to many of the interests Smoot supported, he and others from Utah were quick to respond. The Democratic-sponsored Underwood-Simmons Tariff bill, he said, "threatens disaster to many American industries as complete as we had under the last Democratic tariff law [the Wilson-Gorman Act of 1894]." He thought that "there is no longer any question about the injury to the sugar industry, wool industry" and to the wages which support America's high standard of living. Moreover, the bill was a sectional one, placing commodities from the mid- and far West on the free list and keeping many southern commodities, such as rice, under protection. Smoot and other Republicans were not alone in this view. Western Democrats like James H. Moyle and Progressives like Stephen H. Love took a similar protariff stance.[25] In its final form, the Underwood-Simmons Act of 1913 reduced the sugar tariff from 1.67 cents to 1.25 cents per pound, placing it on the free list after May 1, 1916. Partly as a result of the act and partly because markets were closed at the outbreak of the First World War in 1914, sugar prices and Utah and Idaho stock values dropped to their lowest point since the depression of the 1890s.[26]

At virtually the same time as the price drop, the House of Representatives reopened its investigation of Havemeyer's American Sugar Refining Company. The church leadership, fearing the possible closing of the factories, authorized the presiding bishop, Charles W. Nibley, to repurchase 25 percent of the capital stock of the Amalgamated Sugar Company and the sugar trust's holdings in the Utah-Idaho Sugar Company.[27]

After the war expanded in intensity and the British blockade made competition from continental Europe impossible, this purchase seemed to have been a stroke of genius. The value of U and I stock rose from seven dollars in April 1914 to twenty-nine dollars in November 1916. Under these conditions the company expanded its operations, opening a number of new plants in Utah, Idaho, Oregon, and Washington. Amalgamated opened plants in Wyoming, California, and Utah. The expansion was costly but undoubtedly seemed warranted by conditions during the war. Sugar prices were controlled by the United States Food Administration but markets were plentiful. Price controls lasted approximately two and one-half years, then the price skyrocketed. Between 1918 and May 1920 the price of raw sugar climbed from nine cents to twenty-three cents per pound.[28]

Beyond this, the two companies cooperated in various ways. A director of Amalgamated and president for one year (1914), Joseph F. Smith was president of U and I after the purchase and Anthon H. Lund succeeded as Amalgamated president (1914–1920), so the directorates of the two companies virtually interlocked. The two boards of directors met in December 1916 and agreed to divide their territory on a line between Honeyville and Deweyville in Box Elder County. In addition, the companies agreed together at times on the setting of prices for beets and sugar.[29]

The control of production by Utah-Idaho and Amalgamated led to conflicts with other companies. In June 1919 a complaint was filed before the Federal Trade Commission charging U and I and Amalgamated with conspiracy in restraint of trade under the Sherman Anti-Trust Act. A second suit in May 1920 charged U and I with asking excessive prices for sugar. These conflicts caused bitterness against a number of general authorities, particularly Charles W. Nibley, presiding bishop and general manager of U and I, who was indicted as well.[30]

Since the church was heavily involved in the two companies, beet farmers came to the First Presidency complaining about the management. On March 4, 1920, members of a delegation told the First Presidency that they would refuse to plant beets at the current company prices. The First Presidency discussed the situation, and Anthon H. Lund took their views to the Amalgamated directors. After several offers were made and rejected, on March 13 the companies agreed to offer twelve dollars per ton, the highest to that time, and to split the profits if the market price increased.[31]

By late in World War I, both companies were faced with problems of liquidity. Amalgamated had watered its stock considerably and the capital behind each bag of U and I sugar increased from $8.35 in 1915 to $25.46 in 1919, partly the result of investment designed to avoid high wartime taxes. Pressure from banks and from the Havemeyer interests forced reorganizations of the Amalgamated company leadership in 1918 and 1919. In 1920 Amalgamated reduced its nominal capitalization, probably in a move to squeeze some of the water from its stock, and during the year undertook reorganizational measures to try to satisfy its creditors, including the church and the Havemeyers.[32] By May 1920 sugar prices had begun to fall. Both U and I and Amalgamated sank into difficulties. By December 23 the First Presidency agreed to allow U and I to use church-owned Hotel Utah and ZCMI bonds as collateral for funds to meet payments to beet farmers. At the same time, the company had more than two million sacks of sugar on hand, which it could sell only at a loss.[33]

In the meantime, the suits against U and I and the indictment of the church's presiding bishop caused considerable controversy. Reed Smoot was particularly concerned about the political implications for the Republican party and his senatorial candidacy, and he urged President Grant to make a statement at general conference "on the Sugar question" in Nibley's defense. On October 7, 1920, President Grant read a prepared statement to the Twelve saying that an indictment did not mean guilt and asking members of the church to withhold judgment against Bishop Nibley. A number of the Twelve, including Stephen L Richards, Anthony W. Ivins, Charles W. Penrose, and James E. Talmage, opposed the statement, but all agreed to leave the matter to President Grant's discretion. At the opening session of the conference he read the statement. Some of the Democratic members of the Twelve were quite dissatisfied with it.[34]

In the first six months of 1921 the price of sugar declined from $7.40 to $5.47, and the companies' financial problems deepened. In January Charles W. Nibley and William H. Wattis of Amalgamated failed to secure money to finance the payment to beet growers because of unfavorable bank terms. The church helped in securing funds and invested more of its money in the companies. But these loans merely refinanced long-term obligations; cash was still needed to pay beet growers.[35] On October 11, on the suggestion of Stephen L Richards, the executive committee of U and I agreed that Richards, Heber J. Grant, E. O. Howard of Walker Bank (who was also War Finance Committee Chairman for Utah), and Henry H. Rolapp would visit Washington to try to secure the financing. On October 18, in a meeting with Eugene Meyer of the War Finance Corporation, the committee received $10 million to establish a sugar finance corporation which could lend funds to the two sugar companies. Legal details were left to Richards.[36] Heber J. Grant was particularly pleased at the negotiation of this federal loan. In his diary on October 18, 1921, he wrote that "the psychological effect will be very valuable. The very fact that the government of the United States has seen fit to help the beet sugar industry to the extent of ten million dollars in Utah and Idaho alone . . . will have a very salutary effect in strengthening the confidence of the public in the beet sugar industry generally."[37]

Still, U and I continued to sink into further difficulty, and the church increased its investment to try to save the company. In 1921 the church purchased 150,000 shares of U and I stock from Charles W. Nibley with $200,000, plus $300,000 worth of Hotel Utah 7 percent bonds. By September 1930 the bonds were selling above par, while the U and I stock was being quoted at fifty cents per share. The church had sustained a paper loss of $425,000 on this transaction alone. Between 1918 and 1928 the company was forced to close five plants in Utah, three in Washington, and one in Idaho; still U and I lost money every year between 1925 and 1930. Amalgamated paid no dividends during the 1920s.[38]

In early 1922 it looked as though the situation might improve. The efforts of Heber J. Grant and other church business leaders had saved U and I and Amalgamated from financial ruin. Ironically, some people complained that the church had profited on the U and I sugar deal, when in fact it had required virtually all of Heber J. Grant's time and energy and the church's free capital and goodwill to save the company. By late August 1922 Heber J. Grant could write that there had "been a wonderful improvement" in the condition of the two sugar companies in which the church was "heavily interested." The obligations of the church to eastern bankers had been cancelled, and the church was in debt only to local banks. By the latter part of 1922 the obligations to the War Finance Corporation were cancelled.[39]

By the late 1920s the companies were again in financial difficulty, and the sugar trust pressed both to rejoin in controlling the market. Marriner Eccles of Amalgamated attempted at first to avoid this in August 1929 by asking Heber J. Grant for a gentleman's agreement that each would give first right of refusal to the other on the sale of stock in either company. President Grant said that he could not do this, since the purchase of outstanding Amalgamated stock would cost the church $800,000 to $900,000—money it did not have. On August 24 President Grant met with the officers of American Sugar Refining Company. They offered to purchase his Amalgamated stock at a rate of one share of American for eight shares of Amalgamated. He thought that this was a good proposition, but he had to tell them that he would be forced to wait since he was only trustee for the stock and would have to consult with his counselors and the Twelve.[40]

In August 1929 U and I still faced considerable financial difficulty. Heber J. Grant went east to renew the loans necessary to pay for sugar beets during the fall harvest. He found no difficulty in Chicago, but in New York neither Irving Trust nor Guaranty Trust was anxious to lend money. Chase National Bank agreed to handle the whole account, provided the company would agree to issue acceptances. The money market in the heady days of mid-1929 was so strong that brokers wanted some readily discountable securities which they would use to lend more money.[41] After these problems, Heber J. Grant, Reed Smoot, and Stephen H. Love went again to the federal government for assistance for the two companies. Turning to the Federal Farm Relief Board, they requested a loan of $5 million to pay for the beets. Some problems arose and two weeks later Heber J. Grant was in San Francisco meeting with R. B. Motherwell of Wells Fargo bank and in Los Angeles at several banks securing additional financing.[42]

Similar problems developed again in 1930. In this case the church agreed to subordinate to the interests of the banks the $750,000 owed it by U and I. Anthony W. Ivins said that he "did not regard this as a safe loan, or one that it is proper for the church to make," but the company was in such poor shape that the banks insisted before they would agree to advance the money needed to pay farmers for the fall beet crop. By December 1930 the company was simply unable to meet its obligations. Both Orval Adams and Anthony W. Ivins believed that the best solution was for the company to pass into the hands of a friendly receiver where the debts could be scaled down. Heber J. Grant opposed this since he believed it would reflect negatively upon the church. Grant felt that for the church to guarantee the company's loans was preferable to receivership. After further financial difficulty during the winter of 1930–31, the church ended in early January guaranteeing $1.3 million in U and I obligations.[43] Difficulties continued as the depression deepened. The church again loaned money to U and I in 1931, and the company reduced wages and laid off employees. In addition, it sold its Canadian property, allowing payment on outstanding bonds. In 1932 and 1933 the company took various measures to solve its credit problems until the passage of the Sugar Act of 1934 divided the market between domestic and foreign producers and guaranteed U and I a market for its product.[44]

The Sugar Act was in a sense the culmination of a series of measures designed to overturn the Underwood-Simmons Tariff Act and return protection to domestic producers. Competition with locally produced sugar came from Cuba and the Philippines and, after the war, from the revived European beet producers. Under these conditions, it is not surprising that most westerners would favor a high protective tariff on sugar and other western products. Although nationally the Democratic party had generally stood for a revenue tariff, Democrats from the mountain West usually favored protection for commodities produced in the region. In January 1914, reinforced by the traditional Mormon argument for the promotion of home industries, William H. King went to Washington to lobby against a reduction in the tariff on sugar and wool. During early 1921 Congress had under consideration an emergency tariff act designed to change the basis of the Underwood Act and protect American business in general against dumping—particularly western cattle, sheep, meat, wool, and sugar. Reed Smoot was one of the leaders in the move, and most of the citizens of the state seem to have agreed.[45]

During the 1920s, with business difficulties and failures and constant pressure on the church's assets, church leaders were constantly at the door of the federal government asking for aid, particularly for the sugar industry. Assistance in 1921 from the War Finance Corporation was followed by an increased tariff on sugar in 1922 with the Fordney-McCumber Act, which helped protect the domestic market from outside competition, and with Federal Farm Board loans in the late twenties. In March 1923 Reed Smoot, Heber J. Grant, and Charles W. Nibley had met with the United States tariff board on the sugar question. In 1924 a number of citizens in the eastern United States complained loudly at the high price of sugar and blamed Smoot and the LDS church for the situation. The *Deseret News* defended the tariff, claiming that the already distressed sugar companies would be forced into bankruptcy if more sugar were imported at lower prices.[46]

The situation continued to worsen during the late 1920s and into 1930 as Congress moved to increase the tariff. In August 1927 Heber J. Grant met with Reed Smoot to discuss the problem of Cuban and Philippine sugar, which seemed to be hurting the American industry.

Pressure on Smoot, who was chairman of the Senate Finance Committee considering the Smoot-Hawley Tariff Act, worked its toll. In August 1929 Smoot returned to Utah, having lost more than thirty pounds from the strain. Shortly before the vote on the sugar schedule of the tariff, a visit of Heber J. Grant to Reed Smoot caused a national uproar when Senator John J. Blaine of Wisconsin urged the Senate to declare him a sugar lobbyist. Smoot denied the charge on the Senate floor, but he nevertheless suggested that President Grant telegraph William H. King asking him to vote for the Smoot-Hawley Act on the ground that farmers were doomed to distress if they were not helped.[47]

After the passage of the Smoot-Hawley Act, numerous economists and others complained at the high tariff wall which the United States had built. On the other hand, the church leadership and the intermountain economy were faced with a practical problem. How were those farmers who raised beets to continue to feed their families if they could not continue to sell beets, and what would happen to the church and the economy of the mountain West if the two large sugar companies were to fail? In 1929 the church expended slightly more than $900,000 for its entire educational program. The amount which U and I owed the church was $1.3 million and, in addition, the church owned $700,000 in company stock. Failure of U and I or Amalgamated would have been a disaster not only for the people but for the church itself. It is no wonder that Heber J. Grant, in public pronouncements such as his radio address on January 31, 1930, urged the people of Utah to use Utah-made goods and home manufacture as a means of dealing with unemployment.[48]

Church participation in the salt industry led to similar charges of monopoly and profiteering at the expense of the community and of competing businesses. In fact, the businesses involved in salt manufacture had to struggle to break even, and the church sold its interests in the late twenties to local businessmen.[49]

In many ways the 1920s became the graveyard of church business ventures. Businesses like the Provo Woolen Mills and Consolidated Wagon and Machine seemed to have failed because of antiquated management policies. One of the least understood of these failures was the Saltair Beach Company. General public opinion today in Utah is that the Saltair company was a profitable venture, but this was not the case; it seems to have been kept open for essentially the same reason as the Salt Lake Theater—to try to provide a wholesome alternative to questionable types of entertainment then abroad in the community. It was sold then reacquired by the church before its sale to a local syndicate in 1929.[50]

The church had also been involved in the Utah Light and Power Company, which it eventually sold to a large eastern combine that reorganized the company as Utah Power and Light. As early as November 1901 the church officials began considering the possibility of selling Utah Light and Power, realizing that an outlay approaching $500,000 would be needed to sufficiently increase the generating capacity of the company. They were not prepared at the time to incur such a debt.[51]

By July 1903 the First Presidency was considering the consolidation of Utah Light and Power Company with Alfred W. McCune's Consolidated Railway and Power Company, which operated the street railways in Salt Lake City and Ogden. On July 14, Robert Campbell and LeGrand Young returned from New York with the news that they could probably induce the eastern shareholders to agree to the consolidation, provided the easterners and westerners put up the same amount of money. On July 23, 1903, the First Presidency and Twelve agreed to the merger. Accomplished on December 31, 1903, the consolidation left Joseph F. Smith as president of the new company, Utah Light and Railway, with a number of other Mormon businessmen and leaders on the board. This gave the company a working monopoly of all street railways in Salt Lake City and Ogden and of all electric generating facilities for Weber, Davis, and Salt Lake counties.[52]

Continuation of a monopoly of this sort was, of course, dependent upon the cities, since franchises for such operations had to be granted by the city councils. In 1905 this caused some difficulty as the Utah Light and Railway Company (UL&R) tried to secure a fifty-year franchise from Salt Lake City. Some citizens believed that Gentile businessman Samuel Newhouse could furnish better service at a lower cost and opposed the franchise.[53] In some ways, the opponents were misinformed on the actual cost of granting Newhouse the franchise. This was so because UL&R owned water rights in Big Cottonwood Canyon, which the city wanted. UL&R and the city agreed to consolidate the franchises in a new franchise to run for fifty years, in return for the water rights, some property valued at $100,000, and lower power rates to the city.[54]

By late 1905, however, the mixture of business and religion in the public relations of UL&R had become an embarrassment to the church. Joseph F. Smith received a subpoena to furnish the books of all companies in which the church had an interest; and on October 31 Robert Campbell and LeGrand Young met with the First Presidency to urge the sale of the stocks and bonds of Utah Light and Railway Company. By mid-May 1906 an agreement had been negotiated to sell a majority interest in the company to a trust controlled by Edward H. Harriman. President Smith, in a candid statement, said that the separation of business from religion was the main reason for the sale.[55]

Those businesses which enjoyed most success during this period were well-managed financial and commercial ventures. ZCMI, for instance, continued to prosper even during the dark days of the 1920s, principally because of the enlightened leadership of John F. Bennett. Even here, however, Heber J. Grant was reluctant to approve Bennett's most innovative proposal, that of moving aggressively to open chain stores through Utah, since he feared it "would create a great deal of jealousy among our local brethren who are engaged in business and would really run them out of business." In mid-1928, the company began to plan to move itself out of the wholesale business. By December 1930 sales had dropped off because of depression conditions, but ZCMI was in much better financial shape than many of the church's other enterprises.[56]

Similar fears of competing with local businesses, coupled with adverse ruling by the Utah state insurance commissioner, inhibited Beneficial Life from serving the needs of church members to the degree leaders would have preferred. Organized in 1905, following suggestions of Lorenzo Stohl and John Stringham of the Heber J. Grant Insurance Agency that "our own people" ought to keep the money spent for insurance, Beneficial Life was capitalized at $100,000. Joseph F. Smith became president with John C. Cutler and Lorenzo N. Stohl as vice presidents. As with most other so-called Mormon companies, the board of directors included prominent Mormon and Gentile businessmen.[57]

Since ZCMI and other companies offered mutual insurance programs to employees, Heber J. Grant hoped to be able to do the same for church members in less favored circumstances. As a result, in August 1927 the First Presidency bought out the minority stockholders in

Beneficial Life for the purpose of turning it into a cooperative insurance company.[58]

Almost immediately, roadblocks began to arise. The state insurance commissioner, John G. McQuarrie, and officers of the company protested that legal difficulties might prevent the action. They also complained of the opposition of other insurance companies who would consider the church's activities to be unfair competition. McQuarrie also said that it was wrong for the church to provide insurance for those who were capable of finding other insurance themselves. In March 1928 it looked as though the objection could be overcome by setting up groups of five church members and arranging to have them pay premiums with the church participating. In this way, members who were full tithe payers and who obeyed the church's strict dietary rules could be insured at only a slight cost to the church. Members of the priesthood insurance committee headed by Stephen L Richards nipped this in the bud in April 1928 when they again raised the specter of protests from competitors who would feel discriminated against. By June 1928 Heber J. Grant was so discouraged that he said that he wished that the church had never purchased the minority stock. He decided that the church should give up the whole idea and sell the acquired stock.[59]

In some cases the church leadership was successful in finding imaginative and resourceful businessmen to save companies with problems. By May 1922 Utah State National Bank had landed in serious difficulty, holding $500,000 worth of paper of dubious value. Heber J. Grant, concluding that the bank was vital to Utah's economy, agreed to purchase the paper and bail out the bank for fifty cents on the dollar. In 1925 the church secured the services of Orval W. Adams, formerly with First Security Corporation, to move into the system. In 1928 Adams proposed the consolidation of Utah State National and Zion's Savings Bank with the First Security Corporation, but the First Presidency declined for fear "that it might create jealousy and ill will towards the church." Adams, nevertheless, took what had been a financially unsound venture and built it into the Zion's First National system.[60]

Perhaps the most visible single new business undertaking in which the church was involved was the Hotel Utah. As with most other businesses, it included both Mormon and Gentile businessmen. On

April 19, 1909, the First Presidency proposed the sale of the old Deseret News Corner where the Bishop's Tithing Yard had been located
on the corner of Main and South Temple, with the understanding that
the syndicate would erect a $2 million hotel. Joseph F. Smith agreed to
sell the corner for stock in the company at $750 per front foot, in re-
turn for which the church took 51 percent ownership. Management of
the hotel was apparently sound, and it seems to have prospered.[61]

Broadly considered, the story of the church's involvement in business during the period from 1900 to 1930 reveals a number of important trends, not only in church business affairs but also in the economic development of the intermountain region. The developments of
the period reveal a church faced with conflicting pressures to build the
community, provide wholesome entertainment, mollify potential competitors and critics, and live in harmony with aggressive eastern monopolists. Those pressures were intensified during the financially precarious days of the 1920s, largely because of the church's commitment
to serve the community by keeping the sugar industry solvent.

In regard to the larger economic trends, the church's business successes reveal the beginnings of what some authors have called the
postindustrial age.[62] The manufacturing business had the most difficulty, as witness the sugar, salt, and woolen enterprises. ZCMI succeeded in part because manufacturing had long since gone by the
board, and the most successful were service and financial enterprises,
like Zion's First National, Hotel Utah, and Beneficial Life. On the
other hand, those concerns which tried to purvey nineteenth-century
entertainment in the face of changing early twentieth-century tastes
were also doomed to distress and failure.

In many ways, the economic changes that the church faced during
these three decades could not have come at a worse time. Intent upon
shifting from the nineteenth century, when it had been a prime mover
in intermountain economic development, to the twentieth century,
where the spiritual side of religion received greatest emphasis, the
church was caught in pressures which were impossible to control and
difficult to manage. Hating to see its membership unemployed or
disadvantaged, the leadership cooperated with monopolists like the
Havemeyers, whose activities brought opprobrium not only upon
themselves, but on the church as well. Feeling a sense of community
responsibility, the church continued to operate unprofitable entertain-

ment businesses, like Saltair and the Salt Lake Theatre, then reaped community wrath when it was financially unable to continue their operation. Though some enterprises served as harbingers of a brighter future, the period from 1900 through 1930 was not a pleasant time for the temporal kingdom.

6

Administrative Modernization, 1900–1918

BEFORE 1877 ALL LEVELS of church administration, but particularly the highest echelons, had undergone a number of important organizational changes. Joseph Smith had been designated initially simply as first elder and his associate Oliver Cowdery as second elder. In 1832 Joseph became president of the church with two counselors completing the First Presidency. The Presiding Patriarch, or patriarch to the church, was designated in 1833 to give blessings and preside over other patriarchs, and in 1843 he was first sustained as one of the general authorities. In 1835 the Council of Twelve Apostles and the First Council of the Seventy were organized with responsibility for supervising missionary work and church activities outside areas with large Mormon populations. After 1841 the apostles were drawn into a closer association with the First Presidency, becoming the second governing body of the church, while the First Council of the Seventy, though designated as general authorities, continued to function under the leadership of the Twelve as supervisors of missionary work and Seventies' quorums, especially after a reorganization in 1883.[1]

While the church leadership had called bishops to supervise temporal affairs of the church in local areas since 1831, the general authority offices of presiding bishop and two counselors were not established until 1841. As extensive local organizations developed, the presiding bishopric also regulated the activities of local authorities in their handling of temporal affairs and in their supervision of the functions of the Aaronic, or lesser, priesthood consisting (in ascending order) of deacons, teachers, and priests. Since all male members were eligible for priesthood office, virtually all held an office in the Aaronic or the higher Melchizedek Priesthood (seventies, high priests, and elders).

Local church organization developed over the same period. Stakes, initially the lowest local organizations, were formed in Kirtland, Ohio;

Independence and Far West, Missouri; and Nauvoo, Illinois. Presided over by a president with two counselors and a high council of twelve men, the stakes were responsible for regulation of local affairs. In Nauvoo the leaders further subdivided the city into ecclesiastical wards (a term borrowed from political usage) presided over by bishops who exercised temporal and spiritual jurisdiction over members living in their areas. Neither the wards nor the stakes had responsibility for worship services, which were held in common under the supervision of the general authorities.[2]

After the move to Utah in 1847, local units grew rather haphazardly until 1877, when Brigham Young supervised their reorganization. At the same time, President Young began a trend toward centralization of church administration which accelerated after 1900. This centralization seems to have come about because as the society in which the Latter-day Saints lived became increasingly pluralistic, if not secular, the Mormon community no longer created its own internal regulatory mechanism. Under those circumstances, rational organization and fixed rules replaced a sense of community as the means of establishing norms which the Saints were expected to observe. In retrospect, it seems clear that while the general authorities felt inspired to make the changes they did, they were not completely aware of the consequences. Nevertheless, their ultimate effect is quite apparent today.

Under the 1877 reorganization, most counties with large Mormon populations were designated as stakes, supervised by a stake presidency and high council. Wards were presided over by a bishop and two counselors, who were subordinate to stake officers. In the smaller settlements, each town constituted a ward. In the cities, wards corresponded to geographical subdivisions.[3]

Superimposed on this line authority was what might be considered a staff organization of auxiliaries, which may be viewed as special-interest societies set up to meet the needs of various categories of church members. By the late nineteenth century each of the auxiliaries was organized in substantially the same way. The general organization consisted of a presidency (a president and two counselors) and an advisory board. These were replicated on the stake and ward level. By 1900 the auxiliaries consisted of the Relief Society (a charitable and general interest organization for women which had originally not been an auxiliary at all); the Sunday School (giving Sunday religious instruction to members of all ages); the Young Ladies' Mutual Improvement Association (a cultural, religious, and recreational organization for young women over the age of fourteen); the Young Men's Mutual Improvement Association (a similar organization for young men); the Primary Association (which provided once-a-week religious and recreational instruction for boys and girls under fourteen); and Religion Classes (providing after-school religious instruction for elementary school children).[4]

Administrative practice during Lorenzo Snow's (1898–1901) and Joseph F. Smith's (1901–18) presidencies exhibited both continuity and change. First, the church continued many practices begun in the nineteenth century. The First Presidency counseled regularly with the Twelve. Church leaders visited wards and stakes to supervise the implementation of general church policies and practices and to offer advice and counsel on questions of local and general concern. General authorities conducted a local meeting for all members in the Salt Lake tabernacle. In addition, stakes held regular quarterly conferences, and wards conducted regular weekly worship services.

Secondly, though wards and stakes continued as the basic units of the church, a number of important changes improved their administrative efficiency. The general church leadership began to divide stakes into smaller, more manageable units. This had the effect of freeing the stake president from a too extensive commitment to his ecclesiastical position and of creating a smaller and thus more cohesive community with which the members could more readily identify. The church improved and regularized accounting procedures for funds and membership records, which allowed the bishops of wards and other church authorities more closely to monitor the condition of finances and people.

Third, in its internal affairs, the church moved from a barter system to a money economy. It accomplished this as, and in part because, the church paid off its debt and tithing income increased. This change is significant since most church income came from the tithes and offerings of the Saints, not from church business investments, many of which, as we have seen, were on a precarious financial footing. Moreover, it signified another step in accepting the economic system of the external world and was a way station toward bureaucratization of church administration.

Fourth, the church leadership moved rather vigorously to strengthen the priesthood quorums. Beginning with the seventies, priesthood reform spread to other Melchizedek and to the Aaronic quorums. In practice, this meant that the quorums, rather than the entire community, began to serve as a focus for brotherhood and as vehicles for gospel instruction. In addition, the quorums were more closely identified with and supervised by ward and stake leaders. These changes provided a regular procedure for training future leaders by moving boys over age twelve and young men through the Aaronic quorums into the Melchizedek Priesthood. The church leadership moved priesthood meetings to Sunday, leaving only the meetings of MIA, Relief Society, Primary Association, and Religion Classes to be held during the week. Significantly, none of the remaining weekday meetings was designed primarily for adult males, who were generally at work each day except Sunday.

Fifth, the church leadership moved to separate more completely spiritual and temporal affairs. This was most evident in the development of new rules for church courts, which no longer were to collect debts or take members' property in satisfaction of an ecclesiastical judgment. This, perhaps more than anything else, provides evidence of the change in the nature of the Mormon sense of community.

In 1900 Lorenzo Snow, who had become president of the church in 1898, presided over more than 200,000 members. Born in Mantua, Ohio, on April 3, 1814, and educated at Oberlin College, President Snow had joined the church after a visit to his sister, Eliza Roxcy, in 1836. A non-Mormon who visited him described him as a "man with an exceptionally refined face and gentlemanly bearing," and on the church's seventieth anniversary, Emmeline B. Wells described him as a man "in the zenith of power" who "holds a firm hand and is full of the spirit of progress of this age in the work of God."[5]

Living in the Beehive House on South Temple Street in the heart of Salt Lake City, the president of the church worked in a small office building between his home and the Lion House to the west. A variety of buildings clustered mainly south and east of Temple Square housed other church officials. The First Council of the Seventy operated out of rooms in the Templeton Building; the presiding bishop's office occupied the old tithing yard where the Hotel Utah and the mall to the north now stand; and the church historian's office was located on South Temple Street near the present Deseret Book Store. Some church leaders occupied other offices in the Gardo House on the corner of South Temple and State streets.

Since the church leadership had a small staff, employees left most matters to the discretion of local presiding officers. President Snow insisted that the local officials "assume the burden of their charges and not expect the apostles to do their work." As counselor in the First Presidency, Joseph F. Smith believed that the lowest possible level ought to deal with any problems.[6]

Contrary to the image purveyed by muckrakers like Frank Cannon, the president of the church did not sit like some cloistered Byzantine emperor pulling strings from an office on East South Temple. Rather, as *primus inter pares* he made his decisions in council. Joseph F. Smith said, "The Lord never did intend that one man should have all power," and the president expected to act with the approval of his counselors.[7]

The First Presidency and Twelve expected dissent in their meetings, and each apostle was, as Francis M. Lyman told James E. Talmage, to discharge the "duties that would devolve upon him as an apostle of the Lord Jesus Christ, together with the great responsibilities attached to that calling." He told Talmage of the necessity for harmony in the council, but made it clear that "it would be his privilege to fully express his own individual view" in the meetings. After a decision had been made, however, the leadership expected him "to be united with his brethren." In addition, those matters discussed in council were to be held confidential.[8]

Already eighty-four at the time of his call to the presidency, Lorenzo Snow served during the time of transition. Franklin D. Richards, president of the Council of the Twelve and the visible arm of the church during the days of the intense antipolygamy prosecutions of the 1880s, and George Q. Cannon, whose intellectual and political acumen had served the church for more than forty years, preceded him in death. Between April 12, 1901, when President Cannon died, and October 10, when President Snow passed away, the First Presidency was never fully reorganized. Neither Joseph F. Smith nor Rudger Clawson, sustained as first and second counselors, was set apart. Brigham Young, Jr., as senior apostle, became acting president of the Twelve at the death of Franklin D. Richards, but the Quorum of the Twelve was not reorganized and Elder Young felt somewhat insecure in his position.[9]

The death of Lorenzo Snow necessitated a complete reorganization. On October 17, 1901, the Twelve sustained Joseph F. Smith as president of the church and Brigham Young, Jr., as president of the Twelve.

John R. Winder, a British immigrant and second counselor in the Presiding Bishopric, was called to serve as first counselor in the First Presidency, and Anthon H. Lund, a Danish convert and one of the Twelve, became second counselor. Orrin P. Miller, president of the Jordan Stake, was called to Winder's position, and Hyrum M. Smith, son of Joseph F. Smith, was called to the Twelve.[10]

In general, the president of the church called new apostles through inspiration after prayerful consideration of recommendations by present quorum members. Reed Smoot's call, for instance, came after President Snow asked members of the quorum to suggest names of persons to fill the vacancy caused by Franklin D. Richards's death. Joseph F. Smith told John Henry that "the mind of the spirit" had told him to call George Albert Smith to fill the vacancy caused by the death of Brigham Young, Jr. John Henry said that if this had been a political office, he would advise against the selection, but that he could not "stand in the way of the suggestion of the spirit to" President Smith.[11]

The call of Joseph F. Smith in 1901 constituted the opening of a new era. At sixty-four years of age, he was the first president born in the church, and he represented a second generation of leaders to which apostles Brigham Young, Jr., Heber J. Grant, John Henry Smith, Abraham O. Woodruff, and John W. Taylor belonged. Five years old when a mob had murdered his father, Hyrum Smith, Joseph F. was only thirteen when he lost his mother, Mary Fielding Smith. After he had served missions in Hawaii and England, Brigham Young called him to the apostolate at age twenty-seven. He continued to serve in Europe and Hawaii until he was called as counselor to John Taylor, Wilford Woodruff, and Lorenzo Snow.[12]

President Smith faced an immediate problem of settling the affairs of the Snow estate so he could assume the position of trustee-in-trust to which the votes of the apostles and members of the church had sustained him. Unfortunately, Lorenzo Snow had died intestate and what ought to have been an orderly transition was complicated because of the difficulty of determining which property belonged to the church and which to the Snow estate. Because the church had no legal status other than that of a voluntary organization, church attorney Franklin S. Richards thought that the ownership of all property legally resided in Snow's heirs. Richards suggested that the First Presidency create a corporation sole, but this did not happen until the 1920s. After some difficulty with the heirs, Reed Smoot and John W. Taylor finally negotiated a settlement of the estate, whereupon Minnie J. Snow moved from the Beehive House to make room for President Smith.[13]

The position of president of the church was not as mysterious as contemporary muckraking literature made it appear. The diaries of Anthon H. Lund and President Smith's own correspondence reveal a man and his counselors burdened with decisions ranging from the trivial to the complex. Most of the work was routine but of an overwhelming volume. From early morning until late in the evening, the three men would pour over correspondence, meet with visitors on personal and ecclesiastical problems, and consult with members of the Twelve and the presiding bishopric. In this prebureaucratic era, even the most routine expenditures required the approval of the First Presidency. As a consequence of this pressure, the First Presidency frequently came late to their weekly meeting with the Twelve. Between 1907 and 1913 the church leadership shifted the time and day of the meeting four times to try to accommodate busy schedules. Joseph F. Smith instituted the practice of including the patriarch to the church in the meeting, which ordinarily continued from 10 or 11 A.M. until they had cleared all business—usually about 3 P.M.[14]

Until 1899 the church practiced virtually no budgetary control. Church leaders seem to have made expenditures on an ad hoc basis, and when in December 1898 Lorenzo Snow gave Brigham Young, Jr., papers on the church's indebtedness, Elder Young had to admit that "it is a mystery to me where these millions have gone to say nothing of the 6 or 700,000 dollars income we have every year which for years has vanished like the rest."[15] On January 5, 1899, John Henry Smith suggested that the church appoint an auditing committee to oversee expenditures. All members of the First Presidency and the Twelve agreed, particularly Lorenzo Snow, who admitted he had worked in the dark. The First Presidency appointed Franklin D. Richards, Francis M. Lyman, John Henry Smith, Rudger Clawson, and Heber J. Grant for the task. By December 1901, after the committee had operated nearly three years, the First Presidency still found accounts of the church somewhat in disarray, and the committee persuaded them to open a new set of books. The church had not closed the books for many years, and they erroneously showed the church bankrupt by $43,000! The new books showed that the church actually had more property and income than it owed, and Lorenzo Snow began to pay off obligations held by private creditors.[16]

General authorities who had to devote the majority of their time to church service received salaries. The church had no uniform stipend for general authorities; the leadership based payments on the need of the particular person. In 1899, for instance, Francis M. Lyman and John Henry Smith received $250 per month. At the same time Heber J. Grant did not get the full allowance since he earned money from his business interests. In many cases the trustee-in-trust gave personal loans to general authorities and others. By March 1899 outstanding loans totaled $115,000, much of which, one authority said, would never be paid "in this life." On occasion the church also appropriated money for travel and other special expenses. Nor did the church forget the widows of general authorities, who received a modest stipend.[17]

Local ecclesiastical officers were paid from tithing. Bishops, for instance, received 10 percent of the tithing collected. Members of stake presidencies drew on tithing funds for an allowance which ranged between $300 and $500 per year each in the payment of transportation expenses. The stake tithing clerk received a set salary. In 1904, for instance, Joseph Eckersley of Wayne County received $250 per year as stake tithing clerk.[18]

By 1907 the discretion which the First Presidency could exercise in the use of income had increased considerably. At a reception held at the Lion House on January 10, 1907, Joseph F. Smith announced that the church had completely retired its debt and would save from $30,000 to $60,000 per year in interest. Beyond this, the church had land, buildings, and other property worth about $10 million, and extensive investments in business.[19]

The First Presidency also administered ever-increasing revenues. In 1907 total tithing income stood at $1.8 million or $6.22 per capita. In the years since 1900 it had been increasing at a gradual but rather consistent rate of about 5 percent per year. Fast offerings which helped in poor relief averaged in 1908 19.3 cents per capita, and this had increased at about the same rate. Nevertheless, the First Presidency experienced enormous demands for appropriations which led to delays in the consideration of other important matters.[20]

By 1908 the church had a sufficient cash flow to complete a reform first contemplated in 1888. In January the Presiding Bishopric and First Presidency agreed that they would no longer use tithing scrip (essentially church-issued paper money). This meant that the church moved entirely to a cash basis and that those who provided goods and services no longer had to accept scrip. Part of the reason for the change appears to have been the substantial loss in the value of tithing in kind as it remained in storage. The system seems also to have made easier the valuation of funds transfers between units, an important consideration.[21]

Anxious to see that all members and leaders continued to pay their tithing, the First Presidency asked for reports on nontithepayers. In 1908 they began deducting tithing from the salaries of teachers in the church education system. In 1909 the reports showed that nearly 15,000 church members were nontithepayers, and of those 981 held responsible ward offices and 75 held offices in the stakes. The church leadership expected bishops and ward teachers to labor with these people; but by 1913 forty-six stake officers still paid no tithing, and the number of nontithepayers holding offices in wards had increased to 2,933.[22]

Like the First Presidency, the Twelve kept extremely busy. They met with the First Presidency in the temple one day each week. In addition they held meetings of their own and regular quarterly conferences at which they discussed questions of church policy. At these meetings, they considered such problems as the systematizing of missions, the appointment of mission presidents, the interpretation of doctrine, policy on ordination, jurisdiction of church courts, calls to positions, and standards of worthiness for church members. Also, the apostles attended stake conferences virtually every weekend. Members of the First Council of the Seventy or officers of one of the auxiliary organizations generally accompanied them.[23]

Apostles generally followed a similiar routine at conferences. Anthon H. Lund and Rudger Clawson attended a quite usual conference in March 1901.[24] The visiting authorities arrived for the conference on Saturday. That afternoon the bishops reported on their ward activities and received counsel from the general authorities. At other times these Saturday afternoon meetings included auxiliary leaders as well. On Saturday evening the two apostles attended a conference of the Mutual Improvement Association. Three major meetings and smaller sessions were usually held on Sunday. On Sunday morning the Sunday School conference convened at 10 A.M. The general authorities and stake leaders spoke. The morning general session of conference began at 11 A.M., and the afternoon session at about 2 P.M. On Sunday evening Elders Clawson and Lund went to dinner at the stake president's home. After dinner they spent some time setting stake officers apart. Some stake conferences might include a Sunday evening oratorical contest or other MIA programs. In some cases the conferences would run into Monday, and in outlying areas, with towns separated by distance or difficult terrain, the visiting authorities held separate meetings in various wards on succeeding days. This was the case, for instance, in the Panguitch and Beaver stakes.[25]

Often the general authority spent much of his time at stake conferences dealing with individual problems. At the Cassia Stake in Idaho in 1909, for instance, George F. Richards found that a number of high priests, elders, and seventies belonged to no quorum and that in many cases the bishops had not prepared the young men to receive the Aaronic priesthood at age twelve. In Teton Stake Elder Richards found considerable disharmony and ill feeling because of alleged unethical business dealings by two members of the stake presidency. In the St. Johns Stake in Arizona in 1911, Elder Richards found that six of the members of the high council had not kept the Word of Wisdom and that dissension in the high council had grown because of resentment against President David Udall. In the Teton, Pioneer, and Ogden stakes in 1913, auxiliary associations showed poor enrollment.[26]

Apostles often found the physical aspects of these visits unpleasant. When assignments took them away from railroad facilities, they had to travel long distances by wagon or carriage, sometimes for several days, staying with members or in bad hotels. George F. Richards reported staying at a third-rate hotel during a visit to a Juab Stake conference in Nephi, where he "had a horrible night—*Bugs*."[27]

Problems relating to church courts also came to the Twelve. Though circular letters to stake presidents and bishops around the turn of the century indicated the desire of the First Presidency and Twelve to discontinue the use of church courts for the settlement of temporal disputes, evidence presented during the Reed Smoot investigation showed that the practice, common in the nineteenth century, still continued. In August 1908 the First Presidency asked Francis M. Lyman, George F. Richards, and Anthony W. Ivins to define the jurisdiction of church courts in the collection of debts. Adopted October 15, 1908, their report proposed that church members collect ordinary debts through civil rather than ecclesiastical courts. Where members had filed for bankruptcy but were subsequently able to pay, moral persuasion, rather than court proceedings, was to be used to try to get them to do so. The same course obtained in cases where a moral obligation seemed to exist, even though civil courts had ruled a note invalid. In a case where fraud seemed evident, the offending member could be tried for his fellowship.[28] Church courts still adjudicated more traditional sorts of moral infractions. General authorities sometimes became upset to find that bishops did not pursue cases of adultery or fornication with what seemed sufficient severity, and they urged local officers to deal with such transgressions.[29]

Though the secularization of debt collection had moved the church by 1908 a long way from the condition where members could be tried for their fellowship for a broad range of temporal activities, the jurisdiction of courts was still not well defined, and the practice of using church discipline in secular matters continued, particularly in outlying areas. George F. Richards, for instance, went in 1911 to investigate a dispute in Manassa, Colorado, between members of the stake presidency and a member of the stake seventies' quorum presidency. A seventies president had built an opera house, contrary to the counsel of the ward and stake authorities. The stake president wanted to stop him, but the intervention of Elder Richards allowed him to operate the facility with the stipulation that he would not sell it to an outsider nor conduct "amusements there of any kind contrary to counsel and direction of the priesthood."[30]

In 1917 and 1919 the First Presidency and the Twelve further narrowed the scope of the church court system. They considered one case, for instance, where the court found the evidence insufficient for a conviction, but instead of acquitting the defendant, the court had ruled that the prosecution had not proved the case.[31] In September 1917 Joseph F. Smith wrote about this and other problems in a statement entitled "Principles of Government in the Church." Among other things he said that members had a duty to sustain their bishoprics in decisions unless they had reason to suspect partiality. In such cases they had a right to appeal to the stake presidency and high council, and from there to the First Presidency. Church courts, he said, could try members for their actions, not for their beliefs. They might believe what they wanted as long as they did not try to convert others to their views. In addition courts must prove church members guilty; members were not required to prove their innocence in the church courts any more than in courts of the land.[32] Later, in the April 1919 *Improvement Era*, James E. Talmage wrote about the "Judiciary System of the

Church." The article dealt with the method of conducting trials and concluded with the verdicts which might be pronounced. A church court might excommunicate or disfellowship a member but could not impose fines, deprive members of their liberty, or levy encumbrances on property.[33]

Problems such as budgetary control, removing secular matters from the jurisdiction of the church courts, and keeping stakes manageably small seem relatively common today. A number of administrative practices existed at the time which the church has either abandoned or modified, largely because of subsequent growth and the change in the community. The leadership expected the First Presidency and the Twelve, for instance, to make annual visits to the wards of the church.[34]

In the Salt Lake area weekly general church meetings, probably a vestige of the preward general Sunday meetings, continued into the first decades of the twentieth century. In Salt Lake City the stakes and wards were not to schedule meetings which conflicted with a general tabernacle service conducted each Sunday. Church leaders asked ward and stake officers and members as far as possible to attend. After the division of the Salt Lake Stake in 1904, attendance by local officers tended to decline as wards and stakes became the primary focus of the community and general church services seemed less important to members. A special message from the First Presidency to stake presidents, however, urged attendance as an obligation and cautioned that no stake or ward meeting could interfere.[35]

Perhaps the most anomalous situation among the general authorities existed in the First Council of the Seventy. By the first decade of the twentieth century, neither church practice nor revelation had defined the role of the First Council. Section 107 of the Doctrine and Covenants (vs. 25–27) indicated the First Council of the Seventy formed a quorum equal in authority to the Twelve. In practice, however, the First Council did not meet regularly with the First Presidency and were only infrequently called upon for advice. Considered general authorities, nevertheless, they were assigned to stake conferences and were expected to lead missionary work under the direction of the First Presidency and Twelve. The poor definition of their role led to questions about the extent of the authority of the First Council. In December 1916, for instance, at a conference in Blackfoot, Idaho, at which none of the Twelve were present, B. H. Roberts ordained a bishop, a duty which was ordinarily reserved to a high priest. Upon learning of this, the First Presidency and Twelve considered the question of Roberts's authority to perform such an ordinance. They expressed uncertainty about the matter but decided to let the ordination stand.[36]

Though the first Presidency and Twelve concerned themselves with the church's temporal affairs, principal responsibility for many of these matters fell upon the Presiding Bishopric. By December 1907 reports indicated that Presiding Bishop William B. Preston was so weak that he could no longer function. First counselor Robert T. Burton had carried most of the burden of the office, and after his death in November 1907, the whole load fell upon second counselor Orrin P. Miller.[37] The First Presidency and Twelve gave the matter prayerful consideration, and in December 1907, after securing approval, President Smith called Charles W. Nibley to his office. "Charlie," he addressed his old friend, "the Church of Jesus Christ of Latter-day Saints needs a Presiding Bishop and you have been chosen for the place." Nibley accepted the call and chose Orrin P. Miller for his first counselor and David A. Smith, Joseph F. Smith's son, as second counselor.[38]

Nibley's administration inaugurated many reforms which modernized and rationalized church administration, including the shift from scrip to cash and improvements in record keeping. Previously, though wards kept the membership records, the church expected members to carry their own records from ward to ward as they moved. In many cases records went unexamined and carried inaccuracies. In 1901, following a recommendation by the church auditing committee to correct the records, the church inaugurated a ward "Record Day" during ward conference. A circular letter of February 1902, in addition, encouraged wards, stakes, and auxiliaries to keep their records in order. The church encouraged ward officers to contact members before they moved to see that "they procure their recommends" as membership records were then called.[39] Nibley proposed to deal with such inaccuracies and with the problem of moving records from one ward to another by centralized records control. The wards took the responsibility for records from the members. The church expected the wards to keep membership records, and when a member moved from one ward to another, the bishops were to send the records to the presiding bishop's office, which served as a clearinghouse. In addition, instead of waiting for members to come to them, the bishops were required to make a house-to-house canvass of their wards at least once per year to correct ward records.[40]

Next to the stake president, the ward bishop was possibly the most powerful individual in most Mormon communities. When the power company wanted to move into Mendon in Cache County after 1900, for instance, it contacted the bishop, who helped in signing up the local people for service and who also supervised some of the contracts for providing transmission poles. Less reliant upon central church organization than currently, wards held title to local buildings and other property.[41]

Before 1901 title to ward property had been vested in local trustees, who registered the property in their names with county authorities. Beginning in 1901, however, Utah law allowed any bishop to establish a corporation sole. The title to property was then vested in the presiding officer and would pass to his successor upon his death or release.[42] Similar arrangements were made by stake presidents for stake property.

Wards had to account for tithes and offerings to the general church organization. Beginning in 1898, all bishops and stake tithing clerks submitted monthly reports of cash received. Bishops made inventories and reports of tithes in kind. After 1902 a new system provided more accurate and effective ward accounts.[43]

Bishops were expected to serve an indefinite tenure: church policy provided basically only five reasons for their release—moving from the ward, death, old age, lack of harmony in the ward, or disobedience.[44] The release of a bishop thus became a wrenching experience, since if the incumbent had not moved, died, or been called to a higher position, members often presumed that he had failed in either his personal or ecclesiastical life.

Since a bishop held such an important position and the cooperation of members was essential to the proper functioning of a ward, authorities consulted local priesthood leaders for suggestions before they took the name of a candidate to the Lord in prayer for the confirmation of the spirit on a choice. In one case in 1899, for instance, George Teasdale and Anthon H. Lund asked the stake high council to ballot. After the ballot, however, consultation and prayer with stake leaders led to the conclusion that the man with the highest number of votes was not suitable since he seemed to lack leadership capabilities. The two apostles then returned to the high council, discussed the matter with them, and agreed upon another man. In several cases the priesthood of the ward cast ballots. In one of these the visiting authorities chose the brother with the highest number of votes as bishop and the next highest as his first counselor. They passed over the man with the third highest number since he served on the stake high council and chose instead the fourth highest as second counselor. In another case the authorities passed over the man with the second highest vote since his brother had received the highest number.[45]

Above the ward level the stake was undoubtedly the most important organization. Church leaders expected stake officers to coordinate the affairs of the wards, promote programs for the benefit of the members, and serve as liaison with the general authorities. After the adoption of a general policy in September 1900, the church leadership preferred small to large stakes in order to bring about "an increased growth spiritually," and a greater burden in dividing stakes fell upon the Twelve. Though the Salt Lake Stake had been divided into three (Salt Lake, Jordan, and Granite) in October 1899, by 1904 rapid urban growth dictated the division of the parent stake into four more. At that time the Salt Lake Stake consisted of thirty-seven wards, and President Angus M. Cannon devoted more than three-quarters of his working time to stake business, to the serious neglect of his private affairs.[46] The Twelve found the implementation of the new policy quite difficult since, in the past, stake presidents had held virtually lifetime tenure. As in the case of a bishop, a release seemed to many to suggest either transgression or incapacity. Indeed, the general authorities seemed at first to have concentrated on releasing incapacitated stake presidents. One president released in 1902, for instance, had proved incapable even of "giving out a hymn correctly."[47]

Rudger Clawson and George F. Richards seem to have followed the usual procedure in the stake division on their visit to the Malad Stake in 1908. At a stake conference priesthood meeting on September 25, members of the stake discussed the division and possible choices for president of the new stake. The largest support developed for Bishop William H. Richards of Malad, and after prayerful consideration the two brethren recommended him for president. They then discussed the matter with President Milton H. Welling and his counselor, Moroni Ward, who endorsed the choice. The four men met with Bishop Richards, who accepted the call. On the next day, the membership of the stake sustained President Richards. Welling remained as president of the Bear River Stake, consisting of the Utah portion of the old stake which had straddled the Utah-Idaho border.[48]

Stakes along the Wasatch Front seem to have corresponded most nearly to the general authorities' view of how a stake should function, and those in outlying rural and frontier areas exhibited the greatest differences. In 1907, for instance, the Panguitch stake presidency in outlying Garfield County met with the high council only quarterly and visited the wards only two or three times per year. Members of the high council served in the wards as home missionaries and ward teachers. During a visit to the stake, George F. Richards recommended that the high council meet at least monthly, the stake presidency visit the wards quarterly, and that bishops release high councilmen from ward positions.[49] Perhaps the most creative of the stakes was the Granite Stake in Salt Lake County under President Frank Y. Taylor. Originator of the stake missionary program to bring the gospel to nonmembers in their boundaries, and the seminary program to provide weekday religious instruction for high school students, the Granite Stake also started a monthly family home evening program in 1909. The stake president asked each family to spend Tuesday evening home together. Family members were to teach the gospel and participate in family activities such as songs, scripture readings, games, and refreshments. All three programs were later adopted on the general church level.[50]

Between Brigham Young's 1877 reorganization and the priesthood reorganization of the first decade of the twentieth century, the ward and auxiliary organizations carried out virtually all functions which directly affected the lives of church members and served increasingly as the primary communities for members. Members received gospel instruction at Sunday School, Relief Society, Primary Association, and sacrament meeting. The bishop organized and supervised ward teaching, and the bishopric and Relief Society coordinated virtually all welfare and church service functions. In short, priesthood holders functioned as ward rather than as quorum members. Indeed, many had not enrolled in a quorum, and many quorums met infrequently in poorly attended meetings.

The extent to which the auxiliaries and wards had replaced the general church as the primary community for most members by 1900 can be overstated. Membership in auxiliaries was voluntary; many belonged to none. Attendance at ward services was very low by present standards, generally under 15 percent, especially in the smaller highly Mormon towns. As late as 1900, most members seemed to perceive their primary community to be the church, and because of that Saints could be seen good as members whose lives were quite different from those we tend to view as active today.[51]

Perhaps to strengthen the church in the time of transition and in the increasingly pluralistic society in which the church members lived, thé First Presidency and Twelve recognized the need for increased priesthood activity. In 1900, Lorenzo Snow ruled that seventies owed primary allegiance to their quorums rather than to the wards and auxiliaries. In 1901 the First Presidency and Twelve urged elders, high priests, and other quorums to hold regular meetings and to enroll all priesthood holders living within a ward or stake jurisdiction. If a priesthood holder refused enrollment, the quorum leader was to report him to the high council for possible ecclesiastical court action.[52]

The seventies led out in the revitalization of priesthood work in the church. In part this came about because, though the role of members of the First Council of the Seventy as general authorities was not well defined, their function as leaders of seventies' work in the church was clear. Thus, since unlike other quorums the First Council provided central direction for the seventies, the First Council could develop and disseminate programs and lead out in priesthood reorganization.

In October 1902 the First Council proposed measures to promote systematic instruction and activation. The presidents appointed J. Golden Kimball, Brigham H. Roberts, Rulon S. Wells, and Joseph W. McMurrin from among their number to plan a course of action. By October 15 Roberts reported that he and Kimball had completed a rough draft of a proposed series of lessons. This draft eventually led to the publication of a course of study for the seventies, apparently a first for any of the priesthood quorums in the church.[53]

Throughout 1903, as the seventies tried to bring about this change in emphasis, they encountered difficulties not only from their own members but also from stake presidents and bishoprics who had traditionally directed local church activities. Because the quorums had previously been poorly organized, the local authorities had taken seventies who were supposed to do missionary work to serve as Sunday School or MIA teachers and even as members of bishoprics. One brother suggested, in fact, that instead of holding regular quorum meetings, the seventies might just as well attend and study the MIA lessons. The First Council ruled, however, that seventies should conduct their own meetings and follow the outlined course of study instead of merging with auxiliary organizations.[54]

After leading out in the development of a course of study, the seventies turned to the reform of their meeting schedule. Like most other quorums, the seventies held their infrequent meetings on Monday evenings. Since, however, they were called as missionaries and other assignments were an infringement upon their primary responsibility, seventies could make the case for holding meetings on Sunday as a means of invigorating the quorums. In January 1907 the First Council asked the First Presidency and Twelve to approve a change in seventies' quorums meeting times from Monday evening to the more convenient Sunday morning between nine and twelve. This was such a radical proposal that three hours of discussion preceded approval. The First Presidency then sent a circular letter to local ecclesiastical officers emphasizing that seventies might determine the time of their meeting on Sunday morning and that if they taught Sunday School, bishops should release them. Seventies scheduled the first meeting under this new schedule on November 3, 1907, with B. H. Roberts's course of study as the lesson manual.[55]

The seven presidents recognized that the new procedure and new lessons might create some problems, and in an effort to assist in resolving difficulties, the *Improvement Era* added a new section, "The Seventy's Council Table," edited by B. H. Roberts. But the anticipated difficulties still surfaced. In June 1908 members of the seventies' quorum of the Union Stake objected to bishops attending their meetings. The stake presidency ruled, however, that bishops had a right to attend any meeting held in the ward. Some seventies interpreted this emphasis on quorum meetings as releasing them from the responsibility of attending weekly sacrament meetings. Some also thought themselves relieved from allegiance to a stake since the seventies' quorums were general church rather than stake organizations.[56]

Since other priesthood quorums met on Monday evening, a number of the stake presidents believed that Sunday seventies' meetings caused too much confusion and that the meeting ought to be switched back to Monday. After consideration, the First Presidency and the Twelve agreed and a delegation met with members of the First Council to secure their approval. Since quorum activity had increased after the change, the seventies refused to go back to Monday even though most apostles thought they ought to.[57]

Though these changes did help to increase quorum activity and sense of fellowship among the seventies, they did not address their basic responsibility of missionary work. In 1912 seventies did less than 18 percent of the missionary work of the church. With 8,894 seventies in the church, less than 4 percent (340) actually served on full-time missions. Most worked in auxiliaries and 676 (7.6 percent) served on home missions, which meant working with inactive members.[58] In October 1911 Frank Y. Taylor, president of the Granite Stake, proposed to allow the seventies to perform their primary function by calling and ordaining sixty-one to proselyte among non-Mormons in his stake. With the approval of the First Presidency, other stakes such as Cassia, Duchesne, and Cache adopted this program, and authorities encouraged seventies to accept calls for stake missions rather than spending their time working in the auxiliaries.[59] This reform had two advantages—revitalization of the quorum and unification of the seventies and the stake in a common and complementary purpose.

Though the stake missionary program helped seventies to fulfill their primary function, statistics gathered in 1915 revealed that half of the members of the 192 seventies' quorums in the church had not filled a mission away from home. The First Presidency, the Twelve, and the First Council discussed this matter and decided to take a two-pronged approach to correct this deficiency. First, they sent mission calls to a number of those who had not served, and, second, the First Presidency placed a temporary moratorium on the organization of new seventies' quorums. Instead, the men were to be kept in elders' quorums, where they would be available for service in wards and auxiliaries. This compromise allowed the integration and common purpose among the wards and quorums.[60]

Where the seventies led, other quorums followed. After Brigham Young's 1877 reorganization, twelve-year-olds were supposed to be ordained deacons. Regular movement to teacher and priest at specific ages was not the rule, however, and by the turn of the century, irregularities existed in ordination to deacon. Some bishops delayed the ordination, and some followed such lax procedures that in at least one case a boy had been ordained at age three. Between 1903 and 1906 the First Presidency and Twelve began strongly emphasizing the need to reorganize and regularize Aaronic Priesthood activity. Like other quorums these met only irregularly on Monday evening, and some authorities suggested that inactivity in the Aaronic Priesthood was partly responsible for the "evils in Elders Quorums."[61]

After urging the revitalization of the Aaronic Priesthood quorums for three years, at the October conference in 1906 the Twelve, through President Francis M. Lyman, laid out the procedure which the church has generally followed since that time. Ordination to deacon at age twelve was to be the rule for all worthy young men. They were to serve as deacons for three years when they were eligible for ordination as teachers, also to serve for three years. This was followed by three years as priests. Advancement to the Melchizedek Priesthood could follow at age twenty-one, but those advanced were to be worthy.[62]

In November 1907 a circular letter outlined the procedure which the Melchizedek Priesthood should follow under what came to be called the New Priesthood Movement. Stake presidents were to recommend prospective priesthood holders to the high council for approval. In the case of seventies, since some quorums covered more than one stake, the stake presidents were to consult with each other and make certain that they called only men suitable for missionary work. When seventies could no longer serve as missionaries, the president was to recommend them for ordination as high priests in recognition of their faithfulness. Bishops were to recommend men for ordination to elder to the stake president after securing the sustaining votes of ward members. Final approval for any Melchizedek office required an affirmative vote at a stake priesthood meeting.[63]

The Twelve followed the seventies' lead in formulating regular lessons and other procedures for the reform of other Melchizedek and Aaronic priesthood quorums. During the fall and winter of 1908 the apostles spent time reviewing lessons designed for use for the Aaronic Priesthood in 1909. At the same time the general authorities placed quorums under closer control of bishops and stake presidents than before. High priests and seventies quorums were henceforth contained within stake boundaries, though the seventies could have more than one quorum per stake. More than one elders quorum might exist in a stake, but each quorum must have at least a majority of the number required for a full quorum, which was ninety-six. Quorums of deacons, teachers, and priests were to be within one ward and presided over by the bishops, though the teachers and deacons were to have their own president.[64]

Each quorum except the seventies, who met on Sunday, was to meet every Monday evening for "instruction in the formal study of the doctrines, principles and history of the gospel." In some cases neither the instructors nor the quorum members had prepared for a discussion of the lessons, and the general authorities attempted to deal with these pedagogical and other problems through the "Priesthood Quorums Table" in the *Improvement Era*.[65]

For some time after 1909 the general and stake officers experimented with various proposals for activating the quorums. In October 1909 the First Presidency and Twelve discussed the possibility of moving priesthood meeting to Sunday morning and changing Sunday School to the afternoon. In January 1910 the priesthood committee, consisting of Rudger Clawson, George F. Richards, Brigham H. Roberts, and Anthon H. Lund, recommended a schedule placing priesthood meeting on Sunday morning, Sunday School in the afternoon, and sacrament meeting in the evening in each ward. The Twelve considered the matter in a special meeting with a number of stake presidents and the general superintendent of the Sunday School. Questions raised by David O. McKay of the Sunday School superintendency led to the tabling of the proposal at the time.[66] In order to try to arrive at a consensus, the Twelve conducted a survey of the opinions of bishops and stake presidents. The First Presidency discussed results of the survey, which showed overwhelming support for the status quo, with bishops and stake presidents in the temple annex on February 8, 1910, but reached no conclusion.[67]

Since the general church organization had not resolved the question, a number of stakes tried rearranging the time of priesthood meeting, Sunday School, sacrament meeting, and MIA. The St. Johns Stake, for instance, held priesthood meeting on Sunday evening on three Sundays of the month in connection with YMMIA. On the fourth Sunday, the wards held a joint YM-YLMIA meeting. In 1913 the Ensign Stake adopted a plan of holding MIA and priesthood meeting on alternate Tuesday nights, but this produced disappointing results. In the Liberty, Ogden, and Fremont stakes the other quorums joined the seventies on Sunday mornings. Those stakes found this "satisfactory," with better than average attendance. After these reports, the Twelve reconsidered its reluctance to holding priesthood meeting on Sundays and agreed, in addition, with the possibility of having the Aaronic Priesthood classes as part of Sunday School.[68] The shift of priesthood meeting from Monday night to Sunday morning not only helped priesthood attendance but had also boosted activity in Sunday School. In fact, in light of the results, the MIA considered shifting its meeting to Sunday as well.[69]

Perhaps the most noticeable change which took place with the new priesthood movement was increased activity. The General Priesthood Committee of the church reported in October 1913 that priests especially paid greater attention to priesthood work. Most quorums held regular meetings where five years before not more than 5 percent of the wards had. Attendance at weekly priesthood meeting increased from 16 percent in 1913 to 18 percent in 1915. Sacrament meeting attendance, which stood at 14.5 percent in 1913, increased to 17 percent in 1915. Ward teaching visits increased from 42 percent to 63 percent over the same period.[70]

For members today, this may seem like an extremely poor showing, but the early twentieth century was a time of transition and change which one must judge on its own terms, not by the standards we would apply today. The statistics meant that, for the average Latter-day Saint, attendance at priesthood or sacrament meeting had not been an important part of his church commitment. In the nineteenth century church leaders expected members to give their lives to the church in the development of new communities and in the creation of new church enterprises. This tied them to the general church community. Church attendance and priesthood activities were secondary since their entire beings were wrapped up in the church. The changing statistics and the development of the new programs and procedures by the general and local authorities reveal an increasing reorientation in the church. At the present time, commitment is measured by willingness to devote time to the church for such things as attendance at meeting and participation in teaching, temple attendance, and welfare work. In effect, the Saints of the early twentieth century were laying the groundwork for the church as we know it today.

Moreover, the changes which were taking place had the effect of strengthening both the general church and the local organizations. The reorganization of tithing, membership, and record-keeping procedures increased the importance of the presiding bishop, moving primary responsibility over the definition of church activity from the member as part of the community to the bishop as presiding authority of the ward. The priesthood reorganization, while vitalizing the quorums, also tied them more closely to the ward and stake organization, subordinating them even more to bishops and stake presidents.

The changes also had the effect of narrowing the scope of church organization to a greater degree by defining the church as part of the larger society rather than as a separate community. This is most apparent in the changes which took place in church courts. After the first two decades of the twentieth century, church members were expected to take secular disputes to civil and criminal rather than church courts. Concern for the time local church leaders could spend in their business interests led in part to the reduction of the size of stakes and the willingness to release long-time officers for reasons other than unfaithfulness or incapacity.

7

New Directions in
Church Administration,
1918–30

THE CHANGES WHICH took place in the First Presidency and Twelve in the late teens and early twenties indicate that the method of selecting officers remained essentially the same as in the nineteenth century. Strengthening the authority of the general leadership and of wards and stakes had not changed that combination of seniority and inspiration which had served in the past. A deep commitment to Christ, the church, and the gospel helped promote unity among church leaders and members.

On November 19, 1918, the church lost its sixth president. Seriously ill since mid-summer, Joseph F. Smith had been unable to fill all the responsibilities of president, and day-to-day supervision of church affairs had fallen to Anthon H. Lund.[1]

One might suspect that the question of succession in the First Presidency had been settled in the minds of all by 1918, but that was not the case. In early July 1918, during President Smith's incapacity, Patriarch Hyrum G. Smith discussed his belief that on the basis of his patriarchal office he ought to become the presiding authority of the church upon the death of Joseph F. Smith. On July 3, 1918, Joseph Fielding Smith, David O. McKay, and Heber J. Grant of the Twelve called on presidents Lund and Penrose. The three apostles said that the Twelve differed with the presiding patriarch on the question of succession but that they did not want a controversy. To help settle the matter, they presented a letter which Wilford Woodruff had written on March 28, 1887.[2]

The letter was extremely important because it had come into Elder Grant's possession under similar circumstances. At the death of John Taylor a controversy had surfaced over the reorganization of the First Presidency. Several apostles discussed the matter with Wilford Woodruff, then president of the Council of the Twelve, and he wrote the letter for them, stating that without direct revelation from the Lord he did not believe that the day would come when the president of the Council of the Twelve would not become president of the church. Both presidents Lund and Penrose expressed pleasure at the letter but decided not to discuss the matter with Joseph F. Smith in view of his poor health.

This letter seems to have resolved any doubt that others in the Twelve or the Presidency might have had at the time, and on November 21, 1918, the day before the funeral, the counselors in the First Presidency and the Twelve met together. No one occupied the presidency's chairs in the council room in the Temple, but the apostles took their places according to seniority. The meeting was both a memorial for Joseph F. Smith and an expression of love and confidence in Heber J. Grant, whom all seemed to recognize as the next president.[3] Following the meeting, Elder Grant met with elders Penrose and Lund to plan the church's reorganization. He asked the two to continue to serve as his counselors and asked that Elder Lund, the senior apostle, serve as president of the Twelve. On November 23 the Twelve reorganized the presidency and their own quorum.[4]

Confirmation of President Grant's call followed. Because of the flu epidemic, no general conference was held in October 1918 or in April 1919, but general conference was called for June 1, 1919, to sustain the new presidency. In the meantime, in late May 1919 several people reported spiritual confirmations. Anthon H. Lund reported that at a temple meeting on May 25, 1919, events took place similar to those reported at the meeting "held in Nauvoo when President Brigham Young was transfigured to look like Joseph Smith and the people took it as a sign that he was the true successor to the martyred prophet." Several people at the meeting said that at recent meetings Heber J. Grant had looked like Joseph F. Smith. Theodore Robinson said that at the fast meeting the preceding Sunday at the Granite Stake Conference he was astonished to know that Heber J. Grant was speaking, yet he looked exactly like Joseph F. Smith. Several others including Brigham F. Grant and Edward H. Anderson said the same thing.[5]

Heber J. Grant was the first president of the church born in Utah and the first who had never known Joseph Smith. Raised by a widowed mother, he was active in business affairs, and his diary reveals a man interested in tying religious and secular themes together. He spent much of his leisure time reading works with moralistic themes written by authors such as James Allen, George William Jordan, Harold Bell

Wright, Charles Dickens, and Plutarch. He had read Albert J. Beveridge's *Young Man and the World*, Wilhelm III's *My Ideas and Ideals*, and David Starr Jordan's *The Religion of a Sensible American* and the *Strength of Being Clean*. He also enjoyed William Jennings Bryan's *Prince of Peace*. During his business career, as later, he suffered considerably from physical and emotional stress. In 1915, after experiencing some business reverses and again in 1921, during the church financial difficulties, he faced virtual physical breakdown and had to take vacations for his health in California.[6]

The deaths of several long-established leaders, changes in the First Presidency, and calls to new positions led to changes in the church hierarchy. President Lund, who had suffered for some time from a hemorrhaging duodenal ulcer, died of that disease on March 2, 1921. President Grant was at the time in California, and on March 5, on the way home to attend the funeral, he discussed possible counselors with Charles W. Nibley. Nibley said that everyone expected he would select his cousin Anthony W. Ivins. Grant remarked that if that were done "the Presidency would be strictly Democratic." Bishop Nibley indicated that this would make no difference because Elder Ivins was the wisest man among the apostles. President Grant wrote that he wanted to choose the man the Lord wished. After President Lund's funeral on March 6, Grant spoke with President Penrose, who told him that Ivins was the only one he had thought of. President Grant said that his mind had rested on Ivins and that unless the Lord indicated someone else, he would undoubtedly select Ivins. On March 8, after a discussion with President Penrose, he decided to wait for the "impression of the Spirit," until April conference. On March 10, 1921, at a meeting of the first Presidency and the Twelve, he proposed that Charles W. Penrose become his first counselor and Anthony W. Ivins his second. Rudger Clawson became president of the Twelve, George F. Richards was called as Salt Lake Temple president, and John A. Widtsoe was chosen to fill the vacancy in the Twelve.[7]

Elder Penrose died on May 16, 1925, and that evening President Grant did not get to sleep until well after midnight as he prayed "earnestly" for guidance in the selection of a successor. By May 28 he was impressed to call Anthony W. Ivins to fill Elder Penrose's place and to select presiding bishop Charles W. Nibley as second counselor. He discussed possible replacements for Nibley with Reed Smoot on that day, and on June 4 proposed the call of Sylvester Q. Cannon, then city engineer of Salt Lake.[8]

Between 1918 and 1930 leaders continued the rationalization of church administration. Perhaps the first prerequisites were the separation of the church's estate from that of the president of the church, which as noted before caused some concern at the death of Lorenzo Snow, and the division of ecclesiastical from secular properties. Nevertheless, by 1930 the church had not completed the steps of separating policy making from administrative functions or of creating a bureaucracy; in fact, administrative modernization was not completed until the 1970s, when the president of the church withdrew from active involvement in church-owned businesses and the Twelve ceased to administer church departments.[9] In large part, the financial difficulties of the church made administrative reform impossible. The First Presidency constantly was forced into taking an active part in routine matters such as negotiating loans and allocating funds for building construction. Still, in view of the difficulties the church faced during this period, the accomplishments were significant.

Immediately after assuming the presidency of the church, Heber J. Grant began several measures of reorganization which were to have far-reaching effects on church administration. On November 27, 1918, he announced that the First Presidency would relinquish the presidency of various auxiliary organizations. He intended, he said later, "to give all the auxiliary boards a full organization independent of the President of the Church, though, of course each [would be] under the direction of the General Authorities." David O. McKay then became the president of the Deseret Sunday School Union with Stephen L Richards and George Pyper as assistants. Anthony W. Ivins became general superintendent of the YMMIA with Brigham H. Roberts and Richard R. Lyman as assistants. President Joseph F. Smith had been general superintendent of both organizations. At the death of Anthon H. Lund, Joseph Fielding Smith became church historian, instead of vesting that job in the First Presidency. Some positions, however, the president of the church retained. Heber J. Grant became president of the General Church Board of Education, and he retained the presidency of church-related business such as the Utah National Bank, ZCMI, and U and I Sugar.[10]

Previous difficulties, together with the increasing complexity of church financial commitments, brought about the establishment of two legal entities to administer church property. The First Presidency, the presiding bishopric, and church legal advisers completed arrangements on February 7, 1922, for the creation of Zion Securities Corporation to administer all taxable and nonecclesiastical property. Directors were Heber J. Grant, Anthony W. Ivins, Stephen L Richards, Charles W. Nibley, and Arthur Winter. As a companion measure, on November 26, 1923, the Corporation of the President was organized to hold ecclesiastical property of the church.[11]

The increasing diversity of church activities necessitated closer coordination between the First Presidency and the presiding bishopric. In place of informal exchanges, in 1927 Heber J. Grant set up a regular meeting at first on Tuesdays, and later on Mondays.[12]

The First Presidency also had to consider various cases on appeal from judgments in stake presidency and high council courts. The evidence currently available from President Grant's diary indicates considerable compassion in these matters. On July 26, 1922, for instance, the First Presidency, together with Stephen L Richards, reviewed the case of a member and his wife who had been excommunicated by a high council court in Montpelier, Idaho. They had been charged with adultery, and while there was strong presumptive evidence of guilt, no direct evidence had been produced. Since the burden of proof had to lie with the prosecution, the ruling was overturned.[13]

President Grant did not approve of the use of church courts as agents of retribution. In his diary he recorded the source of that feeling when he told of the excommunication years earlier of one of his closest friends, who had been cut off because he did not pay a full tithing or keep the Word of Wisdom. The friend asked for a year to put his life in order, even though he was already "living a clean sweet life," nevertheless his name was put in "with a lot of others and [the court] cut them off the Church." At the time, Grant, as a young man, had been listening to the proceedings outside the room in his ward in Salt Lake City. He said that he "was never madder at anything in my life than at the action taken" against his friend, and he clearly felt it was wrong to use church courts in such an "indiscriminate" and "vindictive" way.[14]

The first three decades of the twentieth century were extremely important in the development of church policy on buildings, monuments, and historic sites. The church expanded its support of charitable and recreational facilities like hospitals and gymnasia, and it constructed buildings in downtown Salt Lake City to house administrative offices. Church leaders moved rather aggressively to acquire sites at which important occurrences in the early history of the church had taken place, particularly in Vermont, western New York, and Illinois, and to erect monuments to people and events of the past.[15]

Perhaps most important were the creative innovations of the period. The church leadership moved from an ad hoc system in which varying contributions, usually ranging about 30 percent under Joseph F. Smith, were appropriated from general church revenues for the construction of local meetinghouses and stake houses to a system under Heber J. Grant in which the church contributed a standard amount—ordinarily 50 percent—of the cost of a building. The church constructed new temples in Laie, Hawaii; Cardston, Alberta, Canada; and Mesa, Arizona, and the leadership acted vigorously to make certain that the best possible designs and decorations were used, inviting competitive bidding among Mormon architectural firms, generally consisting of men with training in the best traditions of Europe and the United States, and hiring the best available Mormon artistic talent to produce the murals, paintings, and other decorative features of the temples.[16] In particular, two developments epitomize the administrative modernization of the church and its response to the pluralization of the society around the Mormons—the construction of Deseret Gymnasium and the reorganization of the church architect's office.

As the Mutual Improvement Association expanded its physical education program, a number of general board members favored the construction of a gymnasium in Salt Lake City for young men. Some men had begun to frequent the YMCA gym, and many were neglecting Sunday services and drawing away from the church. Stake and ward officers throughout the church were encouraged to see that ward buildings provided light gymnastic facilities to keep young men near their homes and "away from town influences." By late February 1908 the First Presidency and Twelve approved the construction of Deseret Gymnasium in collaboration with Latter-day Saints University, a high school with some collegiate work in Salt Lake City. Finished in 1910, the facility received about one-third general church funds and the remainder was contributed from church members in the Salt Lake area.[17]

The church also experimented with a system of standard plans for meetinghouses. In November 1919 the church announced the appointment of Willard Young as superintendent of the church building department. Perhaps in response to problems found in some buildings like the Blackfoot Tabernacle, which exhibited atrocious acoustics, Young began to standardize plans for buildings, using colonial and neoclassical models. In April 1924, however, Joseph Nielson, who had served as architect for the science building at Brigham Young University and had designed the Beaver Meetinghouse in 1918, called on President Grant to complain. He said that having an architectural department was not fair to local architects and that often the little work an architect could get locally made the difference between his success and failure. Several months later, after considering the situation, President Grant changed the policy and on August 27, 1924, notified architects that the officers of the various wards and stakes could hire local architects to design their buildings should they choose to do so.[18]

In the twenties, principally because of depressed economic conditions, the First Presidency was reluctant to approve new buildings. During the financial crisis of 1920–21 and the Great Depression beginning in 1929, President Grant faced problems in meeting all the demands upon church resources. In November 1921 the First Presidency wrote that the "finances of the church here at home have not been at such a low ebb for ten or twelve years." Conditions improved by August 1922, but by mid-1930 the church was again in financial difficulty. On June 9 President Grant had to tell the presidency of the Panguitch Stake that he could not appropriate money for a seminary building, as he had not yet been able to fulfill promises for assistance made in 1929. He agreed, however, to try to help the stake get a loan. In late December 1930 the church leadership announced a new policy of stopping the erection of "costly L.D.S. meeting houses." By April 1931 the auditing committee reported that expenditures for church buildings and other needs amounted to "much more" than its income. The First Presidency then resolved to curtail new construction even more.[19]

Though most money seems to have gone for capital improvements, full-time general authorities continued to receive a living allowance. Officers with outside business interests seem to have done well, but those like James E. Talmage and John A. Widtsoe, who had to rely upon the church allowance to subsist, were in constant financial difficulty. In July 1916 Talmage recorded preparations for a party at Joseph F. Smith's home. "In preparation for this visit the brethren of the twelve were divided into two classes—the Haves and Haven'ts or the withs and the withouts—one class comprising those who own autos and the other consisting of those who have no such means of conveyance. Members of the second class were assigned with their families to the care of their betters. Wife and I were conveyed to and from the Smith home by Brother and Sister Anthony W. Ivins in their splendid Packard Car."

Widtsoe reported that his allowance as an apostle was one-third his salary for the previous two decades while a professor and president at two educational institutions. He had been forced to sell his car and discharge his servants. Some increases were made in the allowance in 1925, but it remained modest.[20]

An important development during the 1920s was the increasing expansion of the church outside the Utah core area. In July 1922 George W. McCune of Ogden was called to move to Los Angeles to become president of the newly created stake. By 1929 there were two stakes in the Los Angeles area, and Heber J. Grant was particularly impressed by the tremendous growth which had taken place there.[21]

In general, however, the church leadership was not particularly happy with the outmigration of Mormons from Utah. Though there were exceptions, particularly in the case of other mountain states, there was a general feeling of discomfort with the idea of dispersion.[22] In point of fact, the general authorities had little dispersion to worry about by 1930. Most church members still lived in the intermountain region, and a day's train ride from Salt Lake City would take the general authorities to most Mormons. General authority visits to the church's 1,000 wards had become less frequent, but they were expected at every quarterly conference of the 104 stakes, most of which were in Utah, Arizona, and Idaho. Certainly the church had grown in size and complexity since 1900, but it was still a relatively homogeneous intermountain organization of 672,000, more easily administered, in spite of its problems, than the diverse nationwide and increasingly international church of today.

The evidence presented here would seem to indicate that while the modernization of the church's relationship to politics and the business community had been largely accomplished by 1930, its organizational forms were still in transition. The greatest success was evident in ecclesiastical rather than managerial fields. The priesthood quorums had been largely revitalized and set on a track where they could assume a greater portion of the burden for instruction and governance on the local level. The organization of Zion's Securities Corporation and the Corporation of the President were signal achievements, but the First Presidency was still burdened with many decisions of a trivial nature which might more efficiently have come to the attention of their subordinates. Some efforts to solve this problem, at least in connection with the funding for building construction, had been made, but the financial stringencies of the period made the proposed solutions impossible to implement.

8

The Church Auxiliary Organizations

IN THE EARLY TWENTIETH CENTURY, as the Latter-day Saints activated and rationalized priesthood organization, the autonomy of auxiliaries declined and the auxiliaries came increasingly under the direction of general and local priesthood leaders. The First Presidency appointed priesthood advisers for women's auxiliaries (Relief Society, Primary Association, and YLMIA) from among the Twelve. On the general church level under Heber J. Grant, the First Presidency withdrew from the presidency of the Sunday School and the YMMIA, and that function was turned over to the Council of the Twelve as well. Beginning in Joseph F. Smith's administration, the church attempted on two occasions to coordinate the functions of the auxiliaries through correlation committees, but those were abandoned by the Grant administration in 1922, and general supervision was assumed by priesthood leaders.

Changes in the auxiliary publications reflected the changes in organizations. The *Improvement Era*, which had begun as the organ of the YMMIA, became increasingly the organ of the priesthood. The church acquired ownership of the semi-independent *Juvenile Instructor*. The semi-autonomous *Woman's Exponent* was replaced by the church-owned *Relief Society Magazine*, and the *Young Women's Journal* was combined with the *Improvement Era*.

The reduction of auxiliary autonomy took place quite gradually, however, and in the early twentieth century, auxiliary members tended to see their role as encompassing the larger society as well as the Mormon community. Thus, the Relief Society established milk stations with nurses for urban children in predominantly non-Mormon neighborhoods. The Primary Association opened a nonsectarian children's hospital. The Young Men's and Young Women's Mutual Improvement Associations lobbied for the creation of a Saturday half-holiday for employees.

Nevertheless, the Latter-day Saint auxiliary members began to face the conflicting pressures which American Protestantism had already experienced in the nineteenth century. As long as the society in which Mormons lived and the Latter-day Saint community were coextensive, members generally perceived service in the society as building the kingdom. Increasingly, however, the Latter-day Saints came to view their community as something apart from the larger society. Under these circumstances, some members became dubious about the legitimacy of considering compassionate and social service outside wards and stakes as service in the Lord's kingdom. Some, more concerned with personal morality than social service, believed welfare activities diluted religious experience. In a sense, this split was similar to that between social Christianity and evangelical fundamentalism.[1]

Increasingly after 1930, and particularly with the adoption of the Welfare Plan in 1936, the church leadership seems to have shared these concerns. As a result, in recent years church leaders have tended to define work in the larger society as separate from church service. This does not mean that Latter-day Saints do not participate in social and civic service. In fact, most legislators, mayors, PTA workers, and hospital volunteers in predominantly Mormon areas are Mormons, but this kind of service is perceived as outside the members' religious obligation, undertaken as citizens of the nation, not as members of the Lord's kingdom.[2]

In retrospect, much of the activity in the auxiliaries during the early twentieth century was quite similar to that characteristic of progressive America. The promotion of organizational efficiency which underpinned much of the progressive reform had helped to change the character of the church. Like many of the progressives, church leaders and auxiliary workers were concerned with increasingly serious urban problems such as the welfare of families, children, and indigents; public health; and moral reform.[3] In many of these changes, the influence of progressive ideas are difficult, if not impossible, to document except by the comparative approach. This is particularly true of the organizational rationalization which took place. In some, however, progressive origins were explicit. The progressive education and pedagogical movement influenced Relief Society and Sunday School lessons. Debate topics in the MIA addressed such progressive issues as government ownership, business regulation, and direct democracy. Emphasis on the outdoors and recreational activity and the adoption of the Boy Scout program are also clear progressive influences.[4]

Moreover, the argument within the church between supporters of progressive measures and conservatives opposed to them was evident in the discussion of some programs. This is perhaps most clear in a controversy over the MIA manual in 1911. The division there was not between radicals and conservatives but between moderate progressives who thought some government ownership of public utilities was justified in particular cases and conservatives who believed that such ownership was unwarranted.[5]

Given the rather loose organization of church programs in the nineteenth century one is not surprised that the functions of the auxiliaries overlapped with one another and, after the inception of priesthood revitalization, with the quorums. This overlap seems to have developed because each of the auxiliaries was organized and functioned in response to needs which church leaders and members saw at particular times. After their founding each operated under the general direction of its presidency and board with little attempt to define specific roles until the twentieth century. Overlap need not necessarily promote inefficient administration if the emphases within various organizations are complementary, if they address different aspects of the same problems, or if repetition is necessary for learning. But this was not always the case, so as early as 1907 the First Presidency appointed the first correlation committee to coordinate similar activities and suggest means of eliminating duplication of effort.

Most striking by 1930, perhaps, was the degree to which the roles of the various auxiliaries were defined and the overlapping functions reduced or eliminated. The major exceptions were undoubtedly in the nature of the theological training provided by the auxiliaries. Nevertheless, the role of weekday instruction and activity for young children had been given to the Primary Association, and Religion Classes were eliminated. Social and recreational activities for teenagers and young adults came under the supervision of the YL and YMMIA. The Relief Society focused its efforts on compassionate service and provided training for women in community and home life. In the late 1920s the church undertook a short-lived attempt to reduce the overlap in religious instruction by scheduling priesthood lessons during Sunday School or MIA time.

Over the three decades, perhaps the Relief Society changed least. Specific programs were adapted as the Relief Society presidency and board and the First Presidency and Twelve saw altered conditions in

the church and larger community, but the basic thrust of the organization remained the same in 1930 as in 1900.

Joseph Smith had established the Relief Society in 1842 to provide
charitable service and to correct "the morals and strengthen . . . the
virtues of the community." It was initially not an auxiliary at all, but an
organization for women complementary to priesthood quorums. The
society revived in Utah wards in the early 1850s, and in 1867 Brigham
Young reorganized it on a general church level, appointing Eliza R.
Snow as general president. Under Sister Snow's direction, the Relief
Society led out in organizing the Primary Association and YLMIA. In
1892 it was incorporated as the National Women's Relief Society. Active not only in religious affairs, its officers were among the leaders locally and nationally in the battle for women's rights. After the turn of
the century, Relief Society sisters together with other church members
became involved in the peace movement. By the turn of the century,
also, members generally perceived it to be an auxiliary rather than a
basic church organization, though the distinction was not as important then as it was to become by 1930.[6]

Between 1900 and 1930 the Relief Society had five presidents. Zina
D. H. Young (a widow of Brigham Young), who had been active in
nurse and midwife training, presided until August 1901. Bathsheba W.
Smith (a widow of George A. Smith), who had presided over the
women's department of the Salt Lake Temple, served from 1901 to
1910. Emmeline B. Wells (a widow of Daniel H. Wells), who had
edited the *Woman's Exponent* from 1876 to 1914, was president from
1910 to 1921. Clarissa S. Williams, who was active in the work of the
Daughters of the American Revolution, served from 1921 to 1928. In
1928 Louise Yates Robison, who worked particularly in promoting
training for the mentally handicapped, became president.

Under these women the central activity of the Relief Society was its
charitable and educational work. The Relief Society sponsored a broad
program of instruction ranging from civics to mother education, which
it introduced in 1902. Charitable activities included help in civic affairs, on personal and family problems, and in disaster relief.

Since Brigham Young's day the Relief Society had operated granaries in which the women stored wheat in anticipation of possible future need. By 1915 the Relief Society had 157,000 bushels of wheat
stored in granaries throughout the church. At that time, as part of centralization under priesthood control, the First Presidency transferred

the stored wheat from the Relief Society to the jurisdiction of the presiding bishopric. During the First World War, the United States Food Administration purchased most of the wheat.[7]

As with the grain storage program, much of the Relief Society's compassionate service reached people beyond the Mormon community. In December 1913 the Relief Society opened a boarding home for women and girls at 36 West North Temple, just north of Temple Square. The home remained open until October 1921, when the YLMIA's Beehive Home for girls replaced it.[8] This home supplemented the employment service for women which the Relief Society had already begun. In May 1905, after noting the trend of migration from rural communities into the cities, the Relief Society had set up an employment office in Salt Lake City to help young women find work and to monitor wage rates. This paralleled an employment service for men set up by the Presiding Bishopric in 1903. The society also investigated working conditions to see that the young women were not placed in unwholesome surroundings.[9] The society operated a twenty-four hour service for the sick, needy, and unemployed during the economic panic of 1907–8. After the beginning of the Great Depression in 1929 the Relief Society accepted primary responsibility for finding work for women and assisted in giving aid to needy families.[10]

Relief Society medical training helped the larger society greatly. From 1877 to 1898 Sarah M. Kimball and Mary H. Barker had conducted classes in obstetrics, nursing, and physiology. Dr. Romania B. Pratt Penrose had run a school of obstetrics for two decades and was associated as a superintendent and resident physician with the Deseret Hospital, which the Relief Society had operated from 1882 until 1894. Dr. Ellis R. Shipp operated a nurse-midwife school which served various towns.[11]

In 1898 the Salt Lake Stake had established the Relief Society Nurses School, which after 1902 came under the supervision of the Relief Society general board. Dr. Margaret C. Roberts, with the help of Priscilla J. Riter and Emma A. Empey, instructed women called from throughout the church to study nursing. In return for the education, graduates agreed to give charitable service. In 1920 the Relief Society instituted a one-year nurse's aid course. The nurse training program continued until February 1924, when it had to be discontinued because of objections from the National Hospital Training School Rating Bureau.[12]

After 1924 the Relief Society continued to promote nursing in other ways. It maintained two loan funds, one for hospital training and one for graduate nurses who wanted to go into public health work. By 1931 the Relief Society was also cooperating with other private and public agencies to support public health nurses in five counties. In still another county the Relief Society organization cooperated with the school district and the county to establish a dental clinic.[13] A number of local Relief Societies provided low-cost maternity care for expectant mothers. In October 1924 the Cottonwood Stake, in cooperation with a number of other local units, opened one such facility. Operating on a flat rate for service, it ran successfully throughout the remainder of the decade, surviving to the present, though greatly expanded under secular management, as the Cottonwood Hospital.[14]

Particularly through the efforts of Louise Y. Robison, the Relief Society worked for the establishment of state mental health programs. In January 1926 the Relief Society promoted the study of mental health as part of its educational department. Relief Society activities produced increased interest in the field and sentiment in favor of mental tests as part of vocational guidance for children. The Relief Society also promoted adequate custodial and rehabilitative care of the mentally ill. In part because of the efforts of Sister Robison and the Relief Society, the state of Utah passed a bill creating the state training school for the mentally handicapped at American Fork in 1929.[15]

The Relief Society concerned itself with children's health. Beginning in 1916 the Relief Society operated milk stations in Salt Lake City to provide wholesome milk for urban youngsters, particularly Greek- and Italian-Americans. Nurses were placed at the stations during the summer to assist the children with health problems. The Relief Society also promoted the improvement of the milk supply and encouraged increased consumption of milk, particularly by children. This had been a particularly serious problem in the early twentieth century since some dairies adulterated their milk with formaldehyde to prevent spoiling. Various articles in the *Relief Society Magazine* during the 1920s dealt with milk sanitation and means of pasteurization, and urged adequate legislation to protect the purity of the milk supply.[16]

The Relief Society and other church organizations helped in efforts to improve the lives of children. Some of the rural stakes took malnourished children from urban areas to rural homes for two weeks of care. After Heber J. Grant and David O. McKay participated in the

White House Conference on Child Health and Protection, H. E. Barnard, chairman of the conference, came to see President Grant and expressed appreciation for the work being done. He said that some of the programs inaugurated there were being adopted by other states.[17]

Most important, perhaps, was the appropriation of $412,000 from the Relief Society wheat trust fund for health, maternity, and child welfare programs. This action, taken by the Relief Society in April 1922, occurred seven months prior to the passage of the Sheppard-Towner Act, which provided national assistance for maternity and infant care. Quick to appreciate the importance of the legislation, the Relief Society lobbied for Utah's cooperation. Amy Brown Lyman, then general secretary of the Relief Society and a member of the state legislature, sponsored the enabling legislation. In 1923 the Relief Society recommended that women cooperate with the states in administration of the act.[18]

These efforts produced extraordinary results. Cooperation between the Relief Society and public agencies produced in Utah the greatest reduction in the maternal death and infant mortality rates in the nation. By 1931 Utah ranked with five other states in the lowest group. Dr. Theodore B. Beatty, Utah state health commissioner, said that Relief Society women made up the majority of members of the various health center committees and that the cooperation of the society with the state was responsible for the success of the maternity and infant work.[19]

The establishment of the Relief Society Social Welfare Department in January 1919 must be seen against the background of this continuing concern for the larger society. At the beginning of World War I, Joseph F. Smith, who had recognized the need for professional social workers in the church, asked Amy Brown Lyman to specialize in social work. During the war the Relief Society cooperated with the Red Cross in helping families of soldiers, sending workers from various communities to home services courses given in Denver by the Red Cross Western Division. After the war, it became apparent that this work needed expansion, so the church established the Relief Society Social Welfare Department.

In addition to continuing coordination of employment services, providing community welfare services, and serving as the church's adoption agency, the Social Welfare Department introduced the nationally standardized casework method of organization to the church

and to Utah. The casework system, based on private charitable practice and academic sociology, had been introduced into social work in
the United States by 1900 and was refined during the first three decades of the twentieth century. In fact, the development of the social
casework system in the Relief Society predated the development of a
formal system of statewide social service agencies by the state of Utah.
The state system started in 1921 in part because of the influence of
church members like Lyman, who became vice-chairman of the State
Welfare Commission.[20]

In 1919 the Relief Society began a series of regional social service
institutes, used Salt Lake City as a laboratory for its social welfare programs, and promoted the equality of women in the work force and the
larger society. In Salt Lake City social problems tended to be more
complex than in rural areas, but the resources available there were
more diversified as well. Under Lyman's leadership the trained social
workers taught classes in social work to Relief Society volunteers.[21]

In 1921 the Relief Society began an activity which later came under
the direction of the presiding bishopric and which served as the basis
for later welfare programs. The Salt Lake stakes opened a storehouse
for various commodities in 1921. In 1922 the general board of the Relief Society took over the project for the church. Clothes, furniture,
and other items were received and repaired at the storehouse for re-
distribution to the needy.[22]

A tradition of independent activity on behalf of the general welfare,
coupled with progressive ideas on female equality and worth, was undoubtedly responsible for active support of the women's movement.
Women had achieved the vote in Utah in 1870 and after the federal
government's abolition of that right in 1887, equal suffrage was reinstated through the Constitution of 1896. Organized as the Woman
Suffrage Association of Utah and led principally by the Relief Society,
Utah women had promoted the development of universal liberty and
human rights for all deprived of equality before the law. At the National Council of Women's meeting in Washington, D.C., in 1899, Susa
Young Gates and Minnie J. Snow had called for the admission of
women to colleges and universities and the adoption of curricula to
prepare women for the responsibilities of parenthood. In an article in
the April 1907 *Improvement Era* and in her pamphlet *Women in Politics,* Gates contended that, contrary to the image portrayed by the national press, Mormon women enjoyed more rights than most women.

In addition to equal access to education, they ran such organizations as the Relief Society, YLMIA, and Primary Association, served on missions, and worked in various other religious and civic capacities.[23]

Reed Smoot's initial opposition to a national woman suffrage amendment generated a great deal of antagonism from the Relief Society's general board. As a result, he wrote Susa Young Gates explaining that he actually believed in woman suffrage. He opposed, he said, what he considered the excesses of the present movement and thought suffrage a matter for state action. He eventually changed his views and supported the amendment in 1919.[24]

The group of women who stood in the forefront of the emancipation of women in Utah would have been extraordinary in any community. Martha Hughes Cannon, for instance, received her doctorate in medicine in 1880 at the University of Michigan, the only woman in a class of 125. She became a resident physician at Deseret Hospital, married Angus M. Cannon, then president of the Salt Lake Stake, and was the first woman elected state senator in the United States. Instrumental in establishing the State Board of Health, she served as a member of the board of trustees of the State School for the Deaf, Dumb, and Blind, as vice president of the American Congress of Tuberculosis, and as a member of the state Democratic central committee.[25]

In the small southern Utah town of Kanab, Mary W. Chamberlain and a group of women campaigned for election to the town board when the male-dominated board seemed to have mismanaged governmental affairs. Although their candidacy was initially taken as a joke, the women won the election and governed with considerable determination. In their view a major problem with the previous administration had been its unwillingness to deal forcefully with nuisances such as straying cattle, gambling, and the liquor traffic. After taking office, the women startled vested interests by prohibiting cattle and other animals from running unattended on the streets, establishing an estray pound, and fining owners $1.50 for every stray cow. At first many of those who owned the cows refused to pay the fines, and in retaliation the cows or their milk were sold. Chamberlain's board enacted and enforced ordinances prohibiting gambling and sports on Sunday and regulating the sale of liquor.[26]

The Relief Society together with other church leaders supported the home economics education movement. In March 1916 Reed Smoot introduced a bill to appropriate funds to agricultural experiment stations for research in home economics. The Relief Society promoted home economics education within the church. In February 1927 the Relief Society launched a "Clean Home, Clean Town" campaign to try to improve the condition of towns and cities wherever members lived.[27]

Much, perhaps most, of the discretionary time of the average Relief Society woman was devoted to activities within the church. In 1912, for instance, the Relief Society opened a temple and burial clothes department to supply ceremonial clothes to church members. In 1914, at the suggestion of Susa Young Gates, genealogical and temple work were introduced into the Relief Society lesson and activity program. From 1914 to 1920, when the Genealogical Society assumed full responsibility for this work, the Relief Society held genealogical lessons and conventions. In July 1915 the Relief Society joined the Genealogical Society in conducting an excursion for 265 delegates to the International Genealogical Convention held in connection with the World's Fair in San Francisco. The Relief Society inaugurated volunteer temple service under which every member contributed either fifty cents or one day a year in ordinance work. The organization established the Bathsheba W. Smith grant fund, the interest from which was used for temple ceremonies. In 1916 they established a penny temple fund to assist in construction of the Canadian and Hawaiian temples.[28]

The Relief Society visiting teaching program, which included compassionate service and a monthly visit to all sisters in the church, had been inaugurated in Nauvoo. In October 1916 the Relief Society initiated measures to improve the quality of the visits by providing published lesson topics and in 1923 began publishing monthly outlines in the *Relief Society Magazine*. In 1928 the general board inaugurated a forty-five-minute monthly visiting teachers' training meeting to be held in each ward.[29]

Following the lead of the priesthood quorums, in 1914 the Relief Society general board introduced a uniform course of study. Their first course consisted of study in genealogy, home ethics, gardening, literature, art, and architecture. Members of the general board prepared texts. Three of four weekly ward Relief Society meetings were devoted to educational lessons and a fourth was used for business and sewing. In succeeding years the courses included theology, genealogy, literature, history, art, citizenship, parliamentary procedure, home economics, gardening, law enforcement, health, sanitation, poverty, crime, unemployment, social legislation, motherhood, and home education.[30]

Until the mid-teens, local autonomy was the rule in the societies. Property was locally owned by the Relief Society organization, and lessons, based on suggested topics, were written locally. The *Woman's Exponent*, though centrally operated, was a privately owned periodical under general Relief Society direction. The organization enrolled only those women who wished to join, and though all were encouraged, membership in the church did not automatically confer Relief Society membership. By 1920 all of this except the voluntary membership had changed. In March 1914 the Relief Society ceased publication of the *Woman's Exponent* which it had operated since 1872. This semi-private journal, edited originally by Louisa Lula Greene Richards and then by Emmeline B. Wells, had printed poetry and prose, household hints, Relief Society news, and support for the women's movement for more than four decades. It was replaced by the *Relief Society Magazine*, a wholly church-owned journal acknowledged as the society's official organ. Still, much of the emphasis of the Relief Society magazine was similar to that of the previous *Woman's Exponent*. The Relief Society collected funds and maintained its own accounts, but in 1915 the First Presidency directed that all real estate belonging to the society must be held in trust by the ward bishops. It was estimated that at that time the Relief Society owned more than $149,000 in real property, mostly halls and storage granaries.[31]

By the 1920s the First Presidency seems to have become concerned both about independent activity and activity outside the church. In a letter to Dora Henderson in April 1924, President Grant advised that "our sister members advocate all of their spare time to the advancement of our Primary, Mutual, Religion Class, Sunday School, and Relief Society work." He then urged that women not join "any society outside of the regularly organized institution in the church."[32]

Increasingly the emphasis on compassionate service and social welfare alienated some women from the Relief Society. In February 1928 Annie Wells Cannon, a member of the Relief Society general board, came to President Grant with the complaint that President Clarissa Williams ignored her counselors and that Sister Lyman was actually running the Relief Society. In her view, "the spirit of the Gospel and religion seem to have disappeared, and it seems to be a social welfare organization." This concerned President Grant, particularly when presiding bishop Sylvester Q. Cannon, her brother-in-law, supported her views. Nevertheless, Amy Brown Lyman became first counselor and

eventually served as president of the Relief Society. Far from diminish-
ing their social welfare activities, the Relief Society expanded them
during the 1920s.[33]

Thus, in spite of the diminution of its autonomy the period from
1900 to 1930 was an extremely creative and extraordinarily fruitful
time for the Relief Society. In the field of compassionate and social service it was undoubtedly the most important single organization in the
state of Utah. The effect of the activities of the extraordinary group of
women in the Relief Society affected the lives of church members and
non-members as well in ways which improved the LDS community
and the larger society immensely.

While the Relief Society provided charitable assistance, the Sunday
School served as the main auxiliary for teaching doctrine. Following
the establishment of the first Utah Sunday School by Richard Bal-
lantyne in 1849 and the development of ward Sunday Schools in the
1850s, George Q. Cannon of the First Presidency had become interested in the national Sunday School movement in 1866 and established the *Juvenile Instructor* and the Parent Sunday School Union—
later the Deseret Sunday School Union. As other auxiliaries had ma-
tured, they often became competitors for time and attention, many of
them holding meetings on Sunday morning. In 1898, however, the
First Presidency directed that the wards hold Sunday morning free
from meetings conflicting with Sunday School.[34]

Between the mid 1890s and 1930 the Sunday School sought to
broaden participation and improve instruction. Beginning with lessons developed by individual teachers, the general Sunday School organization provided outlines, full scale lessons for teachers, and finally
lessons for students and teachers. Pedagogical training was provided,
and organization was rationalized through the creation of stake supervisory boards and periodic training sessions. As these changes were
made, the subject matter of lessons was adapted to an increasingly urban and pluralistic society facing challenges to traditional morality and
to the family.

In 1896 the Sunday School officers had begun to reexamine the organization in order to define its role and to chart a course of action to
achieve its goals. General Sunday School conventions in 1896 and
1898 published proceedings and a "Treatise" defining the Sunday
School program. The Treatise called upon Sunday School workers to
emphasize religious and theological training, promote right action,

and implant faith in the church and its doctrines and ordinances. Teachers were expected to try to inculcate religious principles by precept and example, not simply to teach theological facts. Songs, stories, and visual teaching aids were to be used to teach religion, and a plan of home reading was devised to support this goal.[35] Before the development of the Sunday School Treatise teachers provided their own lessons. The Sunday School Treatise, however, included outlines and model lessons. By today's standards, the model lessons seem to have negated the avowed aim of trying to teach religious principles rather than theological facts. They were generally factual questions and answers based on the Bible and Book of Mormon.[36]

As part of the stake conference visits during the years from 1899 through 1901, L. John Nuttall of the general board visited Sunday Schools from Alberta on the north to the Mexican colonies on the south. In general, Sunday School activity compared favorably with other organizations in the church at that time. Attendance ranged from 50 to 70 percent of those enrolled. However, many wards were not using the prescribed outlines, some had few song books, and in many, donations to the nickel fund, used to support the organization, were less than 80 percent. Nuttall was dissatisfied with the failure to reach perfection, but on the whole conditions seem to have been relatively good.[37]

The Sunday Schools compared favorably with those of other churches. In 1900 a writer for the national Protestant-related magazine, *The Outlook*, visited a Sunday School in one of the wards in Salt Lake City. He was, in general, favorably impressed. Though the superintendent, he said, was not a man of culture, several of the teachers seemed to be of the "aristocratic type." The remarks of the superintendent and the prayers offered "were fully up to the general level in well-to-do-Sunday-Schools in the East." Though the hymns were unfamiliar to him, they were, he said, "remarkably well sung."[38]

The model for George Q. Cannon's proposal for a Sunday School had been the international movement, and the church authorized members of the Sunday School general board to participate in national and international Sunday School conventions. In June 1902, for instance, George Reynolds represented the Sunday School union board at the International Sunday School Convention in Denver, Colorado.[39]

By 1902 it had become clear that the lesson outlines which the Sunday School had been using provided insufficient guidance for Sunday

School teachers. For the year 1903, as a result, the church undertook a "new departure," with a system of outline plans. Each of four departments received a four-year course of study making possible systematic lessons for sixteen years. With the reorganization of the lesson system came also a change in the method of instruction for the adult theological class. The new model followed the professional meeting. Papers on various topics were read orally by class members, and the class was asked to comment on and discuss them.[40]

In 1901 the status of the *Juvenile Instructor* changed also. Since its establishment in 1866, the *Juvenile Instructor*, like the *Woman's Exponent*, had been a semiautonomous magazine. Tied closely to the church, it was nevertheless independent of the formal organization. In 1901, however, the Deseret Sunday School Union bought the *Instructor* and edited it as an official publication.[41]

In many ways the changes taking place in the Sunday School mirrored the developments in the church as a whole. In line with the increasing concern over urban problems and their effect on the family, after an experiment in the Weber Stake, the general board instituted a parent and child class in 1906. In 1908 the general board prepared a series of lessons for the class. The manual, entitled *Parent and Child*, reveals much not only about the subject matter but also about the pedagogical methods used. The basic model of the previous lessons had been the paper-commentator system. The new *Parent and Child* manual provided for the first time short articles written by members of the Sunday School general board, general authorities, and others. Some essays were based in part on Charles F. Sargent's *Our Home*. A list of discussion questions followed the articles. The lessons combined scripture, citations from *belles lettres* and literary classics, material from science and sociology, and common sense discussions of child development, cooking, literature, cleanliness, and other household topics. Essays for volume 2 for 1909 were also written by a wide variety of people, but volume 3, for 1916, was written principally by Mosiah Hall, associate professor of education at the University of Utah. The final lessons in the manual were rewritten from lectures on child maturation presented by Dr. John M. Tyler for the Utah Educational Association. The bibliography in the first volume is also revealing. The principal sources reflect the impact of developments in nationally prominent universities, especially the University of Chicago, and the progressive education movement. The authors ranged from Elizabeth Harrison to H. F. Cope, from Herbert Spencer to Jacob Riis.[42]

Paralleling priesthood reform and the movement of increased activity in the church organization, after 1905 the Sunday School leadership tried to rationalize its organization. In 1905 some stakes began experimenting with a Sunday School union meeting (essentially a local faculty meeting). In April 1908 stake Sunday School boards were organized and the church's general board recommended a unified plan of union meetings to be held monthly, quarterly, or semiannually, depending on local conditions. In 1909 the Sunday School began instructions in pedagogical method, expanded after 1915 with a textbook authored by Adam S. Bennion, a Berkeley Ph.D.[43]

Before 1908 emphasis had been on course work. After that time the Sunday School expanded its worship service with concert recitations taken from the Articles of Faith, church hymns, and the scriptures. In 1909 memory gems (short inspirational aphorisms) were printed in the *Juvenile Instructor* for use by the ward Sunday Schools. In 1909, also, the sacrament gem, a short phrase repeated by the congregation before the administration of the emblems of Christ's Last Supper was introduced as part of the program.[44]

Enlistment work was expanded in 1907 and 1908. The ward Sunday Schools were encouraged to sponsor "100 percent" and "Bring a Friend" Sundays to promote increased attendance.[45]

In 1928 the Sunday School expanded its musical training and practical speaking experience and involved the students more in Sunday School class instruction. Though sacrament gems and concert recitations had been used, principal emphasis had been placed on course work, and Sunday School had run in most wards from 10:30 A.M. to noon. On January 1, 1928, however, the starting time was pushed back a half-hour. Two-and-one-half-minute talks were inaugurated, and fifteen minutes were allowed for song practice. Also, in addition to lesson textbooks for teachers, used earlier, the Sunday School began providing material for students. Lessons were given out a week in advance for the pupils to study on the theory that they could participate more fully in the next week's instruction.[46]

By 1930 the Sunday School meeting had become a religious service combined with classes to teach the gospel. Teaching from manuals of lessons generally written by church members knowledgeable in the gospel, in secular applications of gospel teachings, and in contemporary pedagogical techniques, class instructors faced their students with much better preparation than their predecessors three decades before. For many members, this meeting became the principal Sunday church service.

Possibly the organizations which changed most during the period from 1900 through 1930 were the Young Men's and Young Ladies' Mutual Improvement Associations. Essentially literary, educational, and theological societies in 1900, by 1930 they had become organizations with a basic athletic and recreational thrust. Though they still provided some theological and literary training, their educational functions had been largely assumed by the increasingly popular public high schools. Second only to the Relief Society in promoting moral and social reform in the larger society, the MIA worked on such moral issues as liquor and tobacco prohibition and social issues like a Saturday half-holiday and a house of refuge for delinquent girls.

The YMMIA evolved from independent adult educational and literary societies which had been founded in various communities. In 1875 Brigham Young called Junius F. Wells to organize the YMMIA. Started first in the Salt Lake Thirteenth Ward, the YMMIA had spread churchwide within a year. From 1880 through 1918 the president of the church was also general president of the YMMIA. Thereafter until 1935 the general president was one of the Twelve.[47]

In 1900 the YMMIA offered a program of religious and secular education for a broad range of cultural and intellectual interests. Like all the auxiliaries, it operated as a voluntary organization, supported principally by funds which officers and volunteers called mutual improvement missionaries solicited. *The Improvement Era*, founded in 1898, served as organ for the YMMIA. Paralleling the broad interest of the organization, the *Era* carried comment on doctrine and public policy together with articles on various sides of a broad range of topics. After the beginning of the priesthood reform movement, the *Era* carried priesthood and later general church information as well.

Closely associated with the YMMIA and sharing its educational and intellectual interests was the YLMIA. Begun in 1869 by Brigham Young in his own family as a retrenchment society, YLMIA was expanded to most wards in the church by Mary Isabella Horne and Eliza R. Snow. The YLMIA was organized on a general church level in 1880 with Elmina Shephard Taylor, a schoolteacher who had been active in the local YLMIA organizations, as general president. The YLMIA published the *Young Women's Journal*, edited by Susa Young Gates until 1929 when the magazine was subsumed under the *Improvement Era*.[48]

Until 1900 the ward MIA sessions consisted of a general class, attended by all, at which a range of cultural and educational topics chosen by the local organization were considered. At the 1900 annual June conference, however, wards and stakes were encouraged to divide classes by age groups "where conditions will permit." Within this framework, MIA workers were admonished to "encourage the understanding and appreciation of culture, literature and music."[49]

In line with these goals, the MIA sponsored various cultural and educational programs. As part of the annual June conference, the Salt Lake Stake sponsored a speaker's contest. In 1904 the four Salt Lake Stake MIAs organized a lecture bureau to bring important critics, commentators, and writers to the city. For the 1904–5 season they brought national figures such as Jacob Riis, Hamlin Garland, and Elbert Hubbard. Eleven hundred people heard Riis's lecture, "The Battle with the Slum," and the *Improvement Era* reported it as "brilliant and instructive, portraying many of the unsavory conditions existing in the large cities, and the thorough and humane methods employed in eradicating the same."[50]

The young men and women of the MIA were also active in promoting moral reform. In October 1901 representatives of the Young Men's and Young Women's Mutual Improvement Associations cooperated with religious leaders from other denominations in a moral reform league. The organization drew up lists of questions to refer to each political candidate on his views regarding liquor and tobacco sales.[51]

As the priesthood reform movement progressed, the First Presidency and Twelve began to consider the possibility of adding recreational and athletic programs to the cultural activities of the YMMIA and reserving theological training to the priesthood quorums and the Sunday School. The Ensign Stake experimented with this proposal during the winter of 1907–8 by holding basketball competition between ward-sponsored teams. The wards participating reported that considerable "enthusiasm" was engendered and "attendance increased nearly 100 percent." In the wake of this experiment, the YMMIA general board in 1908 adopted a resolution encouraging wards to adapt amusement halls for use as gymnasiums and to have physical activities as part of YMMIA. They said that even if regular theological lessons were "somewhat curtailed," no harm would result, because young men would be able to get such training in the priesthood.[52]

In December 1908 the general board redefined their programs and authorized the YMMIA to take up "educational, literary, and recreative studies, permeated by religious thought." In addition to social and cultural programs, "athletic work" was encouraged. In August 1909 committees were organized to coordinate each of the areas of the new thrust. The committees were Class Study, Music and Drama, Social Affairs, Library and Reading Course, Conference and Conventions, Missionary, Athletics and Field Sports, Debates, Contests, and Lectures. A committee was chosen to write lesson manuals.[53]

In an attempt to upgrade the reading in secular and religious topics by MIA members, the organization began the promotion of an annual reading program. In the year 1908–9, for instance, the books chosen were James Fenimore Cooper's *Last of the Mohicans*, John S. C. Abbott's *Cortez*, Charles Dickens's *A Tale of Two Cities*, and Charles Kingsley's *Hypatia*. In 1911–12 the books recommended included Albert Beveridge's *The Young Man and the World* and John A. Widtsoe's *Dry Farming*. In 1912 the course of study included a western novel, *The Winning of Barbara Worth*, which George F. Richards thought was "a good book but there are too many swear words used representing the typical plainsmen and westerners of earlier days." Heber J. Grant read the book *Corporal Cameron* by Ralph Connor (Charles Willam Gordon), which was one of the reading course books for 1912–13, and he was not particularly pleased with the work, which he seems to have considered too simplistic. In addition to books by nationally known and classical writers, the reading program included works by Mormon authors such as Janne M. Sjodahl's *The Reign of the Anti-Christ*, James E. Talmage's *House of the Lord*, *Piney Ridge Cottage* by Nephi Anderson, and *John Stevens' Courtship* by Susa Young Gates. Reports on the reading programs indicated only minimal success. In 1907, 1908, and 1909 only 4 percent, 7 percent, and 5 percent of the active membership read one or more of the books. Joseph W. McMurrin called the statistics "appalling."[54]

The change in attitude about the relationship of the church to the larger society inevitably generated controversy. In 1917–18, for instance, J. M. Tanner's lessons on ethics brought some complaints to the Twelve.[55] Perhaps the biggest controversy developed in 1911. On

September 13 Thomas Hull came in to see the First Presidency complaining that some of the contents of the MIA manual supported socialism. On September 20 the YMMIA board aired the entire matter. The manual committee presented a manuscript which included a consideration of public utilities and favored some governmental ownership. A long discussion over the topic ensued with Brigham H. Roberts, Bryant S. Hinckley, Hyrum M. Smith, and John Henry Evans supporting the manual and Joseph F. Smith, Thomas Hull, and Reed Smoot opposing it. Following the discussion James H. Anderson proposed that President Smith appoint a committee to rewrite the lessons. This was agreed to, and the committee included supporters of both viewpoints.[56]

Nevertheless, there seemed to be general agreement on the propriety of considering all sides of a broad range of topics of progressive concern. In November 1911 the MIA debate committee recommended twelve topics for the coming year. All of them dealt with controversial problems such as direct democracy, governmental ownership of utilities, and compulsory arbitration. In September 1912 John A. Widtsoe reported on the results of debate competitions in the wards, revealing that about two-thirds of the wards in the church had been holding the meets. In some stakes, stake championship contests were held. MIA debate topics in 1917 included national issues such as higher wages, woman suffrage, and public ownership of utilities, in addition to religious questions such as the value of a proselyting mission and the study of the Bible.[57]

This concern that members involve themselves in public questions led to campaigns on various issues. In some cases annual MIA slogans were adopted to emphasize the need for a particular program. Between 1912 and 1917 they included such local issues as a weekly home evening and national movements such as the weekly half-holiday and state and nationwide prohibition. In 1930 the MIA sponsored a traffic safety and law-obedience campaign.

The MIA's cultural programs continued with considerable support into the mid-1920s. Stakes held events such as the Granite Stake music contest in 1911, which drew a total of 300 contestants. In 1913 a number of stakes held "MIA Days" that included contests in storytelling, speech, debate, and music. Also in 1913 the Deseret Gymnasium opened for roadshows that were locally produced dramatic and variety presentations. In 1926 the MIA sponsored annual poetry and essay contests together with musical, dramatic, and other cultural activities.[58]

In 1911 the YMMIA started a program for boys over age twelve, which strengthened the recreational emphasis. Though in April 1911 a committee of the MIA general board consisting of Brigham H. Roberts, George H. Brimhall, and Benjamin Goddard had rejected the Boy Scout movement because they believed that the church already had sufficient activities, on September 2, 1911, the decision was reversed, and the church decided to inaugurate its own Scout organization to be called the MIA Scouts. The new movement to establish the MIA Scouts enjoyed the patronage of Lyman R. Martineau of the MIA athletic committee and Anthony W. Ivins of the Twelve. By March 1913 it had become clear that the objectives of the MIA Scouts and those of the Boy Scouts of America were so close that the advantages of affiliation with the national organization outweighed the disadvantages. Affiliation was consummated in May. Since boys twelve to fourteen years of age were eligible for enrollment in the Boy Scouts, the age at which young men could enroll in the MIA was lowered.[59]

By 1916, largely because of LDS sponsorship, Utah had the highest per-capita membership in the Boy Scouts of any state in the Union. In June 1918 F. A. Moffat, Scout field commissioner of New York, met with Anthony W. Ivins, John H. Taylor, Oscar A. Kirkham, and others from the YMMIA Scout committee to discuss the possibility of forming a council in Utah. Heber J. Grant expressed himself as fearful, if an extra-MIA council were formed, of losing control of the boys to men who believed in smoking and drinking. By April 1921, however, with liquor and cigarette prohibition in Utah, this seemed less likely, and Anthony W. Ivins, Brigham H. Roberts, and Richard R. Lyman, presidency of the YMMIA, announced that all LDS Scout troops would join the national organization and standardize badges and other programs.[60]

To support the Scout programs, and later the YLMIA Beehive programs, many stakes began to operate summer camps. The first seems to have been the Liberty Stake's camp, opened in 1912. The Ensign Stake opened "Camp Ensign," near Brighton in Big Cottonwood Canyon by 1916 on property for the camp donated by Jesse Knight, a Mormon mining magnate from Provo.[61]

As with other recreational programs, the Boy Scouts became increasingly important during the 1920s. By December 1922 the church had 42,000 boys enrolled in Scout troops. By 1926 one in three boys in Utah belonged to a Scout organization compared with a national average of one in five. In February 1930 Vice President Charles Curtis invited Heber J. Grant to a special White House gathering of the Boy Scouts of America in recognition of the work being done by the church leaders.[62]

The YLMIA was not far behind the YMMIA in the development of a recreation program for younger girls. In 1913 the YLMIA joined the Camp Fire Girls, but after six months of operation Charlotte Stewart of the Ensign Stake YLMIA board, a recreation specialist for Salt Lake City and later member of the YLMIA general board, suggested that the program was "too complex." Permission to drop the program was denied at first, but the various stakes began experimenting on their own, and in 1915 the church replaced the Camp Fire Girls with the "Beehive Girls" program. This program included the outdoor emphasis of the Boy Scouts together with gospel and secular lessons geared to future homemaking and vocations. The program was designed, it was said, to make the girls thrifty, industrious, and busy as little bees.[63]

At first the young girls ages twelve to fourteen continued to come under the jurisdiction of the Primary Association. In 1930, however, President Grant ruled that parents might allow girls of those ages to attend either Primary Association or MIA, and this option continued until 1934, when they were finally incorporated into the MIA program.[64]

Some women, such as Priscilla Riter of the Ensign Stake, were concerned with increased juvenile delinquency among girls. After consideration, in 1913 the YLMIA opened the Lucy Mack home for girls, the work of which paralleled the Lund Home for boys operated by Religion Classes. Funding for the Lucy Mack home came from private donations and the Ensign Stake.[65]

With the expanding programs of the MIA, general authorities felt the need to train adult leaders to meet the new challenges. In November 1914 they announced that a six-week MIA leadership-training course would be offered at various church educational institutions. The classes included administration, music, first aid, scout craft, literature, public speaking, debate, drama, methods of teaching, games, social dancing, and athletics.[66]

Increasingly, the athletic and recreational programs inaugurated after 1908 replaced the cultural and educational emphasis on the ward and stake level. On June 3, 1911, the first annual YMMIA inter-stake track meet was held at Wandamere, a park south of Salt Lake City. In 1911 the Daynes Jewelry Company presented to the YMMIA Athletic League a trophy to be awarded to that ward which proved the overall winner in competition in running, jumping, and basketball among the four Salt Lake area stakes. In December 1911 a banquet was held at the Lion House in Salt Lake City in honor of the first MIA class in gymnastic work. In July 1914 a number of stakes held track meets. In 1915 it was learned that some wards and stakes had been giving cash prizes for athletic contests. This was discouraged and stakes were urged to award medals and other items because intercollegiate athletic association rules classified anyone who received money as a professional. After the construction of Deseret Gym, the YMMIA general board helped to promote volleyball.[67]

The increased leisure time following World War I made the expansion of recreational facilities even easier. In July 1923, after an earlier suggestion by George Albert Smith, the church began compiling a survey of recreation and leisure time activity, and indicating how much the church invested in buildings for amusement activities. Melvin J. Ballard of the MIA general board urged each ward and stake to establish a recreation committee to work with bishops and stake presidents to supervise all social activities and to assure that all social functions were in accordance with church standards.[68]

By 1930 it seemed to some observers that basketball was the only YMMIA program available in many of the wards and that it had replaced not only the cultural programs such as music but also the other recreational activities for those over Scout age. Church leaders declared the game beneficial for the casual athlete and favored it because it stimulated activity in the MIA. In March 1931 the all-church basketball tournament in Salt Lake City drew more than 8,000 participants from the wards and stakes.[69]

While they still went to MIA together on Tuesday evenings, by 1930 the young men and the young women had gone in different directions. The manuals continued to carry lessons dealing with a broad range of subjects, but on the local level for the young men the athletic and recreational programs had eclipsed all else. For the young women, however, conditions were different. Never as fully taken up with athletics or recreation as the young men had been, the young ladies continued to receive instruction on a great many subjects and to participate in a variety of activities.

If the principal challenge of the MIA was rapid change, the major problems faced by the Primary Association revolved around the need to develop a distinct role. In 1900 Primary Association functions conflicted with those of Religion Classes, which also provided weekday instruction for children. The two programs overlapped in both age and subject matter, the Primary Association serving children four through thirteen (later four through eleven), and Religion Classes teaching children of elementary school age. In addition, the Primary Association provided instruction on religious and home-centered themes which partly overlapped the Sunday School. Increasingly, however, it was able to find a separate mission by emphasizing home- and service-centered religious messages for the girls and a prescout and pre-priesthood emphasis for boys, together with recreational activities for both groups.[70]

Organized first in Farmington, Utah, in 1878 with Aurelia Spencer Rogers as ward president and shortly thereafter in Salt Lake City and throughout the church under Eliza R. Snow, the Primary Association enrolled 6,900 members in twenty-four stakes by 1881. Louie B. Felt became general president of the Primary Association at the inauguration of the general church organization in 1880. At that time the Relief Society, under Sister Snow, promoted and supervised the Primary Association throughout the church since it was a "woman's" auxiliary. From 1889 until 1909 Sister Felt reported directly to the First Presidency. In 1909 Hyrum M. Smith and George F. Richards of the Twelve were assigned as advisors to the Primary Association, the first advisors assigned to any of the auxiliaries.[71]

The Primary Association experienced many problems until after 1900. These problems resulted in part from the overlap with Religion Classes, in part from financial difficulties, and in part from the absence of a medium for the regular dissemination of information. In 1902, however, the First Presidency approved the publication of the *Children's Friend* to provide lessons and information for leaders and later stories and activities for children. To provide funds for the magazine, Sister Felt borrowed against her house, and May Anderson, her counselor, left full-time employment to edit the magazine. The First Presidency also approved a nickel fund similar to the Sunday School's, to help in financing the Primary Association.[72]

Primary Association leaders developed instruction designed for particular grade levels. For several years various ward associations had experimented with graded instruction, and with the inauguration of the *Children's Friend* in 1902, May Anderson wrote lessons. Initially all classes consisted of both boys and girls, but during the 1920s classes separated by sex and purpose were adopted for boys and girls over age eight. Girls were trained as homemakers and boys for Scouting and the priesthood.[73]

The theories of progressive educators like John Dewey, Francis W. Parker, Marietta Pierce Johnson, and G. Stanley Hall were apparent in the Primary lessons as they were in Sunday School. Exercises, crafts, and participatory activities replaced catechisms of earlier years. Neither the Sunday School nor the Primary Association went the whole way with progressive education, but adopted instead a mix including memorization, group recitations, and stories, together with songs and other activities.[74]

After a particularly poignant experience with a young crippled boy, Sisters Felt and Anderson began the promotion of health care for young people. This led first to the Primary Association's furnishing two rooms in the wing of Latter-day Saints hospital in 1913. In the summer of 1921 Sisters Felt and Anderson began planning for a separate institution, the Latter-day Saints Children's Home and Day Nursery (later the Children's Convalescent Hospital) located in the renovated Hyde home across from the temple on North Temple in Salt Lake City. Dedicated on May 11, 1922, by Heber J. Grant, the home provided the basis for what later became the Primary Children's Hospital. In April 1924 the Primary Association announced the establishment of a fund to operate the hospital: each member of the church was invited to contribute one cent per year for each year of his or her age, which would provide a quarter of a million dollars for the annual operation.[75]

In the operation of the Convalescent Hospital, the church made no distinction as to religious persuasion of the children admitted. In January 1931 presiding bishop Sylvester Q. Cannon suggested making the hospital into a community institution, but though President Grant thought there was some merit to the suggestion, the church continued to run the facility until the late 1970s, when the greatly expanded Primary Children's Medical Center was turned over to an independent governing board.[76]

By 1930 the Primary Association had been firmly established as the auxiliary providing recreational and weekday religious instruction for "little Saints." The classes provided a focus for the lessons and activities, and created an espirit de corps which other organizations, with the possible exception of the scouts, found difficult to match.

The major competitor of the Primary Association in the early 1900s was the Religion Classes, which provided religious instruction following elementary school each day of the week in predominantly Mormon areas, or on Saturday or some evening of the week where students were scattered. Recognizing the overlapping functions and faced with increasing expenses they were unable to meet, the church leadership consolidated the two organizations in 1929.[77]

Evidence of the increasing secularization of the society in which the church operated is epitomized in charges that Religion Classes breached the separation of church and state. The charges often developed because the Religion Classes were held in school buildings under a rental arrangement. By 1904 even many of the church leaders wondered whether the constitution of the state allowed the continuation of the practice.[78]

As the Reed Smoot hearings progressed in 1904 and 1905, the extent of the use of public buildings for the Religion Classes became an issue. A. C. Nelson, state superintendent of public instruction, testified that more than three hundred of the classes were being held in schools, after regular school hours. The state attorney general, however, argued that the statutes of the state allowed the practice since the school district could legally rent unoccupied property. Superintendent Nelson disagreed and sent a circular letter to school district superintendents, pointing to the conflict between the practice and the injunction of the state constitution which prohibited the teaching of religion in public schools. In addition, antagonists attempted to show that Religion Class work was a means of using the public schools to inculcate church doctrine by pointing out that many of the teachers also taught in the public schools.[79] After the revelations of the Smoot hearings, the First Presidency advised local leaders to keep the systems separate. This was not always done, and in February 1924 the state attorney general released a revised opinion stating that such use of schools was illegal. Though contradicted then by the state superintendent of public instruction, the opinion still carried considerable weight.[80]

A spin-off project of the board of Religion Classes, however, outlasted the classes themselves. In 1908 several church leaders considered the establishment of a detention home for wayward boys. They chose a site in an abandoned academy building east of the Salt Lake

City suburb of Murray. Named the Lund Home in honor of Anthon H. Lund, the originator of the Religion Class idea, the facility housed between twenty-two and twenty-eight boys, who engaged in gardening and received regular school instruction.[81]

Religious instruction rather than social service was, however, the principal thrust of Religion Classes during its thirty-nine-year existence. In spite of the resistance of some bishops and stake presidents to the program, it served more than 61,000 elementary school–aged youth. It fell victim to overlapping functions and the church's financial difficulties, but its duties were ably, if somewhat less frequently, continued by the Primary Association.

In large part the educational functions performed by the various auxiliaries may be seen as an attempt to reinforce traditional beliefs and values in the Latter-day Saint community. Leaders perceived challenges as coming in different ways, but most particularly through the introduction of practices which threatened the norms of personal morality and decorum, such as new styles of dress, racetrack betting, lapses in personal chastity, and other practices which seemed to indicate a change in accepted values. An important example of these concerns was the controversy over forms of popular dance in the Mormon wards. Traditionally a significant form of recreation and courtship, dancing was an important Saturday evening activity in most Latter-day Saint towns. Most participated in the dances which were often held in church meetinghouses, with chairs pulled back to the walls, and opened and closed with prayer.[82]

By the mid-nineteenth century waltzes and polkas had been introduced into the United States from Europe and began to vie in popularity with the more traditional square dances and quadrilles. Called round dances in common parlance, the waltzes and polkas were received with considerable skepticism. Apparently forbidden by Brigham Young, round dancing had been allowed by John Taylor and Wilford Woodruff on a limited scale.[83] The question continued to arise in the stakes and in meetings of the First Presidency and the Twelve. In October 1898 the Twelve considered the subject of round dancing. After the discussion Elder Grant doubted whether "it was wisdom to try and prohibit round dancing entirely." Rudger Clawson raised the question again in February 1899, and Elders Grant and Clawson attended a meeting of the St. Johns Stake High Council in January 1900, when the subject came up. They said that the privilege of round dancing ought to be granted, at least to the limit of two or three an evening. "I feel," Grant wrote, "that we could not be too stringent with the young people and retain our influence over them." Practice was not uniform: the officers of the Juarez, Mexico, and the St. Joseph, Arizona, stakes prohibited waltzing "in our social parties," but in Bunkerville, Nevada, waltzing was permitted.[84]

After 1912, the hotly debated question of waltzing became an anachronism as the fox trot and other jazz-influenced dances, together with Latin-American dances such as the tango, came into vogue. Generally referred to as "ragging," or "rag-dances," from the designation ragtime, jazz dance forms were predictably resisted, just as the previous waltzing had been. At Snowflake, Arizona, Horace S. Cummings of the MIA general board found boys who, against the wishes of their bishop, had "tried to dance rag-dances." Cummings used his influence to stop the young men and "got them to promise to take part only in orderly dances."[85]

In retrospect, it is clear that church leaders perceived dancing and other social activities as means to the end of promoting spirituality and morality in the community. The central message was encompassed in the admonition of June 1923 that "if we judge a party successful because of the high quality of its music, the aesthetic appeal of the decoration, the sympathetic and congenial atmosphere of the group, the dignified conduct of the individuals, the dancing party actually becomes a factor for moral uplift and an enterprise which utilizes the pleasure-seeking instinct for spiritual and moral purposes."[86]

If dancing was a debatable social issue, chastity was not. All leaders agreed on the need for strict sexual morality. In a conference address in April 1912, Hyrum M. Smith emphasized the problems associated with venereal disease among those who were sexually promiscuous and pointed to the potential damage to themselves and their children. In a talk before a group of businessmen, Governor John C. Cutler, a prominent lay member, emphasized the need to guard the moral behavior of girls in factories. In February 1908 the stake presidents of Salt Lake City met with members of the council to consider ways to protect young people from some of the vices in the city.[87]

Church leaders were also concerned about standards of personal dress, particularly as it involved modesty and extravagant style. In a monthly fast meeting address in July 1909, Joseph F. Smith spoke "very strong about women dressing" in high fashion while teaching

children. In an address to the student body of LDS University in Salt
Lake City, Anthon H. Lund emphasized the need for sensible and
plain dresses. The concern was probably related to an address given by
the superintendent of Salt Lake City schools, who spoke for modesty
and plainness, both of which were traditionally associated with public
virtue. He feared both the sexual connotation of immodest dress and
the humiliation of poorer students by those who could spend more on
clothes.[88]

At various times, church auxiliary leaders worked for the passage of
Sunday closing, antigambling, and antiboxing legislation. In March
1909 the *Deseret News* urged the state senate to pass a Sunday closing
bill, and in February 1913 the Deseret Sunday School union board appointed Stephen L Richards, Heber J. Grant, and George M. Cannon
to lobby—unsuccessfully as it proved—for the passage of bills prohibiting race track gambling and Sunday amusements. Church and
civic leaders urged the enforcement of existing statutes prohibiting
the "cruel sport" of boxing.[89]

The church leadership referred questions of correlating lessons,
promoting morality, and dealing with social problems to a joint committee which functioned in various forms from 1913 through 1922.
Though in 1907 a committee under James E. Talmage, at the time a
lay member, had been appointed to try to coordinate the lesson work of
the auxiliaries, the church did not undertake a major attempt at correlation until 1913. Composed of representatives of the Twelve, the
First Council of the Seventy, and each auxiliary, the Correlation Committee tried to coordinate convention schedules, prevent duplication in
roles and lesson material, develop teacher training, and establish a
unified church magazine.[90] In June 1913 the committee suggested the
division of fields of study and activities for the various auxiliaries: the
Primary Association and MIA would deal with practical religion, secular subjects, and recreation, and Religion Classes, Sunday School, and
the Aaronic Priesthood would teach scriptural topics and church history. In retrospect, the major concrete results of the Correlation Committee seem to have been the development of a teacher training manual and coordination of auxiliary conferences.

The questions considered by the Correlation Committee involved essentially structural or procedural, rather than social, reform. In September 1916, however, a suggestion of the First Presidency to the Primary Association launched the Social Advisory Committee, probably

the most significant experiment in social engineering between the dissolution of the United Orders in the late nineteenth century and the adoption of the church Welfare Plan in 1936. Functioning between 1916 and 1922, the Social Advisory Committee programs were much bolder in their inception than was the welfare plan, since they involved not only internal church operation but also extensive cooperation and interaction between the church and outside public and private social welfare agencies, businesses, social action committees, and legislative bodies.

The work of the Social Advisory Committee with Stephen L Richards as chairman involved initiatives taken by members of the general church committee and coordination of efforts of stake and ward committees. Consisting of members from the boards of all six auxiliaries, the committee promoted cooperation between the church and state and local welfare agencies, civic betterment leagues, and the state legislature to deal with such matters as prostitution, a girls' home, dance standards, social standards, playgrounds, assistance for the indigent, public amusements, juvenile delinquency, venereal disease, and motion picture censorship. Wards were encouraged to promote recreational activities among the youth to help them in finding healthy outlets for their energy. Adult education programs were promoted to help older people to improve themselves. Sex education, prohibition, and antitobacco campaigns were promoted within the church and in the public schools.

In November 1920 the Social Advisory Committee was merged with the Correlation Committee so that all aspects of education, correlation, and society came under its purview. Under its auspices, the church began systematic studies of the motivation for temple or civil marriage, for payment or nonpayment of tithing, and for other activities of church members. In March 1921 the joint committee, now under the leadership of David O. McKay and Stephen L Richards, again proposed the division of responsibilities for various social and educational functions among the various auxiliaries and priesthood quorums. By October 1922 the First Presidency had been unable to rule on these recommendations, and the committee did very little. In November 1922 the First Presidency decided the central coordination of activities was unnecessary, dissolved the committee, and allowed auxiliaries and quorums to develop their own programs independently.

In rejecting the committee's recommendations, the First Presidency nevertheless recognized the need for division of functions among the quorums and auxiliaries.[91] The priesthood quorums, the First Presidency said, had been set up to teach members, and the auxiliary organizations were to be helps. Auxiliaries were expected to provide means to facilitate the study of gospel doctrines and to control the social, recreational, and literary activities of church members. The Relief Society was to study religious subjects and church doctrine and government, as were priesthood quorums, and to administer charitable and compassionate service under the direction of the bishop. It was also to advance literary, social, and domestic studies for the sisters. The Sunday School had been established to provide children with "proper occupation on the Sabbath," and to teach the fundamentals of the gospel through moral lessons. The MIA was organized to teach doctrines and to provide recreation for the young men and women. The Primary Association was to teach the gospel and to provide recreation for younger children.

By retaining control of appointments to auxiliary presidencies and boards, the First Presidency retained its "right of presidency," which was not to be superseded by a correlation or advisory committee. Neither could such a committee dictate to the quorums or auxiliaries. Though it might be all right to create correlation committees, the First Presidency wrote, it "should be understood that the findings of such committees are subject to the approval or nonapproval of the associations which have created them." In other words, the quorums and auxiliaries were left free to plan and execute their own programs, under general priesthood direction.

General directions, essentially a codification of previous functions, were spelled out in October 1922 in a circular letter sent to the chairmen of the committees on priesthood outlines and courses of study and the general superintendents and presidents of auxiliary associations. In practice, these duties did not differ greatly from those proposed by the Correlation-Social Advisory Committee. The letter began by pointing out that both Melchizedek and Aaronic priesthood quorums are organized to teach duties in the priesthood, then moved to a discussion of the function of the various auxiliary organizations.[92]

Beginning in 1927 the church tried by other means to overcome the duplication inherent in a system where the priesthood quorums, the MIA, and the Sunday School provided sometimes overlapping religious instruction. In September 1927, on recommendation of the

Twelve, the First Presidency approved the holding of all Melchizedek priesthood instruction during Sunday School time. This program was reinforced in 1928, with an experiment in combining Aaronic priesthood instruction with the MIA. Each Tuesday night the young men and women met for separate priesthood-YLMIA instruction, followed by recreational activities.[93]

Both of these programs met vigorous opposition from stake presidents such as Bryant S. Hinckley, Joseph J. Daynes, and Frank Y. Taylor. The program nevertheless continued, in spite of repeated protests. In February 1929 George Albert Smith told Heber J. Grant that in his judgment the program was a failure. President Grant replied that the only thing to do was to keep trying. Since it was a program which the Twelve had recommended, he exhibited considerable annoyance at the stake presidents who said they did not like the program but were willing to continue to try it since they considered it a First Presidency program. After passing through several changes the program was abandoned in 1937.[94]

After the abolition of the Social Advisory Committee, the church members continued to concern themselves with various types of social and moral problems. Instead of coordination through the Social Advisory Committee, however, these activities fell under either one of the existing priesthood leaders, the general board of one of the auxiliaries, or unofficial but church-related groups. Wards, stakes, and church members, for instance, were under constant pressure to contribute to various causes. In April 1922 the First Presidency and Twelve agreed to coordinate endorsement for charitable campaigns through the Presiding Bishopric. Approval was generally given for such undertakings as Christmas Seals, Community Chest (forerunner of United Way), Neighborhood House (a Salt Lake City settlement house), Boy Scouts, and other such community-related ventures.

Although by 1930 the form and functions of the auxiliaries were essentially the same as they are today, the external manifestations of the auxiliary activities were much different. The feature which was so evident during the first decades of the century but generally missing today is the organized outreach beyond the Mormon community. Outside activities still take place on an extraordinary level such as when volunteers are requested for flood control, to attend a women's conference, or to lobby against the Equal Rights Amendment. One would be amazed today, however, to see the Relief Society staffing a neighborhood clinic in a Salt Lake City ghetto, the Primary Association opening a new nonsectarian children's hospital, or the MIA lobbying for shorter hours for workers.

Some members were becoming concerned with this social outreach by the late 1920s, but the major change seems to have taken place during the 1930s, and largely through the influence of J. Reuben Clark. Since the auxiliaries were under firm priesthood direction by that time, however, the change resulted from interaction within the priesthood leadership. The auxiliaries seem to have gone along with the change in emphasis and accommodated themselves to church-centered, rather than social-centered, service.

The end of an era resulted from a conflict in ideology between President Clark and Bishop Cannon. Clark, whose adult life had been spent principally in State Department service away from the Mormon community and the society surrounding it, feared the outside world and especially the power of government. Cannon, who, with the exception of his educational experience at MIT, had spent most of his adult life in solving problems for Salt Lake City government and as a stake president, had seen firsthand the value of community and social cooperation. Cannon joined the three-man advisory committee for the New Deal's Public Works Administration for Utah and instructed stake presidents that relief work was to be supervised by "Qualified and experienced social service workers to be selected by the Stake Presidency and approved by the County Relief Committees [which were governmental organizations] and paid by the County Relief Committee." Presidents Grant and Ivins agreed with Cannon at first, but by 1936 Clark's views had carried the day and the church pulled its social service and welfare programs inward. The church leaders prayed to the Lord about these new programs and obtained spiritual confirmation that He had approved what they had proposed, but in the long run the new direction meant that the Latter-day Saint community would withdraw even further from the larger society.[95]

The Church Administration Building, 47 East South Temple, completed in 1917 to house
the offices of church leaders. Designed in the classical style by Joseph Don Carlos Young
and Don Carlos Young.

Saltair resort on Great Salt Lake, owned at times by the LDS Church.

The old Salt Lake Theatre. Operated by the LDS Church, it was sold and razed in the late 1920s after it became an economic and artistic liability.

Hotel Utah, a fine example of neo-classical revival architecture completed in 1911 and partly owned by the LDS Church.

Bathsheba W. Smith (1822–1910), president of the Relief Society 1901–10.

Emmeline B. Wells (1828–1921), president of the Relief Society 1910–21.

Clarissa S. Williams (1859–1930), president of the Relief Society 1921–29.

Amy Brown Lyman (1872–1959), member of the Relief Society Presidency (president 1940–45), member of the Utah state legislature and leader in the development of social services in the LDS Church.

Ruth May Fox (1853–1958), leader in the Young Women's Mutual Improvement Association (1905–37, president 1929–37).

Martha Hughes Cannon (1854–1934), physician, state senator, plural wife, and progressive Democrat.

9

Definition of a Role
for the Church Educational System

EVEN THOUGH SOME of the church's educational effort centered on the auxiliaries, the LDS church had developed a long tradition of formal education in the nineteenth century. In Kirtland, Ohio, during the early 1830s, the leaders had sponsored an adult educational system called the School of the Prophets, held in the Kirtland Temple, at which Latter-day Saints studied religious and secular subjects. At Nauvoo, the state of Illinois chartered a university at which the Saints took some classes. It did not realize the potential its founders envisioned, but it was at least a rudimentary effort at higher education.[1]

After the move to Utah, the Mormons founded common schools, stake academies, and colleges and universities. By 1854 members of each ward in Salt Lake City had established elementary schools, and in other settlements each town or ward supported common school education. The Mormon-dominated legislature chartered the University of Deseret (later the University of Utah) in 1850, though it was largely moribund until the 1870s. Many stakes sponsored high-school level academies, and Brigham Young himself chartered academies and colleges like Brigham Young Academy (later Brigham Young University) at Provo in 1875 and Brigham Young College in Logan in 1876.[2]

After the passage of the Edmunds-Tucker Act in 1887, the secularization of the public schools brought about a number of changes in the system. The territory of Utah eliminated such religious education as existed from the public schools, and the church responded by expanding its academy system and by instituting the Religion Classes mentioned in the last chapter. By 1900 church-sponsored education consisted principally of the stake academies and colleges, all of which were basically high schools, and religious and secular education through the auxiliaries.[3]

The course of the church educational system from 1900 to 1930 resembled nothing quite so much as a balloon. Expanding during the period to 1920, it shrank rapidly during the 1920s as the church faced renewed financial problems caused in large part by the depression of 1919–21, the continuing hard times in agriculture and mining during the decade, and the onslaught of the Great Depression in 1929. In 1900, although the church mandated consolidation of some districts and focused its budget hearings on controlling outlays, it appeared that the Latter-day Saints would be a major supporter of education at all secondary and higher levels. By 1930, however, the church leadership had charted a future course which anticipated religious instruction at religious educational institutions, called seminaries, near high schools and institutes next to college campuses, together with limited higher education. That trend has changed in recent years with the addition of primary education in some localities outside the United States, but within the Mormon core area, and, indeed, within the entire United States and Canada, the pattern set by 1930 has continued to the present time.

At the turn of the twentieth century, a number of high school-level stake academies formed the backbone of the church educational system. Between 1875 and 1911 the church established thirty-four of these institutions in settlements stretching from Alberta, Canada, to Chihuahua, Mexico. The largest numbers were in Utah, but the Latter-day Saints founded them in such diverse localities as Idaho, Arizona, Wyoming, Hawaii, and New Zealand. In addition, the church operated three colleges—Brigham Young College in Logan, Latter-day Saints University in Salt Lake City, and Brigham Young University in Provo—all of which were basically high schools in 1900. In 1900 the general church appropriated approximately $100,000 for operating expenses of the educational system. In addition, students paid tuition; local stakes appropriated money; various individuals contributed to defray expenses; and the general church organization provided grants for some buildings and capital equipment. In 1910 the church educational system employed 300 teachers and professors in numbers ranging from a high of seventy-five at Brigham Young University to a low of five in some of the smaller academies.[4]

General supervision of the church's educational system rested with the General Church Board of Education, consisting of a superintendent of education and board members. At the turn of the century, Karl G. Maeser, a convert and product of German teacher education from Meissen, Germany, served as superintendent. Maeser's death in 1901 brought about the appointment of Joseph M. Tanner. Horace S. Cummings, a graduate of the University of Utah, replaced Tanner in 1906. Cummings's 1919 resignation brought about a reorganization of the system. The First Presidency appointed Adam S. Bennion, a Berkeley Ph.D., as superintendent but made his position subordinate to a church commissioner of education, Elder David O. McKay of the Twelve, who served with two counselors, Stephen L Richards and Richard R. Lyman. The president of the church served as chairman of the church Board of Education, but the appointment of Commissioner McKay in 1919 relieved President Grant of some of the more routine duties connected with the position. John A. Widtsoe replaced McKay as commissioner in January 1922, and Joseph F. Merrill took Bennion's place as superintendent later in the decade.[5]

In general the church's appropriation system was much like a legislative budget hearing. In 1907, for instance, George F. Richards, Francis M. Lyman, Hyrum M. Smith, and Horace S. Cummings constituted the committee to hear requests. Members of the boards of education of the various stakes sponsoring academies, colleges, or universities appeared before the committee or submitted requests with supporting documents. In the case of Brigham Young University, the university administration appeared personally. After weighing the requests, the committee recommended appropriations to the First Presidency, who made the final allocation.[6]

Under conditions of an increasingly expanded commitment to education immediately after 1900, and even during the attempted retrenchment of the 1920s, general church expenditures for education rose rapidly. By 1907 they had increased 130 percent above the 1900 level to $230,000. In 1912 they were approximately $350,000. By 1922 they had risen to more than $850,000, and by 1930 general church expenditures were $750,000—more than 100 percent above the 1912 level.[7]

Enrollment in the church educational system increased, then stabilized over the period. In 1900 the system enrolled approximately 4,800 students. By 1907 the enrollment had increased to 7,500, by 1910 it stood at 10,000, but by 1917 it had declined to 7,600, largely because of the increase in public high school education. The decline continued into the 1920s because a number of schools were closed. Nevertheless the cost per pupil rose to 1925, and total outlays for education remained substantially the same.

During the first three decades of the twentieth century, church members carried on an active discussion about the general role of education. Many church members emphasized the need for "practical" or progressive education. Even those with a broad educational background, like John A. Widtsoe with a Ph.D. from Goettingen, called for the "new education," which emphasized both specialization and the "useful and practical." Widtsoe did not define practicality strictly in vocational terms, but he included skills valuable to the community and the individual. To be useful, Widtsoe said, "education must have for its purpose the utilization of the resources which are about us." Learning, in other words, ought to emphasize those things which could best improve Mormon society. At the June conference in 1912, Ruth May Fox of the YLMIA began her remarks by observing that "Man's intellect is God-given and is a spark of that eternal intelligence which governs all things." For her, however, college education was less important than self-education and personal commitment. Self-education, she said, included extensive reading in literature designed to stimulate a desire to succeed, such as in the biographies of self-made men. In another vein, J. P. May, in an article in the *Improvement Era* in January 1910, criticized education in the classics, arts, and sciences of those who would not be able to use the subjects, arguing instead for broad but practical training.[8] In July 1914 E. G. Peterson of Utah State Agricultural College (now Utah State University) published an article arguing for vocational education, to "prepare for life." Schooling had, he said, promoted a "snobbery of intellect" that resisted the "intrusion of practical things into the course of study." Now, however, he thought that education had begun to concern itself with the practical, and particularly "with the two most fundamental things in society—farm and home."[9] Comments like these indicate the influence in the church of the educational ideas of the University of Chicago.

Not all members of the church agreed with this view, and as with so many other topics during this period, the pages of the *Improvement Era* opened to a discussion of both positions. In an article in January 1914, Milton Bennion of the University of Utah argued that education should transmit the "heritage [of those things which promote civilized life] from one generation to the next," and should also contribute to the solution of problems caused by the wealthy "who are a generation behind their time, and who ignorantly stand in defense of the older views of property rights, and who resist public regulation of resources held by them." His was a defense of instrumentalism as propounded by John Dewey.[10]

More than anything else this debate over the nature of the educational system reveals the desire of Latter-day Saints to develop an educational system that would equip their children to deal with the world in which they found themselves. While we may think early twentieth-century education primitive, by the standards of the time outside observers rated Utah's system on par with that of other sections of the nation. Ray Stannard Baker pointed out that many of Utah's young men went on to universities like Michigan, Cornell, or Chicago. Even in some of the rural districts such as Lehi and Bountiful, Charles Spahr found schools "well housed and well attended." He found children reading good literature, though he believed that elementary school teachers, "with possibly one exception, were distinctly under grade. . . . [and] One of them bungled fearfully in an attempt to explain to his pupils why the ocean cooled more slowly than the land. Nearly all were deficient in general culture." The exception was an unnamed daughter of B. H. Roberts. "As a teacher," he wrote, "she was in every way one of the best I had seen in any part of the country."[11]

Spahr found, however, a high interest in education and reading. It was easier to establish libraries in Utah than in Pennsylvania, though harder than in Iowa or Montana. The Mutual Improvement Association helped because it encouraged interest in civil government, literature, drama, and theology. In Salt Lake City, with a population of 60,000, the reporter found 640 pupils in high school. Massachusetts and Ohio cities could show no better record. At the University of Utah he found 200 students in the preparatory grades—equivalent to high school.[12] Orlando Powers, an attorney who had come from the Midwest, thought Utah education as good as that in Boston.

Perhaps nothing was more prevalent in the propaganda of gentile groups who sent missionaries to Utah in the late nineteenth century than the belief that education would weaken the Mormon church and eventually wean the children from their "sinful and error-ridden ways." In retrospect, this proposition has to be viewed either as wishful thinking or as a statement of the ideology of progress which pervaded nineteenth-century American thought.[13] Perceptive observers like Richard T. Ely recognized that education had not undermined the faith of Mormons. Pointing out that perhaps no denomination had laid as much emphasis on education, secular as well as religious, as the

Mormons, he saw Mormonism flourishing rather than dying. In addition, he argued, the society was constantly renewed by the missionaries who left to preach throughout the world. "Doubtless," Ely argued, "there is no city in the world where so large a proportion of the residents have had such a wide and varied experience in travel and observation as Salt Lake City."[14]

In 1911 the voters of Utah amended the state constitution to promote state support of high schools. Before then public high schools in the state had been almost nonexistent; private schools and academies operated by religious denominations had filled their place. In 1915 consolidation of school districts, including high schools, became mandatory, and legislation in 1919 and 1921 provided for equalization of the tax burden so the poorer districts could offer an adequate education to their students.[15]

Leaders of the Mormon church held mixed views of the value of public high schools. Though Anthon H. Lund, a product of the Danish educational system, favored the expansion of high schools, Joseph F. Smith did not. Earlier, President Smith had said he thought that although some young men ought to be educated in law so they could help the church, most ought to learn trades rather than professions. In the October conference in 1915, President Smith complained that high schools were being forced on the people and criticized the great amount being spent on schools. "I believe," he said, "that we are running education mad."[16] Heber J. Grant exhibited little of Joseph F. Smith's antagonism to secondary education and tried instead to promote it. In April 1921 he advised John A. Widtsoe, who had just joined the Council of the Twelve, to attend all educational conventions possible whenever the opportunity presented itself.[17]

Even though the rapid expansion of the church's educational system after 1890 had come about in large part to provide a religious alternative to secular education, the need for teachers, particularly in the public school system, motivated more than anything else the expansion of the church's higher educational system after 1900. In a circular letter of August 1902, the First Presidency emphasized that demand for good teachers was "greatly in excess of supply" and encouraged stake presidents to have as many parents as possible send sons and daughters to the church schools for an education. This would, the church leaders emphasized, help the bishops as well since they would have better material to staff the various organizations. After a state law passed in 1903 provided that all cities with populations of more than 2,000 were to support kindergartens, the First Presidency again emphasized the need to secure teachers. They admonished stake boards of education to promote teacher education. Training for kindergarten teachers had been established at Brigham Young University, Latter-day Saints University, and the University of Utah.[18]

The summit of the church's educational system at the turn of the century consisted of the three colleges which, though essentially high schools, provided some collegiate training. Northernmost of the church's institutions of higher learning was the 500-student Brigham Young College at Logan. Its enrollment compared well with the 600 students attending the Utah Agricultural College in 1900. But like most of the church institutions, Brigham Young College had sunk into deep financial difficulty. In February 1900 the trustees met with the First Presidency to try to get them to agree to assume a $20,000 debt. The Presidency refused, but in April 1900 they did agree to give the college a loan to tide them over present difficulties. In addition, college president J. H. Linford agreed to aid the trustees by reducing teachers' salaries and by refusing his own monthly pay. By December 1901 the First Presidency provided an appropriation of $12,400 to assist in operating the college.[19] Though enormous difficulties continued, the school leadership exhibited great optimism. In March 1902 the college spent $6,000 more than the church had appropriated, and financial difficulty continued in spite of a $10,000 gift from Charles W. Nibley in 1906. Even though Utah State Agricultural College had begun to cut into BYC's enrollment, in order to provide teachers for the public schools the church authorized the temporary establishment of a normal or teacher education department in 1911.[20]

Established in 1892, Latter-day Saints University in Salt Lake City had been designed as the summit of the church's educational system. By 1900, however, like Brigham Young College, it had fallen on bad days. When Joshua H. Paul assumed the presidency, the teachers agreed to continue the operation of the university's business department at low salaries if they were paid in cash. After Paul's appointment, however, an appropriation from the church stipulated that LDSU must pay three-fourths of the salaries in scrip. Efforts to secure an equitable adjustment of the grievance failed, and the teachers went

on strike. Then most left to teach at the Salt Lake Commercial College
and the students followed them. The church did not resolve the difficulty until it purchased the commercial college in 1901.[21]

In spite of these problems, the church leadership went ahead to continue the development of LDS University. After an unsuccessful attempt shortly after 1900 to secure temporary space, the church leadership decided to construct facilities for the college on the north half of
the block east of the temple. A number of prominent business and
civic leaders were asked to assist in securing funds for the new facilities, and President Snow allowed the students to meet temporarily in
the Lion House.[22]

The purchase of the Salt Lake Commercial College did not end the
conflict between the faculty and President Paul, who was reportedly
quite dogmatic and dictatorial. Finally, in 1906 the board of trustees
accepted Paul's resignation. Though the faculty wanted John A. Widtsoe
as president, Brigham Young University refused to let him go, and the
board settled on Willard Young, graduate of the U.S. Military Academy
at West Point and a son of Brigham Young.[23] None of these changes
solved the ultimate problem—that of finances.

After World War I the need for educated public school teachers
brought about an expansion of the collegiate offerings, but financial
stringency doomed the church's academy system. As early as 1913, as
the church leaders considered the expansion of facilities at some academies like Murdock Academy in Beaver, Utah, some questioned the
value of continuing to compete with public high schools. In March
1920 Commissioner Bennion and presidents of the stakes sponsoring academies met in Salt Lake City. During five hours of delibera-
tion, they discussed a proposal that the church abandon the academy
system. The church, Bennion explained, could not advance enough
money from general revenues to meet the growing needs; thus, he believed, it ought rather to concentrate on "qualifying school teachers,"
which meant the support of college rather than high school education.
The local church leaders expressed much sorrow at the suggestion,
since they believed the local academies had done much good.[24]

In 1920 the church spent $2 million on school buildings. However,
given the depressed economic conditions during late 1920 and 1921,
such expenditures could not continue. In April 1921 the axe fell on
two of the marginal institutions, St. Johns Academy in Arizona and

Cassia Academy at Oakley, Idaho; the church transferred both to local public school districts. "The change," the announcement said, "is in accordance with the plan of the church commission of education to retire from the high school field . . . and to specialize in the seminary and normal fields." Shortly thereafter the church closed academies in Gila, Arizona; Uintah, Utah; and Snowflake, Arizona. On January 23, 1923, the church announced that Fielding Academy (Paris, Idaho), Murdock Academy (Beaver, Utah), Emery Academy (Castledale, Utah), and Oneida Academy (Preston, Idaho) would be closed. San Luis Academy in Colorado was turned over to the state of Colorado and Big Horn Academy in Wyoming went to the state of Wyoming.[25]

In June 1922, in a speech to graduates at LDSU, Heber J. Grant outlined the course he expected church education to take in the future. The purpose of the church educational system, he said, "was to make better Latter-day Saints. But for this reason, I am convinced there would be no need of having church schools as ordinary education can be secured at the expense of the taxpayers of the state."[26]

The immediate beneficiaries of this policy were the colleges and universities the church continued to operate. In 1920 the church announced the inauguration of a two-year teacher-training course at BYU, LDS University, and Brigham Young College. In addition, the church instituted teacher training at four academies upgraded to junior colleges—Ricks College (Rexburg, Idaho), Snow College (Ephraim, Utah), Weber College (Ogden, Utah), and Dixie College (St. George, Utah). At the same time the church announced that Brigham Young University would offer a complete college curriculum and the other institutions would serve as feeders for the Provo school.[27]

Brigham Young Academy was undoubtedly the most favored of the various church institutions. In September 1903 President Benjamin W. Cluff and his successor, George H. Brimhall, came to the church board of education with the proposition that a collegiate division be added to the academy under the name of Joseph Smith College. The board tabled the proposal at first, then late in the same month reopened the idea with the proposal that the academy be renamed Brigham Young University. A number of general authorities spoke in favor of the proposal, but Joseph F. Smith and Anthon H. Lund emphasized that a change in name would provide no additional money. Elder Lund was particularly emphatic that the institution gain its name "by merit," rather than by action of the board. The board agreed to change the name, and Lund observed wryly that he hoped "their head will grow big enough for the hat."[28]

Perhaps the greatest publicity within the church educational system at the turn of the century came from an expedition undertaken by Benjamin Cluff in 1900. The BYU president proposed leading a group into Mexico and Central America to discover Book of Mormon ruins and artifacts. Cluff invited Joseph F. Smith to send one of his sons on the expedition, but the church president declined on the ground that he lacked the funds. Besides, he confided in a letter to his son, Joseph Fielding Smith, he would prefer they go on missions. A company of three teachers and about twenty students left on April 17, expecting to be gone for two years. They hoped to locate rivers, cities, and places that would "throw light on the divine claims of the Book of Mormon."[29]

In spite of initial support by the First Presidency, on July 18, 1900, in a meeting of the Twelve and First Presidency, Heber J. Grant raised questions about the expedition. His informants, Anthony W. Ivins, Jesse N. Smith, and others, considered the would-be explorers generally unsuited for the purpose. They thought Cluff incapable of leading such an expedition and Elder Grant feared that they might get into trouble or even lose their lives.[30]

Elder Grant, who had been dubious about Cluff since the early 1890s, was unimpressed with their triumphal march through towns as they moved southward from Springville, Utah, to Thatcher, Arizona. After returning from a visit to the expedition, he found that most of the First Presidency and Twelve shared his skepticism but that they had given permission because Cluff asked for it. Grant feared the haughty attitude of Cluff and some of the other leaders. Cluff reportedly bragged that he would unearth the City of Zarahemla and Professor Walter Wolfe was heard to say he would discover new metal plates and receive the gift to interpret them. It would mean, they said, the dawn of freedom for the church. After discussing the matter, the First Presidency and Twelve felt that someone ought to be sent to intercept the party and allow only a small group, or none at all, to enter Mexico.[31]

By early August 1900 Joseph F. Smith and Seymour B. Young had gone to Mexico to consult with Anthony W. Ivins. They then met with President Cluff and urged him either to disband or reorganize the expedition. As a result, nine of the members decided to go on under

Cluff's direction, and the remainder returned to Utah. After waiting at the border, the expedition finally crossed into Mexico and went on to Guatemala and to Colombia; then, after failing to achieve their objectives, they returned. The tangible achievements were specimens of flora and fauna sent from Central America to BYU.[32]

One author on the expedition concluded that Elder Grant's evaluation of the expedition "may have been colored by his lack of confidence in Cluff which arose from his fear that Cluff was introducing too much secularism into the Academy curriculum." In fact, Elder Grant's diary reveals that his lack of faith in Cluff had grown because Cluff's outlook was too idealistic and not secular enough. Cluff had substituted dreams of the discovery of Zarahemla and new golden plates for sound management practices. He was simply not hardheaded enough to please a man inured to the operation of business, as was Grant.[33]

Cluff's successor, George H. Brimhall, did not have the educational background of his predecessor. Like John A. Widtsoe, then president of Utah State Agricultural College, however, Brimhall recognized by 1907 that the growth of high school education in the United States made the expansion of colleges necessary to train teachers. Horace Cummings himself had decreed that high school teachers—including those at the church academies—have college degrees.[34]

Declining enrollments in the collegiate departments of BYC and LDS University, caused largely by the growth of Utah State and the University of Utah, opened the way for BYU, and between 1907 and 1909 Brimhall pushed to have BYU designated as the official church normal school and the major church university. Between November 1908 and February 1909 the church board of education considered the question of educational priorities. In February 1909 the General Church Board of Education agreed to locate teacher training at Brigham Young University and to eliminate all collegiate study work not necessary for teacher training from other church schools.[35] This recommendation of the General Church Board of Education essentially recast the development of higher education. Brigham Young University would henceforth assume a preeminent position as the church downplayed college work at the other institutions. Church leaders in communities outside Provo and Utah County were understandably upset at the decision.

Even the decision to promote collegiate education at BYU came under attack because of cost. On April 27, 1911, the First Presidency appointed a special committee to consider abandonment of the teachers college program at BYU. After thorough consideration, the First Presidency and Twelve decided not only to keep it but also to encourage its expansion. At the same time, because of expense a lid, which proved to be temporary, was placed on the number of students and faculty at the Provo school.[36]

The expansion of the educational functions at BYU, which by this time could honestly have claimed the designation of college—but certainly not of university—necessitated a construction program. The Jesse Knight family donated the land and money for a new neoclassical building on a new campus. Costing $110,000 and named in honor of Karl G. Maeser, the building was begun in 1908 and dedicated in 1911.[37] In 1914, Jesse Knight donated an additional $100,000 to BYU; but in January 1915, the appropriations committee reported that BYU was still $89,000 in debt. The need for expansion of the educational program at BYU was apparent, however, and other new buildings were constructed near the Maeser Building.[38]

A new development inaugurated on the stake level in 1911 facilitated the closing of academies and the expansion of higher education for teacher-training. In 1911 Joseph F. Merrill, a professor at the University of Utah who had been a student at the University of Chicago, became a member of the Granite Stake Presidency with the assignment of supervising education for the stake. Influenced by religious seminaries he had seen in Chicago, he worked out a plan for weekday released-time religious education for students at Granite High School. High school officials agreed to release students for an hour each day. The stake constructed a building near the school for the classes, which were called seminary instruction. Students could come on a voluntary basis to attend classes in Old Testament, New Testament, church history, and Book of Mormon. Later, public high school credit was granted for the two Bible classes.[39] At about the same time, seminary classes were begun at Morgan, and in succeeding years other stakes inaugurated the system. In March 1916 the Brigham City Theological Seminary was dedicated, and in April 1918 the General Church Board of Education agreed to establish seminaries in Pleasant Grove, Heber City, and Roosevelt. By late 1927 the church operated seventy seminaries, and in 1929 it established an early-morning seminary system in Idaho for students who could not be released for an hour from class attendance. These were only the early entries in a system which was eventually to spread throughout most areas in which the church was established.[40]

What remained then to complete the transition from general to limited church support of education at all levels was, first, the development of a system of religious education on the collegiate level and, second, sufficient financial pressure to make the continued operation of most of the church's colleges and universities untenable. The religious education system had a shaky, if not rather stormy, beginning, but by 1930 two institutes of religion—seminaries of the collegiate level, as they were then called—had been inaugurated. The first was established in temporary quarters near the University of Idaho at Moscow in 1926. The church selected J. Wylie Sessions as instructor and in February 1928 laid plans for the construction of a building which was completed in October 1929. The church dedicated an institute building near Utah State Agricultural College at Logan on March 31, 1929.[41]

Institutes did not operate without difficulty. Sessions made a success of the institute at the University of Idaho, but reports in January 1931 indicated that his immediate successor had brought the institute to virtually "complete failure." Only three or four students attended, and the teacher was unable to get along well with either the Mormon or Gentile community. Meanwhile, protests from within the LDS community grew over the institute at Logan. Stake President Oliver H. Budge came to see Heber J. Grant to complain of the teacher, W. W. Henderson, who, Budge believed, was not orthodox on some subjects, including evolution.[42] Nevertheless, this system weathered its early difficulties and is today an important adjunct of every university with sizeable numbers of Latter-day Saint students.

By the early 1930s the church academy system had been largely abolished, and only a few vestiges of the system of higher education remained. In 1927 the name of LDS University was changed to LDS College and then to LDS High School, since no university or college work was offered. In November 1928 President Grant asked the church Board of Education to lay plans for the closing of LDS High School and to meet the needs of the students by expanding the seminary system.

Two departments of Latter-day Saints College remained. They were the McCune School of Music and Art and the LDS Business College. In July 1920 it was announced that LDS University would open a music school in the Gardo House, and in April 1921 the school moved to the McCune mansion, which had been donated to the church by the McCune family with the expectation that it would become the home of the church president. President Grant, however, chose to live in his own home, saying that he could not "make up my mind to spend the tithes of the people, much of which comes from the poorest of the poor for such a purpose" as the upkeep of the mansion. In August 1924 President Grant announced that the school's name was being changed to the McCune School of Music and Art and that he was donating two paintings, Edwin Evans's "Wheatfield" and a copy of Rembrandt's "Elizabeth Bas" to form "a nucleus for gathering paintings for the school." The LDS Business College had continued from the Salt Lake Commercial College and the business department of LDS University which had replaced it.[43]

In May 1924, when the church made a preliminary decision to close Brigham Young College, the presidency of the Cache Stake and a large delegation from Logan came to protest. Finally, the church decided to leave the school open with the stipulation that a substantial proportion of the cost of operation be obtained from private local subscriptions. This succeeded in postponing the demise of the school, but in April 1926 it was announced that Brigham Young College would close at the end of the school year.[44] In February 1929 the Board of Education decided to close Weber College in 1930, and Joseph F. Merrill began lobbying the legislators to get the state to take over its operation. The 1929 legislature did not act, and a delegation from Ogden came to ask the church to reconsider. In addition, the closing of LDS High School met problems in 1931 because the Salt Lake School Board made no arrangements to take over the burden of 1,000 new students.[45]

Turning the schools over to the state was certainly not a happy experience for President Grant and his associates, but as the Depression began in late 1929, it became even more of a necessity. On December 29, 1930, Joseph F. Merrill announced that all church schools except Brigham Young University and Juarez Academy would close in 1931 and 1932. Legislation in 1931 for which Joseph F. Merrill and others lobbied brought about the transfer of Snow, Weber, and Dixie colleges to the state of Utah. The Idaho legislature thwarted the plans to close Ricks College when it refused to accept the college. The same thing happened at the Church College of Hawaii at Laie.[46]

Though faced with difficulties, Brigham Young University continued its growth. Franklin S. Harris attracted faculty members of the stature of Lowry Nelson and Carl F. Eyring, and even though only a minority of the faculty during the 1920s held the Ph.D., Harris secured accreditation and expanded the university's educational offering through an extension division and a summer program at Aspen Grove in Provo Canyon. In addition, Harris expanded the research activities and the library facilities at the university with the construction of the $125,000 Heber J. Grant library. The financial condition of the university was precarious, however, since the annual church appropriation was fixed at $200,000 per year by 1924, though John A. Widtsoe thought that it ought to be increased by increments of $16,000 per year up to $300,000.[47]

Financial problems did not stop BYU from going the way of many other universities by expanding its extracurricular activities. In August 1927 it held its first beauty pageant and crowned blonde Ruth Buchanan as "Mormon Beauty Queen." In August 1919 the General Church Board of Education rescinded an 1898 decision and approved the inclusion of football in the curriculum of the church schools. The university football team made arrangements to play the University of Hawaii in November 1930 and asked the First Presidency to endorse the match. Heber J. Grant agreed to give a letter of introduction to President Castle H. Murphy of the Hawaiian Mission, but refused to "be placed in the position of advocating attendance at football games. We said we thought that was hardly up to the standard of our dignity."[48]

Brigham Young University did not achieve its successes without some costs, some of which came because of its success in recruiting competent faculty. One of the major efforts of George Brimhall had been to bring faculty members qualified by education to offer substantial college work. Between 1907 and 1909 he hired Henry Peterson, an M.A. from Harvard; Joseph Peterson, a Ph.D. from Chicago; Ralph Chamberlin, a Ph.D. from Cornell; and William Chamberlin, trained at Berkeley and Chicago. These four men provided an island of academic excellence in a sea which one "of the leading men of the church" characterized as "a bunch of farmers who gave their leisure time only to teaching and who lacked any genuine devotion to their profession."[49]

It was perhaps inevitable that professors with backgrounds such as the Petersons and the Chamberlins had would come into difficulty at BYU. At any rate, the two Petersons and Ralph Chamberlin began discussion of evolution and higher criticism of the Bible in their classes.

Horace Cummings received a number of complaints from stake presidents, and "some of our leading principals and teachers, and leading men who are friends of our schools," expressing concern about the application of "evolutionary theory and other philosophical hypotheses to principles of the gospel." This led Cummings to believe that the professors had undermined the faith of the students.[50]

On February 3, 1911, the Board of Education met to discuss Cummings's reports. Cummings found the students themselves quite comfortable with the "new light" which the teachers had imparted. Nevertheless, board members were disturbed and appointed a committee to meet with the three to see if they would stop teaching these ideas. On February 10 a committee consisting of Francis M. Lyman, Hyrum M. Smith, Charles W. Penrose, Anthony W. Ivins, George H. Brimhall, Horace H. Cummings, Heber J. Grant, George F. Richards, and Joseph Keeler met with Henry and Joseph Peterson and Ralph Chamberlin. The session lasted nearly five hours, and the three were frank in explaining their belief in evolution and their reservations about some parts of the Bible. According to Heber J. Grant, they manifested "a very good spirit." On February 11 the committee formulated its report, which it presented to the Twelve. They agreed unanimously to ask the three to leave BYU.[51]

On February 20, 1911, the Board of Trustees raised the question again. The board passed a resolution that teachers in the church schools must teach gospel subjects as taught by the First Presidency and Apostles.[52] Thereafter, the whole problem became a matter of public controversy. In an interview published in the *Salt Lake Telegram* on February 23, Henry Peterson denied teaching at BYU anything contrary to the gospel, but thought he could do little about the situation with the unanimous opinion of the Council of the Twelve against him and his colleagues. On March 12, 1911, he resigned from the BYU faculty.

Prior to the resignation, considerable student support had developed for Peterson and his colleagues. On March 3, at a party in Provo, Anthon H. Lund was upset because so many students demonstrated support for the Petersons and Chamberlin. Joseph F. Smith wrote his son Andrew, who had recently left BYU because of bad grades and cutting classes, to "eschew" the Petersons and Chamberlin together with the doctrine of evolution. On March 14 ninety students presented a petition to President Brimhall asking the administration not to accept

Henry Peterson's resignation. On March 15, 125 students from the collegiate department—more than a majority—petitioned in support of the professor. On March 16, the *Deseret News* rebuked the students editorially for publishing their petition in an anti-LDS newspaper.[53]

Brimhall accepted Peterson's resignation from BYU on March 31, however, and Chamberlin submitted his resignation after the school term finished. In the meantime, the church aired its side of the matter, together with the resolution of the BYU trustees, in the *Improvement Era*. Joseph F. Smith commented that evolution and higher criticism, though "perhaps containing many truths—are in conflict on some matters with the scriptures, including some modern revelation." In addition, President Smith took the position that "philosophic theories of life have their place and use, but it is not in the classes of the Church schools." He was particularly concerned that investigation of the problems "tends to upset his [the student's] simple faith in the gospel, which is of more value to him."[54] Realistically speaking, given the attitude of the general authorities about the need for harmony, there was perhaps no other way that the dispute could be resolved. The three professors were generally courteous, but the church leadership could not allow them to remain out of harmony. To the church leaders the professors exceeded the limits of tolerance of divergent views on evolution and higher criticism.

The long-range consequences of the matter were quite important, however, and what seems to have been the most cogent discussion of the consequences came in the 1920s by Ephraim E. Ericksen, who knew those involved and who viewed the problem from the perspective of an academician and a member of the MIA general board. He pointed out that the insistence that certain things must not be taught in church schools had "the unfortunate effect of stimulating hypocrisy among young college men and women." Professors and students alike became unwilling to express thoughts "on important matters of scientific and sociological value for fear of losing their positions and receiving the boycott of the church." This certainly happened to Henry Peterson when in April 1912 the First Presidency threw their opposition against his becoming state inspector of high schools because in his "present mode of thinking and causing doubt in the hearts of the children . . . it would not be a wise thing to do."[55] I say "seems to have been" advisedly since the controversy was obviously clouded by the public airing of charges and countercharges. A great deal of mythology has built up on both sides of the controversy. Unfortunately, though Horace H. Cummings made an outline of the charges, no transcript exists of the hearings. There seems as a result to be little possibility of verifying actually what the three men taught. Ernest L. Wilkinson's assertion that they were dismissed "because of their hostile and belligerent attitude" is belied by the entries in Heber J. Grant's journal that indicated that they had exhibited a good attitude in the hearings. The reason for the dismissal seems to have been a desire to protect the students in church schools from confronting ideas which church leaders thought they were unprepared to evaluate. The long-range outcome seems to have been—as Ephraim Ericksen indicated—to force such ideas as evolution and higher criticism underground.[56]

Brigham Young University also suffered the loss of some of its best faculty members in part because of the lure of better positions with higher salaries and in part as a result of the evolution controversy of 1911. James L. Barker and Edwin S. Hinckley moved to other educational positions, and Harvey Fletcher accepted a post with Bell Laboratories in New Jersey. William Chamberlin left because of the downgrading of his educational status, five years after the dismissal of his brother Ralph. Earl J. Glade left for business and governmental positions in Salt Lake City, and Christen Jensen left for the University of Chicago. Anthony C. Lund left to become director of the Tabernacle Choir. Only through stringent appeals was Eugene L. Roberts kept on until the late 1920s, when he joined the faculty of the University of Southern California. Other faculty were recruited, some from fine universities like Chicago, but it was difficult to replace faculty of the stature of Anthony Lund or Harvey Fletcher.[57]

Somewhat parallel to the difficulties at BYU in 1911, the University of Utah suffered from a controversy between the administration and the faculty in 1915. The developments were significant to the church because Anthon H. Lund, a member of the First Presidency, and Richard W. Young, a stake president, served on the Board of Trustees and because the controversy included charges of church influence in the administration of the university.

In February 1915 President Joseph T. Kingsbury was apparently antagonized by the dislike Milton H. Sevy expressed in a commencement speech critical of Governor William Spry. Some faculty members approved of the talk and Kingsbury recommended that Osborne J. P.

Widtsoe, principal of LDS University and a Harvard M.A., replace English department chairman George M. Marshall, who had reportedly helped Sevy. In addition he urged the firing of Ansel A. Knowlton in physics, George C. Wise in modern languages, and Phil C. Bing and Charles W. Snow in English. On February 24 Widtsoe came to see the First Presidency to tell them about the recommendation and ask their advice. They urged him to accept, but as soon as the matter became public knowledge, members of the faculty became angry and threatened to take action. Meetings of the Board of Trustees seem to have divided into pro- and anti-Kingsbury and pro- and anti-Mormon factions. Wise and Knowlton charged that they were being fired for disagreeing publicly with policies of President Kingsbury and asked the board to investigate. The board agreed to hear them but refused to investigate. On March 17, 1915, the regents voted to sustain Kingsbury, though there was considerable discussion about Kingsbury's methods and relationship with the faculty, which were found to be unsatisfactory.[58] On March 17 fourteen members of the faculty submitted their resignations. Those who resigned included Byron Cummings, dean of the school of arts and sciences, Frank E. Holman, dean of the law school, and Joseph Peterson, professor of psychology, who had been involved in the affair at BYU.

The whole matter evoked national controversy, and it was impossible to divorce the church from the issue. Articles were published in such important national journals as *Outlook, Science, School and Society, New Republic, The Nation*; regional journals like *Sunset*; and educational journals like *School Review* and *Educational Review*. National review journals like *Current Opinion* and *Literary Digest* also picked up the story.[59] Almost immediately, public charges of church influence abounded. Some of the articles pointed out that the professors who were dismissed were non-Mormons and that Widtsoe was a Mormon bishop and principal at LDSU, even though Kingsbury was a Gentile and former Liberal party member.[60]

In fact, the matter went much deeper than this. In a speech given in Salt Lake City and subsequently published in *School and Society*, Frank Holman said that, in his opinion, President Kingsbury had conducted a systematic but covert policy of repression. He had established a policy of prohibiting any political or religious activity which might be offensive to others. One professor who had been asked to speak to a

Democratic rally in American Fork was told this would be displeasing. Another was told not to express his views on national monetary policy publicly. Speeches given at the university were censored. Beyond this, Kingsbury acted autocratically and refused to discuss his views with members of the faculty. In addition, in firing professors, Kingsbury acted on the basis of reports from people close to him rather than holding hearings on the competence of the faculty members.[61] Later, Kingsbury published an article in the same journal denying much of what Holman had said. In defense of his ruling allowing no partisan political or religious activity by professors, he said that he had adopted this policy because of state laws which forbade them. The other charges he denied except the recommendation that one professor not give a political speech. In that case, he said, his views were advisory rather than prohibitory.[62]

Kingsbury also lobbied with members of the board to support his position. On March 19 he came in to see Anthon H. Lund and talked with him about conditions at the university. He indicated that he had accepted the resignations and that he was determined to stand firm. Lund told him that a majority of the regents would back him. Shortly after that, some members of the church leadership tried to get the regents to temporize. Francis M. Lyman and Richard R. Lyman told Lund in order to promote peace it might be better if Widtsoe did not accept the position. Lund thought it would simply make the other side more aggressive; they would take the position that Mormons tried to put a Mormon bishop in the university, then when people objected they backed down. The church had not sought the appointment, Lund said, and ought not to be involved in the affair.[63]

The church, of course, could not be kept out of the matter, if for no other reason than that Mormons constituted a majority of the citizens of the state and that prominent church leaders sat on the board of regents and were active in university affairs. A meeting of the alumni association on April 5 turned into a shouting match between Waldemar Van Cott, Reed Smoot's attorney, representing the regents' position and Dean Holman representing the protestors.[64]

It seemed impossible to put the whole matter down. Controversy swirled over the university for some time and the American Association of University Professors set up an investigating committee headed by Arthur O. Lovejoy of Johns Hopkins University. Though the report exonerated the church, it took the university administration and, by implication, the board of regents to task for failing to realize that possible adverse reaction was not ground for repression of free expression of views on all questions including religious and political issues.[65]

In spite of the resolve of a majority of the regents to support Kingsbury on this occasion, it was only a matter of time before a president who had lost the confidence of a majority of the students and faculty would have to leave. In January 1916 the regents voted to accept the president's resignation and appoint him to a professorship emeritus of chemistry. Kingsbury was, of course, unhappy at the situation. Lund tried to soothe his feelings, but a faculty vote of confidence after the fact seemed merely a sop to a defeated man.[66]

Then, instead of appointing a search committee, Waldemar Van Cott moved that the regents appoint John A. Widtsoe president. W. W. Armstrong and Ernest Bamberger objected, but the motion passed by six to four with N. T. Porter and G. C. Whitmore joining the other two in opposition.[67] Again, the charges of Mormon influence abounded, since the majority who supported Widtsoe were pro-Mormon and the minority tended to be anti-Mormon. In a strong statement Lund denied that Widtsoe's selection had come because of his church connections. In retrospect, it seems likely that while the regents used questionable methods, Widtsoe possessed ample qualifications for the position. A graduate of Harvard and the University of Goettingen, he was president of Utah State Agricultural College at the time.[68]

On March 13 Widtsoe met with the regents and outlined his program for the university. He proposed first the adoption of a university constitution, modeled after that of the University of Illinois, which would define the duties and rights of faculty and administration and provide for orderly means of settling disputes. Even Armstrong became convinced that Widtsoe would do a good job as president.[69]

The whole controversy over the University of Utah presidency points to a difficulty which the LDS church has continually experienced and which it can probably never overcome. Since about 70 percent of the population of Utah is Mormon, it is only natural that most of those in public positions have been Mormons. By the same token, it is only natural that non-Mormons should resent this power and wish for its reversal. Their only avenue to community position is through either cooperation with the church members or diminution of church

power. Under such conditions, it was easy for them to believe that ille-
gitimate church influence was responsible for their failure to exercise
more control in the community.

This feeling was reinforced by rumors and also by generalizing from
existing factual information. Since prominent church members like
W. W. Riter, Anthon H. Lund, and Richard W. Young belonged to the
board of regents, and since Joseph Kingsbury was a friend of church
leaders like Lund, it was easy to believe that support of Kingsbury
came from the church. The fact that Kingsbury had reacted to criticism of prominent church politicians like William Spry and prohibited
free speech which might be critical of the LDS church leadership also
helped to bolster this view.

In fact, what had happened was the secular tendency of conservative men appointed to organizations like boards of regents to support
their appointees even in the face of a groundswell of opposition. Members of such boards often consider such opposition as coming from
malcontents or disturbed activists and they resolve to hold firm. There
is also a balancing tendency to reflect on the situation and after some
time to ease out the embattled leader in order to promote continued
harmony in the organization. This happened in the case of Kingsbury.

It is also not at all surprising that similar charges of church influence surfaced when Widtsoe was appointed to the presidency. He was
selected without a search by majority vote rather than by consensus.
The non-Mormon minority was reconciled to Widtsoe only after he
met with them and convinced them that he would be a good admin-
istrator and fair in his relations with the faculty.

In his study of the secularization of the University of Utah, Joseph
Jeppson concluded that the events of 1915 and 1916 can best be interpreted as a Mormon-Gentile conflict which helped to open the way for
the eventual secularization of the University of Utah. While it is clear
that the Mormon-Gentile issue clouded the local perceptions of the difficulties faced by the university during the period, it seems more
useful to view the conflict as one between autocracy and conservatism
on the one hand and progressivism and academic freedom on the
other. In that light, it is best seen as the reflection of the national educational issues so important to the Progressive era during which the
events took place. The recently founded AAUP provided a vehicle for
the promotion of academic freedom and reinforced, but did not initi-
ate, a similar feeling among many Mormons and Gentiles about the

need for reform at the university. Alumni, the regents, all representing both Mormons and Gentiles, and John A. Widtsoe, a Mormon, supported a constitution, guarantees of academic freedom and due process, and faculty representation to the governance of the university. The AAUP report mentioned the appointment of O. J. P. Widtsoe and the charges of church influence but concluded that it could not judge whether such charges had any substance. Moreover, Jeppson himself presents considerable evidence that the Latter-day Saint community was divided over Kingsbury's highhanded methods and a number of prominent churchmen thought the university administration and regents ought to promote academic freedom.[70]

Difficulties for the church such as those at the University of Utah and at Brigham Young University should not cloud the solid achievements during the period. In the face of enormous financial difficulty and competition with a rapidly expanding public school system, the church leadership on both the general and local levels had charted a course which the church educational system has followed to the present time. The church inaugurated the backbone of its religious education system, the seminaries and institutes; it abandoned competing and expensive collegiate and high school education, and strengthened the role of a single church university with a few smaller junior colleges. Since the closing of academies and colleges required the demise of cherished local institutions, local leaders and citizens were understandably upset. In retrospect, it seems obvious that the decisions were a result of conditions existing at the time, and in general the local people reconciled themselves to the unpleasant but necessary changes.

10

======

Cooperation and Individualism
in Mormon Society

BY 1900 THE LATTER-DAY SAINTS had inhabited the Great Basin for
more than half a century. Perhaps no other people since the seventeenth-
century New England Puritans had shaped the social character of the
North American landscape as thoroughly as the Mormons. The constant conflict with the federal government and with their gentile
neighbors together with strong religious convictions had endowed
them with a combination of fierce independence and group solidarity.
In addition, the persistence of certain aspects of the cooperative tradition coupled with the waxing of an individualism modeled on the
norms of Victorian America seems to have made Mormons so creative
during the period from 1900 through 1930, not only within the church
but also in the larger community. This combination of traditions allowed church members to support both public and private social action and hold the somewhat contradictory ideals of cooperation and
corporate capitalism at the same time. Most importantly, the strengthening of priesthood authority and the tendency to differentiate between the Mormon community and the larger society seem not to have
hindered the creative impulses among the Latter-day Saints.

Between 1890 and 1930 the Mormon people made the transition
which integrated them as fully into the national culture as into national politics and the national economy. In the nineteenth century
many of the Mormon towns had supported their own dramatic companies and theaters, and popular participation in cultural events was
the norm. Although individual wards sponsored dramatic and musical
performances, increasingly in the twentieth century professional and
commercial presentations, particularly movies and traveling vaudeville troupes, tended to replace amateur productions. In cities like Salt
Lake and the smaller Mormon towns as well, these undermined patronage for the local theater. In visual arts painters and sculptors who

had been born in Utah but had studied in Paris and New York, often at church expense, replaced immigrants who had also trained in Europe or the East as well. In spite of some successes in home literature, writers were not particularly distinguished except in the fields of history and theology. Historians and theologians like Brigham H. Roberts, Orson F. Whitney, James E. Talmage, and John A. Widtsoe added a number of seminal works.[1]

That Mormon social attitudes and practices underwent rapid transition seems clear both from statements of church leaders and from actions by Latter-day Saints. Both precept and practice reveal considerable ambivalence on the relationship between wealth and social needs. While church leaders announced publicly that members might organize for collective action on labor questions, some tendency existed to oppose such action in private. By the 1920s, in spite of the theoretical support for a neutral attitude, a number of prominent churchmen supported the union-busting activities of the Utah Associated Industries. Though firmly committed to helping members in distress, during the early stages of the Great Depression the church definitely lacked the resources to assist those in need. In extraordinary but limited crises, such as mine disasters, the church seemed quite able to manage. During the early twentieth century, the church leadership developed a comfortable relationship with the federal government and supported a number of measures of public policy designed to deal with pressing problems such as watershed management, reclamation, and scenic preservation. Some questions, such as smallpox vaccination, however, elicited a mixed response from the church membership.

Inexorably, change overtook the Mormon commonwealth. Mormondom became more than ever before a land of contrasts. The growth of cities had changed the Wasatch Front into an urban region. At the same time the area in Utah south of Nephi remained rural and that south of Marysvale remained virtually a frontier. Through the use of ethnic organizations, the church succeeded in buffering the shock of acculturation for northern Europeans who had moved to Utah. Concurrently, the settlements outside the Wasatch Front moved toward full integration in the life of the church and the nations where they existed. In spite of some difficulties, in the United States and Canada these changes proceeded in a generally orderly manner. In Mexico, however, the conditions became intolerable as the Saints found them-

selves ground between the millstones of opposing forces in that nation's major civil war, and the church virtually abandoned its colonial
experiment.

In the nineteenth century the cooperative commonwealth had been
the ideal. Called the Law of Consecration and Stewardship under
Joseph Smith and the Cooperative Movement and the United Order
under Brigham Young, these programs had promoted equality and
community development. Even corporations like ZCMI, the railroads,
and various manufacturing and communications enterprises were
promoted for community benefit rather than individual profit. Property
in the Mormon towns was privately owned, but cooperation on such
projects as public buildings and irrigation works took place in a spirit
of commitment to the community. Investors made profits from the
businesses, but a sense of community welfare pervaded their establishment and operation.[2]

By the 1890s cooperatives designed to alleviate community distress
by promoting economic equality had generally become joint stock corporations, operated not a great deal differently from other business enterprises. The perceptions of both Mormons and Gentiles indicate this
shift from a cooperative to a capitalistic outlook in Mormon society. In
the 1899 first edition of the *Articles of Faith*, James E. Talmage wrote
that the church fostered a plan which "without force or violence
[seeks] to establish a natural equality, to take the weapons of despotism
from the rich, to aid the lowly and the poor. . . . From the tyranny of
wealth, as from every other form of oppression, the truth will make
men free." Later, as the emphasis on equality declined, these passages
were softened to delete all except a reference to "misused wealth."[3]

In 1901 Mosiah Hall, then professor of education at Brigham Young
College in Logan, emphasized that "widespread intelligence, and the
sweet taste of liberty have given to the people the ideals of life and of
government which will not allow them to endure industrial servitude
and social inequality." By 1904, however, Professor Hall took the view
that disparity of wealth and trusts were inevitable and "not without
some redeeming features," though he still thought that the main value
of corporations was to demonstrate the trend toward community ownership. Lorenzo Snow in February 1901 urged the wealthy to "unlock your
vaults, unloose your purses, and embark on enterprises that will give
work to the unemployed, and relieve the wretchedness that leads to the
vice and crime which curse your great cities." Charles W. Penrose em-

phasized that in Mormon society, church members cooperated freely to achieve the embodiment of Christ's two great commandments.[4]

In the 1895 edition of *A New Witness for God*, B. H. Roberts lamented that "the basis of all our commercial or industrial enterprises, is selfishness." He commented on the condition which "divides civilized communities into two classes—the proud and the envious, . . . the former living in affluence on the proceeds of their wealth, the latter, for the most part, eking out an existence on the insufficient means secured through their labor. Capital, it must be said, feels power and forgets right; labor in its despair grows desperate and violates the law."[5]

In October 1912 an *Improvement Era* article argued that government had not acted adequately to deal with inequalities which had arisen in America. It applauded reformers like Jane Addams and endorsed social legislation "regarding sanitation, proper structure of buildings for the poor, . . . and the limiting of working hours of factory hands" to try to deal with these problems.[6]

Some members of the church emphasized the ideology of progress and the business ethic. D. H. Fowler argued that "the world is getting better." He cited as evidence the existence of material progress—particularly "contrivances that men are continually bringing into use for the saving of time and energy." An anonymous article in September 1909 argued that success would come if a person possessed a strong testimony of the Gospel, was pure, honest, clean, and energetic, and had a "good bank account."[7]

Some Latter-day Saints were quite as emphatic in their denunciation of labor as Roberts was in his criticism of capital. William A. Hyde, president of the Pocatello, Idaho, Stake, wrote that the clamor "for a more equitable division of property" was usually not justified because in many cases those who insisted upon a change did not look behind the immediate condition to realize that "their poverty may to an extent be due to their own negligence of opportunity."[8]

Joseph F. Smith and Heber J. Grant both demonstrated a somewhat ambivalent attitude. Both were active in business and yet concerned about the absence of faith which excessive concentration on amassing wealth might engender. In an article in the April 1908 *Improvement Era*, President Smith wrote that problems had developed from excessive "individualism," and he urged church members to remember their "dependence on God, the church, and others." After a reunion at the

McCune mansion in October 1908, Heber J. Grant lamented that Alfred McCune thought only of earning money. McCune's children had lost their faith, and Elder Grant "was profoundly impressed with the fact that the life of the most humble Latter-day Saint is of far greater value in the sight of the Lord, and a greater success than one devoted to the accumulation of wealth, no matter how many millions they may succeed in making."[9]

Some members exhibited attitudes of resigned equanimity. George D. Kirby argued that there can never be equality of rank, wealth, intellect, or influence, but that there could be "equality of essential happiness, equality of pure and true thoughts, . . . and equality of common destiny."[10]

Even though the church had sponsored cooperation in the nineteenth century, it had taken place within the Mormon community. There had seldom been much sympathy, especially among the leaders, for secular visions of cooperation, whether Marxian or utopian. Thus most required little adjustment to accommodate to the norms of Victorian American society. Rather, those in the church who accepted the increasing pluralism and wished to extend it to their vision to embrace the left wing of American political and economic society experienced increasing difficulty.

In practice, positions on social questions like the relationship of labor and capital ranged from those slightly left of center like Roberts to the far-right views of William Hyde. Few church members supported socialism. An editorial in the *Deseret News* in 1901 argued that socialism was growing because of the growth of monopolies, but predicted that it would fall from its own internal weight. In 1902, however, in answer to a letter from a member, Joseph F. Smith said that, though socialism ought not to be confused with the United Order, he saw "no harm in the wise and intelligent study of socialistic principles, such of them at least as are true and as the teachings of the Gospel and the spirit of the Lord will approve, nor in belonging to a club or society having that as its only purpose." This was perhaps the most generous statement, however, and on another occasion, the First Presidency cautioned that members of the church belonging to the "socialist party who are determined to advocate the principles of their party among our people should confine themselves to the merits of their party principles and not seek to make converts by willful misrepresentations."[11]

In 1911 a particularly active campaign for the Socialist party developed in and around Thatcher, Arizona. Several general authorities thought it unwise. In April George F. Richards wrote to George W. Williams of Thatcher, who saw socialism as a means of achieving the United Order—for him the most perfect form of socialism. Richards argued that if it is "the most perfect form of socialism ever given to man, then why not the Latter-day Saints be satisfied and contented to wait until the Lord through His church is prepared to establish the same?" He advised members of the church not to become socialists, for fear they might "lose the spirit of loyalty and devotion to the church and the Gospel." Williams responded, asking whether members would be dealt with in church courts for belonging to the Socialist party. Richards replied that the church does not excommunicate people for belonging but that some had left of their own accord. Nevertheless, on November 2 the First Presidency wrote to "certain of our brethren" at Thatcher, advising them to join "only with the two great parties Republican and Democratic—for them to avoid socialists."[12]

By the turn of the century even outside observers could see that, though the rhetoric of cooperation often continued, the reality of extensive competition actually obtained. What they did not take into consideration was that the Mormons had not recognized a separation of church and state in their community in the nineteenth century, a point which partly invalidates their argument. In April 1903 Richard T. Ely pointed out that the Mormons' first best state was "the Order of Enoch or United Order," which was nothing less than "working together, living together, having all things in common like certain early Christians." The second best state was "based upon a far-reaching recognition of common needs, involving a generous provision for all public purposes, and also for all classes in the community requiring help, especially the aged." In this state, church members maintained equality of opportunity. Ely argued that by 1903 even the second best state was deteriorating as cooperation "languishes, the wealthier and more enterprising Mormons vie with the Gentiles in absorption of natural resources, and the gaps between economic classes are widening. In Salt Lake City it would appear, upon reliable authority, that Mormons not infrequently call upon Gentiles for relief, and that they are compelled to utilize the public charitable institutions."[13]

Some writers like William E. Smythe and Ray Stannard Baker saw that cooperative ideals persisted in various forms. Land, Smythe pointed out, was widely owned in the community. Public ownership of water for irrigation continued, and shares in the joint stock companies were still quite broadly held. Mormonism, Baker observed, is best understood as "a broad mode of life, a system of agriculture, an organization for mutual business advancement, rather than a mere church."[14]

In the nineteenth century, the church had moved from active support of labor organization to increasing ambivalence and even hostility. The church organized and operated the first unions in Utah. When outside organizations like the Knights of Labor and the American Federation of Labor began to penetrate the Mormon commonwealth, however, some antagonism grew. This came about, in part, because of the anti-Mormon principles of some like the Knights. To some extent, however, it developed from the pro-business attitude of Mormon leaders, most of whom owned or managed businesses and most of whom cooperated with Gentile businessmen in various enterprises.[15]

By the early twentieth century, church leaders still exhibited considerable ambivalence toward labor organization. The *Deseret News* had urged the right of workers and capitalists to organize for self-protection. The *News* was, however, opposed to "the spirit of tyranny and compulsion, which attempts to force workers who do not wish to be bound by the rules of an order or union into its ranks against their will and in violation of law and liberty."[16]

In essence, the battle between capital and labor had already been fought in the late nineteenth century and won by the businessmen. Brigham Young and other church leaders had cooperated with Gentile entrepreneurs in the organization of railroad, sugar, electric, and other companies, and after 1890 Mormon businessmen had moved with Gentiles into the chambers of commerce and other employers' organizations. In many ways the employers had stolen the march, and when the chips were down, though they took a publicly neutral stand, church leaders privately sided with management.[17]

In 1901, for instance, during a railroad strike in Pocatello, Joseph F. Smith wrote to Stake President Hyde, urging that it was "very desirable that our people avoid all combinations and conditions which would be likely to draw them into an attitude of antagonism to their employers. . . ." He hoped that the employees could adjust their differences amicably, but did not want church members to be "mixed up with strikes or combinations that lead to violence and to animosity and hatred and bitterness between the employed and the employer. It is often better," he opined, "to suffer wrong than to attempt to take the reins in our own hands to secure our rights by violence." He called upon Hyde to ask members not to associate themselves with employees who wanted to combine.[18]

In late 1903 and early 1904, in a bitter strike against the Utah Fuel Company in Carbon County, the church took a similar stance. President Anthon H. Lund and Governor Heber M. Wells discussed the strike with President Smith. In a letter to H. G. Williams, adjutant general of the Utah National Guard, the First Presidency endorsed the strong action of the company in holding firm and also expressed approval of the use of troops to control the strikers.[19]

With their diverse business interests, general authorities turned up almost inevitably on the side of management and against labor. In September 1905 the linemen of Utah Light and Railway Company went out on strike. At a meeting of the board of directors, including Joseph F. Smith and others from the general authorities, it was decided not to meet their demands. They realized that this "possibly" might "precipitate other strikes in sympathy." President Smith rationalized the company's position by the often-used anti-union argument "that we cannot consistently turn over the management of our business into the hands of these labor organizations." A strike of streetcar workers in 1907, however, led to mediation by B. H. Roberts and an increase in wages. Some general authorities, like Abraham O. Woodruff, thought the Latter-day Saints should return to the situation in the nineteenth century in which the church sponsored unions. Charles Kelly, president of the Box Elder Stake, in general conference in April 1903 said that unions were secret organizations and that members ought to shun them.[20]

Joseph F. Smith, however, made it clear that neither of these views represented church policy. Officially the First Presidency wrote that the "church, as a church, has taken no stand for nor against labor organizations." President Smith, however, said that he opposed boycotts, sympathetic strikes, and compulsory unionism. He could find, nevertheless, "no reason why workmen should not join together for their own mutual protection and benefit." In August 1910 Charles W. Penrose, speaking in the Tabernacle on the labor question, said that the church should not involve itself in labor issues.[21]

In the late teens and early twenties severe labor strife developed throughout Utah and the nation. Depression followed a sharp inflation, and conflicts arose as wages failed to keep pace with the rapid

rise in cost of living and workers sought through organization to secure more money and better working conditions. The Utah Associated
Industries, an organization formed in 1918, tried to end industrial disturbances by eliminating all workers affiliated with organized labor
through what they called the American Plan.[22]

Strikes during 1919 and 1920 led to conflict, and many church leaders were sympathetic with the Associated Industries. Following the
sessions of the flu-postponed general conference on June 3, 1919, a
group of general authorities "assembled in the font room of the tabernacle" to discuss "the attitude to be maintained by the church in the
matter of oppressive methods followed by some labor unions." "The relation between capital and labor," James E. Talmage thought, "looms
up as one of the serious problems confronting the people in this period
of reconstruction" following World War I. In September 1919 church
leaders became concerned that they might have to end all building
work because of strikes in the construction trades, but this did not ma-
terialize. In spite of the concern, Heber J. Grant reiterated essentially
Joseph F. Smith's position. In the October conference of 1919 and
again in the April conference of 1920, he said that workers had a perfect right to join labor unions, but no one had a right to stop those who
did not join from being employed.[23]

Nevertheless the use of strikebreakers and lockouts during 1919,
1920, and 1921 succeeded in breaking the back of the union movement in Utah. The *Deseret News* and a number of church leaders endorsed the American Plan, and by 1924 the Salt Lake Federation of Labor had been forced to suspend publication of the *Utah Labor News*.
Although it had been able to recoup some strength in 1925, the labor
movement in Utah languished until the 1930s.[24]

A number of church and community leaders supported the Associated Industries. At the April 11, 1922, banquet the principal speaker
was Max J. Kuhl, who spoke of the triumph of the American Plan in
San Francisco and the crushing of strikes. President Grant spoke for a
few minutes and wished Kuhl and his associates "abundant success in
their labors in the future." In November 1927 at the banquet of the
directors of the Associated Industries given to honor Harry Chandler
of the *Los Angeles Times*, Heber J. Grant, Utah Governor George H.
Dern, and Monsignor Duane G. Hunt, rector of the Cathedral of the
Madeleine of Salt Lake City, were honored guests. Paul Shoup, executive vice president of Southern Pacific, attacked unionism by calling

it a means of curtailing progress. Leaders in the Associated Industries who were prominent churchmen included Charles W. Nibley of the First Presidency, a vice president and director; Stephen H. Love of ZCMI, a director; and Henry H. Rolapp of U and I Sugar, also a director.[25]

Though adhering to the Associated Industries movement, church leaders seem to have held an attitude somewhat more moderate than those who wanted to crush all union organization. In September 1922 Heber J. Grant assisted in mediating a dispute between the Union Pacific and shopmen through an agreement that the railroad would take back all striking shopmen and restore pension rights. His concern in this case seems to have been to end the dispute so companies could ship sugarbeets without trouble. Beyond this the *Deseret News* endorsed a movement to abolish the twelve-hour day. "Too much work," the *News* said, "brutalizes men just as too little work barbarizes them." In addition, most church leaders did not generally take the extreme position of many American Plan supporters who refused to hire union members. This, church leaders argued, was a matter for employees themselves to decide, and they often opposed yellow-dog contracts and other antiunion measures.[26]

If the attitude toward labor is not completely clear, the attitude toward local industry was unequivocal. It had not changed from the nineteenth century. From Brigham Young's time onward, the church leadership had promoted manufacturing, commercial, communications, and transportational enterprises. Members were encouraged to patronize local industry, and in some areas discipline was invoked through church court action when members trafficked with Gentiles. Whatever was done, the church leaders anxiously promoted local developments.[27]

Until well into the twentieth century and, indeed, down to the present time, church leaders have concerned themselves also with the economic development of the Mormon core area. In 1922 Heber J. Grant made it clear that the church leadership favored new businesses such as the Ironton plant near Provo. Brigham Young, he said, had announced that Utah would some day abound with industries, and the allegations that Mormons opposed the introduction of outside capital were false.[28]

With their concern for the prosperity of the community, the church leaders demonstrated considerable distress over economic depressions. Some tendency existed to see the depression of 1920–22 as the result of personal sin rather than of market forces, but church members concerned themselves with the sluggish agriculture and mining industries and the severe downturn seven years later.[29]

In March 1928 a Commerce Department representative visited the First Presidency to discuss his impressions of the condition of the economy in Utah. He had noted the prosperity of southern Idaho and northern Utah, but in southern Utah he found "the fences were falling down, houses needed paint," and he "wondered why there was such a falling away." The First Presidency explained that this had resulted from "the almost complete loss of the sheep and cattle industry, which was the main support of southern Utah." They had no manufacturing and insufficient farmland for crop agriculture.[30]

By November 1928 it became obvious to some of the more knowledgeable business leaders in the church that such prosperity as existed could not last long. On November 14 Orval Adams of Zion's First National Bank, a member of the church auditing committee, expressed his alarm to Heber J. Grant at the "frightful speculation" in New York and said that he anticipated "a terrible slump." He cautioned that in a contraction New York bankers would call in loans for Utah-Idaho Sugar and other church financial institutions. He urged Grant not to invest church funds in hotels or other fixed assets because the time would come again when the church would have to extend credit to the sugar company. The President thought "his fears are pretty well grounded. . . . I cannot see how the present speculation can go on without a fearful retraction."[31]

Eleven months later, the catastrophe of late October 1929 hit Wall Street. The economy of the Mormon domain along with the rest of the nation shuddered, then collapsed. On October 29, 1929, Reed Smoot's electric stock declined from $300 to $78 a share in one day. Smoot was one of the lucky ones because he had a job and other large investments. In February 1930 Lewis Wells called on Heber J. Grant. He said he, along with many others, had lost his job at ZCMI, and he noted that unemployment was rising at an enormous rate. He asked for a job in the temple or elsewhere in church service where "there would be little chance of being let out." Grant told him that he "knew of no jobs." On March 19, 1930, the directors of ZCMI reduced their dividend from 3 to 2 percent, and Grant knew that this would mean a decline in the value of ZCMI stock.[32]

Detailing the enormous difficulties caused by the Depression, others came during 1930 asking for concessions. Alonzo A. Hinckley called about the sufferings of the people in Delta, Utah. He thought that many of them would have to repudiate their debts. President Grant expressed sorrow, but he could offer no solution. In October 1930 President Grant agreed to waive part of the principal Harold A. Brown owed on a loan for his Packard dealership in Salt Lake. A recently returned missionary called to ask for help in finding work. President Grant said "it breaks my heart that we are not in a position to give work to any and all who desire it. I know of nothing that is sadder to me than people willing to work who cannot find anything to do." Others came in who were losing their property because of foreclosure on farm mortgages, but he seemed unable to do much except commiserate with them.[33]

President Grant's concern about the financial situation led him to consider possible solutions. In November 1931 he seemed to approve "a very stirring talk" by Robert LaFollette about the means of relieving "the financial situation" by allowing the government to do "practically the whole thing, the same as if there were a war on." His favorite solution was the remonetization of silver, since he believed that the reason for the depression was "the demonetization of silver and destroying of the purchasing power of two-thirds of the people of the world, thereby causing them to work for less and come in competition with the working men of America."[34]

In times of distress as in periods of prosperity, the church leadership was generally quite firm in its support for local businesses. This attitude seems to have stemmed from the historic development of such enterprises with church funds, which led members to view them as community rather than private enterprises. In essence, the Latter-day Saints transferred a religious attitude which had developed in response to nineteenth-century community enterprises to privately owned twentieth-century businesses in which majority ownership often vested outside the Latter-day Saint community. Joseph F. Smith announced his support for home industries during an address before the general conference in 1900. "These clothes that I wear are of homemade cloth," he said; "the wool is from Utah sheep, made up by Utah workmen at Provo factory; the clothes themselves were cut and made by Utah tailors at John C. Cutler's." In his testimony at the Smoot investigation, Richard W. Young said that he "would not see anything inconsistent in the members of the church supporting, and therefore being urged to support, some [business] institution that belongs to the church, and therefore to the members of the church."[35]

In the nineteenth century, relief and care for the needy had been a community responsibility. Since the Mormon community and the larger society were coextensive, members did not concern themselves over whether help came from the bishop or the county government. A similar attitude, sometimes misinterpreted by outside observers, carried over into the twentieth century. During the 1930s the attitudes of J. Reuben Clark came into prominence, church and state were severed, and members were discouraged from accepting governmental assistance. Until then, however, the nineteenth-century attitude persisted, and while conditions had changed and the governments, local and national, became more pluralistic, members in need were still encouraged to seek assistance from them as well as the church.

In fact until well into the 1930s specific instructions from the church placed primary responsibility for assistance on the family, the county, and the church, in that order. One historian is of the opinion that in pressing for a change in the policy of the church to eliminate reliance on the government, J. Reuben Clark, then first counselor in the First Presidency, was reflecting attitudes of Heber J. Grant rather than pressing for a change in policy. Frankly, I find this difficult to believe since Grant and his appointee, presiding bishop Sylvester Q. Cannon, had held a different position until Clark succeeded Anthony W. Ivins as first counselor in the First Presidency.[36]

In spite of Ely's recognition that Latter-day Saints often had to call upon public agencies for relief, the church had committed itself to providing assistance to needy members. Ward bishops, Relief Society presidents, and ward teachers were expected to discern need and provide care. Stakes organized programs for the elderly such as annual old folks days.[37]

Disasters demanded the resources of the entire church. The explosion killing 200 miners at Winter Quarters near Schofield, Utah, in May 1900 and the 1924 Castle Gate explosion brought a prompt response from the general authorities. The First Presidency, church members, and church-owned businesses also assisted people on various occasions. ZCMI, for instance, distributed coal each winter to the poor, and the First Presidency gave occasional direct grants, such as the 1911 gift to a blind girl to allow her to continue her studies at the state school for the blind. Members also took up collections for various purposes, such as assisting missionaries and helping widows. The Salt Lake area stakes provided spiritual guidance and Sunday services for prisoners at the state prison.[38]

Church members worked in the relief efforts during and after World War I. In December 1914 the church leadership appointed Heber J. Grant, Richard W. Young, and George F. Richards to develop methods of collecting and distributing money for relief of the needy in Europe. In 1918 the church sent contributions to the various presidents of European missions for distribution to the needy. In 1920 and 1921 the First Presidency asked for the donation of clothing, shoes, and money for the Swiss and German Saints. Church leaders and leading lay members like William H. King assisted Greek and Jewish relief. The church set aside January 23, 1921, as a special fast day for the collection of funds for European and Near Eastern relief.[39]

Particular attention focused on the people of Armenia. The story of those unfortunate people provides one of the saddest examples of attempted genocide in modern history. In March 1916, as the extermination campaign mounted, the Turkish government prohibited the distribution of money sent for relief. Following the First World War, the Armenian people faced a crosscurrent of attack from Soviet Russia and the Turks. Pleas from the tabernacle pulpit told of thousands of starving Armenian children, and Heber J. Grant pledged himself to provide enough to care for at least five orphans for one year. Many Armenians emigrated to the United States.[40]

Members also concerned themselves with the broader interests of the community in which they lived. Accidents like the Scofield disaster brought about efforts, eventually successful in 1917, to strengthen mine safety regulation which had existed since territorial days. An editorial in the *Improvement Era* in 1900 called for "stringent laws" designed to "insure to every mine strict and frequent inspection by responsible and competent examiners." "Owners of mines," the *Era* went on to say, "should be compelled to have every known safeguard thrown around their laborers and negligence, in any respect, should be visited by severe penalties."[41]

Church leaders often favored government intervention for the general welfare. Joseph F. Smith supported the passage of the Hepburn Act to regulate railroads in 1906. In 1903 Governor Heber M. Wells ordered the state to withdraw from the market all state lands enclosed by forest reserves, a move which Reed Smoot supported. Also in general conference priesthood meeting on April 7, 1902, the church leadership supported the protection of watersheds above Utah's towns by favoring "the Federal Government's withdrawing from the market all public lands in the mountains so that water may be stored there for the farmers."[42]

The church leadership also involved themselves in efforts which encouraged cooperation between local communities, the states, and the federal government. One of the most important was the development of federal reclamation projects. In March 1922 Heber J. Grant conferred with Arthur Powell Davis, chief of the Bureau of Reclamation, on Colorado River projects and thought his views "eminently those that Utah would like to have adopted."[43] Beyond this, John A. Widtsoe served on two important commissions designed to evaluate the effectiveness of reclamation. He was a member of the interstate commission which drafted the Colorado River Compact of 1922. In addition, he served on the Fact Finders Commission established in October 1923 to investigate the success and problems of the Bureau of Reclamation. Serving as secretary and vice chairman of the commission, he and others, including former secretary of the interior James R. Garfield and future reclamation chief Elwood Mead, visited Utah, where they received a warm reception from church leaders. The commission recommended that the bureau write off about $28 million worth of improvements owing to mistakes by engineers and farmers. Widtsoe thought that the "experience gained by the Bureau was well worth the money, for the development of the West is far from being completed." In addition he believed that many problems could have been avoided if politics had not played such an extensive role in the operation of the bureau during its first ten years.[44]

In addition to reclamation, the church leadership, particularly Presidents Grant and Ivins and Elder Smoot, promoted the establishment of national parks in Utah. Smoot helped sponsor the National Park Service Act, and in 1928 and 1930 Heber J. Grant and Anthony W. Ivins attended the dedication of facilities at Grand, Bryce, and Zion's National Parks and Cedar Breaks National Monument.[45]

Some matters of public policy generated more discussion than land withdrawal or railroad regulation. Perhaps the most controversial was the question of smallpox vaccination shortly after the turn of the century.

In the nineteenth century, church members had exhibited an ambivalent attitude toward orthodox medicine. During Joseph Smith's and Brigham Young's times many had shunned medical doctors and opted for priesthood healing, home remedies, or Thompsonian medicine. By the late nineteenth century, orthodox medicine was more widely accepted, but some antagonism still persisted. During the twentieth century, attitudes supporting public health programs became increasingly prevalant, but they battled with older conceptions emphasizing folk remedies and faith healing.[46]

In general, the members of the church lined up behind two positions on smallpox vaccination. Charles W. Penrose, editor of the *Deseret News* and husband of Dr. Romania B. Pratt Penrose, championed those who opposed compulsory vaccination as an "encroachment" upon personal liberty. John Henry Smith of the Twelve and George Q. Cannon of the First Presidency sided with those who believed that the public welfare demanded compulsory vaccination. The situation in Utah was extremely serious since in 1899 and 1900 Utah reported 4,000 cases resulting in twenty-six deaths.[47]

The antivaccination interests succeeded in convincing many in the state that the church leadership opposed vaccination, principally because of the *Deseret News*'s editorial opposition. In fact, Penrose seems to have represented a minority among church leaders, but the legislature passed a bill prohibiting compulsory vaccination, which Governor Heber M. Wells vetoed. The legislature overrode Wells's veto, subjecting Utah children to disease for many years. Twenty years later the First Presidency and Twelve agreed to take a stand in favor of compulsory vaccination.[48]

The controversy is very important because it reveals two strains in Mormon society which emphasize the tension between cooperation and individualism in the church. In the first place, many members tend to value individual liberty more than the welfare of the larger society outside the church, and, second, general authorities often will not speak out when they disagree with another church official who has already made his position public.

The tendency to put individual liberty above the community welfare needs to be qualified, of course. The church had supported withdrawal of the watersheds, railroad regulation, irrigation, and national parks. Nevertheless, in the smallpox matter and many other similar cases, members invoked the doctrine of free agency to oppose compulsion. In addition, a tendency existed—probably because of a residual feeling of millennialism, coupled with a belief in the power of the priesthood—to believe that if members simply lived their religion physical discomforts caused by disease would pass them by. In fact, at least one apostle, Abraham O. Woodruff, and numerous faithful church members died from smallpox in the first decade of the twentieth century.

The unwillingness to open public arguments within the First Presidency and Twelve seems to derive from the need both for harmony in the church's councils and for the image of unity to members and others on the outside. There have been, of course, instances where the members considered questions so important that public controversy has erupted, as in the case of the Political Manifesto. Even in the discussion of the continuation of plural marriage, however, most of the controversy occurred behind the scenes. Thus access to the editorial pages of the *Deseret News*, or to rumormongers, became an important means of winning public opinion to one position or another, or at least of persuading large portions of the public that the church promoted a particular position.

Still, members promoted the opposing strain which supported the needs of the community, and a number of church members took an active part in the public health movement in Utah. Stake president Nephi L. Morris, for instance, served as president of the Utah Public Health Association, and Heber J. Grant served on the board of directors and as vice-president. The association campaigned for legislation to improve the quality of the milk supply for children of Utah's cities. Elder Grant, for instance, thought "that a great many of the diseases of children are due to our poor milk supply, and I would be glad if we had some better city ordinances and state laws on the question of proper sanitary conditions in our dairies." Association members disseminated information on tuberculosis, and in 1911 solicited Salt Lake County assistance in this effort. The First Presidency supported another health association program, the creation of a federal department of public health.[49]

Many of these social concerns reflected an urban environment, probably because the church itself faced an increasingly urban condition. During the nineteenth century Utah played leap frog with the United States as a whole in percentage of people in urban places. Between 1900 and 1910 Utah surpassed the national percentage, only to drop slightly behind by 1920.

Moreover, the principal agricultural region also covered the area of most rapid urbanization. "The Garden of Utah," as one observer called it, stretched along the Wasatch Front from Brigham City, which produced "perhaps the finest flavored peaches in the West," south to Orem. Dry farming was spreading in Juab, Box Elder, and Cache counties.[50]

By 1910 Utah boasted a million acres of irrigated fields and orchards, and irrigable land rapidly disappeared. In Cache Valley, farmers had occupied almost all arable land by 1904 and outmigration had begun to take place. In the Virgin River Valley in southern Utah and southeastern Nevada, almost all water supplies had passed into private hands by 1901, and the only generally available land was for range or dry farm. Beet sugar raising approached its peak, and in settled society in places like Cache Valley it vied with dairying for preeminence. Restrictions prompted by overgrazing on the national forests had already produced a decline in wool production in some Wasatch Front areas.[51]

Even the condition of Mormon irrigated agriculture indicated some problems. Since cooperative labor had generally constructed the irrigation works, as local rather than regional or territorial projects, the irrigation districts, in many cases, did not make the most efficient use of available water. Frederick Haynes Newell had observed this in the nineteenth century, and Richard Ely, another sympathetic observer, made the point again in April 1903.[52]

Nevertheless, considerable interest in better farming methods had appeared in the Mormon community. John A. Widtsoe and others from the Utah Agricultural Experiment Station took the lead in this movement with support from articles in the *Improvement Era* and from pulpit addresses urging members to look upon agriculture as a profession requiring "accurate and scientific knowledge in its pursuit."[53]

South of Marysvale, the Beehive State remained a frontier area, but no large settlements could be found south of Nephi. Lombardy poplars lined the streets and roads of the small Mormon settlements and ranches, and citizens relied on horse power rather than railroad. An outside visitor to Hatch, south of Panguitch, found a small primitive town with houses built chiefly of logs or adobe. Some of the most prosperous ranchers occupied frame buildings, but most citizens still lived in cabins which the first settlers had erected.[54]

Though settlers faced the reality of a harsh life in these rural areas, the mythology to those on the urbanizing Wasatch Front had it quite otherwise. In March 1909 Milton Bennion, professor of educational philosophy at the University of Utah, wrote in the *Improvement Era* praising the advantages of farm life. Agriculture, he said, furnished "opportunity for the most varied mental and physical activity, and for the development of a stability of character unexcelled in other vocations." It developed soundness of body and mind, including "sanity of feeling, a right attitude toward life, the surest safeguard against suicide, insanity, and crime." It offered also the "best opportunity for a free and independent life," and the "most favorable conditions for the rearing of a family."[55]

If the previously agricultural Wasatch Front rapidly became urban while parts of Mormon country remained little more than a frontier area, the social composition of the Mormon area also underwent change. In part these changes can be seen as a result of new immigration patterns. In 1907, while 1,876 immigrants to Utah came from western Europe, an almost equal number (1,877) came from southern and eastern Europe. At the same time, the church promoted a somewhat equivocal policy on emigration. In 1907 the *Millennial Star* urged Saints not to emigrate, and the First Presidency reiterated the plea at various times. The church leadership also seems to have denied all requests for funds to assist members in emigrating.[56]

This was a change from the nineteenth century when the Latter-day Saints had supported an extensive immigration program. Recent research, for instance, has shown that the population of the typical Mormon town in the late nineteenth century consisted of immigrants, principally from the British Isles and northern Europe, and their children. Many had come with help from the church-supported Perpetual Emigrating Fund. All of this was done under an ideology of gathering the pure in heart from the world to combine with the Saints in Zion.[57]

The church came under increasing pressure because of stories, spread in various European countries following the Reed Smoot investigation, that Mormons lured young girls to Utah to recruit them into polygamy. These stories had an impact on the policy of the United States Immigration and Naturalization Service during the Taft administration. In December 1910 immigration officials detained a number of Mormon immigrants at Portland, Maine, and senators Reed Smoot and George Sutherland attempted to free them by appealing to the commissioner of immigration. The senators found that polygamy-entrapment stories had convinced the agents, and they had to explain the rationale for the nineteenth-century gathering and the Church's current opposition to the practice of plural marriage. The commissioner promised that the treatment would not recur.[58]

Nevertheless, the church's leaders continued to recognize a responsibility for the new immigrants and their children and of separate meetings and organizations as they had in the nineteenth century on ethnic and national lines. In general, these ethnic organizations held separate meetings either on a regular basis or on special occasions. In June 1900, for instance, the Scandinavians held a "Scandinavian Jubilee" in honor of the fiftieth anniversary of the church's entrance into their homeland. Saints used the Assembly Hall and Tabernacle for meetings, and many agreed to donate funds for the construction of houses of worship in Scandinavia. Elder Anthon H. Lund, himself an immigrant from Denmark, took an active part in the Scandinavian organization.[59] Also, in October 1904 the church leadership placed the weekly German language services in the Salt Lake Valley under the jurisdiction of the Salt Lake Stake. The church held meetings in other areas and occasionally assigned general authorities to attend.[60]

Relationships within such organizations were not always amicable, and in some cases factions thwarted the process of assimilation into the LDS community and larger American society. The First Presidency in 1902 called new leadership for the Utah Scandinavians and urged them "to perform this labor with the sole end in view of saving our brethren and sisters." The church leadership warned "against the seductive lead of men tinctured with apostasy," and urged to guard against "national hatred." The Presidency also urged that the meetings in Scandinavian languages not hinder older Saints from learning English.[61]

Disagreement between the various Scandinavian national groups created perhaps the most difficult problem within the immigrant community. A dissident faction of Norwegians resisted joining the remainder of the Scandinavians and published their own newspaper, the *Correspondenten*. After considerable negotiation in April 1915, the church worked out an agreement to purchase the printing plant and subscription list and reintegrate the Norwegians into the Scandinavian group.[62]

During the first decades of the twentieth century, at least four ethnic newspapers enjoyed official church sponsorship. In May 1901 President Snow agreed to subsidize the *Bikuben* (Danish and Norwegian), and in March 1902 the church paid off the debts of the *Utah*

Posten (Swedish) and supported the publication. In October 1905 it also liquidated the debts and purchased the *Beobachter*, a German-language newspaper. In March 1914 the First Presidency approved the addition of *De Utah Nederlander* in Dutch and pledged $100 per month to help sustain the publication.[63]

During World War I, however, because of rising Americanist sentiment, the chairman of the state Council of Defense, L. J. Farnsworth, tried to end the publication of foreign language newspapers. A remonstrance by the First Presidency seemed at first unavailing, but Farnsworth agreed finally to allow publication of all except the German-language *Beobachter*. Following the war the *Beobachter* resumed publication. In 1923 the church combined it under one management with the *Bikuben*, the *Utah Posten* and *De Utah Nederlander*. In November 1924 the First Presidency announced the formation of general church supervision for all of the foreign language organizations under a committee chaired by John A. Widtsoe.[64]

The First Presidency recognized the problems which members faced when they gathered to Zion. Many came from foreign countries with high expectations of finding the "pure in heart," and some were disappointed to learn that Utah Mormons could be as wicked as Gentiles. In August 1919 Anthon H. Lund, in an address to a group of Scandinavian immigrants, outlined the problem quite succinctly when he said that if they came here "for the sake of serving God, then they would find Zion here, but if the motive for coming was not to serve God but hope alone of bettering there [sic] condition they would find enough to try and tempt them."[65]

American Indians, many of whom Mormon settlers had dispossessed of their land in the nineteenth century, also lived among the Saints. Some of them converted to the church, and a number settled on reservations or assisted with the construction of meetinghouses. One group of Shoshoni settled at Washakie in northern Utah on land which the church had helped secure. In 1917 the First Presidency transferred the deed to the land to the Indians and counseled them not to sell their property. Some sold, but a number of the Indians remained. In April 1918 the First Presidency donated funds to the Papago Indians in Arizona for a meetinghouse. In 1920 they provided money for a meetinghouse at the Berthold Reservation in North Dakota.[66]

Because of Book of Mormon teachings Mormons believed the Indians to be descendants of the Children of Israel. Nevertheless, it seems that, even with the theoretical commitment which the church members had to the native Americans, Euro-Americans experienced considerable difficulty in fellowshipping them. In October 1930, for instance, Rey L. Pratt of the First Council of the Seventy, then serving as president of the Mexican Mission, urged the Saints to accept the duty of helping the Indians "socially and religiously." Members offered many prayers for them, he said, but often waited for someone else to answer them.[67]

After making their first settlement in the Salt Lake Valley in 1847, the Latter-day Saints had established more than 500 colonies in the West. Concentrated in what Donald Meinig has called a core area in Utah and southeastern Idaho, they reached into southern California and western Nevada and Oregon on the west; northern Mexico on the south; southern Canada on the north; and the Big Horn Basin of Wyoming, the San Luis Valley of Colorado, and the Zuni country of New Mexico on the east. Some colonization had also taken place in the Pacific Islands in Hawaii and New Zealand. In most cases, settlers had gone because of mission calls which assigned them to establish the settlements.[68]

By 1900 the extensive colonization efforts of the nineteenth century had virtually ended. Individual settlement rather than cooperative colonization became the norm. The church did maintain some colonization projects which members had started in the nineteenth century and which continued into the twentieth. These included the Canadian colonies in Alberta, the Mexican colonies in Chihuahua and Sonora, and settlements in northern Wyoming.

Although colonization played an increasingly peripheral role in the church's programs after 1900, it nevertheless absorbed a great deal of the general authorities' time. In 1899 Lorenzo Snow urged church officials not to encourage members to emigrate to Utah. At the same time, the First Presidency and Twelve agreed not to discourage saints from colonizing in Canada or the Big Horn Basin of Wyoming, and in November 1899 President Snow appointed Abraham O. Woodruff to supervise colonization for the church.[69]

Several colonies continued in Utah, including the Iosepa Agricultural and Stock Company in Skull Valley, the Deseret and Salt Lake Agricultural and Manufacturing Canal Company at Delta in Millard County, and settlement in the Uintah Basin. Elder Harvey H. Cluff had started the Iosepa colony in 1889 when he brought a group of fifty

Hawaiians to the United States. In addition to the doctrine of the gathering, perhaps the desire to work in the Salt Lake Temple provided the strongest reason for the colony. The colonists never supported themselves, but President Smith continued to sustain them because of his love for the Hawaiian people. The church leadership tried to improve conditions at the colony, located in a harsh desert environment, by such measures as the opening of new canals and the construction of a meetinghouse in 1908. At its peak during the first decade of the twentieth century the colony supported a population of about 200. The appearance of leprosy and the announcement of the imminent construction of a temple in Hawaii in 1915 made the continuation of the colony both hazardous and unnecessary, and the church dissolved the colony in 1917 after considerable financial loss.[70]

Perhaps the most important new land in Utah opened for settlement during this period was not a church-sponsored Mormon enterprise at all. After the federal government mandated a diminution of the Uintah and Ouray Indian reservation in eastern Utah in contravention of Native American rights, it opened the lands in that area to Euro-American settlement. The church was, of course, interested in seeing that its members got as much of the land as possible. The First Presidency asked Reed Smoot to do all he could to watch out for Mormon interests in Washington, and they set apart a special emissary to look after the interests of the Latter-day Saints. Articles in church magazines and circular letters to stake presidents urged young men of the church to take advantage of the new lands.[71]

Such advertising caused some animosity. The women's auxiliary of the anti-Mormon American party met in protest over the church's activities, and opponents charged the Mormons with dominating the newly opened Vernal land office. The *Deseret News* denied that the church had any special influence in land office matters.[72]

By August 7, 1905, nearly 38,000 people had registered for what became Utah's last great land rush. Because of a fear that violence and bloodshed might result from the migration of so many people into the region, President Theodore Roosevelt ruled that a public drawing would determine the order in which applicants could claim the land. Since only one million acres had been opened and a potential of 5,700 homesteads would thus be available, only one in six of the registrants could receive land.[73]

Even with Abraham Woodruff overseeing colonization between

1899 and his death in 1904, voluntary efforts like the Uintah Basin settlement rather than planned colonization conducted by organized companies characterized the first decades of the twentieth century. After 1910 Mormons generally abandoned even these efforts, and in July 1910 the First Presidency issued a circular letter indicating that the church as such was not involved in colonization anywhere.[74]

In Idaho and eastern Oregon, Mormons settled in the Snake River Valley and the Grande Rhonde Valley. In 1900 some of the Twelve asked Woodruff to try to get more families to emigrate to the Fremont Stake in Idaho, providing it did not weaken other settlements. In 1902 Hyrum M. Smith and Abraham O. Woodruff reported that the area around Emmett, Idaho, offered good opportunities for settlement. A report in the La Grande *Daily Chronicle* in October 1900 indicated that Mormon colonists in the Grande Rhonde Valley were "remarkably industrious and intelligent" and that they were "making a success of beet raising when others have failed."[75]

Some of the settlements dating from the nineteenth century continued to experience difficulty. In January 1900 Heber J. Grant visited the St. Johns Stake in Arizona and learned from President David K. Udall that drought had killed the crops each of the preceding seven years. Elder Grant released the stake members from their mission if they chose to leave, but said he believed that the Lord would bless them if they stayed. He suggested that if they left, they might move to the Gila River Valley. Most indicated that they wanted to stay.[76] In a report to the Twelve, Elder Grant said that he had gone to the area with the idea that the colony should be discontinued. Now he believed the colonists ought to remain, their struggles notwithstanding, because they had a great work to do among the Indians. In response, President Snow said that the colonists had paid $8,000 in tithing in 1899, and he was willing to appropriate half of the amount to complete the nearby St. Johns reservoir and the stake academy. Also, Heber J. Grant was to use his best efforts to secure redemption of a mortgage on David K. Udall's farm, since it contained the water supply for the entire community.[77]

As people from Utah began an outmigration to the Big Horn Basin of Wyoming, many at first tried to discourage it, because it seemed to be robbing settlements of some of their most vigorous citizens. By late 1899, however, the general authorities had lent a sympathetic ear to those urging the advantages of the Big Horn country. By August 1901 the colonies in the basin had achieved some degree of success. Canal and railroad projects had provided water and transportation for the people of the area. In 1905 the Big Horn Basin Colonization Company negotiated a contract with the Bureau of Reclamation for the construction of a dam and reservoir on the Shoshone River to irrigate an additional 46,000 acres. By June 1905 reports indicated that 1,000 people lived in Lovell, Wyoming, the heart of the Big Horn settlement which had been founded only seven years before.[78]

Two settlement areas which still deserved the designation of colony after 1904 were situated in southern Canada and northern Mexico. Mormons had settled the colonies in southern Alberta, all within fifty miles of the United States border, first in 1887. The area around Cardston became a stake in June 1895. Settled in part as a haven for persecuted polygamists, the southern Alberta colonies enjoyed a combination of church and private support. Shortly after the turn of the century, the church and private businessmen acquired land to expand the agricultural base. In 1901 Jesse Knight, a Provo businessman, purchased 30,000 acres of land at Spring Coulee near Cardston for grazing and beet raising. C. A. Magrath, representing the Canadian Northwest Irrigating Company, successfully induced Mormons to settle on the company's land. In 1902 various church leaders organized the Alberta Colonization Company to purchase land from the Canadian government. This private company was necessary because under Canadian law a church could hold land only for charitable, educational, or religious purposes.[79] After 1905, though the Canadian colonies faced some difficulties from weather and outmigration, the situation was essentially favorable. The purchase for $99,000 of the 66,500-acre Cochrane ranch near Cardston provided an additional land base. By 1910 land on the ranch, which in 1905 had sold for $6 per acre, was going for $25 to $40 per acre, indicating an increased demand.[80]

In 1885, two years before the Canadian colonies, Latter-day Saints established settlements in northern Chihuahua in the valleys of the Casas Grandes and Piedras Verdes rivers. Centered around Colonia Juarez, these towns, together with two—Moralos and Oaxaca—which the Saints had established in the 1890s in Sonora, were consolidated in 1895 into the Juarez Stake with Anthony W. Ivins as president.[81]

Under the aegis of Mexico's dictator, Porfirio Diaz, the Mexican Colonization and Agricultural Company, made up of leading general authorities and Mormon colonists, established the colonies. In promoting settlement, the Latter-day Saints maintained close relations with Diaz. In 1901, for instance, John Henry Smith, Anthony W. Ivins, and other leaders made two visits to Diaz. Smith and Ivins told him of expenditures for schools and economic development, and Diaz said he considered the Mormons "industrious, moral, and progressive." The latter seemed to be a *sine qua non* for Diaz and his positivists or *cientificos*.[82]

By early 1908 the colony seemed prosperous. The colonists at Dublan were constructing a new canal, and Ivins was negotiating for the purchase of more land. Missionaries proselyted among the Indians with the tacit approval of President Diaz. In January 1905, for instance, Ammon M. Tenney of Dublan baptized 250 Native Americans.[83] By July 1908, however, Mexico was moving into a full-scale civil war. Unfortunately for the Mormon colonists, they backed the losing side. President Junius Romney of the Juarez Stake told the jefe (local political leader) at Casas Grandes that the Mormons stood firm for the Diaz government and that they would defend the Mexican flag. By that time bands of marauding insurgents had begun raiding Colonia Diaz. Still, the *Deseret News* continued to run stories calling Diaz a great man. Admitting he was a dictator, the *News* commended Diaz for the religious toleration and economic progress under his regime.[84]

By late 1910, as Francisco Madero's forces moved into northern Mexico, the church had sent Anthony W. Ivins to Mexico to advise the people. Ivins again affirmed that the 4,000 colonists, though unarmed, stood by the Diaz government. Since Ivins strongly supported Diaz, the First Presidency sent John W. Cannon to urge members not to take sides. Anxious for the safety of the colonists, they were particularly concerned that the winning side not oppose the church.[85]

Activities of Reed Smoot and the State Department in Washington underscored concern for the colonists. As the conflict grew in intensity, Smoot remained in contact with the State Department and on December 3, 1910, he advised the First Presidency that Diaz could not last long and urged the colonists not to take sides. In April 1911, as Diaz neared abdication, the State Department urged Ivins to get the Mormons to remain neutral. The colonists might defend their homes, but the department warned that the Diaz regime could not last.[86]

During 1910 and early 1911 conflicting reports emanated from the colonies. In late December reports indicated that Porfirista cavalrymen had rushed to the aid of the colonists and were driving out insurgent forces. The *Herald-Republican* published these favorable reports, which may have been an attempt to make the Republican administration look good, since Ivins's journal for the same period indicates a rapidly deteriorating situation. In February 1911 Ivins and Romney again discussed conditions with the jefe at Casas Grandes. After the discussion, they prepared a letter setting forth the unarmed condition of the colonists. They again offered to support Diaz, but asked not to be required to shed blood. On May 25, 1911, Diaz resigned, turning the government over to Francisco Madero.[87]

During the first half of 1912, though Madero maintained peace throughout most of Mexico, the situation in Chihuahua deteriorated even further. In February 1912 bands of guerrillas nominally under Pascual Orozio had begun to search Mormon homes for horses, guns, and ammunition. Irregular troops forced the colonists at Diaz to pay taxes to support the rebel cause. In April the colonists purchased forty-eight rifles, some pistols, and 25,000 rounds of ammunition in the United States to defend themselves, but members of the First Presidency were so concerned that the guerrilla forces might consider this a hostile act that they telegraphed the agent not to buy more weapons until instructed to do so. On May 4 guerrillas robbed and murdered J. D. Harvey in full view of his three small sons, and on July 2 insurgents killed William Adams as he left his home to attend his wife's funeral.

The Madero government seemed powerless to protect the Saints, and the United States government offered little more than diplomatic protests.[88] On May 6, 1912, the American consul warned the guerrillas not to molest the Mormon colonists. On July 8, Smoot and others tried unsuccessfully to obtain assurances of protection from the Taft administration. By July 22 the rebels were looting, and after a request from Junius Romney, the First Presidency and Twelve approved the appropriation of $5,000 to assist in defense. This helped little; on July 28 rebels had begun to disarm the colonists, and refugees from Dublan and Juarez fled for El Paso, Texas. The First Presidency authorized Ivins to expend any funds necessary to assist, and by August 11 the people from Diaz joined those from Dublan, Juarez, Pacheco, and Garcia on the move north. By August 15, 1912, most of the colonists huddled at El Paso "with little except their clothing" and their lives. After the exodus from Mexico began, Smoot requested $100,000 from the government for relief of the homeless.[89]

The ravages of civil war left President Romney with little alternative but to request a release from the mission. The First Presidency granted the request in early August 1912, indicating, however, that those who wanted to return to their former homes should feel free to do so. On October 4 Romney again outlined the status of the colonists and four days later the First Presidency discussed the conditions with the leaders, particularly Bishop Joseph C. Bentley of Juarez, who expressed a desire to return. Again, the First Presidency reaffirmed their previous answer indicating that whether the saints returned "on their own responsibility," or decided to relocate in the United States, "the Church would assist them as far as possible."[90]

On October 10, 1912, the First Presidency issued an open letter to the Mexican colonists, releasing the ward and stake officers of the Juarez stake and urging colonists to use every lawful means to protect their rights and title to property. Those who wished to remain in the United States should take steps to resettle, with the aid of a refugee committee. Those who wanted to return to Mexico could remain as near as possible to the border. The church did not advise colonists to return, but those who did went with the blessing of church leaders.[91]

Throughout these events Reed Smoot had worked with the Taft administration to secure assistance for the bedraggled refugees. Taft assigned the army to provide relief, and Smoot believed that the president had done all he could. Smoot thought he could have persuaded Taft to intervene in the affair, but Ivins had opposed this and had told Smoot that he was thankful for all Taft had done. After the Wilson administration took office in March 1913, Smoot went to visit each of the cabinet officers. He found secretary of state William Jennings Bryan less cordial than the others, but they did discuss the Mexican situation and Bryan asked Smoot to be sure to let him know "about conditions in northern Mexico."[92]

In retrospect, it seems probable that no policy, with the possible exception of full-scale U.S. military intervention, could have prevented the expulsion of the Mormon colonists. The church members had backed the losing side in a civil war and had the misfortune to live in perhaps the most unstable portion of the country during Madero's brief tenure. Madero was deposed by the unprincipled Victoriano Huerta in 1913.

Unlike Taft, Woodrow Wilson began an aggressive policy aimed at forcing Mexico to overthrow Huerta and to adopt a democratic, rather

than a revolutionary, process for settling their disputes and establishing new governments. In April 1914 the policy of the United States led
to a confrontation with the Mexican navy and the occupation of Vera
Cruz by American marines. Later, Pancho Villa's invasion and murder
of American citizens in Columbus, New Mexico, led to an American
expeditionary force under General John J. Pershing which pursued
Villa into Mexico. Where Reed Smoot had previously favored Taft's passive policy, he now wanted to go much further than Wilson in his ag-
gression against Mexico.[93]

Joseph F. Smith was in California during the Vera Cruz episode, and
Anthon H. Lund and Charles W. Penrose had to handle the church's
affairs. They again sent Anthony W. Ivins to Mexico to deal with the
problems of Mormon refugees who might be expelled as a result of the
conflict.[94] During the unstable days of 1915, as Venustiano Carranza
tried to consolidate his power against opponents like Villa and Emi-
liano Zapata, marauding bands of Mexican irregulars raided and murdered throughout the colonies. On March 10, 1916, two telegrams
came from Reed Smoot indicating that the secretary of war wanted the
First Presidency to order the Mormons to leave Mexico because of the
danger of massacres. Anthon Lund telegraphed Bishop Bentley telling
him to do as he thought best. A telegram from J. H. Hurst the same
day indicated that many of the Mormons had already fled to the border
and safety. Church leaders tried to get the remainder to leave, but in
some cases this was impossible because Villa stood between them and
El Paso.[95]

Between March 1916 and January 1917 Pershing pursued Villa in
northern Mexico. Anti-American sentiment rose and guerillas attacked some colonies. As Pershing withdrew, the State Department
recommended that the Mormon colonists leave also. Many left, but
some did not, and several were tortured and slain. In February and
March 1917, as Mexico promulgated a new constitution with Carranza as president, unregenerate Villistas continued their raids on
Casas Grandes, Dublan, and Juarez. In June Hispanic Mexicans at
Colonia Morales disarmed the Mormons and occupied the land, virtually eliminating the colonies in Sonora. By September 1917 only a
tithe remained of 5,000 colonists who had previously occupied farms
and homes in northern Mexico.[96]

Early in April 1917 the United States declared war on Germany and
entered the First World War, which had ravaged Europe since 1914.

Mexico quieted somewhat during World War I, but after the war the First Presidency tried to resolve the remaining problems. In November 1920 they authorized remuneration for the services of Anthony W. Ivins. In 1921 the government of Carranza's successor, Alvaro Obregon, agreed to pay $100,000 for the land occupied by squatters during the civil wars. In June 1921 Obregon asked land owners who remained to file claims with the Mexican government for damage compensation, and in October the government returned 115,000 acres to LDS owners. In November 1922 President Grant, on a tour of the colonies, held conferences in Dublan and Juarez. He found the people generally in good spirits, even though only a small number had returned. Colonia Diaz housed no colonists, as a good number of the buildings had been burned and Hispanic-Mexicans had generally occupied the land. In 1924 attempts to revitalize the colonies by the introduction of a cotton gin led to the immediate cultivation of 700 acres at Dublan.[97]

The Mexican government struck another blow at the colony and the efforts of the church in Mexico in February 1926 when it decided to enforce a set of long-dormant anticlerical decrees. As early as 1855 the Mexican government had supported an anticlerical movement to confiscate property owned by the Roman Catholic church, said to include nearly one-fourth of Mexico's wealth. The Constitution of 1857 and laws drafted in accordance with that basic document declared all church property confiscated and curbed other religious activities. Porfirio Diaz had suspended the laws following his rise to power in 1876, but the Constitution of 1917 and the administrations of presidents Alvaro Obregon and Plutarco Elias Calles brought about the reinforcement of anticlerical sentiment. In February 1926, following some criticism of the government by the Catholic archbishop of Mexico, Jose Mora y del Rio, President Calles issued decrees effective on July 3 prohibiting foreigners from acting in religious functions, placing all schools under the direction of the state, prohibiting churches from owning property, and forbidding church leaders from commenting on political affairs.[98]

The LDS church moved quickly to comply with the regulations. On February 22, 1926, the church evacuated all foreign LDS missionaries. The church closed its schools on February 27, then reopened as private associations on March 4. On August 21 the church issued an official statement indicating "complete compliance" with the laws "requiring all religious teachers to be native born." President Joseph C. Bentley of the Juarez Stake indicated that the church now depended on native-born LDS people to keep the organization functioning.[99]

By the late 1920s only the Mormon settlements in Chihuahua could rightly be called colonies. A tenth of the original settlers remained, and although their existence had stabilized somewhat, anticlerical and anti-American sentiment on the part of the Mexican people and government and problems in the operation of farms and businesses continued to plague them. These colonies would never again play the role in church history they had played in the period between the late 1880s and the late teens.

On the other hand, the Canadian colonies, settlements in the Big Horn Basin, and other smaller ventures such as those near Ramah, New Mexico, and Delta, Utah, had clearly passed beyond colonial status. In those places, the settlers faced problems with aridity and frost common to all settlements and not unique to the Mormons. The church had abandoned marginal ventures like the Iosepa colony, and, in general, the days of church promotion and assistance of settlement had passed. Some groups of settlers still turned to the church for assistance with irrigation ventures, but these were exceptions rather than evidence of a general pattern.

In retrospect, it seems clear that a number of general patterns in the church attitudes toward cooperation and individualism had solidified by 1930. Many of them continued in one form or another to the present time. First, the church allowed, and in many cases even encouraged, the transformation of cooperative and colonization programs from ecclesiastical to private ventures, with individual rather than cooperative ownership. This was particularly the case when such businesses seemed to compete with private enterprise. On the other hand, the church leadership expected a high degree of intergroup cooperation and help, particularly for needy members. Secondly, the church leadership generally took a proprietary attitude toward the Mormon homeland, or Mormon core area. In general, they tended to favor public—at times governmental—action to protect the products and businesses of Utah, Idaho, and Arizona while opposing intervention in the marketplace in general. Thus, tariffs, railroad rate regulation, and watershed control received official support. Finally, in what was apparently an early manifestation of a trend that was to become more apparent in later times, the church leadership took a publicly announced hands-off attitude toward labor organization while privately—often as individuals—they supported management in labor disputes. Favoring cooperation over conflict, they tended generally to see the businessmen as promoters of order and organizing workers as instigators of strife.

In sum, then, the origins of the general patterns which have continued to the present in the church's attitude toward cooperation and individualism seem apparent. Within the church itself cooperation and paternalism remained the rule. Outside the church, particularly in the economic realm, competition and the market were allowed to dominate the general pattern of Mormon life.

11

The Church and Its Missions

SINCE THE LATTER-DAY SAINTS accepted the church as the restoration of primitive Christianity, they felt an immediate need to spread the word to others unfamiliar with the restored gospel. Within two months of the organization in 1830, Samuel H. Smith, a brother of Joseph Smith, left to distribute copies of the Book of Mormon and to contact potential converts. From there missionaries carried the gospel throughout various areas of the Northeast and Midwest and into eastern Canada. In the mid-1830s Wilford Woodruff and others began proselyting in the South.

Perhaps the most important missionary development in the nineteenth century was the opening of the British Mission by Heber C. Kimball and others of the Twelve in 1837. The dislocations of modernization and industrialization seem to have prepared the British for the Latter-day Saints' message. From these proselyting efforts, numerous converts joined the Saints in Nauvoo and, after the movement to Utah, came to settle in the Great Basin. By 1870 these Britishers together with European immigrants, especially those from Scandinavia, made up the majority of the adult population of Utah.[1]

Missionary work continued at an accelerated if difficult pace into the late nineteenth century. In the 1880s the elders opened missions in Latin America, the Pacific Islands, and the Middle East. Violence and exclusion greeted missionaries in Europe and the American South. Between 1890 and 1900 more than 6,000 missionaries left the intermountain West to proselyte throughout the world.

The efforts to spread Mormonism throughout the world passed through three stages during the period from 1900 to 1930. In the first stage, from 1900 to the outbreak of the First World War in 1914, missionaries found their work extremely difficult. In part because of attitudes remaining from the nineteenth century and in part because of the accusations leveled at the church during the Smoot investigation and the succeeding muckraking attacks, anti-Mormon propaganda increased to a fever pitch in many parts of the world, peaking after 1908. In the United States, hostility led to attacks on missionaries and church property in various cities and towns, particularly in the South. In Europe, well-organized campaigns led to mobbings in England, arrests of missionaries in many countries, and the expulsion of missionaries from several countries including Germany and Sweden. These problems, compounded by the poor linguistic, cultural, and educational preparation of many of the missionaries, led to enormous difficulties for proselyting programs.

Many of the problems, including anti-Mormon violence, persisted into the second stage, which began with the outbreak of World War I in Europe and continued until about 1922. Challenges such as securing entry into foreign nations and lack of eligible candidates for missions added new obstacles. The continuation of anti-Mormon campaigns characteristic of the prewar period exacerbated these difficulties, especially immediately after the war.

During the third stage from the mid- to late-1920s missionaries began to experience a more favorable reception. Although, as studies have shown, the image of the church did not become generally favorable in the United States until the mid-1930s, the attitude toward the Mormons had begun to change. The work of nationally known political leaders and businessmen like Reed Smoot, James H. Moyle, J. Reuben Clark, and Heber J. Grant helped in this regard. In addition, the enlightened leadership of mission presidents like B. H. Roberts and James H. Moyle in the eastern United States, Charles A. Callis in the South, and Joseph W. McMurrin in California helped in promoting effective missionary work. Although the world-wide tour of David O. McKay and Hugh J. Cannon in 1920 helped lift the spirits of members, and although missionaries generally escaped violence in the late twenties, the church did not enjoy a favorable image outside the United States until quite recently.

The church membership faced problems in carrying on its proselyting work at the turn of the century, in part because of the relatively inadequate education of those called on missions. As indicated earlier, Utah's educational system ranked on par with those of other states in the nation at the time, but the skills and knowledge required for teaching the gospel were different than the three Rs generally learned in the elementary schools. At the turn of the century the church had not developed systematic lesson programs in either the auxiliaries or the priesthood quorums, relatively few children went on to high school, and the seminary and institute systems did not exist.

A number of church leaders and members recognized this problem and proposed ways of dealing with it. Stake president Richard W. Young suggested a missionary training school, and the members of the First Council of the Seventy proposed that the church school system develop programs to meet this challenge. In cooperation with the First Council, the General Church Board of Education agreed to open a missionary course in 1900 at Brigham Young College in Logan, Latter-day Saints University in Salt Lake City, Brigham Young Academy in Provo, and Latter-day Saints Academy in Thatcher, Arizona. The course as outlined was to consist of seven subjects: themes and arguments along gospel lines, Talmage's *Articles of Faith*, natural and revealed religion, language, biblical history, Book of Mormon history, and church history. The course ran for six months, and though the church schools charged no tuition for the class, stake presidents were expected to provide board and lodging for the students.[2]

After the first experimental class, the church expanded the curriculum to include training in singing, missionary correspondence, theme writing, argumentation, and extemporaneous speaking. The church leadership approved an additional number of academies to host the program in succeeding years. Missionary courses continued throughout the decade, supplemented with a home study program approved in August 1911 and administered by Bishop Edwin S. Sheets of Salt Lake City.[3]

Although the class helped improve the skills and knowledge of those who participated, its success in actually raising the calibre of missionaries was minimal. A survey showed that of the class of ninety which entered the Brigham Young College in September 1900, only thirteen were actually called on missions and all but eleven of the remainder dropped out of the program. The class at Latter-day Saints University produced similar results. In commenting on the class system, B. H. Roberts and J. Golden Kimball reported that most seemed to have regarded the class "as a matter of convenience." Nevertheless, though the class was never entirely successful, it did improve during the years after 1904.[4]

Still, as late as 1930 the level of education among missionaries remained a problem. In November 1930 David O. McKay recommended that the church provide a year's training for missionaries before calling them.[5] The church did not implement this suggestion, but the changes in the church educational and auxiliary system, the adoption of the seminary and institute programs, and the increasing tendency of Americans—Mormon and non-Mormon—to attend postelementary schools helped alleviate this problem.

Many missionaries benefited from advice and teachings of their parents, and others undoubtedly solved some problems by reading from works like the *Elder's Reference* and Francis M. Lyman's "Notes . . . [for] Missionaries." The *Elder's Reference*, for instance, instructed missionaries how to comport themselves, perform ordinances, meet people, distribute tracts, care for themselves, and deal with members of the opposite sex. Lyman's "Notes" provided helpful advice on such matters as mission rules and etiquette. Lyman admonished missionaries to preach the first principles, to avoid too much visiting and sightseeing, and to avoid making promises to do favors when they got home. They were not to encourage the Saints to emigrate immediately, but to "maintain the work abroad in the earth," in order to "gain strength to be able to stand when they do gather to Zion." Married women were not to be baptized without the consent of their husbands, nor children without the approval of their parents.[6]

Later, the church supported these programs by the establishment of a mission home in Salt Lake City. The leaders expected missionaries to go there for a week's instruction prior to departing for the field. In February 1925 a new facility was dedicated at 31 North State Street. LeRoi C. Snow, son of the late president Lorenzo Snow, was called to be president, but after two years an investigation by David O. McKay found his methods "dictatorial and unreasonable." This led to the appointment of John H. Taylor in his stead.[7]

The First Presidency urged stake presidents and bishops to pay attention to the spiritual, intellectual, and physical condition of prospective missionaries as well. Shortly after the turn of the century, the church leaders asked stake presidents not to recommend men in poor physical condition since missionary work required irregular hours and demanding schedules. A circular letter in 1913 discouraged bishops from calling men who did not observe the Word of Wisdom. In addition, they were urged to seek out prospective missionaries with specific linguistic, stenographic, and bookkeeping skills for some missions. After December 1922 each prospective missionary had to have a doctor's endorsement of physical fitness, and after September 1926 each had to be vaccinated for smallpox and inoculated for typhoid fever before entering the mission field. By the late 1920s President Grant still expressed concern over some young men who were sent even though they were "practically unfit . . . for the missionary service." Stake presidents and bishops, he said, needed to be certain that the prospective missionary observed the Word of Wisdom, paid tithing, had "some knowledge of the Gospel," was willing to teach, was in good physical condition, and had funds to stay in the field.[8]

Even with the rules which prevailed, some missionaries found themselves in difficulty. In November 1914 LeGrand Richards wrote from Holland that he had found missionaries in Switzerland and Germany who used "their tea and coffee and tobacco on the sly and exhibit[ed] a very different spirit" from others, particularly those he found in England. In January 1914 Grant Ivins in Japan indicated that five of the elders in the mission had visited houses of prostitution and one of them had contracted a venereal disease.[9]

Initially, the church faced a serious problem securing money to finance the missionary system. At the turn of the century with the Church's heavy debt, President Snow was reluctant to commit funds either for opening new missions or expanding the work already in progress.[10] Nevertheless, pressure to expand the work came from various sources. In 1900 President George Q. Cannon suggested opening new missionary fields by drawing elders from some of the old ones. At the quarterly meeting of the Twelve in October 1901 a number of the apostles favored opening new missions in those areas where the gospel was not being preached. The one glaring deficiency seemed to some to be the countries of South America. President Snow proposed to help in expanding the missionary work by having the apostles, who seemed to be at home much of the time, take their places among the nations.[11]

The church's financial problems prompted a decision in 1900, honored as often in the breach as in the observance, to send missionaries out without money. Missionary support was a great financial burden on the community. In Cache Valley, for instance, approximately 21,000 Saints supported about ninety missionaries—one to every 225 inhabitants. In Colorado the Western States Mission decided to experiment with allowing elders to work during the day to earn the money necessary to support themselves and do missionary work at night.[12]

In spite of the rhetoric of traveling without funds, or in the biblical phrase, "without purse or scrip," and the apparent intention to have elders earn their own way in the mission field, in actual practice the burden generally fell upon the parents, relatives, or savings. Ben E. Rich, for instance, estimated that the cost of supporting a missionary in the southern states in 1904 ranged from $8 to $20 per month. In 1905 Joseph F. Smith had four sons out on missions at the same time. His monthly expenditure per missionary was in the mid- to upper range of Rich's estimate. In 1908 President Smith sent his son Franklin $20 per month. By mid-1909 Franklin Smith was convinced that this was insufficient. He reported that of thirty-five elders he knew in the British mission only five were receiving less than $25 per month and some were receiving as much as $30. Joseph F. Smith thought that this was a tremendous drain on the parents, but there is little doubt that he considered such support to be justified.[13]

At times the burden was too great for families to bear. One missionary who had labored two-and-a-half years in Sweden spent all his money, and his father had none to send him. The family did not even have enough to buy coal to heat the house. Upon learning of the situation, the First Presidency lent the boy $25, and Anthon H. Lund gave the father $5 to buy coal. In at least one case, the First Presidency excused a man called as a mission president when they learned that he would have to sell his house to finance the mission.[14] After 1902 the church's financial situation had improved somewhat, and the church began to provide financial aid to mission presidents and their families.

The church's policy on dress and literature caused some additional expense for missionaries. Church rules did not allow missionaries to wear suits and ties; they were expected to don a Prince Albert coat and top hat. Some of the Twelve opposed such a "uniform" as it singled out the missionaries for persecution and constituted a sizable financial burden. The majority disagreed. Church leaders expected missionaries to provide themselves with the books and tracts they needed.[15]

Upon receiving their calls missionaries were set apart in the Salt Lake Temple annex before they departed for their fields of labor, most of which were in the United States. In January 1901, for instance, of a total of 1,739 missionaries, 985 served in the United States with the largest number (363) in the southern states. In European countries 275 served in Great Britain, 171 in Scandinavia, 80 in Germany, 37 in Switzerland, and 33 in the Netherlands. In the Pacific Islands 43 served in Samoa, 37 in New Zealand, 32 in Hawaii, and 21 in Australia. The smallest number (5) labored in Turkey. Similar proportions seem to have obtained in other years during the first decade of the century at least.[16]

A number of the general authorities believed that at least 1 percent of the church population ought to be on missions all the time. In 1909 George F. Richards calculated that this would be nearly 3,000, where at the time there were slightly under 2,000. Only eight of the sixty stakes had 1 percent of the population on missions, and some had as few as one-half of 1 percent. Richards realized that this effort would cost the church a great deal, but he was convinced that a campaign to pay tithing comparable to the effort then being waged to get people to keep the Word of Wisdom would provide the funds.[17]

Even though the church did not reach Richards's goal, as the financial problems receded in 1906, mission expansion accelerated. In 1906 more than a thousand missionaries entered the field, and between 1907 and 1913 an average of more than 900 entered annually, which was higher than the average of any equivalent previous period in the church's history.[18]

During World War I, the number of missionaries in the field declined. In 1916 the number had dropped to 722, and in 1918 only 245 served. During the 1920s this trend reversed, and an average of more than 1,000 missionaries went out each year between 1922 and 1930. Changing church policy helped increase this number. In August 1928, for instance, the First Presidency challenged each ward in the church to send two missionaries during the year.[19]

At the turn of the century, church leaders had done little to systematize the techniques of missionary work. In a meeting of the Twelve in April 1900, John W. Taylor suggested that such systematization was necessary and proposed a meeting of the First Presidency, Apostles, and presidents of the Seventy to accomplish the purpose. A committee consisting of Francis M. Lyman, John W. Taylor, and Matthias F. Cowley was appointed to plan the coordination effort.[20]

After conference meetings on April 9, 1900, the general authorities held a session with mission presidents. They discussed methods of proselyting and promotion of missionary work and made suggestions for better missionary procedures. Suggestions included lectures delivered in the large cities and letters of introduction from Governor Heber M. Wells to the governors of all states.[21]

Some members of the church believed that going from door to door passing out tracts—"tracting" in common parlance—was quite out of date. In an article in the *Improvement Era* in June 1910, Eugene L. Roberts, chairman of the BYU athletic department and a former Swiss missionary, argued that in the climate of Progressive America missionaries in the field often felt frustrated because their tracts and teachings did not relate to the central problems of the people. Tracts tended to concentrate on "dogma and authority." People, Roberts argued, "no longer ask which is the true church; but they are keenly interested in what principles must underlie social systems." He suggested that temperance was a relevant question. He also suggested that the elders might follow the lead of some missionaries in New Haven, Connecticut, who attended classes at Yale, worked with the YMCA, and worked "shoulder to shoulder with the Yale boys in the missionary activities among the slums of New Haven."[22]

Though they did not accept Roberts's suggestions, in an attempt to improve the success rate of missionaries, the First Presidency in late 1918 and throughout 1919 began to change some procedures. In November 1919 the church adopted a new system to follow up missionary contacts. The names of those who were contacted in certain missions in the United States were sent to Zion's Printing and Publishing Company at Independence, Missouri. From there the publisher sent copies of the *Liahona* (a monthly magazine) and other free literature to each individual. Thereafter, the staff sent a letter of inquiry asking if they wanted to subscribe to the *Liahona*. Money for the program came partly from the First Presidency and partly from special contributions.[23] Beyond this, church administrators and mission presidents developed a number of innovations. In 1924 and again in 1930 the church prepared sets of slides which they offered to missionaries. Following his appointment as Eastern States Mission president in 1928, James H. Moyle produced sixteen-millimeter movies on the ruins of Central America. He also instituted a series of radio programs.[24]

In spite of suggestions like those made by Eugene Roberts and the use of motion pictures, slides, and radio broadcasts, missionaries generally used tracting as a means of contacting potential converts. As a result, missionaries tended to focus on church-sponsored literature, particularly the Book of Mormon. In part because of complaints about the bad grammar in a work revealed by the Lord, B. H. Roberts proposed a new interpretation of the translation process. On May 30 and 31, 1907, Roberts presented his views at a joint meeting of the First Presidency, Council of the Twelve, and First Council of the Seventy. To many of the brethren, Roberts's position that Joseph Smith did not actually see the words in English through the Urim and Thummim but was inspired with the thoughts and rendered them in his own language explained the poor grammar in the book. Anthon H. Lund described Roberts's presentation as "masterly," and George F. Richards commented that the group "agreed that his theory is most nearly correct of any considered if not perfectly correct." Roberts published this position in his book *New Witness for God in America*.[25] Roberts also wrote volumes 2 and 3 of *New Witness* to help members and missionaries in their understanding of the Book of Mormon and charges leveled against it. Roberts reviewed the problems ranging from the absence of horses, goats, and some other animals before the European conquest of America and the absence of iron and steel among the Indians. He also rebutted the various theories of the origin of the book, including the Campbellite theory that Joseph Smith wrote the book, the Spaulding manuscript theory, the Sidney Rigdon authorship theory, and the Riley theory that the book developed from Joseph Smith's hallucinations.[26]

In September 1909 James E. Talmage finished the manuscript for *The Great Apostasy* for use in missionary and educational work. This book dealt with the apostasy of members of the primitive church from the teachings of Christ, and the syncretism of Christian, pagan, and Greek ideas. Originally designed as a lesson manual for the YLMIA, in 1910 the book was published in a small missionary size for use in proselyting work.[27]

After the Book of Mormon, perhaps the most important tract was Joseph Smith's *Story*, which the church reprinted substantially as it appears in the *Pearl of Great Price*. In the tract version there followed an explanation of the church's history after the ordination of Joseph and Oliver, including the visitations in Kirtland, the death of Joseph Smith, and the migration to Utah. Thereafter it included a discussion of the Solomon Spaulding theory, together with the story of the discovery of Spaulding's manuscript in Honolulu, its present location, and the explanation that it did not resemble the Book of Mormon.[28]

Perhaps the most prolific tract writer for the church was Charles W. Penrose, successively editor of the *Deseret News*, member of the Council of the Twelve, European Mission president, and member of the First Presidency. His tract, *What Mormons Believe*, discussed the basic principles of the gospel, together with the apostasy, restoration, redemption of the dead, the Book of Mormon, celestial marriage, church government, auxiliary organization, continuous revelation, and divine authority.[29] Some of the most widely distributed and longest continually used literature ever published by the church were Penrose's twelve *Rays of Living Light* tracts. The pamphlets covered basic principles by taking the reader through a systematic program of gospel study. The first tract included a discussion of the need for true religion and an attack on the doctrine of justification by faith alone. Tract Number 2 dealt with the nature of God and the Godhead. Continuing the discourse on the first principles, tracts Numbers 3 and 4 discussed the doctrine of repentance, baptism, the gift of the Holy Ghost, and other spiritual gifts. Tract Number 5 dealt with the nature of authority and outlined the difference between the Melchizedek and Aaronic priesthoods. Number 6 considered the apostasy from the primitive church and emphasized the prediction of this apostasy by Christ and the Apostles. Numbers 7, 8, and 9 dealt with the restoration, the story of the Book of Mormon, and the need for continuous revelation in the church. Numbers 10 and 11 discussed work for the dead, the mercy of God, and the eternality of the family. Tract Number 12 considered the positive aspects of the public image of the Mormons.[30]

Another tract which continued to serve the church missionary system was Ben E. Rich's *Friendly Discussion*. Rich, at various times mission president in both the southern and eastern states, wrote the tract in the form of a dialogue between a missionary and others about the gospel. The tract moves through the first principles, dealing with the nature of God, baptism, apostasy, and other topics.[31]

Missionaries used several tracts less widely known today. One was R. M. Brice Thomas's *My Reasons for Leaving the Church of England*. This discussion, written by a British convert, began with a consideration of the question of apostasy as it related to the Church of England and Thomas's desire to determine the nature of primitive Christianity. From there Thomas considered the basic doctrines of the primitive church, followed by a discussion of the principles which changed as a result of the apostasy. Thomas then told of his conversion to the Church of Jesus Christ, and the features of the church which impressed him.[32] Another less widely known tract was B. H. Roberts's *The Mormon Character*. This defense of the Mormons likened the defamation then being used against them to the charges of cannibalism leveled at early Christians. From that point, Roberts used statistical evidence, quotations from friendly outsiders, and a discussion of such matters as plural marriage and the Mountain Meadows Massacre as a means of defending the church against defamatory charges.[33]

Samuel O. Bennion, president of the Central States Mission, thought the church should use Joseph Smith's "inspired translation" of the Bible. The First Presidency said that it was not, properly speaking, a translation at all, but rather an inspired revision of parts of the Bible which the commandment of the Lord led the Prophet Joseph Smith to make in the margin of the King James translation. In their view Joseph Smith had not completed the revision at the time of his death, and though the church owned a copy of the manuscript, the spirit of the Lord had not indicated they should use it.[34]

The First Presidency and Twelve organized the missionary system with additional supervisory assistance from the First Council of the Seventy. The church leadership divided the United States into missions made up of several states. Missionaries served under the general supervision of a mission president and under the immediate supervision of a senior missionary within the locality, or "conference," as they were then called. Conferences would be equivalent approximately to what would be referred to as a district or zone in the current mission system. While the missionaries were generally men in their early twenties, the presidents were usually prominent laymen or members of the First Council of the Seventy.

In Europe the system was somewhat different. One of the Twelve served as European Mission president with offices in London. Otherwise, the mission system was organized much as in the United States except single countries or groups of countries rather than groups of states usually constituted missions.

Missions in other parts of the world were generally supervised by a mission president called from among the leading laymen or members of the First Council of the Seventy. At times, as with the opening of the Japanese Mission by Heber J. Grant, and the opening of a number of missions in Latin America by Melvin J. Ballard, members of the Twelve would preside over missions, but this was not generally the case.

The greatest success in conversions appears to have come in the United States and western Europe. In 1900 statistics for Europe revealed that the number per missionary ranged from a high of nine in the Netherlands to a low of 1.5 in Great Britain. Membership in the missions grew from 58,000 to nearly 81,000 between 1907 and 1913, an increase of 40 percent. At the same time, church membership in the stakes, presumably by natural increase and immigration, increased from 289,000 to 351,000, or 21 percent. The number of members in missions grew from 82,000 in 1914 to 107,000 in 1921, a 30 percent increase. From 1922 to 1929 the membership in missions grew by 32 percent.[35]

Perhaps the one feature of the mission system which is difficult to explain in rational terms is the conversion process. Converts were touched by the spirit and came to see Mormonism as true and as a means of altering and enriching their lives. In 1905 a national magazine published a first-person account of a conversion. The family was converted because of the promise of the establishment of the "Kingdom of God on earth . . . somewhere in the mysterious wonderful West." Mormonism promised "a fresh world beyond the veil of faith." In addition, the close correspondence of the Book of Mormon and the New Testament assisted conversion.[36]

The Southern States Mission was the most successful in the church during this period. The success of the mission is an example of the strengthening of two opposing forces at the same time. Perhaps nowhere on the earth was the church more despised and persecuted than in the American South at the turn of the century. In February 1898 the *Alcorn Democrat* of Corinth, Mississippi, urged the lynching of the elders in Jackson "quicker than . . . the most poisonous reptile which ever crawled upon the earth." The man who protected a Mormon elder or failed to guard his household was "not only a disgrace to the state but a menace to civilization," said the paper. In his annual address to the legislature in January 1900, the governor of Mississippi denounced the missionaries and recommended legislation prohibiting their preaching in the state. The month before the *Alcorn Democrat's* article, however, Elder Rodney Ashley reported from Marshall County, Mississippi, that he and his companion had just converted a lady who was looking for the true religion. She had not been able to find it, and as a last resort she contemplated joining the Catholic church. The elders contacted her, taught her the gospel, and she accepted. An employee of the Associated Press, she then began to write articles favorable to the church.[37]

Usually, the lot of the missionaries was difficult and the editorial mentioned above revealed the general attitude of southern people.

Throughout the period from 1898 to 1907 there were numerous attacks upon missionaries throughout the South. A pair of elders were kidnapped and a chapel dynamited in Georgia. Missionaries were driven from Sweetwater, Tennessee; stoned near Dover, Tennessee, and Bessemer, Alabama; shot at in Tennessee; and barely escaped mobs in Webster County, Kentucky, and Chester County, South Carolina. Two missionaries were denied the right to preach in Marietta, Georgia. In July 1905 the elders in a small town in Mississippi were jailed and fined for preaching. In January 1906 a group of North Carolina citizens burned the LDS chapel at Harker's Island. This created such a stir that the First Presidency ordered members not to hold meetings there until things quieted down.[38]

Still, the church flourished. In 1899, 500 missionaries labored in the South. In that year the southern states missionaries baptized more than 1,100 people, bringing the total members in the South to more than 10,000. In spite of the attacks, missionaries reported that conditions for preaching the gospel had never been better than in Georgia in the fall of 1900.[39]

For much of the 1920s Charles A. Callis, later a member of the Council of the Twelve, served as president of the Southern States Mission. During 1927 nearly a thousand converts joined the church in the southern states, and by 1930 authorities reported phenomenal growth in the South.[40]

The Eastern States Mission bounded the southern states on the north. Stretching through thirteen states from West Virginia to Canada, it did not enjoy the degree of success which the southern mission had. Nevertheless, in the last six months of 1897, the mission averaged twenty convert baptisms per month.[41]

The missionaries in the eastern states were not persecuted like those in the South. An article in the Pawtucket, Rhode Island, *Tribune* in October 1899, for instance, reported that the church had obtained a relatively large following in Rhode Island and the editor expressed his respect for the church.[42] However, some exceptions did exist. In June 1905, for instance, the chief of police in Springfield, Massachusetts, denied the Mormons and other missionaries the right to hold street meetings. In 1903 Mayor Seth Low of New York City also withdrew all permits to preach in the city streets. In 1916 and 1918 missionaries were fined in Pennsylvania.[43]

In April 1922 the First Presidency offered Brigham H. Roberts the choice of becoming president of the mission or replacing John Q. Cannon as editor of the *Deseret News*. Roberts and the Twelve decided that, in view of his relatively poor health and advanced age, he should head the mission. Almost immediately, protests appeared from Roberts's Republican detractors. On May 29 the First Presidency received a long letter from J. Reuben Clark, Jr., then with the State Department, expressing opposition to Roberts's nomination, and Reed Smoot and George W. McCune, the current Eastern States Mission president, seconded Clark's view. Nevertheless, Roberts was set apart and sent to the field, and President Grant sent a letter to Clark asking him not to overreact to Roberts's call.[44] After a successful mission of five years, Roberts was released and Henry H. Rolapp called in his place. Roberts expressed the view that the period had been both the happiest and saddest in his life. During his mission two of his wives died, and yet he had been able to undertake an important work among the Jewish people of New York City.[45]

Missionary work in the area was not easy. In February 1922 the ministerial association of Syracuse, New York, issued a resolution demanding that missionaries be refused permission to preach in the city. In October 1924 the Mormon-baiting Lula Shepard held a series of lectures throughout New England and New York outlining the "horrors" of Mormonism. By 1928 and 1929, however, thanks to the efforts of Roberts and Rolapp, who remained about a year and a half, and James H. Moyle, who came in November 1928, conditions had changed somewhat. Attempts to stop proselyting work in Freeport and Syracuse, New York, and in Philadelphia proved unsuccessful.[46]

Moyle's mission was itself something of a miracle. In November 1928 Heber J. Grant called Moyle, who told of his unfavorable financial situation. Moyle, however, talked the situation over with his family and particularly with his son, Henry D. Moyle, who urged him to accept the call. James H. Moyle did so and told Heber J. Grant that in spite of his own situation "he felt the greatest work in the world was bringing souls to a knowledge of the gospel and he did not want to shirk the right kind of work."[47]

Further to the west, the Central States Mission encompassed the states north of the Ohio stretching westward to the Great Plains. Though the missionaries found considerable indifference and were less successful in gaining converts than in the South, they experienced fewer serious difficulties. In fact, they reported some success and friendly feelings from Oshkosh, Wisconsin, and Chicago, the mission headquarters. The antagonism they encountered in opening Indianapolis in 1898 seemed to have been the exception rather than the rule. Some interest was aroused in September 1906, when Joseph F. Smith visited Nauvoo, the city in which his martyred father was buried, to hold a conference. The meetings were well received, and reports indicated that the "spirit of God was manifest as it has only been once before since the saints were driven out in 1846."[48]

Further to the west on the High Plains and in the Rockies was the Western States Mission with headquarters in Denver. There, reports indicated that the missionaries were enjoying some success and very little persecution. In Anaconda, Montana, in six months of 1899, eight baptisms were reported. In western Colorado, missionaries reported good success.[49]

North and west from Utah stretched the Northwestern States Mission. In 1900 a branch of the church was opened in Portland, but undoubtedly the most important development in that mission during the period was the establishment of a branch in Boise, Idaho. In February 1903 B. H. Roberts visited the Idaho capital at the request of the First Presidency, to try to locate members and hold meetings. Melvin J. Ballard, then mission president, had preceded him into the area and had found sixty-five saints, most of them employed in the state government. Many of the saints had resided in Boise for years without knowing that other members lived there. Shortly thereafter, the church organized a branch of more than 100 members.[50]

The missionaries enjoyed some success in California. Street meetings were held in San Francisco in 1900, and the church was reported doing well there and in Sacramento. Los Angeles boasted the strongest branch in the mission, but there were also branches at Oakland, San Jose, Fresno, San Bernardino, and Santa Ana. By the 1920s the church was well established in California with many cities in the Bay Area and in Los Angeles sustaining wards.[51]

Missionaries encountered stiffer resistance in several European countries than in the American South. Missionaries were not allowed in Spain or Russia, and they had some difficulty in Hungary. President Rulon S. Wells of the German Mission reported in 1898 that meetings could be held in Hanover, Berlin, and Breslau, but it was unlawful to hold divine worship in Saxony, and missionary work in Chemnitz and Dresden was particularly difficult. Missionaries might speak there, but government officials prohibited singing and praying, as well as invitations to other than dissenters.[52]

Though missionary work continued in selected German states, the missionaries began to have serious trouble. In March 1900, for instance, the government banished two elders from Hanover. An appeal to the American consul provided no help because the law allowed the banishment of obnoxious foreigners. In early 1903 pressure in Germany increased and large numbers of missionaries were deported or imprisoned under an order issued by the Prussian cabinet. As a result, a committee consisting of LeGrand Young, Franklin S. Richards, Rudger Clawson, Reed Smoot, and John Henry Smith appealed to secretary of state John Hay for help. Smoot worked through Secretary Hay to get Ambassador Charlemaign Tower to try to secure good treatment for the missionaries. President Theodore Roosevelt told John Henry Smith that his administration would do everything possible to protect the missionaries as long as they violated no law. At the same time, Francis M. Lyman, the European Mission president, and Hugh J. Cannon, German Mission president, worked to try to stop the application of the order which allowed judges to expel or imprison missionaries without due process of law.[53]

By July, however, the conditions had deteriorated and President Cannon in Berlin had received official orders to leave the country within three weeks. The church attempted to continue the work by appointing a German elder to take nominal charge while President Cannon provided actual supervision from Switzerland. Fortunately, the situation lasted only two years, and by early 1905 the ban had been lifted. In April 1905 Elder Cannon reported that proselyting was once more allowed and the mission was growing.[54]

In 1907 efforts at expulsion had begun again in Germany. By October German members had been subjected to continual harassment and three missionaries had been expelled. Harassment continued into early 1909, when Robert J. Thompson, United States consul in Hanover, tried to outline some of the reasons for the anti-Mormon actions. Charges included disorderly conduct and encouraging emigration. In May 1909 Smoot called on secretary of state Philander C. Knox to try to secure the assistance of Ambassador Napoleon Hill at Berlin to see that "Mormon missionaries are treated as other missionaries," and Knox promised to deal with the matter at once. In November 1910 President Thomas E. McKay of the Swiss-German Mission reported

that six more missionaries had been banished from Berlin and persecution of the remaining elders continued. In July 1910 President
Rudger Clawson of the European Mission visited Berlin to investigate
the situation. He, too, was arrested, spent a night in jail, and was ordered to leave the city and not return. Police then conducted a raid on
an LDS meeting and took the missionaries to prison, where they were
confined for eighteen hours, then told to leave Prussia.[55] Finally, in December 1910 twenty-one missionaries, including the mission presidency, were expelled from Germany. Moving to Vevey on Lake Geneva
in Switzerland, they continued their efforts to bring the gospel to the
Swiss and German people. Winifred Graham (Mrs. Theodore Corey),
an anti-Mormon writer in England, called the Prussian expulsion of
the Mormon missionaries "indeed a noble example to other countries
who only play with fire, and do not extinguish it, heedless of un-
doubted danger."[56]

In 1900 the area north of Germany belonged to the Scandinavian
Mission, which then had a total of fifty-eight branches with 5,400
members. The mission encompassed not only Denmark, Norway, and
Sweden, but also Finland and Russia. In a 1903 tour of the European
Mission, Francis M. Lyman blessed Finland and Russia for preaching
the gospel. In January 1905 Sweden, Finland, and Russia were separated from Denmark and Norway to form the Swedish Mission. The
change was undoubtedly related to the successful movement for Norwegian independence from Sweden, which brought about the division
of the two countries in 1905.[57] By 1905 meeting houses had been
erected in Copenhagen, Christiana (Oslo), and Stockholm at considerable cost to the church.[58]

Although the church enjoyed some success in Scandinavian countries, persecution there was similar to that in Germany. Some of the
most intense opposition to the church prior to World War I appeared in
Denmark. In March 1900 Danish officials banished two elders because they encouraged people to emigrate and because of the church's
belief in and former practice of polygamy. The mission president wrote
to the government indicating that the church no longer preached the
two doctrines, but his effort was unsuccessful.[59]

In spite of some opposition from clergymen, active persecution
seems to have subsided until 1908, when Hans P. Freece, a Danish
convert, published the anti-Mormon *Letters of an Apostate Mormon
to His Son*. Freece wrote that his disillusionment began after he emi-

grated and failed to find the degree of spiritual gifts, community harmony, and equality he had expected in Utah. The revelation of information on plural marriage and conditions during the reformation of the late 1850s added to his dissatisfaction.[60] After the publication of his book, Freece began an extensive campaign against the church. In 1911 he tried to influence the Danish ambassador to the United States to adopt an anti-Mormon stance. Leo T. Hampel, a Gentile on the Salt Lake City police force, contacted the ambassador and told him that Freece's story was a pack of lies. Undaunted, Freece went on a lecture circuit in Denmark in 1911. Making assumptions from the Reed Smoot hearings, Freece claimed that both Joseph F. Smith and Francis M. Lyman were criminals. Andrew Jenson, Oluf J. Anderson, Anthon J. T. Sorenson, and Joseph K. Nicholes spent considerable time defending the church from Freece's charges, and received some support from the newspapers in Denmark for their efforts.[61] In addition, Freece and his supporters opened an anti-Mormon mission in Salt Lake City to try to convert Danish immigrants. In these efforts Freece's group obtained some assistance from the Danish consulate in Utah, which helped those wishing to return to Denmark. Since Danish law prohibited emigration, the Danish ambassador opined that Danish converts arriving in America would probably be sent home anyway.

Difficulties grew in Sweden as well as in Denmark, but were more serious as they increased in intensity. At the turn of the century, the church had experienced some progress, but Swedish regulations prohibited missionaries from visiting churches, mission houses, or schools in the country. In December 1910, however, petitions to the king from representatives of the Lutheran church asked the deportation of all Mormon missionaries. Although a mass meeting in Salt Lake City protested the deportation request, in September 1911 the Swedish government began deporting some missionaries.[62]

Similar anti-Mormon movements were evident in Norway, Holland, Switzerland, and Hungary, but they were unsuccessful. In Holland the minister of justice asked the American government to give official notice of the polygamous practices of the Mormons, but the Dutch government refused to act officially because of laws providing for religious liberty in the Netherlands. In Switzerland in December 1907 several elders were arrested in Chur in the canton of Grisons and convicted in the local court. An appeal to the supreme court of Switzerland, however, overturned the lower court ruling on the ground that any religious association was free to worship in Switzerland. In Hungary in 1911 the church also won a case which provided official recognition. In addition, the church was able to open a mission in Paris, France, in 1911, reportedly the first since all Protestant sects had been outlawed.[63]

Great Britain constituted undoubtedly the major center of missionary activity in Europe. During much of the prewar period, opposition to the Mormons grew in England, but the work seems to have been the most successful of any country in Europe. In 1899, for instance, a man from Wales charged that the Mormons were converting young girls to go to Utah. He claimed that his daughter had been enticed to leave Wales to marry a Mormon. The daughter denied this, but the bad publicity seems to have done the church little good.[64]

Beginning in 1908 anti-Mormon activity leading to violence developed in England, especially in a number of towns in East Anglia and the north of England. Anti-Mormon articles began appearing in the British press, and these were continued in succeeding years, culminating in the publication of Winifred Graham's *The Mormons*. Hans Freece was also active in the anti-Mormon campaign in England. The campaign reached its height between 1911 and 1914 and found support from at least thirty members of Parliament, principally of the Unionist faction of the Conservative party. Articles, books, and speeches warned British girls to be aware of LDS missionaries who were recruiting women to go to the United States for polygamous marriages. In addition to the publicists, a number of Anglican and Catholic clergymen including Dr. James E. C. Welldon, dean of Manchester, and Father Bernard Vaughan joined the battle against Mormonism.[65]

The church attempted to answer the charges by requesting an investigation of missionary work in England and publishing some articles on the subject. The First Presidency published a letter to the editor of the *London Times* countering the charges, denying that the emigrants were principally girls, and affirming that the church currently disapproved of plural marriage. In April 1911 a reporter for the *London Times* interviewed Anthon H. Lund in Salt Lake City on the subject.[66]

Perhaps the worst outrages took place at Birkenhead and Nuneaton. In Birkenhead in April 1911 a mob attacked the meetinghouse, smashed the windows, and injured a number of people. At Nuneaton in June 1912 the mob battered the missionaries, and tarred, feathered, and stoned sixty-year-old Elder Albert Smith. In the latter case, the courts convicted the leader of the anti-Mormon mob, R. H. Smith, for assault and forced him to pay damages.[67]

Though a number of rallies took place and the whole affair finally reached the floor of Parliament, insufficient support was found for anti-Mormon legislation. Winston Churchill, then British home secretary, indicated in 1910 under questioning on the floor of Parliament that the government had discovered no grounds to credit the charges that the Mormons were converting young women to lure them to Utah for polygamous marriages.[68]

Though the disturbances occasionally got out of hand, they were not spontaneous outbreaks, but were rather well organized. Ordinarily, the attacks would be prefaced by a rally with anti-Mormon speeches and a resolution that the Mormons leave the city. When the missionaries refused to go, they were subjected to outrages of various sorts, the worst being similar to those seen at Birkenhead and Nuneaton. The missionaries were forced to leave several small towns but were able to remain in most others. In spite of Joseph F. Smith's assertion in a letter to John P. Meakin in March 1911, that the attacks had actually increased interest in the church, statistical evidence indicates that the number of baptisms decreased. In 1910, 963 converts joined the church in England, but the average of the years from 1912 through 1914 was 61 percent lower.[69]

In Turkey violence was generally aimed not at the missionaries but at members, most of whom were Armenian Christians. Since 1894 the Armenians had been the target of an intermittent campaign of genocide. Anthon H. Lund found 101 members in Turkey in 1898, and in 1900 five missionaries served under President Ferdinand F. Hintze. By 1905 the Book of Mormon had been translated into Turkish. The successive waves of anti-Armenian attacks led the First Presidency to appropriate small amounts of money to assist the group, and in 1912 they acquired 1,200 acres of land at Moapa, Nevada, for emigrating Armenians.[70]

Perhaps the opening of the Japanese Mission in 1901 presented the most difficult situation. Heber J. Grant was called as president, even though he was heavily in debt as a result of losses during the 1890s. Louis A. Kelsch, Horace S. Ensign, and Alma O. Taylor accompanied him.[71] By early August the party had arrived in Yokohama and had settled in a boarding house. At first a number of groups exerted considerable pressure to try to prevent them from establishing the mission, but through connections of the Utah Sugar Company they were able to get in. Thereafter they made connections with people like William Rockhill Nelson of Kansas City, whose diplomatic service had given him entry into many areas in Japan. On September 1, 1901, Elder Grant dedicated the country for preaching the gospel.[72] By October 8, the preliminary efforts had been completed and the decision was made to proceed with teaching. Since Japan was largely non-Christian, they decided to teach the Bible to the people first and then to introduce other aspects of the gospel. On April 25, 1902, the missionaries performed the first baptisms in Japan.[73]

The experience of leading this mission was a difficult one for Elder Grant. He was never able to learn the Japanese language, and though the missionaries baptized some people, the mission was not particularly successful. In 1906, of the nine missionaries then resident in Japan, five were unable to speak the language and four were doing nearly all the missionary work. In many cases elders were released from the mission before they had developed any linguistic facility.[74]

In spite of the difficulties the church had experienced in Germany, Sweden, and England during the period down to 1914, the most serious disruption of church activity came during the First World War. Joseph F. Smith announced in October 1914 that the church had withdrawn missionaries from most of central and western Europe. In 1917 the British government refused to provide visas for Americans planning travel to Australia and New Zealand, thus keeping missionaries out of those areas. Missionaries from the United States found it difficult to get into England, and after the entry of the United States into the war in April 1917, the missionary force in the United States dwindled as well.[75]

In June 1916 George F. Richards left, without his family, to preside over the European Mission. For the next three years he shared wartime life in Europe with the British Saints. Between August and November 1916 he reorganized thirty-three branches, replacing the elders from the United States with local members. He called women to officiate in auxiliary organizations, including the Sunday School and YMMIA, and assigned them to do branch teaching and to pray and preach in the meetings. Women, most of whom were employed in the shops and munition factories, were called as missionaries, and each agreed to spend at least one hour each week in tracting. The last group of missionaries from the United States arrived in December 1916, and even they were restricted in their movement as they had to register with the alien office in each town into which they moved. Because of wartime dangers, Elder Richards himself was unable to visit Ireland until late September 1918.[76] In spite of—perhaps even because of—the hardships and dislocations, activity in the church actually increased in England under local leadership. Tithes increased by 20 percent in 1917 over 1916. Baptisms at 319 were higher than in 1916 (297) or 1915 (298).[77]

Following the war, however, the missionaries had difficulty in getting permission to reenter the countries from which they had been excluded. In May 1919 Richards tried to make a tour of several western European countries, and while he was permitted to enter Holland and France, he could not get into Switzerland. During the same month, Reed Smoot and George Albert Smith worked in Washington to try to secure permission to send missionaries and a new president to England. Permission was given, then withdrawn twice before it was finally granted. On the other end Richards worked with the British minister of labor, who had denied landing permits for the missionaries. Finally, on June 6 the first group was allowed to land conditionally.[78]

Throughout August 1919 British papers contained much anti-Mormon propaganda, and the admission of additional missionaries was difficult to secure. Reed Smoot continued to work with the British embassy in Washington, attempting to gain unrestricted access, but he found the consular officials adamant in their belief that such permission was unnecessary. He also found considerable objection to the idea of sending missionaries to any of the Commonwealth countries. General permission was not granted until June 1920.[79]

Securing admission to other countries was also difficult. In May 1920 permission was finally secured to allow missionaries to return to Holland, from which they had been excluded since December 1916, and on May 3 permission to go to Australia was again given. Thereafter, Smoot spent considerable time visiting the legations of Switzerland, Denmark, Norway, and Sweden, trying to secure entry for missionaries.[80]

By late 1921 fully three years after the end of the war, the situation was still not satisfactory. In October 1920 active missionary work was resumed in Germany, from which missionaries had been expelled before the war, but throughout 1921 Smoot still worked for permission to allow free entry of missionaries to Sweden, Norway, Denmark, Switzerland, Holland, and South Africa. Restrictions of various sorts remained. In general, these countries allowed some to enter, but special permission was required for each entry and the numbers were limited below that necessary to maintain an adequate missionary force. In April 1921 Sweden reversed its previous decision and excluded all missionaries.[81]

During the mid-1920s an active anti-Mormon movement continued to challenge the church in Great Britain and on the continent. Challenges for debates in January 1922 were followed by anti-Mormon mob violence in Plymouth and other cities in February and March. In June 1922 a group of Edinburgh University students raided the LDS meetinghouse and assaulted two elderly members. In June 1924 the British press published stories charging the abduction of a girl by Mormons. Missionaries experienced difficulty in securing permission to enter any of the Scandinavian countries, and feeling against the church ran high in Germany.[82]

The church, of course, tried to change the situation. David O. McKay, who had returned less than a year before from a tour around the world, was called in November 1922 as European Mission president. In 1923 John A. Widtsoe and Reed Smoot were called to visit Europe in order to try to stop official and press approval of the violent anti-Mormon activities. In London Widtsoe and Smoot held a conference with owners of the leading British newspapers and with Stanley Baldwin, former prime minister, who had served with Smoot on the allied reparations council following World War I. Particularly sympathetic was Lord Beaverbrook of the *Express*. After Beaverbrook and some of the other newspapermen learned that much of what they had been printing was untrue, they agreed not to accept anti-Mormon material. Smoot and Widtsoe visited several other countries, including Norway.[83]

From this effort, and the generally changing image of the Mormons in the United States and elsewhere, came an easing of tensions and a virtual end to the persecution of Mormons in Europe. James E. Talmage, who replaced McKay in the fall of 1924, and Widtsoe, who returned as mission president in 1927, found things much different. Newspaper articles seemed much more favorable, and missionaries seem to have experienced fewer problems during the late 1920s.[84]

The situation was, of course, not ideal, and continued sporadic anti-

Mormon activity was still evident. Several editorials attacked the church, claiming the practice of polygamy still persisted. There were, in addition, some anti-Mormon gatherings in England in 1929. Still, by 1930 the European Mission, which included the British, Swiss-German, German-Austrian, Netherlands, Danish, Swedish, Norwegian, French, Armenian, and South African missions, had 30,000 members and 700 missionaries.[85]

Several new missions were opened during the period. The French Mission reopened in 1923, the German-Austrian Mission reopened in 1925, and the Czechoslovakian Mission opened in 1929. Though there was some difficulty in Bavaria in 1924, the principal difficulty in these areas was in Czechoslovakia with its large Catholic population, which caused problems for the missionaries by entering law suits against them.[86]

In December 1925 Elder Melvin J. Ballard reopened the South American Mission. In September 1925 Ballard, German-speaking Rulon S. Wells, and Spanish-speaking Rey L. Pratt were called to go to South America to dedicate the land for the preaching of the gospel. They went first to Buenos Aires, where they baptized six German-speaking people, then on to Peru and several other South American countries, returning home in August 1926.[87]

The other missions on the American continent were in Mexico and Canada. The situation in Mexico was, of course, closely related to the conditions in Mormon colonies there. In Canada the principal problems developed in the east and central regions where the church was less well-known. In March 1922 it was reported that British anti-Mormon efforts had spread into Toronto. In June 1924 marriages performed by Mormon elders were held to be illegal in Winnipeg, a decision which was, however, overturned within a month.[88]

In the Pacific Islands missionary work continued in many areas, including Samoa and Tonga. Some difficulties arose in Tonga when, in 1922, Queen Salote Tupou instituted a ban against new American missionaries coming to the country. This was quite serious because the 1,000 native members there were generally new in the church and found it difficult to work together within the organizational structure. Efforts on the part of Reed Smoot and others eventually bore fruit in October 1924, when the ban was lifted.[89]

Missionary work was not successful in all areas and the lack of success in Japan seems to have been responsible for the closing of the mission there. Problems included the inability of the missionaries to understand the culture, the difficulty of translating LDS religious concepts into Japanese, and the antagonism toward Americans. In addition the country itself was disrupted internally as a result of the Tokyo earthquake of September 1923. In June 1924 the First Presidency announced the closing of the mission, which they justified as a result of the "almost negligible results of missionary effort." By 1927 the only organizations remaining were the MIAs, which were presided over by Elder Fujiya Nara at Tokyo, who in December 1927 was appointed presiding elder with jurisdiction over all church affairs in Japan.[90]

In 1920, after the immediate postwar turmoil, the church leadership planned an assessment of conditions in the church missions. Members of the Twelve and others were sent out. In October 1920, for instance, David O. McKay and Hugh J. Cannon were called to visit the islands of the Pacific, and Orson F. Whitney went to the Northern States Mission. In early November President Grant suggested that Elders McKay and Cannon visit missions around the globe. After visiting the Pacific islands, the two brethren went to China. In Peking, at what was possibly the high point of the journey, the two church emissaries held a service in a grove of cyprus trees in the heart of the city and Elder McKay dedicated China for the preaching of the gospel. After circling the earth, the two returned from their journey at Christmas time, 1921, having traveled nearly 62,000 miles.[91]

The publicity given the McKay-Cannon world tour within the church and favorable reports in some British newspapers masked to a great extent the underlying difficulties which the LDS church continued to face throughout the world. Although the conditions in the United States had improved by the late 1920s, active anti-Mormonism still hampered recognition of the Latter-day Saints as a legitimate expression of Christianity. Ouside the United States, if violence had subsided from the pre-World War I peak, seething anti-Mormon sentiment still remained to confront missionaries and members alike.

A number of factors fueled anti-Mormonism. The Reed Smoot investigation revived charges of plural marriage, and anti-Mormon propaganda played on those fears of the threat to the virtue of young women who seemed ripe for conversion and transportation to Utah for marriage to lecherous patriarchs. Many European countries prohibited the emigration of their citizens, and proselyting which emphasized the concept of the gathering led to opposition there. In the United States and elsewhere, traditional Protestant and Catholic churches seemed threatened, which led to ecclesiastical, and in some cases, official opposition. Indeed, continued opposition on the part of clergy and committed laity to a new religious tradition was to be expected and continues to exist today. What continued to persist by 1930, however, and what is generally absent today was the perception of the Latter-day Saints as a deviant and immoral sect.

Broad acceptance of the legitimacy of the Latter-day Saint church required a fundamental change in the perception others had of the nature of Mormonism. This included not only the question of the morality of the Mormon people but also the belief that the Latter-day Saints were recruiting potential converts for emigration. A change in the latter image required a basic revision of Mormon millennial doctrine and the recognition of that revision in the world outside the Mormon community. As long as church members believed they should gather to Zion as a place of refuge against the holocaust prior to the Second Coming, membership outside the American West would remain small and would be drawn principally from the lower ranks of society. Under those conditions, the legitimacy of the church would continue to remain open to question among patriots and among those who saw power and status as a prerequisite for legitimacy.

By 1930 this change had not taken place. Church members continued to think of the intermountain West or Utah in general and the Wasatch Front or Salt Lake City, in particular, as synonymous with Mormon country. Most missionaries came from Utah, and pronouncements by church leaders discouraged members from migrating from the mountain West. Most importantly, on an informal level, church members still continued to speak of Utah as "Zion" and to hope for a chance to gather there with the Saints.

This was a particularly serious obstacle in countries outside the United States as nationalism became an increasingly potent force in the minds and hearts of people throughout the world. Pronouncements discouraging emigration of people who were not sufficiently faithful or could not find employment did not alter the basic perception of church members and Gentiles alike that Mormons viewed the United States as a choice and blessed land to which the righteous should look for refuge. Modification of that position, and hence the internationalization of Mormonism, did not occur until the late 1960s, and it persists to some extent even today. Until that change, Mormons outside the United States would continue to carry the added burden of being viewed as members of an American church.

12

Reshaping the Latter-day Saint Image

FROM ONE POINT OF VIEW, the missionary work of the church might be considered part of a public relations effort. Missionaries tried to tell the story of the church through the literature they disseminated to make people sympathetic to its aims and doctrines and eventually to convert them to the organization. The previous chapter detailed the problems they encountered and the degree of their success.

During the nineteenth century most other principal public relations efforts were designed essentially for officials and political leaders. Thus church leaders lobbied in Washington to try to defeat the 1882 Edmunds and 1887 Edmunds-Tucker acts. During the late 1880s and early 1890s they cultivated political leaders to try to achieve statehood for Utah, to obtain amnesty for former polygamists, and to secure the return of the church's confiscated property.[1]

With some notable exceptions, however, their public activities were aimed to produce converts and only secondarily to create a favorable public image among nonbelievers. In general, public relations seems to have been furthest from the mind of church leaders as they systematically excluded Gentiles from participation in the economic and political life of Utah Territory, flaunted the practice of polygamy, and preached unusual and anathematic doctrines like blood atonement and the Adam-God theory.[2]

By the late 1890s this had begun to change, and the public relations efforts and the public image of the church passed through three broad stages in the period between the 1890s and 1930. Most important, the church leadership showed increasing concern about how the Mormons looked to others. During the first stage, from the late 1890s to about 1904, though attacks continued, the image of the church improved somewhat. Favorable comments like Richard Ely's well-researched *Harper's* article appeared, and the church leadership began to open a public relations campaign through its Bureau of Information in Salt Lake City and by publishing articles. During the second stage, which lasted from 1905 through about 1914, the image of the church suffered considerably as muckraking attacks followed the revelations of the Smoot investigation. Some favorable comment continued, but it was decidedly in the minority. The third stage began in about 1915. Mormon loyalty during World War I, coupled with activities of nationally known church leaders, politicians, and businessmen, brought about a rethinking of the previous negative image, and the image continued to improve through the 1920s and 1930s.[3]

At first, some church leaders expressed doubt about the idea of conducting a public relations campaign at all. In connection with the World Columbian Exposition in 1893, the Mormons had given equivocal signals. Several church leaders and the Tabernacle Choir attended, but they gave only reluctant approval to B. H. Roberts's abortive attempt to present the church's position at the exposition's World Parliament of Religions.[4] As late as 1900 some church leaders seemed closed to outside approaches. Brigham Young, Jr., and Francis M. Lyman, then senior members of the Twelve, both thought tourists should not be shown the Salt Lake tabernacle. Lyman thought that members who did so ought to be reported to their priesthood leaders for possible disciplinary action.[5]

Already, however, others had begun to change their views. Between 1898 and 1901 a number of members, particularly from the First Council of the Seventy and the YMMIA general board, suggested that the church open a bureau of information in Salt Lake City. In response to these suggestions, Joseph F. Smith appointed a committee to consider the question. By early 1902 church members formulated plans, and in June the leaders opened a small booth manned by representatives of the Salt Lake Stake.[6] By early 1903 it had become apparent that the small structure could not meet the volume of public demand. After considering various proposals, in July 1903 the First Presidency approved the construction of a permanent building, which they erected on Temple Square near the south entrance. Dedicated on March 26, 1904, the new building began immediately to provide information to visitors. In addition, the church leadership opened a branch office at Saltair resort. In 1903 the First Presidency approved a request that the bureau of information hold religious services for visitors. The bureau reported that more than 200,000 people had visited Temple Square during 1905, and the church representatives at the bureau gave away more than 100,000 tracts. During the summer of 1922 the bureau of information, by then administered by the Temple Block Mission, not infrequently served 3,000 people per day.[7]

That the church needed such public relations activity seems obvious today if only because of the visible manifestations of anti-Mormon sentiment and even of contempt for the Latter-day Saint people. The most celebrated examples came on the heels of the national exposure associated with the Smoot investigation of 1903–7. In 1906, for instance, Sarah Bernhardt visited Salt Lake City, and she refused to enter the Tabernacle or any other Latter-day Saint building.[8]

National women's organizations initiated a number of attacks. In 1904 the National Federation of Women's Clubs adopted a resolution barring Mormons from membership. In March 1905 the Interdenominational Council of Women declared war on the LDS church, alleging that polygamy still constituted an essential element of church doctrine. In April 1906 the Daughters of the American Revolution urged the abolition of Mormonism. Throughout the first decade of the twentieth century, the Women's Christian Temperance Union agitated for a constitutional amendment prohibiting polygamy.[9]

Continuing from the nineteenth century and stepping up somewhat during the period of the Smoot investigation, Evangelical Protestant journals carried on a barrage of abuse. The attacks of true believers, they often exhibited the characteristic pre-World War I belief in progress. In many cases the articles predicted the imminent demise of the church. One of these, an article by Baptist minister Bruce Kinney in August 1906, said the abandonment of the faith by members and the failure of missionaries to convert as many as formerly would bring about the end of Mormonism.[10]

Attacks often centered on allegations of deviant social practices and ideals of church members. Josiah Strong warned that if polygamy continued, Mormons would overrun all of the western states. Some charged that the "church thrives directly from the revenues of vice." Saltair and Reed Smoot's drug store both sold liquor, the church operated both, and it was alleged that property leased from church officials harbored houses of ill repute. Mormon women were often maligned for their alleged sexual impurity.[11]

Protestants believed they had a calling to convert Mormons to "Christianity" and to undermine the secular power of the church. In October 1900 the Reverend John D. Nutting, a Congregational minister of the Utah Gospel Mission, averred that the Mormons were feigning the abandonment of polygamy as a shield to protect themselves from the laws of the land. At a Presbyterian teachers conference, missionaries were encouraged to distribute tracts in order to convert Mormons from their ways, and a group of Methodists called Mormonism "A Black and Devilish Spot." Attacks also took the form of the citation of such assumed features of church doctrine and practice as blood atonement, which was alleged to be a mask for official murder; control by the priesthood; the alleged evil mysteries of the temple ceremonies; and the allegations that Mormons did not believe in Christ or his atonement. Later, Nutting went as far as to say the church was "simply modern *phallic paganism.*"[12]

Books published and distributed for the national market also carried attacks. Perhaps the two most offensive were I. Woodbridge Riley's biography of Joseph Smith and William Alexander Lynn's *Story of the Mormons,* both of which contained misinformation and unfavorable interpretations. American history texts, like Henry W. Elson's work on American history, continued to attack the church. In 1916 John Quincy Adams of the Auburn Theological Seminary published *The Birth of Mormonism,* which was noteworthy principally for its lack of information and flippant style.[13] Some attacks were oversensationalized and probably designed as much for the profit of their authors and distributors as to challenge the Mormons. These included motion pictures and books which focused on accounts of the Mountain Meadows Massacre, plural marriage, and atrocities of the Danites.

Perhaps the most humiliating incident was the desecration of the Salt Lake Temple by the New York impresario, Max Florence, who had pictures taken of the interior. In September 1911 Florence offered to sell the pictures to the church, threatening that if the Mormons did not purchase them, he would sell them to post card manufacturers. The First Presidency refused to accept the offer "to deal with thieves or traffickers in stolen goods." In October 1911 *Leslie's Weekly* published some of the pictures, and by mid-1912 the city had been "flooded with cheap, gaudy postcards containing pictures of the temple interior."[14]

More serious, however, was the challenge raised by an analysis of the three cuts published in the Book of Abraham by the Rt. Reverend Franklin S. Spalding, Episcopal bishop of Utah. During 1912 Bishop Spalding circulated the three facsimiles to a number of Egyptologists to find out whether the Joseph Smith explanation coincided with their reading of the material. Those who rendered opinions on the validity of the translation included A. H. Sayce of Oxford; W. M. Flinders Petrie of the University of London; James H. Breasted of Chicago; Arthur C. Mace, Metropolitan Museum of Art; C. A. B. Mercer, Western Theological Seminary; John Peters, formerly of the University of Pennsylvania; Edward (probably Eduard) Meyer, University of Berlin; and Frederich Freiherr Von Bissing of the University of Munich. In November 1912 Spalding published a pamphlet containing the views of the Egyptologists, who concluded that Joseph Smith's translation had been wrong and that the facsimiles came in fact from an Egyptian funerary document or book of the dead dating from much later than Abraham's time.[15] At first, the church leadership simply greeted the Spalding pamphlet with silence. After Spalding began distributing the work to Mormon college students, the First Presidency responded. Following on the heels of the dismissal of the three BYU professors for teaching evolution and higher criticism, Spalding's challenge seemed particularly serious.[16]

Joseph F. Smith recognized that the church could only answer for itself by gathering as much information as possible on the topic. Their efforts were hampered because the Mormons lacked the ability to deal competently with the charges since no one in the community at the time could translate ancient Egyptian. Through the good offices of Reed Smoot and Isaac Russell, a Mormon journalist living in New York City, Smith secured some of Gaston C. C. Maspero's Middle Eastern works, Ernest A. T. W. Budge's *Book of the Dead,* and other books on ancient civilizations. Janne M. Sjodahl and B. H. Roberts immediately began a counterattack. They submitted the problem to leading church writers and initiated a series of articles which ran successively from February through September 1913 in the *Improvement Era.* Members of the First Presidency and Twelve reviewed some of the articles before publication. In addition to Roberts and Sjodahl, Frederick J. Pack, Junius F. Wells, John Henry Evans, Levi Edgar Young, Dr. Robert C. Webb (actually J. C. Homans, a non-Mormon journalist), John A. Widtsoe, Richard W. Young, Osborn J. P. Widtsoe, Nels L. Nelson, Sterling B. Talmage, and Isaac Russell wrote articles for the series.[17]

From the perspective of today, perhaps the most cogent argument was that of John Henry Evans. Recognizing that none of the church writers could read Egyptian, while the scholars to whom Spalding had sent the cuts could, Evans conceded that the Joseph Smith translation of the facsimile plates might not be correct. He pointed out, however, that even if that particular translation were not accurate, it did not mean that Joseph Smith's teachings were incorrect. Many of the others were either petty or irrelevant to the central issue of Spalding's argument.[18]

Some of the anti-Mormon activity seems in retrospect to have been frankly narrow minded, but it reveals, nevertheless, the depth of the animosity toward the Latter-day Saints. In late 1910, for instance, as the battleship *Utah* neared completion, the state of Utah presented the officers a silver service with high relief engravings of the Brigham Young Monument on some pieces. Because of Young's reputation as a polygamist, immediate and progressively intense protest originated from ministers, including the Washington Ministerial Association, and women's groups, including the Daughters of the American Revolution.[19] As the protests grew, Reed Smoot and other Utah representatives responded. Smoot talked with President Taft, who said that he would "take no notice of the protest." Nevertheless, as the outcry intensified, George Von L. Meyer, secretary of the navy, thought to refuse the gift until Smoot took two non-Mormons, Daniel C. Jackling, a member of the committee which had selected the service, and John Hays Hammond, a respected mining engineer, to discuss the matter with him. The secretary seemed to want to smooth over the controversy by accepting all the pieces except those with Brigham Young's picture. Jackling refused to consider this proposal and told Meyer that the government must either accept the entire service or the state would withdraw it. Smoot and Hammond supported Jackling. The House of Representatives investigated the matter, and John Henry Smith of the First Presidency together with his son, Elder George Albert Smith, came to testify. The Utahns stood their ground, and the government accepted the service on November 6, 1911. Utah non-Mormons, with the exception of Mrs. Simon Bamberger, boycotted the presentation ceremony.[20]

Not all non-Mormons refused to insist upon fair play for the Latter-day Saints. Mrs. Bamberger's feelings seem to have grown, for instance, from a sense of outrage at the bigotry of Gentiles in the state. Many of these appeared before 1903. An article in the *Washington Post* in December 1900 congratulated the Mormons on being good Christian people. In an article in *Munsey's Magazine* in June 1900, C. C. Goodwin, formerly an anti-Mormon *Tribune* editor, said that conditions were generally good and that the Mormons were a successful, prosperous, and generally likeable people. William Glasmann of the *Ogden Standard* deplored the examples of hatred between the Gentiles and Mormons. Taking the view that conditions were really quite favorable, he said that the charges that Gentiles in Utah were ready to take up arms against the Mormons were overblown.[21]

Even after the Reed Smoot hearings, some national magazines defended the Mormons. Articles in 1908 and 1911 in *Outlook*, a Protestant journal associated with Theodore Roosevelt, branded as false the charges of extensive new polygamy and overweening political power. Mormons had recently sought political power to protect themselves, the article said, but their activity was not unlike that of Congregationalists in New England. Favorable articles also appeared in the *Outing Magazine* and the *Jewish Herald*.[22]

Many observers agreed that the Mormons had accomplished much in the fields of irrigation and community development. Church leaders, for instance, welcomed the visit of Richard T. Ely to Salt Lake City in September 1902. Ely met with general authorities and tried to inform himself on the condition of the community. Mormons were generally impressed by Ely's article in *Harper's Magazine*. The First Presidency, for instance, said that "Professor Ely took a great deal of pains to inform himself on the subject on which he has written by making a personal visit here. . . ."[23]

Beyond this, church members seem to have been accepted by many representatives in the fields of business, particular professions, and politics. George Q. Cannon and John Henry Smith were both active in the Trans-Mississippi Commercial Congress as were some second echelon church leaders like stake president L. W. Shurtliff and Utah governor John C. Cutler. John Henry Smith and some other church leaders were active in the National Irrigation Congress. John A. Widtsoe was invited on occasion to present papers at national conventions of chemists.[24]

Nevertheless, given the national image of the Mormon people with the Smoot hearings, it seems probable that an article in the *Era*, a national literary magazine, in 1903 was essentially accurate. "At present," James B. Halsey wrote, "it is hard to find anything between extravagant eulogy from its devotees and sympathizers on the one hand, and fierce denunciation and abuse from religious despisers and Gentile prejudice on the other." In fact, most of the information which appeared in the national press on the Mormons was so negative that visitors to Utah were often astonished at the reality of conditions there. The *Outlook* reported on a lady passing through Salt Lake City who was surprised to find that one Mormon gentleman "was most courteous and kind to her and to the members of her party."[25]

After Joseph F. Smith became president in 1901, the church became increasingly active in defending itself in the national media. In part this came about because, as John R. Winder put it, the leadership concluded that it was "better to represent ourselves than be misrepresented by our opponents." If anything demanded a reply it was charges and revelations incident upon the Reed Smoot investigation.[26]

In part to counteract this unfavorable publicity, the church addressed its position to the world through an open letter in 1907. A committee consisting of Orson F. Whitney, David O. McKay, Brigham H. Roberts, Franklin S. Richards, LeGrand Young, Nephi L. Morris, and James E. Talmage wrote the address. The First Presidency and the Twelve reviewed the statement in late March and published it on March 26. Whitney read it on April 5 in the conference session.[27]

The address was essentially an effort to explain church doctrine and to answer charges made in the Smoot hearings and by Protestant and women's groups. Beginning with the Mormon doctrines of revelation, restoration, and the Godhead, the discussion moved to the plan of salvation, the authority of the priesthood, the gathering, and preparation for the millennium. The statement then digressed to denigrate the efforts to "differentiate the 'Mormon' priesthood and the 'Mormon' people, by allowing that the latter are good, honest, though misguided folk, while alleging that their leaders are the personification of all that is bad." It pointed out that the "great majority" of male members hold the priesthood and that the "Priesthood and people are inseparable, and vindicated or condemned, stand together."

The statement then moved to attack various challenges. Arguing that the church did not use duplicity in its missionary efforts, the statement said that the church welcomed "enlightened investigation" and promoted education. Mormonism did not destroy the sanctity of the marriage relation, but rather regarded the lawful union of man and woman as a means to the highest and holiest aspirations.

In explaining the church's relationship to economic development, the statement denied that the church was a commercial institution but indicated that the church "claims the right," nevertheless, "to counsel and advise her members in temporal as well as in spiritual affairs." The settlements established throughout the mountain West were discussed. The statement justified investment in various enterprises on the basis of the impossibility of securing sufficient private capital.

The address then moved to church government. Nominations to church office were by revelation, but no ordination to any office in the church could come without the affirmative vote of a regularly organized branch. "True," the statement admitted, "that elective principle here operates by popular acceptance, rather than through popular selection, but it is none the less real." Tithing, in addition, was not a tax levied on members, but rather a free-will offering.

Church members' relationships to the national government were next considered. Mormons were not disloyal to the government. The Book of Mormon declared America to be the land of Zion, a land dedicated to righteousness and liberty. Church members believed in an inspired Constitution. The statement argued that the only example of disloyalty which had been found was the practice of plural marriage, which members did as a matter of conscience until 1878 when the Supreme Court of the United States affirmed the constitutionality of the Morrill Act. Afterward, the practice was continued in the hope that the court might reverse its decision. "What our people did in disregard of the law and of the decisions of the Supreme Court affecting plural marriages, was in the spirit of maintaining religious rights under constitutional guaranties, and not in any spirit of defiance or disloyalty to the government," the statement asserted. It may be true, the statement admitted, that some members violated the law after the Manifesto, but there are always people who disobey the law. It does not follow that the integrity of an entire community need be questioned because of the actions of a few members of that community.

The last part of the statement was essentially an answer to charges that the church's millennialist doctrines required disloyalty to the government. Denying the assertion that the church believed in the overthrow of earthly governments or domination of the state, the statement said that the church held to the doctrine of the separation of church and state and noninterference of church authority in political matters. The church also asserted a doctrine of freedom and independence of members in the performance of their political duties. The church insisted that "politics in the states where our people reside shall be conducted as in other parts of the Union: that there shall be no interference by the state with the church, nor with the free exercise of religion." Where that was not the case, and where "political parties make war upon the church, or menace the civil, political, or religious rights of its members as such," the church asserted "the inherent right of self-preservation . . . and her right and duty to call upon all her children, and upon all who love justice and desire that perpetuation of religious liberty, to come to her and to stand with her until the danger shall have passed."

Continuing this theme, the statement contradicted what seemed to outsiders the logical consequences of the doctrines of the Kingdom of God and millennialism. Those outside the church and some church members and authorities had urged that since the president of the church could receive revelation upon any subject and since the revelations were paramount to faithful members of the church, it was impossible for any Mormon to "give true allegiance to his country, or to any earthly government." In response to this, the church leadership simply cut the Gordian Knot by asserting that they refused to be bound by interpretation others placed on their beliefs. The statement further denied that the belief in divine revelation or anticipation of the millennium weakened allegiance to any country. Church leaders did not know when Christ's kingdom would come any more than did other Christian millennialists.

The response to the statement by the Protestant churches of Salt Lake City was predictably negative. On June 4, 1907, the *Tribune* published a review prepared by the Salt Lake Ministerial Association which characterized the church's statement as full of "evasions," "hypocrisy," and "dishonesty." It was, the attackers charged, a "halfhearted" attempt "to make the world believe in their patriotism, their piety, their unselfishness, their benevolence, their purity, when they do not believe these things of themselves, knowing their own corruption, treason, blasphemy and corroding selfishness, avarice, lusts of power, and of the flesh." In the June conference of the MIA, B. H. Roberts answered the ministerial association's review. The *Improvement Era* subsequently published the answer, and the church offered to publish the review, providing the association would pay half the cost of printing, which they refused to do. Roberts later published all three documents in his *Defense of the Faith*.[28]

Church leaders also tried to answer the plethora of criticisms in the muckraking magazines between 1910 and 1913. In 1910 Joseph F. Smith attempted to answer charges in *Pearson's Magazine*, but the

editors refused to publish his reply. He believed, however, that a state-
ment to answer these attacks would help the church. In 1910 Charles
W. Penrose tried to reply to Frank J. Cannon's articles in *Everybody's
Magazine*.[29]

Early in 1911, as the campaign expanded, the Twelve considered
the mounting charges, and Reed Smoot suggested that they ought to
receive some sort of systematic answer. The Twelve agreed that Smoot
could have an article appear under his name ghostwritten by L. Ray
Armstrong and also that the church would undertake a full answer.
Smoot also had been privy to the letter Theodore Roosevelt wrote to
Isaac Russell denying that he had knowingly assisted the church in
illegal activities in return for church political support. During the April
Conference, 1911, Joseph F. Smith wired Smoot in Washington that a
statement would be read, and Smoot interceded with representatives
of the Associated Press in Washington and New York asking them to
instruct their local reporters to carry the story.[30]

The statement, which Heber J. Grant read and which members at
the conference approved on April 9, 1911, answered the principal
muckraking charges. Calling the charges slander against the church,
the statement denied that there had been any compacts in return for
statehood. The only document which could be construed as a compact,
it said, was the petition for amnesty framed in December 1891, which
was signed by the Presidency and Apostles. The statement also said
that since October 6, 1890, the church had not authorized plural marriages. Admitting that some such marriages had taken place in Mexico, the statement said that when rumors of these surreptitious unions
reached the church leadership, Lorenzo Snow published a declaration
in the *Deseret News* on January 8, 1900, calling on all to stop. The Second Manifesto of April 1904 reaffirmed this position. New offenders
were being disciplined or excommunicated. The document also reiterated some points already covered by the statement of 1907. Each citizen cast his vote as he chose. No church member had been disciplined
for voting for or against a candidate or proposition. Charges of disloyalty or treason on the part of the church were untrue, as church
members had served in both the Spanish-American and Civil wars.
Tithing was accounted for and was not used for illegal purposes.[31]

Perhaps the most important effort to answer charges—at least that
with the greatest long-lasting effect—was the one made by Brigham H.
Roberts. Roberts wrote in response to a series of articles on the origins

of the Book of Mormon by Theodore Schroeder. Formerly a Salt Lake City lawyer, then living in New York, Schroeder published the articles, based on the time-worn and long-discredited Solomon Spaulding theory, from September 1906 through May 1907 in the *American Historical Magazine*. The publisher of the magazine, David E. Nelke, invited Roberts to reply. Nelke published his reply in the issues from September 1908 to March 1909. Thereafter, Nelke asked if Roberts wanted to publish a complete history of the church, providing the church would pay for the research and also for the printing plates. Roberts and the church agreed, and the magazine also increased its publication schedule from bimonthly to monthly. The series of articles, which ran from July 1909 to July 1915, was later updated and became B. H. Roberts's *Comprehensive History of the Church*. Since the series was heavily subsidized by the church, some church leaders, still unconvinced of the need for such public relations efforts, raised questions as to its value.[32]

One innovation seeming at the time to promise much for future church publicity was the newly developing medium of motion pictures. After an abortive effort in 1910, in July 1912 the church approved the production of a film entitled "One Hundred Years of Mormonism," filmed by Harry A. Kelley of the Ellage Motion Picture Co., Los Angeles. The film was exhibited in February 1913 before a meeting of the Deseret Union Sunday School Board. James E. Talmage, who saw the film, thought it "not a complete success." It contained, he reported, "many crudities and historical inaccuracies." Nevertheless, he believed, "the general effect will be good." Thereafter a number of other pro-Mormon motion pictures were made.[33]

After news of Max Florence's illicit picture taking, James E. Talmage suggested that the church take good quality pictures of the interior of the temple and make them available to the public. The church leaders did this and, in addition, commissioned the book *The House of the Lord*, which was to include not only pictures of the interior of the Salt Lake Temple but also a statement on the purpose and meaning of temples.[34]

In 1917 the Oxford University Press cancelled a contract with the church to publish a special edition of the Bible containing scriptural references between the Old and New Testaments in a section entitled, "Ready References," edited by Joseph Fielding Smith and James E. Talmage. The decision apparently came because of protests against the scriptural compilation, which tended to support the Mormon point of view. Nevertheless, Cambridge University Press agreed to continue publication of the volume.[35]

After 1914 several non-Mormon authors wrote books favorable to the church. In 1916 J. C. Homans published *The Case Against Mormonism*, which, despite its title, was a book supporting the church. Homans had previously written for the church, and this book may well have been commissioned. In 1919 and 1921, after research in the LDS church archives, Thomas E. Farish, state historian of Arizona, published a complimentary section on the Mormons in his *History of Arizona*. In 1921 George Wharton James had James E. Talmage and Anthony W. Ivins review portions of his manuscript on Utah before publication of his favorable *Land of Blossoming Valleys*. In May 1924 the writer Morris W. Werner came with a letter of introduction from Mahonri M. Young. The First Presidency helped in securing information on Brigham Young for a projected biography. The resulting biography is perhaps the most favorable of the LDS leader yet produced by a non-Mormon. In 1926 the *Saturday Evening Post* published a complimentary article entitled "Mormons and What Not." In 1930, when Hoffman Birney wrote an article on the Mormons which emphasized the Mountain Meadows Massacre, the First Presidency was able to keep the *Saturday Evening Post* from publishing it. By May 1927 Heber J. Grant could say (in fast meeting at the Ensign Ward) that the attitude of the press toward the church had changed and the church could now expect to see in print virtually "everything we request them to publish."[36]

Beyond this, many of the wounds from previous years were healed during the 1920s and early 1930s. George F. Richards attended the funeral of Sarah Jenne Cannon and had a cordial conversation with Frank J. Cannon. William F. Bryant, a Nebraska author who in his book *The Historic Man of Nazareth* had severely criticized Joseph Smith and Brigham Young, sent a letter to the church leadership indicating that his views had changed. In November 1924 Heber J. Grant attended the funeral at St. Marks Cathedral of Ambrose Noble McKay, manager of the *Salt Lake Tribune*, who, Grant said, had been absolutely fair in his treatment of the Mormons. In January 1927 Mormons were declared eligible for membership in the Young Women's Christian Association in Utah.[37]

In general the church seems to have had more success in finding

forums to tell its own story after 1914 than before. Following the se-
rialization of Roberts's *Comprehensive History of the Church* in the
American Historical Magazine, the First Presidency asked James E.
Talmage to prepare a series of articles designed to answer anti-Mormon
critics. Throughout 1917 Talmage worked on the articles under the
supervision of the Council of the Twelve and First Presidency. Talmage's views did not find universal agreement among the general authorities. Anthon H. Lund, with his broad linguistic background, realized that Talmage would have a difficult time in demonstrating the
difference between faith and belief since some languages like German,
Danish, and Greek had only one word for the two English words.[38]

The church negotiated with various newspapers for publication of
the articles. Even here Talmage encountered some difficulty since several agreed to publish and then withdrew following loud anti-Mormon
outcries and pressure from advertisers. At first only the *Atlanta Constitution* and the *San Francisco Chronicle* agreed to print the series,
but as the year 1917 wore on, more than a dozen others signed on.[39]

In general Talmage's efforts succeeded. During the newspaper campaign, the Denver Philosophical Society asked Talmage to address
them on the topic of the *Vitality of Mormonism*, which was the central
theme of the newspaper articles, and the national journal *Current
Opinion* reviewed this speech. Beyond this the Gorham Press of Boston,
which had earlier published John Quincy Adams's attack on the church,
approached Talmage about collecting the articles into a book under the
title of the Denver talk. The First Presidency endorsed the *Vitality of
Mormonism* after its publication in 1919 and encouraged members to
use the book in classes and homes and for general reading.[40]

Nevertheless, attacks which had forced some papers to suspend
publication of the articles continued after the appearance of the book.
Representatives of Protestant missionary organizations derided the
volume as masking the real intent of Mormonism and presenting "an
insidious danger cleverly concealed," since it did not admit the continued practice of polygamy.[41]

This seems not to have deterred at least some Protestants and other
Christians from accepting Talmage and other Mormon representa-
tives. In November 1919 Talmage represented the church at the Third
World's Christian Citizenship Conference in Pittsburgh, Pennsylvania,
as he and Emmeline B. Wells had done at the 1915 Panama-Pacific
Exposition in San Francisco. Talmage spoke at the convention and, in

spite of attacks by representatives of some denominations, he comported himself with dignity. One of Heber J. Grant's achievements was a well-received speech to the Kansas City Knife and Fork Club in 1920.[42]

The efforts to change the church's image, which had borne fruit by the end of the First World War, brought some harmony with other churches in Utah. Even the *Missionary Review of the World* published some mildly favorable articles, and in April 1919 Reed Smoot addressed a gathering at the Methodist church in Salt Lake City. In September 1921 the Reverend W. F. Blukley of the Episcopal church in Provo tried to combat opposition to Utah Mormons. He had concluded that the Mormons were maligned too much by popular lecturers and hoped that the national organization of the Episcopal church would adopt his view.[43]

Mormon relations with Catholic and Jewish representatives in Utah had never been generally as bad as they were with the Protestants. In July 1915 Reed Smoot made arrangements for a special organ recital for a large delegation of Catholic visitors, including the Papal delegate to the United States and the bishop-elect of the Roman Catholic diocese of Salt Lake City. Joseph F. Smith participated in the dedication of the hall for the Jewish congregation Montifiore. In August 1920 Orson F. Whitney and Heber J. Grant were invited to speak at a Palestine celebration held in the Assembly Hall. In April 1921, also, President Grant warned church members not to take part in the persecution of Jews, strengthening his position because of the church's belief in God's providence and Zionism.[44]

During and after World War I the church leaders expanded their contacts and the nature of their support to a broader range of national political figures. In 1917 Franklin K. Lane and William Gibbs McAdoo of Wilson's cabinet and Vice President Thomas R. Marshall visited Utah, where the general authorities received them. In 1919, following charges that the Mormons were importing girls from England for polygamy, Herbert Hoover came to the defense of the church, contradicting the charges and pointing to LDS charitable service in wartime. In 1920 William Jennings Bryan, whose writing Heber J. Grant admired, and Senator Robert L. Owen attended April conference as spectators. Bryan expressed his approval of many of the sentiments he had heard.[45]

Beyond this the church received considerable favorable public acclaim because of the conservation work of Reed Smoot and the support

for conservation by church leaders. During the Wilson administration
Smoot worked with Horace Albright and others to secure passage of
the National Park Service Act. In 1919 Smoot sponsored legislation
creating Zion's National Park, and in September 1920 he and President Grant, together with other dignitaries, attended the dedication of
the park. Following the ceremonies Stephen T. Mather of the National
Park Service called on the First Presidency, and President Grant gave
him a number of books.[46]

As part of the effort to improve the information about their own history, the First Presidency began consideration in early 1921 of the publication of a one-volume history of the church. In March they talked
with James E. Talmage about his availability to write the volume. The
press of his other assignments made this impossible. By early April the
decision had been made to have the volume written by Joseph Fielding
Smith and John A. Widtsoe. Brigham H. Roberts had to be told that
the church could not afford to publish the history he had written for
the *American Historical Magazine*, and he was much upset by the decision. Roberts, who had undoubtedly done more than any other single
church member to that time to publish the general history of the
church, felt that a great injustice had been done to him. After the decision had been made, President Grant regretted that the presidency had
not considered Roberts for the assignment, but it was impossible to
make the change without creating other ill feelings.[47]

Beyond this Franklin S. Harris's and Newbern I. Butt's *The Fruits of
Mormonism* enlarged on a genre of writing begun by John A. Widtsoe
in his books *Joseph Smith as Scientist* and *A Rational Theology*
and continued by Roberts's *American Historical Magazine* articles
and Talmage's *Vitality of Mormonism*, which attempted to explain
the church in terms understood by the outside world. *The Fruits of
Mormonism* contained an explication of the principles of the Gospel
thought by the authors to be responsible for the success of the church.
These included the mission of Christ, the idea of resurrection, the
eternity of marriage, eternal progression, continuous revelation, the
Word of Wisdom, and the thirteenth Article of Faith with its emphasis
on accepting all truth from whatever source. The book used statistics
from Utah to emphasize the impact the church had on the community.
The authors discussed such matters as support and achievement in
education and development of leadership in the community. They
stressed the colonization of the Great Basin area and its redemption

through cooperative effort. They argued, citing the twelfth Article of Faith, the 134th section of the Doctrine and Covenants, and World War I, that the Mormons were patriotic. Though they were forced to admit that the divorce rate was high in Utah, they argued that it was not among the Mormons by showing that it was lower in rural areas.[48]

By the 1920s this campaign had borne fruit and the church leadership carried considerable political clout outside Utah. On March 1, 1929, for instance, Heber J. Grant received a letter from historian James H. McClintock announcing that the Arizona legislature had just passed a bill naming a bridge across the Colorado at Marble Canyon Lee's Ferry Bridge. The church leadership did not like the name because of its association with John D. Lee, who had been executed for his part in the infamous Mountain Meadows Massacre. Heber J. Grant immediately left for Arizona after telegraphing Charles W. Nibley to send an article which Anthony W. Ivins had written on the Mountain Meadows Massacre and also information on Jacob Hamblin, a famous Mormon emissary to the Indians. Upon reaching Phoenix on March 2, he called on McClintock, visited Governor George W. P. Hunt, and met with a number of senators and representatives. Thereafter he contacted the *Arizona Gazette*, and on March 4 he again called on members of the legislature. His lobbying continued with representatives of the highway commission on March 5, and all finally favored a change in the name. In the afternoon of March 5, he spoke before a joint session of the legislature and told of his opposition to the name, arguing for a name which was "distinguished and constructive." The newspapers agreed, since advertising for the state would be better. His efforts proved successful, and the name was changed.[49]

Perhaps of all the antagonists, the most vocal opposition had come from spokesmen of the Reorganized Church of Jesus Christ of Latter Day Saints. Arguments often centered around the right of succession in the presidency of the church and on the practice of polygamy. In 1905 Frederick M. Smith, son of RLDS president Joseph Smith III, wrote an open letter condemning the LDS church. Attacking his cousin Joseph F. Smith and LDS doctrine, he said that the LDS church was not representative of churches descended from Joseph Smith. Attacks also came from the president of the RLDS church, Joseph Smith III.[50]

The striking development, however, is that relations with the RLDS church seem to have improved considerably by the 1920s, and that, as much as anything, is a sign of the change in the church's public image. When the RLDS church began constructing the auditorium on the temple lot in Independence, Frederick M. Smith, then RLDS church president, visited Utah to inspect the tabernacle organ with a view to including a similar instrument in their facility. In February 1929 the presiding bishop of the Reorganized Church called on James E. Talmage and Heber J. Grant to obtain suggestions for instituting the United Order. President Grant had to admit that Brigham Young had died before he was of an age where he was aware of such things, and that he did not have any practical suggestions on the operation of the organization.[51]

By the late 1920s a number of changes had taken place. Church members had opened what before 1890 had been a relatively closed society. The attitudes of Elders Young and Lyman mentioned before seem to have been typical. Before 1900, beyond the personal contacts with businessmen and political leaders, public relations efforts outside the LDS community had usually consisted of tracts and writings designed to convert people to Mormonism rather than to explain Mormonism to nonbelievers.

The most important early signal of a change in that position was the opening of the Bureau of Information in 1902. Residual antagonism based on misinformation, sectarian animosity, and the revelations of the Reed Smoot investigation undoubtedly set back the effort to change the church's image. After 1914, however, the church was able to build upon the foundation of positive treatment by such authors as Richard Ely to publish favorable articles and to expand its public contacts and support.

While the change to a favorable image had not been completed by 1930, a rather clear trend was evident. The contributions of leaders like B. H. Roberts, James E. Talmage, John A. Widtsoe, Heber J. Grant, Reed Smoot, and James H. Moyle cannot be overrated. Personal contacts by members living outside Utah, such as those of Mahonri M. Young and J. Reuben Clark, undoubtedly helped, as did books like Talmage's *Vitality of Mormonism* and Harris and Butt's *Fruits of Mormonism*, which were written to explain Mormonism rather than to recruit new converts. Perhaps the most important signs of the changes which had taken place were found in the more cordial attitude within that deepest of all chasms, the cleft between the RLDS and LDS churches.

On the most basic level, however, the experiences of the church with public relations during the first thirty years of the twentieth century reveal much about the changes which had taken place in Mormonism. No longer did one hear the strident rhetoric of the reformation of 1856, the pox on both your houses attitude of the Saints during the Civil War, or the nailing the flag to the mast of polygamy by John Taylor. Rather, we find conciliatory but firm public statements, open relations with the outside community, and concerted efforts to explain the Latter-day Saints to the outside world.

In retrospect it seems clear that these changes were closely tied to the ongoing reconsideration of church doctrine and practice already partly discussed and to be considered more thoroughly in the following chapters. Increasingly, the reconsideration of doctrine and practice brought Mormons closer to the mainstream of American society in their social, political, and economic attitudes, while at the same time maintaining certain doctrinal positions and practices unique to Mormonism. These changes had their backlash in the defection of Fundamentalists committed to such doctrines as plural marriage and Brigham Young's speculative Adam-God theory, but the majority of the Latter-day Saints accepted them enthusiastically.

13

The Adoption of a New Interpretation
of the Word of Wisdom

THE ABOLITION OF PLURAL MARRIAGE, of church domination of politics, of social exclusiveness, and of heavy church involvement in the economy left a number of breaches in the boundary between Latter-day Saints and others. Although it was undoubtedly not consciously so conceived, the reinterpretation of members' responsibilities under the Word of Wisdom, a set of dietary regulations given in a revelation to Joseph Smith, provided a new and increasingly more significant boundary. Paradoxically, perhaps, the boundary created by insisting on strict abstinence from liquor brought increased credibility with Evangelical Protestants, the one group most antagonistic to Mormons, since they had been pressing for prohibition since the late nineteenth century. It did, however, create a boundary with an increasingly secular and hedonistic American society and with religious groups that did not adopt Evangelical attitudes toward liquor and tobacco.[1]

The Word of Wisdom itself originated in a revelation Joseph Smith received in February 1833. At the time the region around Kirtland, Ohio, where Smith and the church leaders resided, together with much of the northeastern United States, was a hotbed of temperance and health reform sentiment. Moreover Smith and his wife Emma became offended by the frequent use of tobacco by guests who visited their house for instruction. The revelation against the use of alcohol, tobacco, and hot drinks (Joseph Smith interpreted the phrase "hot drinks" to mean tea and coffee about five months after he gave the revelation) also cautioned against eating too much meat and advocated the use of herbs, fruits, and grains. In return members were promised physical and intellectual strength.[2]

Currently available evidence indicates that adherence to the Word of Wisdom in the nineteenth century was sporadic. At various times resolutions were passed, advice and counsel were given, and members were disfellowshipped or even excommunicated at least in part because of their failure to observe the Word of Wisdom. In general, however, adherence in the sense of abstaining from tea, coffee, liquor, and tobacco was honored as much in the breach as in the observance by leaders and members alike, particularly after 1840. Some members or groups committed themselves to strict adherence to the Word of Wisdom, but they were doing so as individuals bound to "a principle with promise."[3]

Although Brigham Young declared the Word of Wisdom to be a commandment and secured the approval of some of the Saints to that proposition, he announced no revelation on the subject, and actual observance did not coincide with public pronouncement. An 1851 conference and in some cases other conference addresses or reminiscences of addresses are often cited as the date the Word of Wisdom became binding as a commandment. However, during Brigham Young's lifetime, after the conference, he and other church leaders and members failed to observe the Word of Wisdom as we interpret it today. The Word of Wisdom was again reemphasized in the late 1860s and early 1870s, but this reemphasis seems to have been more closely related to the larger effort to discourage imports than to emphasize the health aspects of the principle. From the death of Brigham Young until after the turn of the century, adherence was intermittent. In 1883 and 1884 the general authorities, following the lead of President John Taylor, emphasized the need to adhere to the Word of Wisdom. Thereafter, it seems generally to have lain dormant.[4]

The status of the Word of Wisdom in the late 1890s seems evident from contemporary sources. At a meeting on May 5, 1898, the First Presidency and Twelve discussed the Word of Wisdom. One member read from the twelfth volume of the *Journal of Discourses* a statement by Brigham Young that the Word of Wisdom was a commandment of God. Lorenzo Snow, then president of the Council of the Twelve, agreed, saying that he believed the Word of Wisdom was a commandment and that it should be carried out to the letter. In doing so, he said, members should be taught to refrain from eating meat except in dire necessity, particularly since Joseph Smith taught that animals have spirits. Wilford Woodruff, then president of the church, said he looked upon the Word of Wisdom as a commandment and that all members should observe it, but for the present, he said, no definite action should be taken except the members should be taught to refrain from the use of meat. The minutes of the meeting record that "President Woodruff said he regarded the Word of Wisdom in its entirety as given of the Lord of the Latter-day Saints to observe, but he did not think that Bishops should withhold recommends from persons who did not adhere strictly to it."[5]

Though it seems clear that some church leaders like Heber J. Grant and Joseph F. Smith insisted upon complete abstinence from tea, coffee, liquor, and tobacco, all general authorities did not agree. During a discussion in 1900 after he became president of the church, Lorenzo Snow again emphasized the centrality of not eating meat, and in 1901 John Henry Smith and Brigham Young, Jr., of the Twelve thought that the church ought not interdict beer, or at least not Danish beer. Other apostles like Anthon H. Lund and Matthias F. Cowley enjoyed Danish beer and currant wine. Charles W. Penrose occasionally served wine. Emmeline B. Wells, then a member of the presidency and later president of the Relief Society, drank an occasional cup of coffee, and George Albert Smith took brandy for medical reasons. Elder George Teasdale agreed with President Woodruff and thought that no one ought to be kept from working in the Sunday School because he drank tea and that eating pork was a more serious problem than drinking tea or coffee.[6]

We find then a diffuse pattern in observing and teaching the Word of Wisdom in 1900. Some general authorities preached quite consistently against the use of tea, coffee, liquor, tobacco, and meat. None supported drunkenness, and no one insisted on the necessity of vegetarianism. In practice, however, they and other members also occasionally drank the beverages which current interpretation would prohibit. Observance of the Word of Wisdom was urged by way of counsel by President Snow and others. Some apostles like John Henry Smith believed that the more important question was one of free agency and that those who continued to insist upon strict adherence to the Word of Wisdom were ignoring more serious principles. President Snow also opposed sanctions against the use of alcohol and was upset when the general board of the YMMIA asked for an end to the sale of beer at Saltair.[7]

Most vocal among general authorities in his opposition to the use of tea, coffee, alcohol, and tobacco was Heber J. Grant, who would become one of the leaders of the state prohibition movement. He was particularly outraged at the church members who served liquor and at some of the Twelve who opposed the prohibition of alcohol at Saltair.

He was also concerned at the indifference some of the general authorities demonstrated to the feelings of Protestant ministers who complained about the Saltair saloon.[8]

The death of Lorenzo Snow brought to the presidency Joseph F. Smith, whose views on the Word of Wisdom were close to those of Heber J. Grant. The path to the current interpretation of the Word of Wisdom leads from Smith's administration. Dropping the emphasis on abstaining from meat, he urged the need to refrain from the use of tea, coffee, alcohol, and tobacco. In 1902 he reversed President Snow's stand and closed the saloon at Saltair, a move which the Protestant clergy heartily approved. Apparently following this lead, in June 1902 the First Presidency and Twelve agreed not to fellowship anyone who operated or frequented saloons. In the same year Joseph F. Smith urged stake presidents and others to refuse recommends to flagrant violators, but to be somewhat liberal with old men who used tobacco and old ladies who drank tea. Habitual drunkards, however, were to be denied temple recommends.[9]

Under these conditions the general authorities were clearly moving toward current policy and practice. By mid-1905 members of the Twelve were using stake conference visits actively to promote adherence, which they interpreted as abstinence from tea, coffee, liquor, and tobacco. In September 1905, for instance, George Albert Smith advised the stake presidency, high council, and bishops in Star Valley, Wyoming, "to no longer tolerate men in presiding positions who would not keep the Word of Wisdom." George F. Richards preferred the technique of interviewing and urging compliance rather than insisting on lack of toleration. In keeping with the change in emphasis, the First Presidency and Twelve substituted water for wine in the sacrament in their temple meetings, apparently beginning on July 5, 1906.[10]

After 1906 a strong prohibition movement developed in the United States, centered in Evangelical Protestant groups. In 1906 only Iowa, Kansas, and Maine had statewide prohibition, but by 1919 twenty-six states, principally in the Midwest, far West, South, and upper New England, had adopted the reform. Although increasing scientific evidence on the adverse effects of alcohol helped the movement, moral rather than scientific considerations seem to have sustained it. The period between 1911 and 1916 represented the post-Civil War apogee of alcoholic consumption in the United States and fear of moral decay, broken homes, and wasted fortunes fueled the prohibition movement.[11]

As indicated above, the Latter-day Saints were already working internally before 1906 to oppose the consumption of alcoholic beverages and to interdict the use of tea, coffee, and tobacco among members. The interpretations given by nineteenth-century leaders to the Word of Wisdom and Brigham Young's declaration that it was a commandment provided part of the basis for this emphasis in the church.

Another important motive for those on all sides of the question seems also to have been the desire for acceptance. Strongest opposition to the seating of B. H. Roberts and Reed Smoot had come from Evangelical Protestant groups, and some leaders, such as Elder Grant, were particularly sensitive to their feelings. In addition, the strongest support for state—and later nationwide—prohibition among church members was found among Democrats and progressive Republicans. They were searching for acceptance by church members who were increasingly pressured to vote Republican in support of Reed Smoot and his Federal Bunch and for national approval by Protestants who had so long opposed the church. Among Federal Bunch Republicans, however, the situation was much different. Generally in control of the legislature, the governorship, and the congressional and senatorial seats until 1916, Smoot supporters were reluctant to upset their majority position by alienating members of the business community sympathetic to the liquor traffic or by creating a climate congenial to anti-Mormon political parties.[12]

The organization of the statewide prohibition movement in Utah began in December 1907, when the Reverend Dr. George W. Young of Louisville, Kentucky, assistant general superintendent of the Anti-Saloon League of America, came to Utah. Throughout early 1908 the league organized its three departments—agitation, legislation, and law enforcement—in Utah, and Heber J. Grant, who took an early interest in the movement, became a trustee for Utah and an officer of the Utah organization. In the late fall and early winter of 1908 the Reverend Dr. Louis S. Fuller, superintendent of the league for Utah and Idaho, met at various times with members of the First Presidency and Twelve and with Elder Grant. They agreed to support a local option bill in the 1909 legislature.[13]

Initially prohibition had wide support within the church. Edward H. Anderson expressed surprise in a January 1908 *Improvement Era* editorial that Utah was still one of the completely "wet" states. He thought that the "Latter-day Saints will unitedly and enthusiastically join in bringing about . . . [the liquor traffic's] complete extermination." A number of the Twelve met with members of an organization called the Salt Lake City Betterment Committee and agreed to implement a resolution which had been passed in October 1907 general conference to do all in their power to stop the liquor traffic. As Anthon H. Lund, second counselor in the First Presidency, said, "this means 'prohibition.'" At the temple fast meeting on January 5, 1908, Richard W. Young, president of the Ensign Stake, and Joseph F. Smith both endorsed prohibition.[14]

A number of factors, however, led some church leaders to support only local option or even to oppose public action on the liquor question rather than to favor prohibition. William Spry, John Henry Smith, and a number of Republican leaders thought that prohibition would not prohibit and that the law would subject property to confiscation. Some like Francis M. Lyman urged individual regeneration rather than prohibition, though he later changed to favor prohibition.[15]

Perhaps the most important pressure against prohibition came from Gentile Republicans, particularly businessmen whose interests included liquor manufacture or sales. Fred J. Keisel, for instance, said it would be a political blunder to support statewide prohibition. After June 1908 the *Intermountain Republican*, the church-owned organ of Reed Smoot's Federal Bunch, stopped publishing articles favorable to prohibition, and the Republican party dumped Governor John C. Cutler, partly because of his support of statewide prohibition, in favor of William Spry, who nominally supported local option.[16]

By the time the legislature met in January 1909 the church leadership was moving in two directions. Francis M. Lyman, by now converted to prohibition, called Bishop John M. Whittaker to work with the legislature and with Elder Grant, Presiding Bishop Charles W. Nibley, and others who favored prohibition. The *Deseret News* published articles and interviews favoring prohibition. However, President Joseph F. Smith, Reed Smoot, and others more sensitive to the political problems became equivocal in their support. Reed Smoot said he believed the prohibition movement would hurt the church by bringing further charges of church influence in politics. John Henry Smith opposed prohibition but considered Smoot's objections somewhat hypocritical since the apostle-senator "had no objection to Priesthood influence when he wanted to be elected. Then he said all . . . [the Gentiles] honored was power." Eventually, the legislature sidetracked a prohibi-

tion bill introduced by non-Federal Bunch Republican George M. Cannon in favor of a local option bill sponsored by Smoot's lieutenant
Carl A. Badger. Though the Badger bill passed, William Spry pocket-
vetoed it, to the chagrin of many supporters. In 1911, however, the legislature revived and passed the Badger local option bill and this time
Spry signed it.[17]

The fight over prohibition between 1911 and 1917 almost replayed
the local option battle between 1908 and 1911. Republican church
leaders closely allied to the Federal Bunch favored prohibition in
public, but were equivocal in private. Fear of a backlash against the
church which might lead to the creation of a new anti-Mormon party
and fear of alienating Gentile businessmen from the Republican party
seem to have been the principal motives. In 1915 Spry pocket-vetoed a
widely supported statewide prohibition bill. By 1916 the majority of
Republicans could no longer support Spry, and Nephi L. Morris, president of the Salt Lake Stake, Progressive party gubernatorial candidate
in 1912, and an avowed prohibitionist, received the Republican party
nomination but lost the election. By that time virtually all church leaders and a large majority of all Utah citizens also supported prohibition,
and Democratic governor Simon Bamberger and the Democratically
controlled legislature enacted statewide prohibition in 1917.

In the meantime emphasis on the Word of Wisdom during Joseph F.
Smith's administration continued essentially as in 1902. In a letter
dated December 28, 1915, President Smith indicated again that young
"or middle-aged men who have had experience in the church should
not be ordained to the Priesthood nor recommended to the privileges of
the House of the Lord unless they will abstain from the use of tobacco
and intoxicating drinks." Since prohibition had outlawed the legal use
of alcohol, emphasis in church magazines and talks after 1917 centered on tobacco, and members were urged to support groups like the
No-Tobacco League of America, the YMCA, and the Salvation Army in
their efforts to eradicate the use of tobacco.[18]

After the inauguration of Heber J. Grant's administration in 1918,
however, the situation began to change. In 1921 the church leadership
made adherence to the Word of Wisdom a requirement for admission
to the temple. Prior to this time, as indicated, stake presidents and
bishops had been encouraged in this matter, but exceptions had been
made. Apparently under this new emphasis, in March 1921 George F.
Richards, serving both as an apostle and as president of the Salt Lake

Temple, phoned two Salt Lake City bishops about two tobacco users who had come to the temple. He told the bishops "to try to clean them up before they come here again."[19]

Between 1921 and 1933 the requirement of adherence to the Word of Wisdom for full fellowship in the church was made even more explicit. In the 1928 *General Handbook of Instructions*, sent to guide bishops and stake presidents on church policy, the passage on requirements for temple recommends reads: "It is important that all those who may desire to enter the temple for endowments or other ordinances should be encouraged by the bishopric to observe the principle of tithing as well as all other Gospel principles." The next edition of the *Handbook*, published in 1933, read that members desiring temple recommends "should observe the law of tithing. The applicant should also observe all other principles of the Gospel, should keep the Word of Wisdom, not use profanity, should not join nor be a member of any secret oath bound organization and should sustain without reservation the general and local authorities of the church."[20]

With prohibition an accomplished fact, the church leadership also moved during the 1920s to incorporate the use of tobacco under legal sanctions. Church members and leaders threw their strong support behind a bill introduced by state senator Edward Southwick of Lehi to prohibit the sale of tobacco in Utah. The church's Social Advisory Committee, students from Brigham Young University, and other church groups lobbied for the bill, which passed in 1921. By early 1922, however, it was clear that the Southwick law had worked very poorly and massive disobedience brought about its revision in 1923, to provide for controlled access and to produce revenue for the state.[21]

The church continued its campaign against tobacco use. An article in the *Improvement Era* for March 1923 argued that tobacco users naturally linked themselves with evil persons such as profaners, criminals, vagrants, and prostitutes. Other articles said that men did not want women to smoke because it seemed unladylike. In 1923 the MIA adopted abolition of tobacco as its annual theme. Appeals to scientific authority were also used, including references to nicotine poisoning and smoke damage to mucus membranes and lungs.[22]

Late in the 1920s church leaders urged alternative antitobacco legislation. In 1927 Elders Richard R. Lyman and Melvin J. Ballard asked church attorney Franklin S. Richards for information on the possibility of legislation preventing the advertising of cigarettes on billboards.

Richards believed that the Supreme Court would declare such a law unconstitutional, but the 1929 legislature passed one anyway. The *Relief Society Magazine* in May 1929 said it hoped that the courts would uphold the law and regretted that the Idaho legislature had not passed a similar law. In November 1929, however, Judge David W. Moffatt of Utah's Third District Court ruled the billboard law unconstitutional.[23]

In spite of the legal setbacks church leaders continued to preach and act against tobacco. Heber J. Grant in January 1930 warned bishops that young men using tobacco were not to be called on missions. Ruth May Fox, president of the YWMIA, asked Mormon girls to abstain from smoking and drinking in order to "remove temptation from our husbands and brothers." At the June 1930 MIA conference, President Grant urged all members to "study and know the laws regulating tobacco, liquor and safety." He said that "cigarettes degenerate the brain in an uncontrollable manner." He particularly urged that girls not be allowed to smoke, because, he said, "it destroys the God-given power to bring forth sons and daughters into this world."[24]

Undoubtedly the most difficult public problem related to the Word of Wisdom was the enforcement of state and nationwide prohibition against those who chose to ignore the law. At least twice during the 1920s the First Presidency injected itself into election campaigns to assist in defeating candidates for Salt Lake County sheriff alleged to be lax in the enforcement of prohibition legislation and electing those who promised more vigorous action.[25]

Heber J. Grant stood clearly on the side of strict enforcement, and as pressure on prohibition enforcement mounted in the late twenties and early thirties, he assisted with church resources. On January 5, 1928, Stephen L Richards, Milton Bennion, and Heber Chase Smith of the Social Welfare and Betterment League called to discuss conditions in Salt Lake City. They told him of organized crime protected by a pliant police force, and President Grant confided to his diary that he lost considerable sleep over the matter. Bennion provided information on law-breaking for *Deseret News* editorials, and Heber J. Grant insisted in conversations with his brother, B. F. Grant, the paper's business manager, that the *News* take a strong stand in favor of prohibition enforcement.[26]

Some members were disturbed with the actions of the authorities in providing financial support for the league's efforts, but the church leadership continued to help. In August 1931 the First Presidency, the

Sunday School, the Relief Society, and the MIA agreed to tax themselves to support league efforts. President Grant felt, however, that they could not continue "perpetually using church funds for something that ought to be done by the Government."[27]

Though the church leadership continued to fight to remain dry, Utah became the thirty-sixth state to vote for repeal of the Eighteenth Amendment and thus to seal the end of prohibition. Church leaders were not uniform in their assessment of the experiment. Heber J. Grant was very upset that Utahns had not followed his counsel to retain prohibition. Joseph Fielding Smith said that with "all its abuses and corruption," prohibition had nevertheless "been a boon to society and it would be a calamity of the gravest kind to repeal or modify it now." B. H. Roberts favored repeal, and Anthony W. Ivins, first counselor in the First Presidency, questioned its usefulness. He pointed out that enforcement had cost more than one-half billion dollars by 1931, with which, he thought, the country could have constructed 100,000 miles of paved road, or endowed 500 colleges with one million dollars each.[28]

In addition to liquor, tobacco, tea, and coffee, some members of the church urged that the prohibitions of the Word of Wisdom ought to be broader. In March 1917 Frederick J. Pack of the University of Utah published an article in the *Improvement Era* dealing with the question, "Should LDS Drink Coca-Cola?" His answer was no. His argument was not that the Word of Wisdom prohibited such drinks, but that such drinks contained the same drugs as tea and coffee.[29]

Still, church members were not long in making the link between stimulants and additives on the one hand and the Word of Wisdom on the other. On October 15, 1924, representatives of the Coca Cola Company called on President Grant to complain that Dr. T. B. Beatty, state health director, was using the church organization to assist in an attack on Coke. They asked President Grant to stop him, but he refused at first, saying that he himself had advised Mormons not to drink the beverage. Beatty, however, had been claiming that there was four to five times as much caffeine in Coke as in coffee, when in fact, as the representatives showed, there were approximately 1.7 grains in a cup of coffee and approximately .43 grains or about a fourth as much in an equivalent amount of Coke. After a second meeting President Grant said that he was "sure I have not the slightest desire to recommend that the people leave Coca Cola alone if this amount is absolutely harmless, which they claim it is." Beatty, however, insisted that he would still recommend against its use by children. The question was left unresolved, and evidence indicates that while the First Presidency has taken no official stand on the use of cola drinks, some members urged abstinence.[30]

In addition, some scientists and health food faddists insisted that the Word of Wisdom included much more than the church leadership generally supported. Often they attempted to incorporate the prescriptions requiring the use of herbs, fruit, and whole grains and scientific evidence indicating the harmful effects of substances not mentioned in the revelation. In 1930, for instance, John A. Widtsoe published a tract entitled *The Word of Wisdom*, which interdicted the use of refined flour and foods and "all drinks containing substances that are unnaturally stimulating." On November 23, 1930, James W. Fitches and Don C. Wood called on President Grant and asked permission to use Widtsoe's tract and to get the First Presidency to invest in their "Nature Way" health food company. Grant refused, saying that many points in Widtsoe's pamphlet and in their campaign "might be criticized because the actual teachings in the Word of Wisdom would hardly justify the conclusions drawn."[31] In the latter case, scientific evidence on the harmful effects of certain types of food and food additives probably played an influential role in the attempt to broaden the coverage of the Word of Wisdom. By the same token, similar scientific evidence also seems to have played an important role in the developing insistence that members abstain from tea, coffee, tobacco, and liquor.

What role did revelation play in the matter? Section 89 of the Doctrine and Covenants was clearly given as a revelation to Joseph Smith. Advice that the members of the church adhere to the Word of Wisdom was also undoubtedly given under inspiration. There is, however, no contemporary evidence of which I am aware that a separate new revelation was given changing the Word of Wisdom from a "principle with promise" to "a commandment" necessary for full participation in all the blessings of church membership. One author on the subject has argued that the vote in 1880 sustaining the Doctrine and Covenants as binding on the church membership was equivalent to a vote making the Word of Wisdom a commandment. If, however, the members were voting on the words contained in the book, what they did was to agree that the Word of Wisdom was "a principle with promise," not that it was a commandment.[32]

The Twelve and First Presidency obviously gave prayerful consideration to the conclusion that the Word of Wisdom ought to be a commandment binding on church members. Nevertheless, the major problem in interpreting the influence of revelation in these deliberations is the absence of references to revelations or even spiritual confirmation of specific positions in the diaries of those who participated in the meetings. The references are rather statements or reminiscences of statements by previous authorities. In sum, it is much easier to find references to previous statements than to see the presence of new specific revelation. The inclusion of coffee and tea and the exclusion of cocoa, for instance, from the prohibited substances can probably be attributed to statements of Joseph and Hyrum Smith and Brigham Young rather than to specific revelations.[33]

Other influences are much easier to document. Elder Grant's diary reveals the influence of Evangelical Protestant sentiment in his attitudes toward liquor and tobacco. These attitudes had begun to develop in the Evangelical churches and certain sectors of the business community as early as the 1830s. The nationwide temperance movement of the 1830s and the prohibition movement of the early twentieth century were linked to Evangelical attitudes.[34] Utahns in general and Mormons in particular were late additions to the prohibition movement rather than its early leaders. The influence of the attitudes of these groups is easiest to see when one contrasts the insistence on abstinence from liquor and tobacco with the rather tolerant attitude toward eating meat.

The sources of political attitudes related to the Word of Wisdom are also rather evident. Few of the general authorities seem to have opposed the use of the state to enforce their moral code, and although some opposed the use of legal sanctions to enforce health restrictions like vaccination, Elder Grant believed in the use of state power to regulate the quality of milk and to control tuberculosis. He and many others also supported public sanctions against the use of alcohol and tobacco. The political sources of the attitudes of Reed Smoot and Joseph F. Smith in the period before 1916 are also evident. Both feared tearing apart the Republican party and the possible rebirth of a new anti-Mormon party from the ashes of the old Liberal (1870–93) and American (1904–11) parties. By 1916, however, public sentiment was so strongly in favor of prohibition that such fears were secondary to their religious beliefs, which insisted upon adherence to the Word of Wisdom.

How, then, does one draw all these influences together to understand what happened during the period under consideration, and what part did revelation play? Public and private statements indicate that the church leaders were concerned about the moral tone of the community in which they lived. In an attempt to improve the tone, they sought guidance from scriptures, from statements of earlier leaders, and from the Lord as they carried on their deliberations. In addition, contemporary political and social movements like the prohibition and antitobacco movements seemed to them to offer help in solving the problems they perceived. Thus the confluence of a number of forces, religious and secular, rather than a single force led to a change in the interpretation of the Word of Wisdom. The decisions made under the confluence of these forces have had an important long-range effect since nothing, with the possible exception of the wearing of the temple garments, serves to distinguish Latter-day Saints and thus set them apart from the larger community more than does observance of the Word of Wisdom.

Two matters deserve some discussion at this point. First, it should be understood that while certain aspects of the Word of Wisdom undoubtedly ingratiated Mormons with Evangelical Protestants, the abstinence from tea and coffee served as well to define a boundary between Mormons and those groups. Secondly, while Joseph Gusfield's interpretation that prohibition is best understood as a means used by an increasingly displaced middle class to regain status might be attractive, that condition hardly obtained in Utah. No matter how much Mormons might have been challenged by newly wealthy mining entrepreneurs, Protestants, the American party, and increasing numbers of southern and eastern European immigrants, they were clearly the dominant group in Utah society. Prohibition provided a basis for cooperation between Mormons and Protestants, but Norman Clark's interpretation that prohibition is best understood as a movement to improve the moral tone of society and that the movement was extremely wide based seems more nearly to fit the Utah situation. After all, the governor who signed Utah's prohibition act into law was a naturalized American of central European Jewish extraction.[35]

An understanding of the way in which the current interpretation of the Word of Wisdom developed is significant, in addition, since it provides a case study of doctrinal and policy development in the church. In those cases where we have detailed information on such development, evidence seems to suggest that change has ordinarily come about through the prayerful consideration over time of contemporary problems in the context of tradition (including previous scriptures and statement), immediate conditions (including political, social, and economic problems), and alternative courses of action. Other examples for which we have good documentation include the decision to locate in Utah, the current Welfare Plan, and even the doctrines of God and man.[36] Thus, the student of Latter-day Saint doctrinal and policy development will provide a more thorough picture by conceiving the task broadly rather than limiting the context by looking only at the scriptures and at public statements. If a study of the interpretation of the Word of Wisdom can tell us anything, it is that such change does not take place in a vacuum.

14

Definition and Explication
of Church Doctrine

LIKE THE QUESTIONS CONNECTED with the Word of Wisdom, the consideration of other matters of doctrine created boundaries between the Latter-day Saints and certain other religious and secular groups. Within the community, the definition of doctrines played an important role in promoting a sense of place and security among many Latter-day Saints. Nevertheless, the attempt to define certain doctrines and practices created some tension. Two instances are particularly significant.

One example was the attempt to reconcile the apparent conflict between scientific naturalism and the biblical account of the creation. Church members worked from two divergent traditions on this matter. On the one hand, the persistence of the Baconian ideal of the congruence of divine revelation and scientific discovery underpinned the work of a group of progressive theologians who tried to reconcile scientific thought and church doctrine. On the other hand, several conservative theologians condemned as heretical the attempt at reconciliation as long as it involved a rejection of the supremacy of selective scriptural literalism. In their view, certain scriptures denied the possibility of death and thus of fossil remains older than the presumed time of Adam's transgression.[1]

The second instance involved the conflict between the increasing emphasis on priesthood authority and standardization and regularization of forms of worship on the one hand and Pentecostal experience, healing ordinances, and open personal prophecy on the other. In some ways, this development is reminiscent of the Antinomian controversy in New England Puritanism or the Holiness movement in late nineteenth- and early twentieth-century Methodism. Order and respectability seem to have conflicted with open personal religious experience.[2]

During the period from 1900 to 1930, a number of doctrines seem to have been foremost in the minds of the Latter-day Saint people. Judging by the volume of writing and correspondence on the subject, the interrelated questions of scientific naturalism, Darwinism, the relationship between science and religion, and higher criticism of the Bible were the most important. Closely related to these were the doctrines of God and man. Third was millennialism and its corollary, the Kingdom of God on earth.

A number of other issues involved to a greater extent the interaction of doctrine and practice. One of the most important was the question of salvation for the dead and the role of the temple ceremony in the lives of Latter-day Saints. A second question was the role of secret societies in the lives of Latter-day Saints. Finally, church members considered a number of questions in relation to the Book of Mormon.

As the new century dawned, Darwin's *Origin of Species* had been in print for four decades, and scientific advances together with changing attitudes had moved the United States well along the road to the secularization of scientific analysis. By the last two decades of the nineteenth century, Mormon academicians like James E. Talmage and John A. Widtsoe had begun to leave home to study the natural sciences at major universities.

As early as 1881 Talmage had resolved to "do good among the young," possibly by lecturing on the "harmony between geology and the Bible." Anxious to use the "priesthood, as a touchstone," Talmage hoped to keep himself "open to suggestions at all times." By 1884 he had concluded that the much-discussed conflict between science and religion did not exist, but that in some cases religionists manufactured it. After listening to a discourse by a Protestant minister on Darwinism, Talmage thought that the misinformation the cleric presented "bred the disgust with which most scientific people regard them—because they will dabble with matters from which their ignorance should keep them at a safe distance." After returning to Utah Talmage served in the church and in education before his ordination as an apostle. In 1898, during a conversation with George Q. Cannon, Talmage urged the authorities to give "careful, and perhaps official consideration to the scientific questions on which there is at least a strong appearance of antagonism with religious creeds." Cannon agreed with the suggestion, and Talmage recorded at least one interview with the First Presidency on the subject. Talmage spelled out his views of the relationship between science and religion in part in the *Improvement Era* in February 1900, where he argued that "Faith is not blind submission, passive obedience, with no effort at thought or reason. Faith, if worthy of its name, rests upon truth; and truth is the foundation of science."[3]

John A. Widtsoe was just as interested in the problem. Norwegian immigrant and graduate of Harvard and Goettingen, Widtsoe "set out [to make his] contributions from the point of view of science and those trained in that type of thinking." Between November 1903 and July 1904 he published in the *Improvement Era* a series of articles under the title "Joseph Smith as Scientist." The articles argued that Joseph Smith had anticipated in writings and revelations the scientific theories and discoveries then current.[4] After revision, Widtsoe's articles were published as a book and used as the MIA manual in 1908. It was Widtsoe's "conviction that there is no real difference between science and religion." The "great, fundamental laws of the Universe," Widtsoe maintained, "are foundation stones in religion as well as in science." What Widtsoe attempted was a reconciliation of pre-Einsteinian science with the principles of the gospel. The major thrust of his work was to show that Mormon doctrine either anticipated scientific principles or was generally in accord with them.[5]

Widtsoe first considered the questions of energy and matter. Pointing out that Mormonism accepted the doctrine of philosophical materialism, he said that in "Mormon theology there is no place for immaterialism; i.e. for a God, spirits and angels that are not material." The discussion led to the conclusion that Joseph Smith's enunciation of the eternity of intelligence in May 1833 anticipated the acceptance of the principle of the conservation of energy by ten to twenty years. Moving then to a theory which scientists had introduced to explain the movement of light as waves through space, he proposed the view that Joseph Smith anticipated the theory of the universal ether through the principle of the pervasive nature of spirit.[6]

Not all features of the book were so speculative, however, and some played an important part in reshaping, or restating, LDS doctrine. Continuing with a tradition dating from Orson and Parley Pratt, Widtsoe reinterpreted an essential portion of Mormon theology to argue that supernatural events were antithetical to the gospel. He wrote that miracles were simply phenomena not understood, that Joseph Smith taught the invariability of cause and effect, and that all operations take place according to law. Sweeping away such mystical or apocalyptic events as the Kirtland Temple experiences, Widtsoe said that Joseph Smith "taught doctrines absolutely free from mysticism, and built a system of religion in which the invariable relation of cause and effect is the cornerstone." Thus, he said, Joseph Smith was in full harmony with the scientific principle that the universe is controlled by law.[7]

The central discussion of the book, requiring more than fifty pages, dealt with evolution. Beginning with an interpretation of the Book of Abraham, Widtsoe argued that Joseph Smith was aware that the earth was created in an indeterminant time period and that the terms *day* and *night* are figurative. In his view of evolution Widtsoe worked from Herbert Spencer's views rather than from those of Charles Darwin. Asserting that "the philosophy of Herbert Spencer is considered the only philosophy that harmonizes with the knowledge of today," Widtsoe argued from Spencer's basic position that all things are in ceaseless change and moving toward a state of increasing complexity. The evolution from less to more complex forms, he argued, is "undoubtedly . . . correct" and "in harmony with the known facts of the universe." "It certainly throws a flood of light upon the phenomena of nature," he wrote. In itself the theory of evolution was incomplete because it "tells little of the force behind it, in obedience to which it operates." Widtsoe left little doubt of his belief that the Holy Spirit directed evolutionary changes.[8]

In critiquing Darwin, Widtsoe separated the theory of natural selection from that of evolution. Evolution, or the Spencerian idea of change in the direction of increasing complexity, did not presuppose natural selection. Arguing that Darwin's theory of natural selection had been brought into question by "recent discoveries . . . which throw serious doubt upon natural selection as an all-sufficient explanation of the wonderful variety of nature," Widtsoe proposed rather an alternative evolutionary doctrine that he called "the moderate law of evolution," which included an evolving God and human development toward godhood. Joseph Smith, he said, did not extend his ideas to the lower animals and plants, but Widtsoe believed that they advanced just as man has done. He argued that there could be no jumping from order to order, though he admitted the "limits of these orders are yet to be found."[9] With these conclusions Widstoe took a position between the outright rejection and full acceptance of natural selection. Widtsoe carefully chose his terminology, using "orders" rather than species as the terminal point of evolution, thereby leaving considerable latitude for the acceptance of some sort of change.

Some negative comment greeted Widtsoe's work, and he and others responded. Widtsoe and Edward H. Anderson answered criticism of dating the age of the earth with the statement that the scriptures do not require acceptance of a six-day or a 6,000-year creation. "Day" in the Mosaic record, they said, meant a time of indefinite duration. Widtsoe argued that the time may have been "hundreds of thousands or even millions of years in length," and he doubted the hypothesis that the earth was formed from large fragments of other worlds because "it would not be the way of nature as we know it. God, who is nature's master, does his work in a natural manner."[10]

Both Joseph F. Smith and Widtsoe attempted to answer criticism of Widtsoe's hypothesis that the universal ether was the spirit of God. President Smith said that the discussion was allegorical. Widtsoe believed that both the ether and spirit were included "in the works of God." Though poorly known to human understanding, the "marvel to us is that Joseph, the boy Prophet, unacquainted with the learning of men, should embody in the theological structure which he gave to the world, a fundamental doctrine, the practical counterpart of which men of science have been compelled by their discoveries to include in their man-made philosophy."[11]

By September 1909 the First Presidency had decided to issue a general statement on the problem of natural selection. Instead of choosing someone with a scientific background like Widtsoe or Talmage to prepare the statement, however, they picked Orson F. Whitney. From September 27 through October 15 members of the First Presidency and the Twelve, together with Widtsoe, Talmage, and George H. Brimhall, met to review the draft. It was presented to the Twelve on October 20 and approved.[12] The statement, entitled "The Origin of Man," was published in the November 1909 *Improvement Era*. All but part of the next to last paragraph deals with man, and the gist of the article is that Adam was the first man and that he was created in the image of God and was, thus, not something other than we are today. The method of creation is not discussed, but with regard to animals, the statement proclaims that "the whole animal creation will be perfected and perpetuated in the hereafter, each class in its 'distinct order or sphere,'" thus accepting Widtsoe's orders rather than Darwin's species as the boundary of natural selection in nonhuman creatures.[13]

Other general authorities shared an interest in the problem. From 1903 through 1906 the Mutual Improvement Association published as a lesson manual a revised and expanded version of B. H. Roberts's

New Witness for God. Like Widtsoe and Talmage, Roberts discussed scientific naturalism and the related topic of higher criticism of the Bible. Roberts agreed that the earth must be tremendously old, not simply 6,000 years, a position which he believed accorded well with Joseph Smith's conception of the inhabitation of other planets. Chapter 1 of volume 2 considered higher criticism and recent archaeological finds, which he argued tended to substantiate the authenticity of the Bible.[14]

Attacking the problem from a literalist point of view, J. C. Homans, a non-Mormon writing for the church, did some of the most controversial work on the subject. In an article published in the September 1914 *Improvement Era*, Homans asserted that though evolution was all right as a zoological theory, its proponents had encroached upon other disciplines. "Natural scientists," he argued, "have not hesitated to invade the fields of logic, philosophy, ethics, theology, etc., in which they have shown themselves, not merely 'laymen' but also amateurs of the crassest variety. . . . They are very good natural scientists, undoubtedly, but amazingly poor philosophers, and wretched logicians." Attacking evolution on the basis of logic, he argued that the facts of the variation in forms "do not argue for the philosophical dogma of organic evolution with any certainty or consistency; while the main allegations upon which this dogma is erected are, simply speaking, not true." In his view there was ample evidence of variation, but none of progression from simple to complex forms since there was an absence of proved linkages.[15]

Objections to Homans's views came from churchmen in the scientific community. Elder Talmage read Homans's article to the First Presidency on September 22, and Anthon H. Lund commented that it did not strike him as particularly logical in its assertions. Frederick J. Pack of the University of Utah came in the same day and said that the article was fighting an old issue, but not touching the real "pith of evolution." On September 27 Pack met again with President Lund and told him that he was convinced that Homans was harming intelligent young people who studied evolution because of his unwarranted and ignorant assertions.[16]

Elder Lund's discussions with Pack seem to have had some impact because in January 1915, when Talmage read a Homans manuscript to him on the origin of life, Lund rejected it. He considered the article "abstruse," and did not believe the readers of the *Era* would follow the thoughts. In addition, echoing Pack's views, he believed it did not "meet points at issue between the old ideas and the Evolutionists." Homans, he thought, believed that the evolutionists held ideas which would kill religion. Unfortunately, Lund believed, Homans was not willing to deal with the problem of harmonizing the ideas and "truth must harmonize with itself. This is the great problem. It will be solved," he believed.[17]

In 1915 John A. Widtsoe extended the argument on God, creation, and evolution written in *Joseph Smith as Scientist* by publishing *A Rational Theology* for use as a manual for the Melchizedek Priesthood. Starting essentially with the position that all truth must harmonize, he argued that the church expressed "a philosophy of life" which must be in "complete harmony with all knowledge." The gospel, Widtsoe argued, recognized the eternity of time, space, and matter. The universe is both material and eternal. God organized it; He did not create it. Since God had used pre-existing matter to organize the universe, He was not, in the theological sense, its creator. In the long run He too was governed by law and thus not, in the usually understood sense, omnipotent since law, rather than God, was fundamental. Widtsoe then equated this view of creation with Spencer's views of the development toward increasing complexity which he correlated with the LDS doctrine of eternal progression. As man acquired knowledge, he acquired power and thus moved toward a more advanced state. This acquisition of power, Widtsoe argued, allowed the endless development of man.[18]

The creation process was not accomplished in a way man might yet comprehend since he had not developed that complex an understanding. Rather, Widtsoe explained, "great forces, existing in the universe, and set into ceaseless operation by the directing intelligence of God, assembled and brought into place the materials constituting the earth, until, in the course of long periods of time, this sphere was fitted for the abode of man." God's work had been in harmony with natural law, and the creation had been accomplished by the "forces of nature act[ing] steadily but slowly in the accomplishment of great works," always under the direction of God.[19]

With this as a framework, Widtsoe considered the creation of man. Without trying to explain how the creation process took place, he argued that the biblical account of the creation of man from the dust of the earth and man's infusion with the breath of life were to be interpreted figuratively. The exact method of man's creation was unknown and probably at man's current stage of development could not be known. Nor, he said, "is it vital to a clear understanding of the plan of salvation."[20]

From there, it was but a short step to his view, drawn from an interpretation of the Book of Mormon, that the fall came about through natural law and to the view that the biblical account of the fall was also only figurative. For Widtsoe there "was no essential sin" in the fall, except as an effect follows the violation of any law, whether deliberate or not. Thus, the "so-called curse" on Adam was actually only an opportunity for eternal progression.[21]

The most controversial portion of the work, however, was simply a corollary of the previous views. If God had created neither the universe nor man in the theological sense of making them from nothing, man must be co-eternal with God. God was not "a God of mystery," but operated on a different level of advancement from man. It followed that "the man who progresses through his increase in knowledge and power, becomes a collaborator with God." Man's progression was God's progression, and man's method of procreation was God's. Thus, "we must also have a mother who possesses the attributes of Godhood."[22]

In his original draft, Widtsoe had gone much further than in the published version. He had included a discussion of intelligences which had existed before men became spirit beings and an explicit statement of the corollary of the previous views that there was a time when there was no God. These views, novel at the time, were too speculative for the general authorities to accept. On December 7, 1914, Joseph F. Smith, then in Missouri, telegraphed to Anthon H. Lund to stop the publication of Widtsoe's book. Lund called in Edward H. Anderson, who furnished the proof sheets. After reading the discussion of the evolution of God from intelligence to superior being to God, Lund became disturbed. "I do not like," he said, "to think of a time when there was no God." On December 11 Joseph F. Smith had returned from Missouri and ordered the elimination from the manuscript of those aspects considered too speculative.[23]

Discussions of the nature of the Godhead and of the relationship between God and Jesus Christ pointed to the need for an authoritative book on the nature and mission of Christ. During the years from 1904 to 1906 James E. Talmage had delivered a series of lectures, entitled "Jesus the Christ," at the Latter-day Saints University. Shortly after that, Talmage received an assignment from the First Presidency to incorporate the lectures into a book which was to be published for the use of the church in general. Owing to other assignments Talmage suspended work on the project, but by September 1914 the First Presidency had asked him "to prepare the matter for the book with as little delay as possible. Experiences demonstrated that neither in my comfortable office nor in the convenient study room at home can I be free from visits and telephone calls. In consequence of this condition, and in view of the importance of the work, I have been directed to occupy a room in the Temple where I will be free from interruption."[24]

Talmage began work on the volume in the temple on September 14, 1914. On April 19, 1915, slightly over seven months later, he "finished the actual writing." In his diary he said that he believed he could never have completed the writing had it not been for the privilege of working in the temple. "I have," he wrote, "felt the inspiration of the place and have appreciated the privacy and quietness incident thereto." By May 4, 1915, the manuscript was under consideration by the First Presidency and Twelve. The consideration progressed until June 24, when it was completed and the revised text was approved.[25] On August 13, 1915, the First Presidency issued a statement urging all members to read the book. Talmage's work dealt not only with Christ's life and ministry, but also with major aspects of the doctrinal importance of his life, his antemortal existence, his Godhood, his ministry, and his activities in a resurrected state.

Widtsoe's work on the nature of God and Talmage's discussion of Christ together with his earlier work on the Godhead preceded an authoritative statement on deity. A clarification of this point was necessary because of the apparent confusion in various scriptures relating to the unity of the Father and the Son, the discussion of Jesus Christ as Father, and the ambiguity over the roles of the Father and Son in the creation. The church undertook to do this in 1916, through a statement prepared by the First Presidency and Council of the Twelve and published to the church membership. The effect of the statement was to make clear the separation of the two beings and to indicate the roles of God and Christ.[26]

Widtsoe's and Talmage's intellectual predecessors had been Orson Pratt and his brother Parley P. Pratt, whose volume, *Key to Science of Theology*, had attempted to reconcile church doctrine with the discoveries of science as he knew them. Parley Pratt's views on the Godhead, however, were not in harmony with the church's twentieth-century position, and Charles W. Penrose undertook a revision of Pratt's work. Completed by January 1915, it was reviewed by other members of the First Presidency.[27]

Perhaps the most significant changes which had derived from clarifications in doctrine—completed as part of James E. Talmage's *Articles of Faith* and amplified in Widtsoe's work—were the revisions of the discussion of the Holy Ghost and the nature of spirit. Pratt had viewed spirit as a "fluid" which could pass from one body to another through the nerves. This discussion was deleted and the term "spiritual essence" replaced "spiritual fluid" where it appeared. Beyond this, Pratt had described the Holy Ghost as the controlling agent through which God operated the universe. In the revision the Holy Ghost was still reported as the "great, positive, controlling element of all other elements," but the discussion of those attributes which would necessitate an incorporeal, all-pervasive essence were deleted. The passage indicating that there are "vast quantities of this spirit or element not organized in bodily forms, but widely diffused among the other elements of space" was deleted.[28]

The clarification of the doctrine of the nature of the Holy Ghost and the relationship between the three members of the Godhead made necessary the revision of the fifth Lecture on Faith, then included in the Doctrine and Covenants. The first part of the volume titled *Doctrine and Covenants* had consisted of "Lectures on Faith" which had been presented by Joseph Smith and others in Kirtland, Ohio. The second part of the book, entitled "Covenants and Commandments," consisted of the first 132 sections of the present Doctrine and Covenants, which were followed by an Appendix including Sections 133 through 136.[29]

A meeting of the Council of the Twelve and First Presidency in November 1917 considered the question of the Lectures on Faith, particularly Lecture 5, which spoke of the Godhead as consisting of Father, Son, and Holy Ghost, only two of whom were personages. The Holy Ghost, Lecture 5 said, was the mind of the Father and Son. At that time the brethren spoke of appending a footnote to Lecture 5 in the next edition. Later, this idea was abandoned as a revision of the entire work was undertaken by the First Presidency and the Council of the Twelve.[30]

Already the First Presidency had appointed a committee, consisting of George F. Richards, Anthony W. Ivins, James E. Talmage, and Melvin J. Ballard, to prepare a new edition of the Book of Mormon, and this same committee was given the responsibility for a new edition of the Doctrine and Covenants. The immediate reason for the revision was not the contents of the Lectures on Faith, but rather the condition of the volume itself and of the plates on which it had been printed for many years. Discrepancies now existed between the present Doctrine and Covenants and Roberts's edition of *The History of the Church*. Revision continued through July and August 1921, and it was finally printed in late 1921 in essentially the form which it retained until 1981. The Lectures on Faith were deleted from this edition on the ground that they were "lessons prepared for use in the School of the Elders, conducted in Kirtland, Ohio, during the winter of 1834–35; but they were never presented to nor accepted by the Church as being otherwise than theological lectures or lessons."[31]

Important in the consideration of the doctrines of God and Christ was the role of Christ in the salvation of mankind. Considered as part of the First Presidency's 1916 statement on God and Christ and as part of Talmage's *Jesus the Christ*, it also became a part of Joseph F. Smith's prayerful consideration during the illness preceding his death. On October 3, 1918, while ill at home, Joseph F. Smith began pondering the mission of Christ to those who were dead, particularly as considered in I Peter 3:18–20 and 4:6. "As I pondered over these things," he wrote, "the eyes of my understanding were opened, and the Spirit of the Lord rested upon me, and I saw the hosts of the dead, both small and great." These spirits of faithful men and women met with Christ, and Christ organized them to carry the missionary work to the spirits in prison. In addition, Christ ministered unto these people and "gave them power to come forth, after his resurrection from the dead, to enter into his Father's kingdom."[32] On October 31, 1918, Joseph Fielding Smith brought the revelation to the Twelve. He read it to the council, and the apostles "accepted it as true and from God."[33] During the presidency of Spencer W. Kimball, this revelation was added to the church's Doctrine and Covenants as Section 138.

By the 1920s the issues of the creation, evolution, and biblical literalism had evoked a cultural crisis not only within the church but in the United States as a whole. Fundamentalists and Modernists battled one another in the press and across the pulpit. In the trial of John Scopes in Dayton, Tennessee, Fundamentalist William Jennings Bryan countered Modernist Clarence Darrow.[34] Most striking in light of the national controversy is the broad range of views church members held on these questions. In October 1922, while Heber J. Grant was in Washington, the First Presidency received a letter from Joseph W. McMurrin asking about the position of the church with regard to the literality of the Bible. Charles W. Penrose, with Anthony W. Ivins, writing for the First Presidency, answered that the position of the church was that the Bible is the word of God as far as it was translated correctly. They pointed out that there were, however, some problems with the Old Testament. The Pentateuch, for instance, was written by Moses, but "it is evident that the five books passed through other hands than Moses's after his day and time. The closing chapter of Deuteronomy proves that." While they thought Jonah was a real person, they said it was possible that the story as told in the Bible was a parable common at the time. The purpose was to teach a lesson, and it "is of little significance as to whether Jonah was a real individual or one chosen by the writer of the book" to illustrate "what is set forth therein." They took a similar position on Job. What is important, Penrose and Ivins insisted, was not whether the books were historically accurate, but whether the doctrines were correct. Nevertheless, higher criticism, they pointed out, was merely scholarly opinion and could say nothing about the doctrinal accuracy of the ideas in the books. In conclusion, they said, "to answer yes or no," to the higher critics, "is unwise and should not be undertaken by one representing the church."[35]

Unwilling to commit the church to a particular position on the questions of higher criticism or evolution, the First Presidency welcomed a number of points of view. In June 1922 Joseph Fielding Smith gave William Jennings Bryan's book, *In His Image*, to Heber J. Grant. The book, based on Bryan's lectures at Union Theological Seminary, discussed the authenticity of the Bible, the nature of Jesus Christ, evolution, and other topics from a Fundamentalist point of view. Two days later, having read the book, the First Presidency wrote commending Bryan and indicating that they were "thankful for such men as William Jennings Bryan, and invite upon you the blessings of Almighty God in your good and valiant work." An editorial in the *Relief Society Magazine* in August 1924, commenting on the heresy trial of Episcopal bishop William Montgomery Brown, indicated that though he might have been right in some of his criticism of minor points of the Bible, some basic doctrines like the virgin birth and the divinity of

Christ could not be sacrificed. In November 1924 Joseph Fielding Smith staked out a position on biblical inerrancy more conservative than the First Presidency's letter.[36]

Indicative of the wide range of views on the subject, Frederick Pack mounted one of the strongest attacks on biblical literalism and anti-evolutionary sentiment in *Science and Belief in God*, published by Deseret News Press in 1924. While affirming his strong belief in God, Pack pointed out that biblical literalism presented a number of problems. He cited the difficulty of finding space to gather all earthly species on the ark. He pointed out that if rain had fallen for forty days and forty nights, to submerge the highest mountain peaks, which are five miles above the surface of the ocean it would have to have rained twenty-five feet per hour. Not only were even the most severe rains known on earth scarcely one-tenth of that volume, but the quantity of water available on the earth for the purpose was too small. In addition, even if the water had been boiling, it could not have evaporated in the time stated in the account. Most theologians, he said, looked upon the account as teaching a hidden truth. Perhaps, he suggested, periodic flooding in recorded time or the rapid melting at the end of the ice age might have been meant, and Noah may have simply gathered domestic animals.[37]

Nevertheless, warning against "worshipping at the shrine of newness," he denied most emphatically that such suggestions ignored the question of the authenticity of the Bible. He said that "quite the contrary," these tried "to go directly to the heart of it." Students of the Bible are not justified in interpreting the narrative of the ancient Israelites in terms understood by modern civilizations. Conditions are far different at present and it is unreasonable to expect that God revealed His will to the Hebrews in terms of modern knowledge. They would have been culturally incapable of understanding such revelations. "Deity cannot make complete explanations until the human mind has developed to the stage where it is capable of grasping the full truth."[38]

Pack's major purpose seems to have been to disarm both the intransigent Fundamentalist and the crusading Modernist. The conflict between science and religion develops, Pack said, when a theist believes that the basis of his faith is being attacked by the scientific conception of the operation of the universe. In Copernicus's time the prevailing view of the geocentric universe came under attack. Today the threat to a particular biblical interpretation came from evolution and higher criticism. In Pack's view, if the theist could overcome the sense of threat he could just as easily overcome the problems with evolution and higher criticism as earlier religionists did with the Copernican universe. "If the doctrine of organic evolution is true," Pack said, "it is not unreasonable to believe that *its method of operation is the manner in which God is bringing about His purposes.*" On the same basis Pack attacked theists who believed in two sets of laws, one by which God operated and one by which nature operated. The only safe position for the theist, Pack said, was that if scientific theories are true, they reveal the work of God. On the other hand, if the religionist attacks the scientists as earlier generations did Copernican theory and evidence later shows that the scientists are right, then the theistic position, and with it the faith of other believers, is undermined. He believed such attacks were particularly dangerous in view of the scientific evidence on prehistoric life.[39]

Pack's book, however, was not a defense of irreligion. Pack differentiated, as Widtsoe and Talmage had, between evolution and natural selection. Darwin's explanation that evolution operates through organic change could be entirely wrong, Pack wrote, and yet the idea of evolution could be entirely right. Evolution through natural selection does not necessarily involve the creation of new species. Rather, it may simply direct them after their creation. The fundamental weakness of the doctrine of natural selection, Pack wrote, is that it does not explain the method of creation. The major problem of organic evolution, he said, is the insistence of some that it was not directed. Pack, on the other hand, affirmed that evolution, however it functioned, was directed by God.[40]

Pack followed a path already trod by Talmage, Widtsoe, and Roberts in declaring a position which could incorporate both the scientific evidence and religious teachings. In the same spirit in 1930 Widtsoe wrote another book called *In Search of Truth: Comments on the Gospel and Modern Thought.* After discussing the findings of science and the conflicts with the ideas of some religionists, Widtsoe argued that the only essential is a belief in God and His work. The method by which God operates is open to question, and above all, the church will accept any truth.[41]

In addition to publishing these two books, which took an essentially Baconian stand, the church published much more on a wide range of views, some of them closer to the selective literalists. The Scopes trial during the summer of 1925 brought about a renewed interest in the problem of evolution, and the First Presidency published a statement on July 18 and again in September affirming that Adam, the first man, was, like contemporary man, in the image of God. The statement was perhaps more remarkable for what it did not say than for what it did. Certainly neither Pack, Widtsoe, Roberts, nor Talmage would have had any trouble accepting it. The statement did not say that the creation had taken place in six literal days or even in six thousand years nor did it reject the idea of evolution. It affirmed that man was created in the image of God, but said nothing of the method of creation.[42]

At the same time, Bryan's handling of the prosecution of John Scopes evoked a responsive chord in some segments of the Mormon community. George F. Richards read the speech Bryan planned to deliver at the trial the day after his death. He endorsed the speech fully, sent a copy to his son Oliver, who was on a mission in Germany, and secured permission from Heber J. Grant for its publication in the October 1925 *Improvement Era*. Bryan's final argument is perhaps most important not as a rejection of evolution, which it was, but as an affirmation that the world needed Christ then more than ever before.[43]

The *Improvement Era* opened its pages to further discussion of the same problem. In the October 1928 issue Nephi Jensen posed a dichotomy between false science and true science and a false interpretation and a true interpretation of Genesis. In the October 1930 *Improvement Era* Frederick J. Pack again dealt with the problem of time by insisting that the use of a six-day period or even six thousand years contradicted modern scripture and offering the Latter-day scriptures as a means of settling the Fundamentalist-Modernist controversy.[44]

In essence, works by Widtsoe, Pack, and Talmage had chosen to suspend judgment and not to try to reconcile the biblical account with the geological record. B. H. Roberts proposed a method of reconciliation, in what he perceived to be his final masterwork. In April 1927 Roberts, just completing his term as Eastern States Mission president, secured permission from Heber J. Grant to remain in New York to finish a book he had begun. President Grant agreed to allow him to do so and in addition supplied a stenographer. Completed by 1928, the manuscript, which Roberts entitled "The Truth, the Way, the Life: An Elementary Treatise on Theology," dealt essentially with Christ and the centrality of his mission to Latter-day Saints. Part of the manuscript, however, caused immediate controversy in the Council of the Twelve.[45]

Roberts attempted to reconcile the biblical and geological records by refurbishing a doctrine Brigham Young had preached as early as 1852. Roberts held that the discussion of the creation of Adam was irrelevant since Adam had in fact come from another sphere to inhabit the earth. Most importantly, Roberts insisted, the earth had been inhabited by pre-Adamic forms of life.[46] On this point a clash developed between Roberts and Joseph Fielding Smith, who rejected the possibility of pre-Adamic life. Implicit in Elder Smith's view was the position that the period since the creation had not been long, and explicit was the statement that "there is no warrant in the scripture" for the view "that this earth was peopled with a race—perhaps many races—long before the days of Adam." Rejecting any attempt to reconcile the geological or paleontological record with the gospel, Elder Smith said that he did not "care what the scientists say in regard to dinosaurs and other creatures upon the earth millions of years ago that lived and died and fought and struggled for existence. . . . *There was no death in the earth before the fall of Adam.*" At the same time, he insisted on a literal interpretation of certain scriptures and took to task those who tried "to stretch the word of the Lord to make it conform to these theories and teachings." Presented first on April 5, 1930, at a genealogical conference, Elder Smith's views were published in October 1930.[47]

In May 1930 Roberts, somewhat upset at the controversy among the Twelve on the matter, visited Heber J. Grant. He asked that his manuscript be published with no changes. President Grant was sorry that Roberts took the position that he did, not because he disagreed with Roberts's views, but because he realized they were "problematical and cannot be demonstrated." He was willing, he told Roberts, to publish the book—after all, the church had supported its writing—provided the First Presidency and the Twelve could "come to an understanding as to what shall go into it." They reached no understanding and the controversy continued into January 1931, when both Smith and Roberts stated their positions before the council. In the meantime, Elder Smith had published his article and Roberts had attacked Smith's position.[48]

Thereafter the First Presidency took the question under consideration. In his diary, President Grant said that "after reading the articles by Brothers Roberts and Smith, I feel that sermons such as Brother Joseph preached and criticisms such as Brother Roberts makes of the sermon are the finest kind of things to be let alone entirely. I think that no good can be accomplished by dealing in mysteries, and that is what I feel in my heart of hearts these brethren are both doing." After further consideration during February and March the First Presidency decided to allow the matter to rest.[49]

Further discussion was essentially ended at the time with a speech straddling the issue of pre-Adamic man made by James E. Talmage in August 1931 and later published as *The Earth and Man*. He made clear his view that scientific evidence ought to be taken into consideration in any discussion of the creation, thus taking a position between elders Smith and Roberts by denying Elder Smith's attacks on the scientific method and recognizing the speculative nature of Roberts's position.[50]

From the point of view of President Grant, the question of whether one or the other was right or wrong was irresolvable. What was important was that the two had drawn the church into an irreconcilable controversy and created ill will among members who lined up behind one or the other. In fact, on August 16, 1931, he attended an address by Nephi L. Morris in the Tabernacle which he considered "a very scholarly effort indeed." Morris expressed the view that "the earth is about two billion years old." President Grant said that he was "not thoroughly converted myself to the wisdom of such addresses, and yet I have no objections, seeing he is a lay member now, to his speech being published." As long as Morris's views could not be construed as the official position of the church he had no objection to their publication. With Roberts and Smith, however, the matter was quite different.[51]

Moving to the consideration of other doctrinal questions, one notes considerable change in emphasis from 1900 to the 1920s on doctrinal points relating to the millennium and the Kingdom of God on earth. Lorenzo Snow's views were considerably more apocalyptic than either Joseph F. Smith's or Heber J. Grant's. During 1900, in articles and speeches, President Snow stressed his belief in the nearness of the millennium. In October 1900, replying to a letter of Isaac Riddle of Provo with a check for $25,000 to help construct a temple in Jackson County, Missouri, he reported that John R. Winder had donated $1,000 for the same purpose and that many felt that the "time has come to commence to redeem the Land of Zion." On November 7, 1900, following the Republican electoral victory, Lorenzo Snow, in an apocalyptic mood, said, "THERE ARE MANY HERE NOW UNDER THE SOUND OF MY VOICE, PROBABLY A MAJORITY WHO WILL HAVE TO GO BACK TO JACKSON

COUNTY AND ASSIST IN BUILDING THE TEMPLE." He made a similar prediction in the October 1900 conference, in his January 1901 greeting
to the world, and in a fast meeting in the temple in March 1901.[52] On
the other hand, Joseph F. Smith and his counselors downplayed the
imminence of the millennium. Part of Charles W. Penrose's revision of
Pratt's *Key to the Science of Theology* involved the removal of some
passages predicting its nearness. By the 1920s the nearness of the millennium was deemphasized even more. In keeping with the changing
emphasis, questions related to the imminence of the millennium were
generally avoided. With the exception of the sort of ritual pronouncements on the "signs of the times," discourses dealing with the millennium were usually general rather than apocalyptic.[53]

Church leaders also reinterpreted the doctrine of the Kingdom of
God to push its earthly application into the millennium. Instead of arguing, as church leaders like Parley P. Pratt in the nineteenth century
had, that the priesthood-directed Kingdom of God was the only legitimate government on earth, in December 1901 the First Presidency
stated that though the church might instruct in temporal as well as
spiritual matters, it "does not infringe upon the liberty of the individual
or encroach upon the domain of the State." Charles Penrose's revision
of Pratt's *Key to the Science of Theology* also removed passages asserting the legitimacy of priesthood authority in temporal affairs. Ecclesiastical and political systems were and are to be separate, church
leaders said. The church has been established preparatory to the Kingdom of God, but there is to be no domination of the state. James E.
Talmage argued that though the church is to be regarded as the beginning of the Kingdom of God on earth, "until the coming of the King,
there is no authority in the church exercising or claiming temporal
rule among the governments of earth."[54]

On a practical level, the decline of millennialist spirit brought about
some change in the emphasis on gathering church members to Utah.
Though members of the church were encouraged to secure land in
those areas where the church was organized and to emigrate to colonies which were newly opened, Presidents Snow and Smith wanted to
make sure certain jobs were available for those who came. Anthon H.
Lund suggested that missionaries ought to encourage only those well
versed in the gospel to gather. During the first decades of the new century, restraint seems to have been practical rather than doctrinal. The
church took an essentially neutral attitude on emigrating to Zion—

that is, no inducements were used, but members who decided to emigrate were not stopped.[55]

Lest it be thought that this was in some ways the beginning of the current concept of multiple Zions, it should be emphasized that the leaders still urged the establishment of compact communities in the West. In a discourse at Burlington, Wyoming, in September 1903, Joseph F. Smith said that settlement in the mountain West was part of the gathering. The members of the church needed to promote solidarity and community life and not become a law unto themselves. The leaders advised members to build cities and close-knit communities, not to spread themselves throughout the world. The principal institution of community life was still the Mormon town.[56]

During the 1920s the church leadership sent out even more negative signals in regard to gathering to Zion. In September 1925 the First Presidency warned those who came to Zion that they would have additional difficulties because of their foreign birth and the language barrier. In late 1929, after the stock market crash and the onset of the Depression, they urged German Mission president Fred Tadje to allow only those who could purchase homes or who had secure employment to emigrate. Still, they refrained from making explicit statements rejecting the doctrine of the gathering.[57]

Coincident with a decline in emphasis on the imminence of the millennium and equivocation on the gathering was a tendency to discourage Pentecostal and charismatic gifts which members had experienced since early days. Those who remember, for instance, the first meeting of Brigham Young and Joseph Smith will recall that the Prophet declared that Young had spoken in the pure Adamic language. Throughout the nineteenth century, speaking and blessing in tongues and open prophecy had been prevalent in church gatherings. In addition, women in the church had been encouraged to participate in the healing of children and the anointing of sisters prior to their confinement for childbirth. Rebaptism and baptism for health had been common until the mid-1890s.[58]

Even though Wilford Woodruff had questioned the practice of rebaptism in the 1890s, after the turn of the century it was used quite extensively both as a sign of repentance and as a healing ordinance. Marriner W. Merrill, for instance, brought his daughter Lenora Eveline to the temple to be baptized for the cure of an afflicted eye. In 1903 Heber J. Grant took William A. Nuttall to the temple to be baptized for his health. In 1913 Anthon H. Lund told one sister that she must submit to rebaptism for having withheld information on her artificial insemination from her husband.[59]

On one occasion President Lund gave the rationale for the practice of rebaptism as a means of healing. He pointed out that though baptism was not mentioned in the revelations for healing, Jesus had said that it was easier to forgive sins than to heal someone. Since baptism is for the remission of sins and sickness is often the result of violation of a law of nature or of God, Elder Lund justified rebaptism on the ground that when faith accompanies baptism, it may be used for the restoration of health.[60]

Nevertheless some authorities, apparently uncomfortable with these views, thought the temples should be closed to healing ordinances. In 1915, for instance, Francis M. Lyman said that members ought not go to the temple for their health. President Lund pointed out that on Tuesdays ordinances for health were scheduled, and Elder Lyman withdrew his objection. In May 1918 Alvin Smith said that members ought not be encouraged to come to the temple when the elders could as well come to their homes to administer to them. Lund, again, disagreed with this view.[61]

President Lund, however, seems to have been among the last of the general authorities who favored rebaptism and temple healing ordinances. In December 1922, a year and a half after his death, the First Presidency issued a circular letter saying that "baptizing for health is no part of temple work, and therefore to permit it to become a practice would be an innovation, detrimental to temple work, and a departure as well from the practice instituted of the Lord for the care and healing of the sick." The letter indicated that no more recommends were to be issued for baptisms for health or administrations to the sick in the temples. Several reasons seem to have been paramount in abolishing the practice. There was concern that some members believed that going to the temple for an administration was superior to an ordinance given by a priesthood holder outside. In addition, the use of the temple for performing vicarious work for the dead had increased greatly, and the pressure for baptism and administrations for health occupied temple facilities.[62]

At the same time that general authorities were discouraging temple attendance for healing, they were restricting the women's participation in such ordinances. Joseph Smith had instituted the practice of women healing at least by 1842, and both Brigham Young and Wilford Woodruff had encouraged it. At the turn of the century it was generally expected that women would participate to one degree or another in the healing ordinance. In January 1900 Emmeline B. Wells reported that she and Bathsheba Smith washed and anointed Martha H. Tingey, who was "suffering from a weakness of some sort." Emily Richards received a blessing from Zina D. H. Young, Bathsheba Smith, and Emmeline Wells. Sisters Wells and Smith also washed and anointed Lydia Spencer Clawson prior to her confinement. "Sister Smith anointed," Wells reported, and she "sealed the anointing."[63]

In a letter in 1901 Joseph F. Smith said that anointing and healing the sick was to be done under the direction of a member of the Melchizedek Priesthood, but that he might call upon an Aaronic Priesthood holder or a woman to assist him. "In my own case," he wrote, "I have frequently when alone administering to the sick invited my wives to lay hands on with me in the prayer for their recovery." Later, the First Presidency indicated that there was no objection "whatever to a mother administering oil to her children in the absence of her husband." In 1905 the First Presidency also approved the ordinance of "washing and anointing sisters for health and for confinement." Any "good sister who had received her endowments and who is in good standing in the church might officiate in washing and anointing previous to confinement, if called upon, or if requested to do so, by the sister or sisters desiring the blessing."[64]

As Joseph F. Smith's administration progressed, further questions about the propriety of women performing healing ordinances arose. As early as 1907 the First Presidency had begun to question the practice. In 1911 President Lund said that anointing prior to confinement could comfort and strengthen women, but that it ought not be confused with temple ordinances, and the words used in washing and anointing in the temple ought not be used in this ordinance whether the sisters who performed it had received their endowments or not. Nevertheless, in October 1914 the First Presidency seemed to set the question to rest by issuing a circular letter ruling that sisters had the same right to administer to the sick or to anoint women prior to childbirth as priesthood holders did. In keeping with this position, Anthon H. Lund noted that Elizabeth McCune and Susa Young Gates visited his wife during an illness and blessed her. He reported that it "seemed to cheer Sanie."[65]

In general, these ordinances had been performed under the direction of the Relief Society, but in 1922 the First Presidency moved to curtail that practice. On December 29, 1922, a circular letter indicated that the church did not approve of sisters being set apart by the Relief Society to anoint the sick. Nor should any women participate in the ordinance unless they did it in the spirit "of invocation and prayer" rather than on the basis of authority. In November 1923 the First Presidency moved even further on the path of restricting women by indicating that they neither encouraged nor discouraged women from performing these ordinances, but ruled that it was unnecessary for those participating to be Relief Society members as had previously been the case.[66]

Central to this whole question was the problem of whether women who had been endowed received the priesthood with their husbands or whether they received only the blessings of their husband's priesthood. Currently available evidence indicates that a number of nineteenth-century church leaders including Joseph Smith believed that the endowment actually bestowed the "privileges, blessings, and gifts of the priesthood" on the women. By the early twentieth century, however, most church leaders were inclined to disagree. Thus the restrictions placed on the performance of blessings on the part of women is quite understandable.[67]

This is not to say that healing ordinances were discouraged. Rather, with the caveat that members also ought to "show our works by calling in a competent physician," church leaders encouraged calling in the elders for healing. The *Improvement Era*, for instance, reported a number of miraculous healings including one by Joseph F. Smith in Rotterdam during his visit to Holland. On August 18, 1915, while Anthon H. Lund was officiating in the temple, Leah Matthews of Midway, Utah, came into the temple on crutches. She said that she had been told in a dream to come to the temple and have Lund administer to her, and promised she would be healed. Lund agreed, and as he did so he "looked at her face which showed me she had faith that the dream was from the Lord." Immediately after the ordinance, Matthews said, "I am healed." She put her crutches under her arms and walked away without help. She said it felt good to have the strength to walk again. After the experience, he confided to his journal, "I feel thankful for this manifestation of the power of God. I feel so small and humble to be an instrument in the hand of the Lord to bring her this blessing."[68]

Basically, the same decline in usage and acceptability took place in glossolalia that took place in healing by women and baptism for health. Currently available evidence indicates that in the nineteenth century, speaking in tongues was quite common. At the turn of the century, such experience was still widespread in the church. In August 1899 L. John Nuttall recorded that Elizabeth Hamman blessed him and Karl G. Maeser in tongues. Following that, Zina Y. Card laid her hands on their heads and interpreted the blessings. Emmeline B. Wells reported an experience in the Tabernacle in February 1900, where a missionary had spoken in tongues and given interpretation. The gift of tongues was manifested in a conference in Pueblo, Colorado, October 1900, and Anthon H. Lund witnessed a sister speaking in tongues in Lehi in February 1903. In January 1901 Joseph Eckersley listened as his wife sang in tongues. His little boy "made the simply childlike truthful statement . . . that his mama sang as he had never heard her before, that it was beautiful and sounded like a violin and piano and other kinds of music all being played at one time." Emmeline Wells saw another incident of blessing in tongues by Lillie Freeze in 1903. In June 1908 Anthon H. Lund heard a woman speak and sing in tongues in the Tabernacle.[69] In general, however, the incidence of this sort of experience had begun to decline in the early twentieth century, though glossolalia declined more rapidly among men than among women. In a study of the MIA, Scott Kenney found that such experiences continued to be found among members of the YLMIA general board longer than among members of the YMMIA general board.[70]

By the early 1920s the general authorities were actively discouraging such Pentecostal experience within the church. In a letter to Heber Q. Hale of the Boise Stake in March 1923, the First Presidency referred to an incident which had occurred in the stake and urged that it be discontinued. In the Nampa Relief Society one sister had pronounced a revelation in tongues, following which the president of the Relief Society interpreted the speech. The First Presidency said in its letter that the gift of tongues was given to the church for the purpose of "preaching among peoples whose language is not understood. This being the case," they said, "it was entirely unnecessary . . . to resort to speaking in tongues on the occasion referred to, as all present spoke the same language." In addition they said "it was not the sister's place to pronounce a revelation" of the sort given and they urged the stake president to advise the sister "to let speaking in tongues alone and to confine her speech to her own language."[71] In addition to the interdiction of glossolalia, the 1923 letter included a caveat against certain types of public revelation and prophecy. These public prophesies should be distinguished from personal religious experiences which continued into the new century and were not discouraged.

In contrast, at the turn of the century public revelations and prophecies were still to be heard in some gatherings. In a meeting at the Temple in January 1898 John W. Taylor prophesied that Heber J. Grant would be relieved from debt. Elder Grant's "entire being was on fire while brother Taylor was prophesying . . . and the tears filled my eyes, and they were tears of the deepest gratitude to the Lord as I felt impressed that the blessings promised by Bro. Taylor were promises made by inspiration and that the Lord would see that they were fulfilled." At a fast and testimony meeting Anthon H. Lund heard a testimony by Hamilton Park, who said he had seen and spoken with the Savior. George Q. Cannon had been visited by Joseph Smith while on a ship lying in San Francisco harbor waiting for a wind to take him to Hawaii.[72]

Marriner W. Merrill had spiritual experiences which impressed those who heard. In January 1900 he reported a dream in which he had seen the Devil and a large company camped near the Logan Temple. The Devil wanted admission to the temple, and Merrill reported that he was a fine-looking, rather large man who acted like a "perfect gentleman." Merrill experienced also the visitation of his son, who had died, who told him that he was working with many relatives beyond the veil. Merrill said that he had been comforted by the visitation.[73]

At times members experienced mass spiritual feelings. In the October conference 1905 a number of people said that during a speech of Joseph F. Smith, "the Spirit of the Lord touched the hearts of the people, and there was intense feeling so much so that many quivered with emotion, and there was weeping in all the building."[74]

Some church members reported personal or family spiritual experiences. Heber J. Grant wrote of an intense spiritual experience in January 1916 at the time of his wife's death. Reed Smoot reported an experience in April in connection with the healing of his wife. In August 1917, when a brother told Joseph F. Smith that his house was full of evil spirits, the president told him to use the power of his priesthood and drive them out, adding that such spirits can have no power over a person who lives a pure life. In 1919 Melvin J. Ballard experienced a

manifestation of the Savior shortly before his call to the Council of the
Twelve as had George F. Richards in 1906. Heber J. Grant's daughter
Emily had felt a "strong premonition" that she would not live after she
went to the hospital in 1929. Her sisters thought "that perhaps she was
a little irrational, but we [members of the family] realize now that she
is gone and that she was perfectly rational."[75]

Many church members were uncomfortable with religious experiences when they served as a basis for circulating rumors or to entice
church members into questionable investments. In 1902, for instance,
Joseph F. Smith denied rumors that Joseph and Hyrum Smith had
been resurrected or that he had seen the Savior face to face and had
shaken hands with him.[76] Perhaps the most serious problem developed
in Utah County when Bishop John Koyle reported a vision of a mine on
the mountain east of Spanish Fork which he believed would produce
enough wealth to save the church. The mine, still in existence, proved
worthless, but Koyle was able to induce a number of church members,
including Heber J. Grant's nephew Carter E. Grant and J. Golden
Kimball of the First Council of the Seventy, to purchase stock. President Grant was particularly dismayed at the activities of the mine
promoters.[77]

While the fear of fraud and idle rumors may have played a part in the
decline of the general acceptance of the public revelations and prophecies, a more basic objection seems to have come about because of the
change in the church itself which had taken place in the period since
the 1890s. First, except for personal religious experiences, the church
leadership clearly wanted religious manifestations to come within recognized lines of priesthood authority and within doctrinally defensible
limits. Second, the reconstruction of Latter-day Saint doctrine which
had taken place following the lead of Talmage, Widtsoe, and Roberts,
while addressing the reconciliation of church doctrine with scientific
theory, had brought supernaturalism into question. Since the views of
the three progressive theologians had not been officially accepted, the
church leadership could tolerate and even encourage personal spiritual experiences. On the other hand, public displays of prophecy or
glossolalia tended to the discomfort of some members and perhaps
even to disharmony in the organization.

As Thomas Kuhn has argued in his *Structure of Scientific Revolutions*, new paradigms develop because old models do not answer important questions. The major problem with new views, however, is

that they often cannot answer some of the questions which the old ones could. This problem can also be viewed from the perspective of Victor W. Turner's theory of limnality, or crossing the threshold from one condition to another.[78] How does one incorporate supernatural experiences into a paradigm which denies their legitimacy outside priesthood authority and which proposes the reconciliation of scientific and religious truths? A rational approach to such a problem provided answers to part of the questions. Talmage spoke of the actuality of miracles, and Widtsoe took the view that miracles were not unnatural events. In his view, "the miracles of the Savior were done only by superior knowledge. Nothing is unnatural." Prominent lay members like Frederick J. Pack reinforced such views. Pack said that "a great service would be rendered Christianity if the term supernatural were expurgated from all languages," because, he said, supernatural experiences were simply the operation of natural laws we do not understand.[79]

This position on charismatic experiences might have been acceptable in some cases, but was upsetting to some members who experienced personal spiritual manifestations. In December 1914, for instance, one brother came and asked Anthon H. Lund for the interpretation of a dream. In the dream the brother saw the Devil come unrecognized to him and lie down beside him. The man called upon the Lord, but the Devil did not go, but spoke to him and asked him to kiss him. The brother did so, and the kiss filled him with loathing. Then, realizing whom he had kissed, the brother said, "Now I know who you are. I command you to depart," which the Devil did. The man asked Lund for the interpretation of the dream. Lund told him that though dreams were sometimes full of meaning, they are mostly caused "by an overloaded stomach." It hardly seems likely that this explanation satisfied the brother.[80] Another instance occurred in January 1918 at the death of Hyrum M. Smith. Questions arose as to the cause of Elder Smith's death. Several of the speakers at his funeral said that he was needed for work on the other side, but Charles W. Nibley pointed out that Smith had refused medical attention and said that if he had not done so, he would still be alive. Joseph F. Smith nodded his agreement to the remarks, but it seems clear that such an explanation might not comfort a bereaved family.[81]

Although a rational approach to religious experience might gratify some, it could clearly not meet the needs of all. With the increasing reluctance of church leaders to accept Pentecostal experience, the increasing insistence that religious experiences be confirmed within the bounds of priesthood authority, and their discouraging of public prophecy and revelation, many members sought other outlets for religious impulses. Many of these forms of personal religious experiences remained despite their official disapproval, but members turned increasingly to institutional forms such as bearing of testimonies in the monthly ward fast and testimony meeting and to genealogical work and vicarious ordinances for the dead in the temples.

The Genealogical Society of Utah provided support for the temple work. Organized under the auspices of the church in 1894, following Wilford Woodruff's announcement of the need for each person to be sealed to his own parents rather than to some prominent church leader, the Genealogical Society expanded its activities in the twentieth century.[82] Although Anthon H. Lund and Anthony W. Ivins served successively as presidents of the society, they were both engaged in numerous other church assignments, and the principal force behind the society was Joseph Fielding Smith and, in addition, during the 1920s, Archibald F. Bennett.

In January 1910 the Genealogical Society began publication of the *Utah Genealogical and Historical Magazine* with Elder Smith as assistant editor and business manager. Elder Smith had already visited the principal genealogical libraries of the United States during the summer of 1909, and from those visits he had introduced improved methods of filing and record keeping to the society.[83]

During the 1920s the work of the Genealogical Society expanded greatly. The society sponsored regular conventions of genealogical researchers, and Bennett actively worked to interest young and old in family reconstitution. In October 1919 the church organized the Lamanite Society to encourage genealogical activity among native Americans, and by March 1924 reports indicated that more than 12,000 Indian names had been collected for vicarious ordinance work. By September 1929 Richard L. Evans had worked out a plan to allow European Saints to do genealogical research in return for Americans performing vicarious endowments and sealings in the temples. Since many family records were in Europe and all the temples were then in western North America, this seemed an equitable trade-off.[84]

These promotional activities, growing interest in family ties, and the need for religious experience led to the increase in temple activity. In

February 1911 Anthon H. Lund suggested, in view of the increased pressure on the Manti Temple, that wards be given a certain day each month to attend. In 1911 the Salt Lake Temple opened for one session per day on Wednesdays, Thursdays, and Fridays for endowments and sealings and on Mondays and Tuesdays for record taking and baptisms for the dead. By February 1913 the single sessions had become so crowded that the First Presidency and Twelve decided to open the temple for two sessions per day.[85]

Following World War I attendance at the Salt Lake Temple increased greatly. Participation in vicarious endowment ceremonies grew 300 percent between 1918 and 1922 to 413,000 per year. The number of baptisms for the dead expanded also as young people were encouraged to organize stake excursions to the temple. The number of sessions per day and days per week that the temple was open for endowments increased during the 1920s. By January 1923 the Salt Lake Temple was opened for one session on Wednesday, Thursday, and Friday evenings, making nine sessions per week. So many people wanted to attend the temple on January 17, 1924, that the facilities could not accommodate them. By 1926 the general authorities had agreed to open the temple for endowments four days per week rather than the previous three. In addition, as we have seen, the capacity of the temple facilities and the number of temples was expanded during the 1920s.[86]

The increased emphasis on temple attendance affected church members. Prior to the 1920s regular temple attendance had generally not been expected. Indeed, Reed Smoot testified in 1905 that he had not been back to the temple to do endowment work since his marriage. President Heber J. Grant, who had been quite infrequent in his temple attendance before the 1920s, began to go regularly.[87]

In general, members of the church were expected to do the temple work vicariously for their own relatives or pay to have someone else do it. In April 1926, however, the church leadership designated the St. George Temple as the place where mission presidents might send the names of faithful deceased members with no relatives in the church to have the temple work done for them at the church's expense.[88] This was eventually expanded into the enormous temple work of today, where the cost of virtually all temple work comes from general church funds. The church leadership also continued the practice of doing vicarious work for outstanding political leaders, started by Wilford Woodruff at the time the St. George Temple opened in 1877. In September 1926, for instance, Heber J. Grant, George F. Richards, and Reed Smoot received endowments in behalf of a number of national leaders including Warren Harding, Theodore Roosevelt, Ulysses S. Grant, Julia Dent Grant, and Ulysses S. Grant's parents, Jesse Root Grant and Hannah Simpson Grant.[89]

Vicarious work for the dead also seemed a way to meet the purposes of celestial marriage without actually entering into polygamy. As early as December 14, 1909, George F. Richards had suggested that it would be appropriate for members of the Twelve who had only one living wife to have some "good dead woman sealed to them while they are here and can look after their own interests." He thought Francis M. Lyman could present the suggestion to the First Presidency and Twelve because he wanted his "brethren [to] avoid the disappointments which must follow neglect of opportunity." Already on February 20, 1907, Richards had been sealed to May Gowans, deceased daughter of President E. G. Gowans, who with Elder Lyman had agreed to the sealing. The extent of the practice is not currently known, but some posthumous sealing to living authorities continued as late as April 1925.[90]

The increasing interest in temple work brought about a desire to review the temple ceremony so it could better meet the needs of the church members. As late as 1923 parts of the temple ceremony had never been written down. They had been passed on by word of mouth from temple worker to temple worker and were often different in the various temples.[91] During the administration of Heber J. Grant, the Salt Lake Temple president—then his counselor Anthon H. Lund— was given the responsibility of reviewing the temple ceremony and clothing. Continued by President George F. Richards after Elder Lund's death in 1921, the revision was not completed until 1927.[92]

Three purposes seem to have been paramount. First was the need for "the means of getting uniformity in all the temples." Second was a desire to accommodate a greater number of patrons in the temples, which meant a reduction in the length of the ceremony, then reportedly six to nine hours long. Third was a wish to redesign the clothing used in temple ceremonies and the garments worn as underclothing by endowed members to better meet the needs of church members while maintaining doctrinal standards. Elder Richards was particularly interested in determining what was essential and what unnecessary in the ordinances.[93]

The redesign of the temple clothing and garments was completed first. In April 1923 the First Presidency referred the question to a committee consisting of Elder Richards, Rudger Clawson, Joseph Fielding Smith, and Orson F. Whitney. The suggestion for the reconsideration apparently came because of Elder Richards's questions raised after a conversation with Sister Maria Dougall in October 1922. At that time he learned that Joseph Smith had not designed the garments and temple clothing. In fact, a group of sisters led by Emma Smith and including Bathsheba Smith had fashioned both the garments and the temple clothing, and presented them to Joseph Smith for his approval. The collar on the garments had been put on because the sisters could think of no other way to finish it at the top, and they added ties because they had no buttons. The original cap in the temple clothing had looked something like a crown, but Joseph Smith had them redesign it to look more like a baker's cap.[94]

On April 14, 1923, Richards discussed the garment design with the First Presidency. At that time, they considered such changes as removing the collar, using buttons, and allowing women to use elbow-length sleeves and shorter legs presumably to coordinate with women's fashions, which had changed considerably by the 1920s. On May 17, 1923, the entire council and Presidency approved the new design.[95]

In a circular letter dated June 14, 1923, the First Presidency discussed the refashioned garments. They pointed out that the Lord had revealed no fixed pattern for the garment. The presently used style differed from those in use earlier in the church when a garment without a collar and with buttons was frequently in use. In the letter, members were told that they might use either the old or new style in the temple, though the First Presidency preferred the old style for ceremonial use.[96]

The revision of the temple ceremony itself required considerably more time. In April 1921 Richards enlisted the aid of Duncan M. McAllister, chief recorder of the St. George Temple, to try to provide a uniform administrative practice. These first revisions did not make any fundamental changes in the ceremony, and Richards presented them to the First Presidency on June 25, 1921, after which they were accepted. Administering to the sick was changed from the temple's Garden Room to the assembly room in the temple annex, possibly an indication of the increasing disfavor with which this method of performing the healing ordinance was viewed. Several procedural changes were made at the same time.[97]

By late 1921, however, a review of the entire temple ceremony was clearly necessary. On November 15 at a meeting of the First Presidency and Council of the Twelve, a list of twenty-two questions was presented for consideration, including suggested changes in ordinances. After the meeting the First Presidency met with President Richards, his counselors Joseph Fielding Smith and Albert Davis, and the temple recorders. Elder Smith, Duncan M. McAllister, and President Richards were appointed to formulate a list of recommendations. These were to be approved by the First Presidency, then presented to all temples.[98] The committee membership changed on occasion, but at times included David O. McKay, Stephen L Richards, John A. Widtsoe, and James E. Talmage, in addition to Elders Richards, Smith, and McAllister. Anthony W. Ivins reviewed the recommendations before their submission to the First Presidency and Twelve.

Although the entire revision was not completed until 1927, some changes were adopted during the intervening years. Alterations involving the simplification and clarification of parts of the ordinance were adopted, for instance, in June 1922. In April 1923 Elder Richards secured permission from the First Presidency to write down all ceremonies which had heretofore been unwritten. Giving the matter prayerful consideration, he expected to provide a single unified ceremony for all temples.[99] On December 16, 1926, the Richards committee presented its report to a meeting of the First Presidency and Twelve, and they approved it with a few minor changes. After Richards had rewritten the ordinance books in line with the revisions, he met on January 25, 1927, with Heber J. Grant, and they completed work on several important points in the ordinances, thus "making a finish of the work which has been under consideration of the committee of five of the Twelve for several years."[100]

The revisions completed in January 1927 are extremely important since they seem to have placed the temple ceremonies in substantially the form in which they are used today. Beyond this, they seem to have been the first attempt to codify the ordinance which had apparently taken different directions at various temples since 1877, when it had been written from memory for the St. George Temple.

Problems relating to the temple ceremony were only part of the questions facing church members in the early twentieth century. At various times, in addition, the church leadership confronted the difficult problem of determining the limits of the activity of members in organizations outside the church. In many cases church adherents were attracted to secret societies for low cost insurance which they offered.[101] The church leadership found this rationale at odds with the emphasis on the need for social solidarity within the Mormon community. Lorenzo Snow, for instance, emphasized that by joining such organizations, members compromised the independence of the church because their "allegiance to the Lord and His Priesthood" could thus not remain "unsullied." Church members who joined secret societies were often denied entrance to the temple and positions of leadership in auxiliary organizations. A 1907 letter indicated that though the church opposed secret societies, leaders should differentiate between converts who had belonged before joining and those who entered afterward. Joseph F. Smith's feelings in this matter seem to have been essentially the same as those of Lorenzo Snow, and he cautioned against such insurance programs.[102]

The revival of the Ku Klux Klan shortly before World War I and its expansion into Utah in the 1920s led to official concern about this organization. The *Deseret News* in an editorial in June 1924, at the height of the Klan power in Utah, condemned the Klan as dangerous on the basis of the Mormon position opposing secret societies. American people, the *News* said, lose precious rights in organizations such as the Klan. Whether members of the church belonged to the Klan or not, they certainly did not belong and carry on the Klan hate campaigns with official support.[103]

Beyond these questions the church faced a number of problems with regard to the Book of Mormon. In 1903 the church sponsored a convention on the Book of Mormon. Its major importance was the development of a standard pronunciation of Book of Mormon names by a committee under the chairmanship of George Reynolds. The pronunciation has become standard to the present time. In addition, B. H. Roberts, George Reynolds, John M. Mills, and Joel Ricks were asked to consider the location of Nephite lands and cities. Apparently they were unable to reach a conclusion, since the problem arose again in the early 1920s with differences of opinion on this and other topics. Most importantly, Roberts recognized some of the problems posed for the Book of Mormon by current scientific knowledge and interpretation. In an attempt to address those problems he prepared two manuscripts which he presented to the church leadership.[104]

The church also completed revisions and republications of the book. Early in the century Anthon H. Lund was involved in editorial correction of the book. In March 1920 a committee was appointed to revise and correct the book for a new edition. The committee, including George F. Richards, John M. Mills, and James E. Talmage, recommended changes in grammar and wording of some passages, printing in double columns, and other items. A decision was made, for instance, to append Joseph Smith's description of the Angel Moroni, a statement on the contents of the book, a key to the pronunciation of names, based on the Reynolds committee's work and a synopsis of chapters. With the decision to revise the Doctrine and Covenants, the First Presidency and Twelve also agreed to publish the two books and the Pearl of Great Price together as a triple combination.[105]

The consideration of church doctrine and doctrinally related practice reveals as well as anything the changes which had taken place in the church in the years since 1890. Within a religious organization based on the concept of leadership through revelation and discipleship through common consent, it has proved much easier in practice to institute administrative and other temporal changes than to redefine doctrine. The limits to the implementation of change in the church clearly are not determined by the revelations received by the church's president, or even by the desires of some of the general authorities. As Heber J. Grant and his counselors realized in the controversy over evolution and higher criticism, achieving internal harmony was more important than staking out definitive positions. Elders Smith and Roberts could ignore this since they held basically their own interests and views foremost rather than the interests of the larger church organization. In view of this condition, it is not at all surprising that the First Presidency refused to make sweeping doctrinal pronouncements on disputed subjects. In view of the broad range of issues under consideration, the various statements on the doctrines of man, God, and Christ are remarkable for their brevity and pointed focus rather than for their sweeping announcement of new doctrines and narrow positions. They reaffirmed certain fundamentals such as the atonement of Christ, the fatherhood of God, and the unity of the human family. They shunned statements on the age of the earth or biblical literalism.

On the surface, the most radical changes seem to have been the displacement of Pentecostal experience and public prophecy and revelation, and their replacement by institutional forms of religious experience in fast and testimony meetings and especially in the increased temple and genealogical work. On further reflection, however, the reasons ought to be apparent. The early twentieth century was imbued with the need for scientific and rational analysis of all phenomena. The publication under church auspices of the works of Talmage, Widtsoe, Roberts, and Pack indicates the degree to which church members sought scientifically respectable analyses of belief and practice. In the early twentieth century glossolalia was difficult to rationalize in scientific terms except by those who saw it as a form of irrational emotional excitement. In recent years research in the field of religious studies has arrived at a different conclusion, which recognizes such practices as legitimate religious experiences demonstrating deep faith and commitment. Then, such experiences were incompatible with the type of scientific rationalism increasingly popular in church circles. Under those conditions the hegira of Heber J. Grant from comfort at the personal revelation he received from John W. Taylor to the discomfort at glossolalia and public prophecy in the Boise stake is understandable.

Not surprisingly, the women of the church resisted these changes most. Western culture has anointed women as guardians of tradition, and these changes from a supernatural to a scientific point of view seem to have been most difficult for them. At the same time women were faced with the loss of privileges such as healing and anointing prior to childbirth which they had held since Joseph Smith's time. Theirs was a double burden as they faced the rationalization not only of religious experiences, but of administrative practices as well. They made the adjustment also, as leaders like Susa Young Gates led out in genealogical and temple work and Amy Brown Lyman promoted the scientific study of social problems.

By 1930, for the general church membership, the transition of the Latter-day Saint people from conditions and attitudes in the nineteenth century to those prevalent in the early twentieth century had generally been completed. Those who disagreed with the transition formed a minority in the church or had left to organize Fundamentalist groups. From a persecuted, apocalyptic, polygamous sect in the nineteenth century, the Latter-day Saints had become an increasingly respected church. Theologically, Mormons perceived themselves as the restoration of primitive Christianity. To the outside observer they might be perceived as a new Christian tradition.[106] Administratively and practically, however, they fit in well and were increasingly accepted by the society which had worked so hard a generation before to destroy them.

Bureau of Information on Temple Square, ca. 1902. An early attempt at public relations.

Elder David O. McKay (third from left) and missionaries in Japan during his 1920–21 world-wide tour.

The Hawaiian Temple. Designed by Harold W. Burton and Hyrum C. Pope, and dedicated in 1919, it was the first of three temples, all outside Utah, completed between 1915 and 1927.

James E. Talmage (1862–1933), member of the Council of the Twelve, 1911–33, geologist, educator, and theologian.

John A. Widtsoe (1872–1952), member of the Council of the Twelve, 1921–52, scientist, university president, and theologian. Sitting for a bust by Torlief Knaphus.

Joseph Fielding Smith (1876–1972), member of the Council of the Twelve (1910–70) and president of the LDS Church (1970–72). Actively involved in the Genealogical Society and as a conservative theologian on questions like evolution.

George F. Richards (1861–1950), member of the Council of the Twelve (1906–50), president of the European Mission during World War I, Salt Lake Temple president during the 1920s, and principally responsible for the revision of the temple ceremony.

Inauguration of radio broadcasting in Utah, 1922. President Heber J. Grant (with microphone) and dignitaries atop the Deseret News Building.

Epilogue

===

IN 1930, AS MEMBERS OF THE CHURCH of Jesus Christ of Latter-day Saints greeted the centennial of their church's founding, they could look back with satisfaction on the successes of more than three decades of transition. Leaving a single church political party in 1891, the church members had now joined the mainstream of American life with its two major nonideological parties and various issue-oriented factions. Members had generally accepted the discontinuation of plural marriage, and while some older men still had more than one wife, they were a fast-dying breed representing a bygone age. Their important health code, the Word of Wisdom, and increased genealogical and temple activity in many ways replaced political solidarity and polygamous marriage as the distinctive features of Mormon society.

Most evident were the signs of stability and prosperity such as the numerous buildings and monuments constructed through the efforts and sacrifice of church members over three decades. The church built three new temples—all outside Utah—together with numerous meetinghouses and stake tabernacles. Stakes had been organized outside the mountain West, and property had been acquired for an impressive new chapel in Washington, D.C. Most of the important sites from church history had been acquired, including the farm worked by Joseph Smith and his parents' family when he had his First Vision, the nearby hill from which he took the plates of gold, and the Illinois jail where he was murdered.

The priesthood quorums of the church had been reorganized and recharged with their duties. Young men at age twelve could now expect to begin their journey through the various offices of the Aaronic or Lower Priesthood until they were called to the Melchizedek or Higher Priesthood in time for missionary service or marriage. More young men went on proselyting missions than ever before, and a vigorous corps of mission presidents had broadened and strengthened the work throughout much of the world. Elders, seventies, and high priests, members of the adult priesthood, met weekly in quorum meetings to study the gospel and carry out church assignments.

Internal changes of considerable importance had taken place in the church auxiliaries. The women's organization, the Relief Society, had led the way in the development of a modern social welfare system. The work of the young people's society, the Mutual Improvement Association, had been expanded beyond its previous cultural emphasis to include recreational activities. Because of the public assumption of responsibility for education in Utah and the mountain West, the church had turned most of its secondary schools over to the state and had successfully begun a program of religious instruction for students in high school and college. The demise of the Religion Class program, with its weekday religious instruction for elementary students, laid increasing responsibility at the door of the children's auxiliary, the Primary Association. In the place of a rather unorganized class system, the Sunday School had graded instruction with well-written lessons and training for its large teacher corps.

In view of the relative isolation of church members in the nineteenth century from the currents of social change in the remainder of the nation, the alteration of Mormon society by 1930 was nothing less than miraculous. Mormons and Gentiles were now working together in social and community betterment causes such as prohibition, nonpartisan government, the development of parks, and a multitude of other social and cultural causes.

This same integration of Mormon and non-Mormon society had taken place in the business world. No longer was it proper to talk about Mormon domination of the economy. The majority of business enterprises, including those generally considered church undertakings like Salt Lake City's Hotel Utah and Zion's Cooperative Mercantile Institution (ZCMI), were in fact joint ventures financed by investment from Mormons and non-Mormons from Utah together with outside capital.

Church leaders singled out three events for special centennial observance: the visitation of the Angel Moroni, the delivery of the plates of gold, and the organization of the church. On September 21, 22, and 23, 1923, several thousand people gathered at the Sacred Grove and the Hill Cumorah, just outside Palmyra, New York, to commemorate the centennial of the first visit of Moroni to Joseph Smith. Planned by

Brigham H. Roberts, then Eastern States Mission president, three meetings were held each day alternating between the Hill Cumorah, where the Prophet received the golden plates, and the Sacred Grove, where he experienced his First Vision. On the morning of Sunday, September 23, a special meeting was held in the Sacred Grove. Dignitaries and leaders from throughout the church attended.

This centennial was followed in 1927 by an observance of the delivery of the plates to Joseph Smith. On September 22, 1927, meetings were held at the Hill Cumorah and the Sacred Grove. Henry H. Rolapp, then president of the Eastern States Mission, conducted the meetings and speakers included John H. Taylor, Charles H. Hart, Brigham H. Roberts, and President Heber J. Grant.

Undoubtedly the most important celebration, however, was the centennial of the founding of the church. In February 1929 the church leadership agreed to publish B. H. Roberts's six-volume *Comprehensive History of the Church*, in commemoration. The history was updated from articles published a decade and a half earlier to 1930, though the part after 1900 is somewhat sketchy. The project cost $60,000. Heber J. Grant thought that the church would never break even on the venture, but believed that it would "be of great value as a historical record." In November 1929 the first volume was off the press, and at the general conference in April 1930 it was announced that five volumes had appeared and that the sixth, including information on the centennial celebration, would appear a few days later.

In addition to the publication of Roberts's history, the church celebrated the centennial in several other ways. The general conference included special services on Sunday, April 6, commemorating the church's founding. The morning session featured a special message from the First Presidency together with a solemn assembly in which the authorities of the church were approved, or "sustained." President Anthony W. Ivins spoke on "God's Purposes Unfolding in History," and Heber J. Grant pronounced a blessing on the world. In the afternoon session Charles W. Nibley and Rudger Clawson spoke, and Orson F. Whitney read his poem, "The Lifted Ensign," extolling the triumph of the gospel of Jesus Christ. On Sunday evening and through May 5 performances of a special pageant, "The Message of the Ages," were presented. Outlining the various dispensations of time, the pageant dealt with the falling away and the restoration of the gospel. Music for the performances was provided by an orchestra under the baton of Frank W. Asper and the Tabernacle Choir under the direction of Anthony C. Lund, with Tracy Y. Cannon at the organ.

Each church member was encouraged to participate in the celebration in one way or another. Copies of the program and centennial addresses were sent to all wards except those with radio equipment, who were asked to meet together at 10 A.M. Mountain Standard Time on Sunday and participate in the program.

The acceptance of the church by outsiders and the good will enjoyed by church members were indicated by the events which surrounded these proceedings. The *Salt Lake Tribune*, which had been bitterly anti-Mormon only a few years earlier, published a serialized history of the church written by Levi Edgar Young, professor of history at the University of Utah and member of the First Council of the Seventy. Pathe Pictures filmed the pageant, "The Message of the Ages," on the steps of the state capitol.

In many ways, the centennial observance was characteristic of the change which had taken place. Mormons could now freely reflect upon both the similarities and the differences between their beliefs and those of others. Gentiles too were interested in the development of the church and could read about and work with their Mormon neighbors with much less rancor than had existed before. The symbolic importance of a general authority being asked to write a history of Mormonism in the *Salt Lake Tribune* spoke volumes about the success of Latter-day Saints in reconstructing the kingdom.

APPENDIX

Officers of the Church of Jesus Christ of Latter-day Saints, 1890–1930

Table 1
Members of the First Presidency, 1890–1930

President	First Counselor	Second Counselor
Wilford Woodruff (1889–1898)	George Q. Cannon (1889–1898)	Joseph F. Smith (1889–1898)
Lorenzo Snow (1898–1901)	George Q. Cannon (1898–1901)	Joseph F. Smith (1898–1901)
	Joseph F. Smith (1901–not set apart)	Rudger Clawson (1901–not set apart)
Joseph F. Smith (1901–1918)	John R. Winder (1901–1910)	Anthon H. Lund (1901–1910)
	Anthon H. Lund (1910–1918)	John Henry Smith (1910–1911)
		Charles W. Penrose (1911–1918)
Heber J. Grant (1918–1945)	Anthon H. Lund (1918–1921)	Charles W. Penrose (1918–1921)
	Charles W. Penrose (1921–1925)	Anthony W. Ivins (1921–1925)
	Anthony W. Ivins (1925–1934)	Charles W. Nibley (1925–1931)

Source: *Deseret News 1974 Church Almanac*

Table 2
Members of the Council of the Twelve Apostles, 1890–1930

1. Lorenzo Snow (1849–1898)	2. Franklin D. Richards (1849–1899)	3. Brigham Young, Jr. (1868–1903)
Rudger Clawson (1898–1943)	Reed Smoot (1900–1941)	George Albert Smith (1903–1945)
4. Moses Thatcher (1879–1896)	5. Francis M. Lyman (1880–1916)	6. John Henry Smith (1880–1910)
Matthias F. Cowley (1897–1905)	Stephen L Richards (1917–1951)	Joseph Fielding Smith (1910–1970)
George F. Richards (1906–1950)		
7. George Teasdale (1882–1907)	8. Heber J. Grant (1882–1918)	9. John W. Taylor (1884–1905)
Anthony W. Ivins (1907–1921)	Melvin J. Ballard (1919–1939)	Orson F. Whitney (1906–1931)
John A. Widtsoe (1921–1952)		
10. Marriner W. Merrill (1889–1906)	11. Anthon H. Lund (1889–1901)	12. Abraham H. Cannon (1889–1896)
David O. McKay (1906–1934)	Hyrum M. Smith (1901–1918)	Abraham O. Woodruff (1897–1904)
	Richard R. Lyman (1918–1943)	Charles W. Penrose (1904–1911)
		James E. Talmage (1911–1933)

The above table shows the name of each member of the Council of the Twelve Apostles under the name of the person he succeeded on the council. Position in the council was according to seniority. Those numbered 1 through 12 constituted the Twelve in 1890. Dates in parentheses indicate inclusive dates of membership in the quorum.

Source: *Deseret News 1974 Church Almanac*

Table 3
Members of the First Council of the Seventy, 1890–1930

Seymour B. Young (1882–1924)	Christian D. Fjeldsted (1884–1905)	John Morgan (1888–1894)	Brigham H. Roberts (1888–1933)
Rey L. Pratt (1925–1931)	Charles H. Hart (1906–1934)	Edward Stevenson (1894–1897)	
		Joseph W. McMurrin (1898–1932)	
George Reynolds (1890–1909)	J. Golden Kimball (1892–1938)	Rulon S. Wells (1893–1941)	
Levi Edgar Young (1910–1963)			

The above table shows the name of each member of the First Council of the Seventy under the name of the person he succeeded on the council. Position in the council was according to seniority.

Source: *Deseret News 1974 Church Almanac*

Table 4
Members of the Presiding Bishopric of 1890–1930

Presiding Bishop	First Counselor	Second Counselor
William B. Preston (1884–1907)	Robert T. Burton (1884–1907)	John R. Winder (1887–1901)
		Orrin P. Miller (1901–1907)
Charles W. Nibley (1907–1925)	Orrin P. Miller (1907–1918)	David A. Smith (1907–1918)
	David A. Smith (1918–1925)	John Wells (1918–1925)
Sylvester Q. Cannon (1925–1938)	David A. Smith (1925–1938)	John Wells (1925–1938)

Source: *Deseret News 1974 Church Almanac*

Table 5
General Presidency of the Relief Society, 1890–1930

President	First Councelor	Second Counselor
Zina Diantha Young (1888–1901)	Jane S. Richards (1888–1901)	Bathsheba W. Smith (1888–1901)
Bathsheba W. Smith (1901–1910)	Annie Taylor Hyde (1901–1909)	Ida Smoot Dusenberry (1901–1910)
Emmeline B. Wells (1910–1921)	Clarissa S. Williams (1910–1921)	Julina L. Smith (1910–1921)
Clarissa S. Williams (1921–1928)	Jennie Brimhall Knight (1921–1928)	Louise Yates Robison (1921–1928)
Louise Yates Robison (1928–1939)	Amy Brown Lyman (1928–1939)	Julia A. Child (1928–1935)

Source: *Deseret News 1983 Church Almanac*

Table 6
General Superintendents of the Deseret Sunday School Union

President	First Assistant	Second Assistant
George Q. Cannon (1867–1901)	George Goddard (1872–1899)	John Morgan (1883–1894)
	Karl G. Maeser (1899–1901)	Karl G. Maeser (1894–1899)
		George Reynolds (1899–1901)
Lorenzo Snow (1901)	George Reynolds	J. M. Tanner
Joseph F. Smith (1901–1918)	George Reynolds (1901–1909)	J. M. Tanner (1901–1906)
	David O. McKay (1909–1918)	David O. McKay (1907–1909)
		Stephen L Richards (1909–1918)
David O. McKay (1918–1934)	Stephen L Richards (1918–1934)	George D. Pyper (1918–1934)

Source: *Deseret News 1983 Church Almanac*

Table 7
General Presidencies of the Young Women's Mutual
Improvement Association, 1890–1930

President	First Counselor	Second Counselor
Elmina Shephard Taylor (1880–1904)	Maria Young Dougall (1887–1904)	Martha Horne Tingey (1880–1904)
Martha Horne Tingey (1905–1929)	Ruth May Fox (1905–1929)	Mae Taylor Nystrom (1905–1923)
		Lucy Grant Cannon (1923–1929)
Ruth May Fox (1929–1937)	Lucy Grant Cannon (1929–1937)	Clarissa A. Beesley (1929–1937)

Source: *Deseret News 1983 Church Almanac*

Table 8
General Superintendency of the Young Men's Mutual
Improvement Association, 1890–1930

Superintendent	First Assistant	Second Assistant
Wilford Woodruff (1880–1898)	Joseph F. Smith	Moses Thatcher
Lorenzo Snow (1898–1901)	Joseph F. Smith	Heber J. Grant
Joseph F. Smith (1901–1918)	Heber J. Grant	B. H. Roberts
Anthony W. Ivins (1918–1921)	B. H. Roberts	Richard R. Lyman
George Albert Smith (1921–1935)	B. H. Roberts	Richard R. Lyman
		Melvin J. Ballard

Source: *Deseret News 1983 Church Almanac*

Table 9
General Presidency of the Primary Association, 1890–1930

President	First Counselor	Second Counselor
Louie B. Felt (1880–1925)	Lillie T. Freeze (1888–1905)	Clare C. M. Cannon (1880–1895)
	May Anderson (1905–1925)	Josephine R. West (1896–1905)
		Clara W. Beebe (1906–1925)
May Anderson (1925–1939)	Sadie Grant Pack (1925–1929)	Isabelle Salmon Ross (1925–1929)
	Isabelle Salmon Ross (1929–1939)	Edna Harker Thomas (1929–1933)

Source: *Deseret News 1983 Church Almanac*

Notes

Chapter 1: The 1890s and the Challenge to the Mormon World View

1. On the life of Wilford Woodruff see Matthias F. Cowley, *Wilford Woodruff, Fourth President of the Church of Jesus Christ of Latter-day Saints: History of His Life and Labors as Recorded in His Daily Journals* (Salt Lake City: Deseret News Press, 1916); and Thomas G. Alexander, "Wilford Woodruff and the Changing Nature of Mormon Religious Experience," *Church History* 45 (March 1976): 55–69. For a general history of the Latter-day Saints, see James B. Allen and Glen M. Leonard, *The Story of the Latter-day Saints* (Salt Lake City: Deseret Book, 1976).

2. For a discussion of the journey see Wilford Woodruff, Journal (hereinafter cited as Woodruff Journal), August 3 through September 21, 1890, Archives of the Church of Jesus Christ of Latter-day Saints, Salt Lake City, Utah (hereinafter, LDS Archives). A published typescript of the journal is Wilford Woodruff, *Wilford Woodruff's Journal*, ed. Scott G. Kenney. 9 vols. (Midvale, Utah: Signature Books, 1983–85).

3. For a discussion of Mormon relations with these California politicians see Edward Leo Lyman, "Isaac Trumbo and the Politics of Utah Statehood," *Utah Historical Quarterly* 41 (Spring 1973): 128–49; idem., "The Mormon Quest for Utah Statehood" (Ph.D. dissertation, University of California at Riverside, 1981).

4. Woodruff Journal, September 21–25, 1890. In addition, George Reynolds, Charles W. Penrose, John R. Winder, and George Q. Cannon edited the document for publication and several minor suggestions were made by several members of the Council of the Twelve. D. Michael Quinn, "LDS Church Authority and New Plural Marriages, 1890–1904," *Dialogue: A Journal of Mormon Thought* 18 (Spring 1985): 44–45.

5. For a discussion of these matters see Gustive O. Larson, *The Americanization of Utah for Statehood* (San Marino, Calif.: Huntington Library Press, 1971).

6. Martin Buber, *Paths in Utopia*, R. F. C. Hull, trans. (New York: Macmillan, 1950), pp. 134–35; Robert Redfield, *The Little Community: Viewpoints for the Study of a Human Whole* (Chicago: University of Chicago Press, 1955), p. 4. There is some problem with Redfield's definitions in relationship to the Mormon community, since the Latter-day Saints' group was neither small nor self-sufficient, though it sought the latter.

7. On religious attitudes toward politics see George M. Marsden, *Fundamentalism and American Culture: The Shaping of Twentieth-Century Evangelism, 1870–1925* (New York: Oxford University Press, 1980); for an interpretation of the Mormon response see Klaus J. Hansen, *Mormonism and the American Experience* (Chicago: University of Chicago Press, 1981).

8. For a general discussion of the church debt in the 1880s and 1890s see Leonard J. Arrington, *Great Basin Kingdom: An Economic History of the Latter-day Saints, 1830–1900* (Cambridge: Harvard University Press, 1958), pp. 400–403; see also Ronald W. Walker, "Crisis in Zion: Heber J. Grant and the Panic of 1893," *Arizona and the West* 21 (Autumn 1979): 257–78.

9. Heber J. Grant, Diary (hereinafter cited as Grant Diary), January 4 and August 8, 1898, LDS Archives; Brigham Young, Jr., Journal (hereinafter cited as Young Journal), July 12, 1898, LDS Archives.

10. Young Journal, July 14, 1900; Anthon H. Lund, Journal (hereinafter cited as Lund Journal), September 6, 1900, LDS Archives; Arrington, *Great Basin Kingdom*, pp. 403–9.

11. Young Journal, July 2, 1899; Marriner W. Merrill, Journal (hereinafter cited as Merrill Journal), July 2, 1899, LDS Archives; John Henry Smith, Journal (hereinafter cited as J. H. Smith Journal), July 2, 1899, Smith Family Papers, Western Americana Collection, University of Utah Library, (hereinafter cited as U of U).

12. Young Journal, April 12, May 6, 1900; Lund Journal, June 26, 1900.

13. Young Journal, October 15, 1898, May 22, 1900.

14. Woodruff Journal, October 5, 1890.

15. Melvin Clarence Merrill, ed., *Utah Pioneer and Apostle: Marriner Wood Merrill and His Family* (n.p.: privately printed, 1937), p. 141; Gordon B. Hinckley and John Henry Evans, *John Henry Moyle: The Story of a Distinguished American and an Honored Churchman* (Salt Lake City: Deseret Book, 1951), pp. 213–15.

16. Gene A. Sessions, ed., *Mormon Democrat: The Religious and Political Memoirs of James Henry Moyle* (Salt Lake City: Historical Department of the LDS church, 1975), pp. 182–84; Lyman, "Mormon Quest for Statehood," chapter 6.

17. Young Journal, August 10, 1898; J. H. Smith Journal, August 12, 1900; Lund Journal, November 1, 1900.

18. Hinckley and Evans, *John Henry Moyle*, p. 224; Glen Miller, "Has the Mormon Church Re-entered Politics?" *The Forum* 20 (1895–96): 501. For a general discussion of the development of these issues and the emergence of the Republican party to political dominance, see H. Wayne Morgan, *From Hayes to McKinley: National Party Politics, 1877–1896* (Syracuse: Syracuse University Press, 1969).

19. Calvin Reasoner, *The Late Manifesto in Politics—Practical Working of "Counsel" in Relation to Civil and Religious Liberty in Utah* (Salt Lake City: privately printed, 1896), cited in U. S. Senate, Committee on Privileges and Elections, *In the Matter of the Protests Against the Right of Hon. Reed Smoot,*

A Senator from the State of Utah to Hold His Seat. 4 vols. (Washington, D. C.: Government Printing Office, 1904–6) 1 : 941; see also Ibid. 1 : 285 (hereinafter cited as Smoot Proceedings with the volume and pages).

20. Ibid. 1 : 248–53, 910, 955; Merrill, *Utah Pioneer and Apostle,* pp. 160–63; Woodruff Journal, October 3, 1892, March 22, 1893; James E. Talmage, Journal, April 6, 1893, Manuscripts Division, Brigham Young University Library (hereinafter Talmage Journal); Jan Shipps, "The Mormons in Politics: The First Hundred Years" (Ph.D. dissertation, University of Colorado, 1965), pp. 223–24; Lyman, "Mormon Quest for Statehood," chapter 6.

21. John M. Whitaker, Journal, November 1, 1893, cited in Kenneth W. Godfrey, "Frank J. Cannon, a Political Profile" (seminar paper, Brigham Young University, 1965), p. 21; Merrill, *Utah Pioneer and Apostle,* pp. 184, 192; B. H. Roberts, *A Comprehensive History of the Church of Jesus Christ of Latter-day Saints, Century I,* 6 vols. (Salt Lake City: Deseret News Press, 1930) 6 : 330–31; Miller, "Has the Church Re-entered Politics," p. 503; and Smoot Proceedings 1 : 751–54.

22. Whitaker Journal, November 1, 1895, cited in Godfrey, "Frank J. Cannon," p. 30.

23. Merrill, *Utah Pioneer and Apostle,* pp. 197–99, 205, 207, 209; Smoot Proceedings 1 : 170, 563; Milton R. Merrill, "Reed Smoot, Apostle in Politics" (Ph.D. dissertation, Columbia University, 1950), p. 4; and Roberts, *Comprehensive History* 6 : 335–36. Thatcher saved his church membership by recanting in the summer of 1897.

24. Grant Diary, August 2, 13, November 11, December 9, 29, 1898, February 18, 1899; Young Journal, August 2, 1898, February 23, 24, 1899; Lund Journal, March 30, 1899; Frank J. Cannon and Harvey J. O'Higgins, *Under the Prophet in Utah: The National Menace of a Political Priestcraft* (Boston: C. M. Clark Co., 1911), pp. 221–24, are mistaken in their belief that McCune was the church's candidate. Heber J. Grant and several other Democrats used their considerable influence on McCune's behalf, but he received no official church support.

25. Lund Journal, March 30, 1899.

26. Davis Bitton, "The B. H. Roberts Case of 1898–1900," *Utah Historical Quarterly* 25 (January 1957): passim; A. Theodore Schroeder, "The Mormon Breach of Faith," *The Arena* 23 (February 1900): 114–18. See also Truman G. Madsen, *Defender of the Faith: The B. H. Roberts Story* (Salt Lake City: Bookcraft, 1980), pp. 243–72.

27. Woodruff Journal, October 25, 1891; Doctrine and Covenants (1981 edition), Official Declaration 1 and notes; Smoot Proceedings 1 : 21–22.

28. The Doctrine and Covenants is a book of revelations given to Joseph Smith. First published in 1835, it went through a number of editions. The term "celestial marriage" was often used to refer to plural marriage since it related the practice to the highest degree of salvation in Mormon theology.

29. Talmage Journal, October 20, 1891, January 9, 16, 1899; Lund Journal, January 13, 1899, January 9, 1900; J. H. Smith Journal, January 9, 10, 1900;

Smoot Proceedings 1 : 107, 408–10; Merrill, *Utah Pioneer and Apostle,* pp. 127, 147. For a comprehensive discussion of those engaged in encouraging or practicing new plural marriage see Quinn, "LDS Church Authority and New Plural Marriages," pp. 37–96.

30. For discussions of plural marriage after the Manifesto see Kenneth L. Cannon, "Beyond the Manifesto: Polygamous Cohabitation among General Authorities after 1890," *Utah Historical Quarterly* 46 (Winter 1978): 24–36; and Victor W. Jorgensen and B. Carmon Hardy, "The Taylor-Cowley Affair and the Watershed of Mormon History," *Utah Historical Quarterly* 48 (Winter 1980): 4–36; for evidence of further plural marriages during the 1890s see Smoot Proceedings 1 : 110–11, 389–90, 406, 422, 2 : 141–43, 68; Joseph F. Smith to Reed Smoot, April 9, 1904, Joseph F. Smith Letterbooks, LDS Archives (hereinafter cited as Joseph F. Smith Letterbooks); Cannon and O'Higgins, *Under the Prophet,* p. 177; Lund Journal, September 28, 1906; Grant Diary, October 9, 1898; George Q. Cannon to Anthony W. Ivins, December 27, 1897, Ivins Family Papers, Utah State Historical Society, Salt Lake City, Utah (hereinafter cited as Ivins Papers); Anthony W. Ivins, excerpts from the A. W. Ivins Recordbook of Marriages, Ivins Papers; and H. Grant Ivins, "Polygamy in Mexico," (MS in Ivins Papers).

31. Lund Journal, July 12, December 30, 1899; Young Journal, November 23, December 30, 1899.

32. Journal History of the Church of Jesus Christ of Latter-day Saints, January 8 and 11 and August 13, 1900, LDS Archives, (hereinafter JH with the date); Young Journal, January 11, 1900; Merrill Journal, January 9, May 17, 1900; Smoot Proceedings 1 : 487–88, 2 : 47, 3 : 198–200, 4 : 5–8; Lorenzo Snow to George E. Waite, September 19, 1900, First Presidency, letters sent, LDS Archives (hereinafter FP, letters sent). The term "sealing" is used in connection with marriages for time and eternity performed by priesthood authority.

33. Note in FP, letters sent, November 24, 1899.

34. The following is based on D. Michael Quinn, "The Mormon Church and the Spanish-American War: An End to Selective Pacifism," *Pacific Historical Review* 43 (August 1974): 342–66.

35. Thomas S. Kuhn, *The Structure of Scientific Revolutions,* 2nd ed. (Chicago: University of Chicago Press, 1970), especially chapters 5–10. For a critique of Kuhn's theory see W. H. Newton-Smith, *The Rationality of Science* (Boston, London, and Henley: Routledge and Kegan Paul, 1981), chapter 5.

36. Kuhn, *Structure of Scientific Revolutions,* p. 110.

37. Peter L. Berger, *The Sacred Canopy: Elements of a Sociological Theory of Religion* (Garden City, N.Y.: Doubleday & Co., 1967), p. 29; see, in addition, all of chapters 1 and 2.

Chapter 2: The Search for a Pluralistic Political System, 1900–11

1. Kent Sheldon Larsen, "The Life of Thomas Kearns" (Master's thesis, University of Utah, 1964), pp. 52–53.

2. Lund Journal, December 5, 22, 27, 1900; Young Journal, December 29, 1900; J. H. Smith Journal, December 27, 29, 1900; Smoot Proceedings 2: 226, 240.

3. Thomas Kearns to Nephi Morris, January 2, 1901, Nephi L. Morris Papers (hereinafter Morris Papers), J. Willard Marriott Library, University of Utah, Salt Lake City; J. H. Smith Journal, January 17, 1901; Lund Journal, January 3, 1901; Merrill, "Reed Smoot" (chapter 1, note 23, p. 319), p. 8; Reuben Joseph Snow, "The American Party in Utah: A Study of Political Party Struggles During the Early Years of Statehood" (Master's thesis, University of Utah, 1964), pp. 30, 33; Shipps, "The Mormons in Politics" (chapter 1, note 20, p. 319), pp. 231–33.

4. Lund Journal, January 23, 24, February 6, 1901.

5. Noble Warrum, *Utah Since Statehood: Historical and Biographical* 4 vols. (Chicago: S. J. Clarke, 1919) 1 : 125; Lund Journal, January 16, 1902; Smoot Proceedings 3 : 187; JH, May 16, July 2, September 6, October 3, 25, November 2, 1902; John Henry Smith to Francis M. Lyman, September 3, 1902, Smith Family Papers, University of Utah; Merrill, "Reed Smoot," pp. 12, 22; Larsen, "Life of Thomas Kearns," pp. 96–97.

6. JH, January 12, 1903; J. H. Smith Journal, December 4, 1902; Lund Journal, December 9, 1902; Mark A. Hanna to John Henry Smith, December 18, 1902, Smith Family Papers.

7. JH, November 2, December 2, 19, 1902, January 2, 1903; Lund Journal, November 14, 21, 1902.

8. Cannon and O'Higgins, *Under the Prophet* (chapter 1, note 24, p. 319), pp. 251–56, 258; Sessions, *Mormon Democrat* (chapter 1, note 16, p. 318), p. 216.

9. Smoot Proceedings 1 : 591–93.

10. Ibid. 1 : 1, 12–18, 25, 663.

11. Merrill, "Reed Smoot," pp. 96–97; Joseph F. Smith to Samuel E. Woolley, July 10, 1903, Joseph F. Smith Letterbooks; JH, March 12, May 20, 1903, May 24, 1904, January 4, 5, 7, 11, 15, 19, 21, 22, 24, February 3, 18, March 11, 16, 17, April 19, October 27, 28, 1905; *Current Literature* 36 (January-June 1904): 379.

12. Joseph F. Smith to Reed Smoot, January 30, 1906, cited in James R. Clark, *Messages of the First Presidency*, 5 vols. (Salt Lake City: Bookcraft, 1966–71), 4 : 125; Lund Journal, February 28, 1903; Merrill, "Reed Smoot," pp. 34–35, 38; Joseph F. Smith to Samuel E. Woolley, August 27, 1903, Joseph F. Smith Letterbooks; and Shelby M. Cullom, "The Meaning of Mormonism," *The Independent* 60 (April 26, 1906): 980.

13. First Presidency to Reed Smoot, November 17, 1903, FP, letters sent.

14. Reed Smoot to James H. Anderson, November 17, 1903; Smoot to Richard W. Young, November 18, 1903; Smoot to John C. Graham, November 24, 1903, Reed Smoot Papers, Harold B. Lee Library, Brigham Young University, Provo, Utah (hereinafter cited as Smoot Papers).

15. Smoot Proceedings 1 : 31–32, 57, 58, 61, 67.

16. Ibid. 1: 116–17, 122–23.

17. Smoot to J. H. Anderson, March 18, 1894, Smoot to Edward H. Callister, March 22, 1904, Smoot Papers; Merrill, "Reed Smoot," pp. 52–53. Joseph F. Smith to Reed Smoot, April 9, 1904, Joseph F. Smith Letterbooks.

18. Smoot to Callister, March 22, 1904, Smoot Papers.

19. Joseph F. Smith to Reed Smoot, April 9, 1904, Joseph F. Smith Letterbooks.

20. Smoot to Callister, March 22, 1904, Smoot Papers; Joseph F. Smith to C. Hermansen, November 13, 1905, Joseph F. Smith Letterbooks.

21. Loman Franklin Aydelotte, "The Political Thought and Activity of Heber J. Grant, Seventh President of the Church of Jesus Christ of Latter-day Saints," (Master's thesis, Brigham Young University, 1965), p. 30.

22. First Presidency to Francis M. Lyman, November 12, 1903; Anthon H. Lund and John R. Winder to Heber J. Grant, September 10, 1906, FP, letters sent; Reed Smoot to John Henry Smith, November 19, 1903, and to James Clove, November 21 and 22, 1903, Smoot Papers; JH, January 14 and 21, 1905; Smoot Proceedings 1:684, 4:154; JH, January 16, 1905; Heber J. Grant to John Henry Smith, August 1, 1906, Smith Family Papers.

23. Lund Journal, March 22, 1904.

24. Merrill Journal, February 20, December 6, 1904; First Presidency to George Teasdale, January 6, May 11, 1905, FP, letters sent; Reed Smoot to George Teasdale, May 17, 1905, Smoot Papers; Joseph F. Smith to Reed Smoot, March 20, April 9, 1904, Joseph F. Smith Letterbooks; idem to Julius C. Burroughs, April 15, 1905, cited in Clark, *Messages* 4:85.

25. Smoot Proceedings 1:42.

26. Ibid. 1:600, 866, 870, 897.

27. Ibid. 1:166, 275; Joseph F. Smith to Reed Smoot, March 20, 1904, Joseph F. Smith Letterbooks; *Improvement Era*, April 1903, pp. 469–73.

28. Smoot Proceedings 1:733, 2:262.

29. Ibid. 2:666, 938.

30. Smoot Proceedings 1:726–27; JH, January 21, 1905.

31. Merrill, "Reed Smoot," p. 91.

32. Ibid., pp. 87, 99.

33. JH, February 20, 1907; Lund Journal, February 20, 1907; George F. Richards, Journal, February 20, 1907, LDS Archives (hereinafter Richards Journal); and Joseph F. Smith to Reed Smoot, February 23, 1907, Joseph F. Smith Letterbooks.

34. JH, January 3, 22, February 13, 14, 1907; George F. Gibbs to Reed Smoot, January 4, 1907, cited in Clark, *Messages* 4:135.

35. Lund Journal, August 30, 1911; and Smoot Diary, September 2, 28, November 1, 1911.

36. Merrill, "Reed Smoot," pp. 101–2.

37. JH, December 12, 1902, January 8, February 11, 27, 1905; Lund Journal, January 18, 1905; Snow, "American Party," pp. 61–63; Smoot Proceedings 2:989.

38. Larsen, "Life of Thomas Kearns," p. 106; Lund Journal, June 10, 29,

July 9, 13, 21, 26, August 18, 25, 1904; Joseph Eckersley, Journal, August 14, 1904, LDS Archives (hereinafter cited as Eckersley Journal).

39. Ellen Gunnell Callister, "The Political Career of Edward Henry Callister, 1885–1916" (Master's thesis, University of Utah, 1967), pp. 38, 48; Merrill, "Reed Smoot," p. 221.

40. Merrill, "Reed Smoot," pp. 170–71; Lund Journal, October 27, 1905, March 17, 1906.

41. Callister, "E. H. Callister," p. 73; JH, January 24, 1908.

42. Snow, "American Party," p. 69; Larsen, "Life of Thomas Kearns," p. 123; *Improvement Era*, November 1904, p. 74.

43. JH, January 18, 1905; Joel Francis Paschal, *Mr. Justice Sutherland: A Man Against the State* (Princeton: Princeton University Press, 1951), p. 49.

44. Larsen, "Life of Thomas Kearns," pp. 110–13; Snow, "American Party," p. 121; JH, March 7, 1905.

45. Joseph F. Smith to Charles W. Penrose, March 10, 1907, Joseph F. Smith Letterbooks; JH, February 21, 25, 1908.

46. Charles W. Nibley, "Reminiscences of Charles W. Nibley" (MS, LDS Archives), pp. 85–86; Merrill, "Reed Smoot," pp. 142–44.

47. Lund Journal, March 27, 1908; Emmeline B. Wells, Diary, March 29, 1908, Brigham Young University (hereinafter cited as Wells Diary); Merrill, "Reed Smoot," p. 129.

48. Merrill, "Reed Smoot," p. 146; JH, March 30, 1908.

49. J.H. Smith Journal, May 6, 1908; Shipps, "Mormons in Politics" (chapter 1, note 20, p. 319), p. 260; Lund Journal, May 6, 18, 19, October 6, 1908; Richards Journal, July 22, October 3, 6, 1908; Grant Diary, October 3, 1908; JH, October 6, 29, 1908; Snow, "American Party," p. 183.

50. Grant Diary, June 9, 11, October 2, 1908; Snow, "American Party," p. 179; JH, October 8, 12–14, 19, 23, 24, November 14, 1908.

51. Grant Diary, October 31, November 2, 1908; Lund Journal, October 25, November 3, 1908.

52. Snow, "American Party," p. 178; Lund Journal, September 21, 1908; JH, September 23, October 10, 1908.

53. Lund Journal, March 23, June 29, July 2, 3, 10, September 14, 1908; Callister, "E. H. Callister," pp. 86, 90–94; and Snow, "American Party," p. 178.

54. Ibid., pp. 198–99; Sessions, *Mormon Democrat*, pp. 212–13; Joseph F. Smith to C. E. Loose, November 5, 1908, Joseph F. Smith Letterbooks; Richards Journal, November 4, 1908.

55. JH, November 16, 1908; Sessions, *Mormon Democrat*, pp. 212–13; Richards Journal, January 6, 1909.

56. Richards Journal, January 6, 1909; Cannon and O'Higgins, *Under the Prophet*, p. 307.

57. Lund Journal, January 30, December 9, 1909. For a general discussion of the prohibition issue in Utah see Bruce T. Dyer, "A Study of the Forces Leading to the Adoption of Prohibition in Utah in 1917" (Master's thesis, Brigham Young University, 1958), and Jan Shipps, "Utah Comes of Age Politically: A

Study of the State's Politics in the Early Years of the Twentieth Century," *Utah Historical Quarterly* 35 (Spring 1967): 91–111.

58. On the nineteenth-century situation in Idaho see Merle W. Wells, *Anti-Mormonism in Idaho, 1872–92* (Provo, Utah: Brigham Young Univeristy Press, 1978). See Joseph F. Smith to William Budge, October 24, 26, 1900, Joseph F. Smith Letterbooks.

59. Joseph F. Smith to Ben E. Rich, October 20, 1900, to William Budge, October 23, 1900, to Walter Hoge, November 7, 1900, March 14, 1902, Joseph F. Smith Letterbooks; J. H. Smith Journal, September 19, 1900; Lund Journal, November 9, 1900, October 29, 1902, October 15, 1906; George Gibbs to E. M. Pugmire, December 22, 1900, to Alfred Budge, November 9, 1900, FP, letters sent.

60. JH, January 22, 1907, March 25, 26, April 7, 1908; Lund Journal, February 5, 1908; *Toncray* v. *Budge*, 14 *Idaho Reports* 621 (1908), see especially 648 and 655.

Chapter 3: The Politics of Change and Reconciliation, 1912–30

1. For a general treatment of Utah politics in the twentieth century see Frank H. Jonas, "Utah: The Different State," in Jonas, ed., *Politics in the American West* (Salt Lake City: University of Utah Press, 1969), pp. 327–79.

2. On J. Reuben Clark's activities and Heber J. Grant's attitude toward the New Deal see D. Michael Quinn, *J. Reuben Clark: The Church Years* (Provo, Utah: Brigham Young University Press, 1983), pp. 68–69, 73–75, 78, 86–87.

3. Joseph F. Smith to Reed Smoot, August 1, 1911, Joseph F. Smith Letterbooks; *Improvement Era*, June 1912, pp. 737–83; Smoot Diary, September 24, 1912.

4. Joseph F. Smith to Reed Smoot, March 25, 1912, Joseph F. Smith Letterbooks; Lund Journal, June 16, 18, 22, 1912.

5. Warrum, *Utah Since Statehood* (chapter 2, note 5, p. 321) 1:160–63; C. Austin Wahlquist, "The 1912 Presidential Election in Utah" (Master's thesis, Brigham Young University, 1962), p. 88; Wayne Stout, *History of Utah*, 3 vols. (Salt Lake City: privately printed, 1967–71), 2:344; for a study of the Progressive party and its role in the election of 1912 see John Allen Gable, *The Bull Moose Years: Theodore Roosevelt and the Progressive Party* (Port Washington, N.Y.: Kennikat Press, 1978).

6. *Improvement Era*, October 1912, pp. 1120–21.

7. Lund Journal, October 25, 27, 1912.

8. Smoot Diary, September 28, 1912; Lund Journal, September 28, 1912.

9. D. Craig Mikkelson, "The Politics of B. H. Roberts," *Dialogue* 9 (Summer 1974): 40–43.

10. Ibid.: 43.

11. Smoot Diary, October 6, 1912; Lund Journal, October 5, 6, 1912.

12. *Ogden Standard*, October 8, 1912, cited in Wahlquist, "1912 Presidential Election," p. 82.

13. Ibid., pp. 52–53, 56, 60, 63, 65, 96; Callister, "E. H. Callister" (chapter 2, note 39, p. 323), pp. 130–31, 134.

14. Vote totals are cited in Warrum, *Utah Since Statehood* 1 : 164.

15. Lund Journal, June 8, 1912; Merrill, "Reed Smoot," pp. 256–58.

16. Reed Smoot to E. H. Callister, January 10, 1908, cited in Merrill, "Reed Smoot" (chapter 1, note 23, p. 319), p. 153.

17. Richards Journal, February 22, 1913.

18. For Smoot's position on various progressive issues see Thomas G. Alexander, "Reed Smoot, the LDS Church, and Progressive Legislation, 1903–1933," *Dialogue* 7 (Spring 1972): 47–56; Smoot Diary, March 23, October 9, 1913.

19. Joseph F. Smith to Fred J. Kiesel, March 4, 1914, Joseph F. Smith Letterbooks; *The Progressive* (Salt Lake City), March 7, 1914.

20. Callister, "E. H. Callister," p. 138; Merrill, "Reed Smoot," p. 155.

21. Mary L. Morris to Nephi L. Morris, March 13, 1914, Nephi L. Morris to Francis M. Lyman, March 20, 1914, Morris Papers; Sessions, *Mormon Democrat* (chapter 1, note 16, p. 318), pp. 215–16.

22. *Salt Lake Tribune*, January 3, 1915; Warrum, *Utah Since Statehood* 1 : 171.

23. *The Progressive*, February 28, 1914; Frederick M. Davenport, "The Junction of Jew and Mormon," *Outlook* 114 (December 20, 1916): 863–64.

24. Lund Journal, June 20, July 26, 1916.

25. Ibid., July 28, 1916; Callister, "E. H. Callister," p. 162.

26. Joseph F. Smith to Hyrum M. Smith, August 4, 1916, Joseph F. Smith Letterbooks; Lund Journal, August 7, 8, 1916; Joseph Eckersley Journal, July 29, August 8, 1916, LDS Archives.

27. Merrill, "Reed Smoot," pp. 219–20, 270; Paschal, *Sutherland* (chapter 2, note 43, p. 323), p. 96; and Callister, "E. H. Callister," p. 148.

28. Grant Diary, May 4, July 8, 27, 29, 1916; Frank Thomas Morn, "Simon Bamberger: A Jew in a Mormon Commonwealth" (Master's thesis, Brigham Young University, 1966), pp. 115–18; Brad E. Hainsworth, "Utah State Elections, 1916–1924" (Ph.D. dissertation, University of Utah, 1968), pp. 12–16; Lund Journal, August 10, 15, 1916.

29. See the sources listed in note 26 plus Callister, "E. H. Callister," p. 163.

30. Warrum, *Utah Since Statehood* 1 : 178; Merrill, "Reed Smoot," p. 277.

31. Joseph F. Smith to E. Wesley Smith, November 7, 9, 1916, Joseph F. Smith Letterbooks.

32. Grant Diary, November 7, 1917, December 8, 30, 1916.

33. Ibid., November 9, 10, 1916, March 3, 1917; Lund Journal, January 1, 1917; JH, January 2, 4, 1917.

34. Lund Journal, September 20, 22, 1917; Grant Diary, October 1, 1917, November 5, 1920; *Improvement Era*, November 1917, p. 92.

35. *Improvement Era*, September 1914, pp. 1074–76.

36. Joseph F. Smith to *Los Angeles Examiner*, September 15, 1914, cited in Clark, *Messages* (chapter 2, note 12, p. 321) 4 : 311; JH, October 5, 1915; *Improvement Era*, February 1917, pp. 423–25.

37. John M. Whitaker, Journal, Brigham Young University (hereinafter cited as Whitaker Journal), October 15, 1916; Clark, *Messages* 5:61.

38. JH, April 8, July 20, 1918; Charla Woodbury, "A Study of the Development of Nativism in Utah's Institutions, 1917–1925" (Seminar paper, Brigham Young University, 1968, copy in author's possession), pp. 6, 12, 15.

39. Lund Journal, February 24, 1916, June 3, 1917, August 28, September 10, 1918; JH, May 23, 1916, March 31, 1917, August 5, 13, 1918; Smoot Diary, August 14, 1918.

40. JH, May 12, June 1, 1917; Richards Journal, July 20, 1917, August 8–9, 1918; Lund Journal, July 30–31, August 1–2, 6, 8, 1917; Richard Maher, *For God and Country: Memorable Stories from the Lives of Mormon Chaplains* (Bountiful, Utah: Horizon Publishers, 1976), p. 14; *Improvement Era*, November 1915, p. 44, July 1917, p. 851; Roberts, *Comprehensive History* (chapter 1, note 21, p. 319) 6:456.

41. *Improvement Era*, December 1914, p. 182; JH, April 6, 23, September 25, October 15, 1917, February 26, 1918; *Relief Society Handbook*, 1921 ed., p. 45; *Relief Society Handbook*, 1931 ed., pp. 43–44, 47; *Relief Society Magazine*, April 1918, p. 226, April 1919, pp. 218–19; Jessie L. Embry, "Relief Society Grain Storage Program, 1876–1940" (Master's thesis, Brigham Young University, 1974), pp. 42–58; Lund Journal, October 22, 1917.

42. Grant Diary, April 9, 12, 1917; *Improvement Era*, April 1918, pp. 541–42.

43. *Improvement Era*, March 1917, p. 464; Talmage Journal, June 9, 1917; Grant Diary, June 9, October 7, 1917; Lund Journal, June 13, 1917; JH, October 20, 1917; Roberts, *Comprehensive History* 6:467–68; *Relief Society Handbook*, 1931 ed., p. 46; and Stout, *History of Utah* 2:407.

44. Lund Journal, August 16, September 11, 1917, and 1917 passim; Joseph F. Smith to Reed Smoot, June 23, 1917, cited in Clark, *Messages* 5:78; JH, March 20, 22, 1917; Smoot Diary, April 29, May 4, 1917, January 4, April 18, 1917, April 17, 1918.

45. Reed Smoot, "Party Politics in War Issues," *Forum* 59 (May 1918): 584.

46. Grant Diary, January 16, 1918.

47. Lund Journal, April 22, May 4, June 11, 13, 1918; for a general history of the Nonpartisan League see Robert L. Morlan, *Political Prairie Fire: The Nonpartisan League, 1915–1922* (Minneapolis: University of Minnesota Press, 1955).

48. Sessions, *Mormon Democrat*, p. 208.

49. Ivins Journal, September 4, 1930.

50. Merrill, "Reed Smoot," pp. 220, 279; Hainsworth, "Utah State Elections," pp. 55–57, 156; Smoot Diary, March 4, 17, 1921; Stanford John Layton, "Governor Charles R. Mabey and the Utah Election of 1924" (Master's thesis, University of Utah, 1969), pp. 9, 30–34; Dan E. Jones, "Utah Politics, 1926–1932" (Ph.D. dissertation, University of Utah, 1968), p. 42; Robert W. Wells, Jr., "A Political Biography of George Henry Dern" (Master's thesis, Brigham Young University, 1971), p. 54.

51. Grant Diary, October 11, 12, 1919; Lund Journal, October 12, 1919; for a general treatment of the League of Nations controversy from a different point of view than that presented here see James B. Allen, "Personal Faith and Public Policy: Some Timely Observations on the League of Nations Controversy in Utah," *BYU Studies* 14 (Autumn 1973): 77–98. See also the discussion in Frank W. Fox, *J. Reuben Clark: The Public Years* (Provo and Salt Lake City: Deseret Book and Brigham Young University Press, 1980), pp. 273–308. Throughout the following discussion, it should be noted that Clark was an irreconcilable and Smoot a reservationist on the league.

52. Lund Journal, October 12, 1919, July 28, 1920; Smoot Diary, August 20, 24, 1919, July 29, 1920; JH, August 24, 1919.

53. Smoot Diary, July 29, 1920; Lund Journal, July 28, 1920.

54. Lund Journal, July 31, 1919, August 5, 1920; Smoot Diary, July 29, 30, August 5, 1920.

55. Lund Journal, August 5, 1920; Smoot Diary, August 5, 1920.

56. Grant Diary, October 23, 1920; Smoot Diary, October 23, 24, 1920; Lund Journal, October 21, 1920; on Smoot's contacts with Casey see Smoot Diary, April through July 1919, passim.

57. James H. Moyle to Heber J. Grant, April 29, 1920, and Grant to Moyle, May 13, 1920, in Sessions, *Mormon Democrat*, pp. 258–65.

58. On the campaign see Thomas Sterling Taylor and Theron H. Luke, *The Life and Times of T.N.T.: The Story of Thomas Nicholls Taylor* (Salt Lake City: Deseret News Press, 1959), pp. 33, 60, 74, and passim; and Stanford J. Layton, "Governor Charles R. Mabey and the Utah Election of 1924," pp. 1–7; Lund Journal, August 12, October 16, 20, 1920; Smoot Diaries, September 20, 1920.

59. Grant Diary, July 9, 1920; Smoot Diary, October 14, 1920.

60. Grant Diary, May 22, June 16, 17, 19, 26, July 10–12, 22, 1922; for a discussion of the election from the point of view of J. Reuben Clark see Fox, *Clark*, pp. 414–20.

61. Hainsworth, "Utah State Elections," pp. 148–53, 165; Grant Diary, October 2, November 2, 1922.

62. Smoot Diary, October 12, 24, 27, 1922.

63. First Presidency statement, October 28, 1922, FP, letters sent.

64. Grant Diary, October 27, 28, 29, November 1, 2, 3, 1922, October 23, 29, 30, November 5, 1930; Richards, Talmage, Smoot diaries, November 1, 2, 1922, October 30, 1930; JH, November 3, 1922.

65. Grant Diary, November 3, 5, 1928; Jones, "Utah Politics," p. 84.

66. Smoot Diary, March 29, 1923.

67. Larry C. Gerlach, *Blazing Crosses in Zion: The Ku Klux Klan in Utah* (Logan, Utah: Utah State University Press, 1982), p. 39; JH, October 1, 17, 22, November 3, 5, 1923; John S. H. Smith, "Cigarette Prohibition in Utah, 1921–23," *Utah Historical Quarterly* 41 (Autumn 1973): 358–72.

68. Jones, "Utah Politics," pp. 18–24; Merrill, "Reed Smoot," pp. 160–62, 284.

Chapter 4: Recurrent Encounters with Plural Marriage

1. On the attitudes toward the practice of plural marriage see E. Victoria Grover-Swank, "Sex, Sickness and Statehood: The Influence of Victorian Medical Opinion on Self-Government in Utah" (Master's thesis, Brigham Young University, 1980); for an opposing view see Larson, *The Americaniza-tion of Utah for Statehood* (chapter 1, note 5, p. 317), p. 281.

2. *Improvement Era*, October 1901, p. 909; Smoot Proceedings 3:45; Young Journal, January 11, 1900, uses the term *celestial marriage*, as syn-onymous with plural marriage; for the incidence of polygamy among the Latter-day Saints see Stanley Ivins, "Notes on Mormon Polygamy," *Western Humanities Review* 10 (Summer 1956): 229–39.

3. Doctrine and Covenants (1981 ed.), Official Declaration 2; *Salt Lake Tri-bune*, July 23, 1978.

4. Smoot Proceedings 1:21; Eckersley Journal, September 2–6, November 9, 1903, December 26, 1904; Ivins Journal, notes from January to May 1903; Wiley Nebeker to John Henry Smith, May 27, 1903, Smith Family Papers; John Henry Smith to Wiley Nebeker, June 3, 1903, J. H. Smith Letterbooks; Lund Journal, September 4, 1903; J. H. Smith Journal, October 1, 1903. For a general treatment of plural marriage see Kimball Young, *Isn't One Wife Enough?* (New York: Henry Holt, 1954), and Lawrence Foster, *Religion and Sexuality: Three American Communal Experiments of the Nineteenth Cen-tury* (New York: Oxford University Press, 1981).

5. Lund Journal, April 18, 1901; Young Journal, March 13, 1901.

6. Eugene E. Campbell and Richard D. Poll, *Hugh B. Brown: His Life and Thought* (Salt Lake City: Bookcraft, 1975), p. 18; Grant Diary, July 23, 1924.

7. Smoot Proceedings 1:110–11, 389–90, 406, 422, 2:68, 141–43, 295–96; Grant Diary, October 9, 1899; George Q. Cannon to Anthony W. Ivins, De-cember 27, 1897, Ivins Family Papers; Anthony W. Ivins, excerpts from the A. W. Ivins Recordbook of Marriages, Ivins Family Papers; H. Grant Ivins, "Po-lygamy in Mexico," MS, ibid.; Joseph F. Smith to Reed Smoot, April 9, 1904, Joseph F. Smith Letterbook; Cannon and O'Higgins, *Under the Prophet* (chap-ter 1, note 24, p. 319), p. 177; Lund Journal, September 28, 1906; Smoot Diary, March 14, 1911. D. Michael Quinn, probably the most knowledgeable authority on the subject, estimates that "more than 250 plural marriages oc-curred from 1890 to 1904 in Mexico, Canada, and the United States by autho-rization of the First Presidency, and by action or assent of all but one or two members of the Quorum of the Twelve Apostles." "On Being a Mormon Histo-rian," (MS in possession of the author). See also Victor W. Jorgensen and B. Carmon Hardy, "The Taylor-Cowley Affair and the Watershed of Mormon History" (chapter 1, note 30, p. 320); Kenneth L. Cannon II, "Beyond the Manifesto: Polygamous Cohabitation among General Authorities after 1890" (chapter 1, note 30, p. 320); Hansen, *Mormonism and the American Experi-ence* (chapter 1, note 7, p. 318), chapter 5. For details on the new plural mar-riages see Quinn, "LDS Church Authority and New Plural Marriages," p. 40 ff.

On the Cannon-Hamlin marriage see Quinn, "LDS Church Authority and New Plural Marriage" (chapter 1, note 4, p. 317), pp. 83–84.

8. Glen Miller, "The Mormons: A Successful Cooperative Society," *World's Work* 5 (December 1902): 2881; William R. Campbell, "Mormonism and Purity," *Missionary Review of the World* 25 (February 1902): 133–37; Joseph F. Smith, "The Real Origin of Plural Marriage in America," MS, Joseph F. Smith Letterbooks; Charles W. Penrose, "The Aim, Scope, and Methods of the Mormon Church," *Arena* 27 (January 1902): 605–6; Joseph F. Smith, "The Mormonism of Today," ibid. 29 (May 1903): 449–56; Joseph Smith, III, "Plural Marriage in America," ibid.: 556–65; Richard T. Ely, "Economic Aspects of Mormonism," *Harper's* 106 (April 1903): 667–78; Ray Stannard Baker, "The Vitality of Mormonism: A Study of an Irrigated Valley in Utah and Idaho," *The Century Magazine* 68 (June 1904): 177; Charles B. Spahr, "America's Working People: X, The Mormons," *The Outlook* 64 (February 3, 1900): 305–17.

9. Estimate of the percentage is based on work by D. Michael Quinn. Ivins Journal, notes from January to May 1903; Eckersley Journal, September 2–6, November 9, 1903; Lund Journal, September 4, 1903; J. H. Smith Journal, October 1, 1903.

10. Smoot Proceedings 1:24–25, 120, 129–30, 144, 184, 201, 320–22, 324, 328, 350, 478, 487–88; Merrill Journal, May 17, 1900.

11. JH, January 5, February 13, 15, March 7, 15, May 8, 9, July 17, August 20, October 31, November 16, 1905; *Improvement Era*, June 1905, p. 639.

12. Lund Journal, April 4, 5, 6, 7, 1904.

13. Joseph Fielding Smith, comp., *Life of Joseph F. Smith, Sixth President of the Church of Jesus Christ of Latter-day Saints* (Salt Lake City: Deseret News Press, 1938), pp. 374–75.

14. Reed Smoot to Jesse M. Smith, March 22, 1904, cited in Merrill, "Reed Smoot" (chapter 1, note 23, p. 319), p. 58.

15. Francis M. Lyman to John W. Taylor, May 3, 1904, FP, letters sent; First Presidency, circular letter, May 5, 1904, Smith Family Papers; George F. Gibbs to Anthony W. Ivins, June 3, 1904, First Presidency to Ivins, June 9, 1904, FP, letters sent; Lund Journal, June 18, 20, 1904, March 27, 1902; Francis M. Lyman to George Teasdale, July 9, 1904, Smoot Papers; Grant Diary, February 20, 1900; First Presidency to Andrew Kimball, July 21, 1902, cited in Clark, *Messages* (chapter 2, note 12, p. 321) 4:45; and First Presidency to John W. Taylor and George Teasdale, October 22, 1904, FP, letters sent.

16. Smoot Proceedings 3:194; Richards Journal, April 8, 1906.

17. Joseph F. Smith to Heber J. Grant, October 4, 1905, Joseph F. Smith Letterbooks.

18. Lund Journal, August 22, 1905; George F. Gibbs to Anthony W. Ivins, December 18, 1905, FP, letters sent; Joseph F. Smith to George C. Smith, December 17, 1905, Joseph F. Smith Letterbooks; Richards Journal, April 10, June 2, 1906.

19. Lund Journal, April 5, 1906; First Presidency to Heber J. Grant, April

12, 1906, FP, letters sent; JH, April 6, 10, 1906; Richards Journal, March 22, April 8, July 5, 1906; J. H. Smith Journal, December 10, 1906. Elder Richards reported a personal spiritual experience involving a vivid dream of the Savior on March 22 which he later perceived to have been a foreshadowing of his call.

20. Snow, "The American Party" (chapter 2, note 3, p. 321), p. 138; Callister, "E. H. Callister" (chapter 2, note 39, p. 323), pp. 77–78; Lund Journal, November 23, 1906.

21. Richards Journal, July 14, 1909, February 8, 1910. The material in this paragraph about the scope and nature of the investigation is based on numerous diary entries in Richards's journal, which is the best available source for the trials held by the Twelve. The trials were also matters of public record since the most notorious of them were published in the pages of the *Deseret News*; Smoot Diary, September 14, 29, 1909; Lund Journal, February 8, 1910; Richards Journal, 1910 passim; First Presidency, circular letter to stake presidents, October 5, 1910, in Clark, *Messages* 4:217.

22. Grant Diary, July 7, 8, 9, 12, 1909; Richards Journal, July 21, 1909; Ivins Journal, July 21, 22, 23, 1909. The generalization about the usual response of those called to testify is based on a review of the journals of the committee members. Again, the Richards journal is the best source. For those years in which it was transcribed the Grant diary is also excellent. On the Higgs trial, which was a model, see Smoot Diaries, August 25, September 1, October 6, 1909. Higgs eventually left for Canada. See also Smoot Diaries, October 1, 3, 1910, for another case.

23. Joseph F. Smith, *Gospel Doctrine: Selections from the Sermons and Writings of Joseph F. Smith*, comp. John A. Widtsoe, et al. (Salt Lake City: Deseret News Press, 1919), p. 351; J. H. Smith Journal, May 7, 1911; Lund Journal, July 13, 1911; Whitaker Journal, September 24, 1912.

24. Smoot Diary, November 15, 16, 1910; Lund Journal, November 16, 1910; see also Ivins Journal, January 1911. The generalization is based on a review of numerous instances cited in the journals of participants in the decisions.

25. JH, February 11, May 7, October 31, 1908, January 22, February 27, 1909, November 12, December 13, 1910; Lund Journal, February 22, 1907; Julius C. Burrows, "Another Constitutional Amendment Necessary," *The Independent* 62 (May 9, 1907): 1074–78; Harvey J. O'Higgins, "A Reply to Colonel Roosevelt Regarding the New Polygamy in Utah," *Collier's* 67 (June 10, 1911): 35–37; Roberts, *Comprehensive History* (chapter 1, note 21, p. 319) 6:143; Cannon and O'Higgins, *Under the Prophet*.

26. Smoot Diary, October 6, 1910; Joseph F. Smith to Ben E. Rich, December 20, 1910, Joseph F. Smith Letterbooks; Lund Journal, September 27, 1910; Burton J. Hendrick, "The Mormon Revival of Polygamy," *McClures Magazine* 36 (February 1911): 458–64, (January 1911): 345–61.

27. Alfred Henry Lewis, "The Viper on the Hearth," *Cosmopolitan* 50 (March 1911): 439–50, "The Trail of the Viper," ibid. (April 1911): 693–703, and "The Viper's Trail of Gold," ibid. (May 1911): 823–33.

28. On this point see A. J. Simmonds, *The Gentile Comes to Cache Valley: A*

Study of the Logan Apostasies of 1874 and the Establishment of Non-Mormon Churches in Cache Valley, 1873–1913 (Logan, Utah: Utah State University Press, 1976).

29. See, for instance, the case of Joseph Summerhays, Smoot Diary, October 12, 1910, and compare the punishment of elders Taylor and Cowley mentioned below.

30. Smoot Diary, March 14, 1911.

31. Fred C. Miller and Robert R. Black, comps., *The Trials for the Membership of John W. Taylor and Matthias F. Cowley*, 2nd ed. (n.p., 1976), pp. 1, 18, and passim; Richards Journal, September 22, 1909, May 10, 11, 1911; Smoot Diary, October 13, 1910.

32. JH, January 20, February 2, April 20, 1912, January 19, 1913; Smoot Diary, December 10, 1913.

33. Berger, *The Sacred Canopy* (chapter 1, note 37, p. 320), pp. 48–49. For a discussion of the shift in world views specifically dealing with the Mormon situation see Jan Shipps, "In the Presence of the Past: Continuity and Change in Twentieth Century Mormonism," in Thomas G. Alexander and Jessie L. Embry, *After 150 Years: The Latter-day Saints in Sesquicentennial Perspective* (Midvale, Utah: Charles Redd Center for Western Studies, 1983), pp. 3–35. See also Shipps, *Mormonism: The Story of a New Religious Tradition* (Urbana: University of Illinois Press, 1985). For some discussion of some of the similarities and differences in my own and Shipps's point of view see my review of her book forthcoming in *Dialogue*.

34. Grant Diary, March 16, 1921, January 12, November 27, 1928.

Chapter 5: *The Temporal Kingdom*

1. Arrington, *Great Basin Kingdom* (see chapter 1, note 8, p. 318), pp. 13–14, 72–76, 298–302, 385–400; idem., "Utah and the Depression of the 1890s," *Utah Historical Quarterly* 29 (January 1961): 3–18.

2. Arrington, *Great Basin Kingdom*, pp. 243–44, 384–85.

3. On these developments see Robert H. Wiebe, *The Search for Order, 1877–1920* (New York: Hill and Wang, 1967).

4. For a discussion of support of business values within the mainline churches see Irvin G. Wyllie, *The Self-made Man in America: The Myth of Rags to Riches* (New York: Free Press, 1966), especially chapter 4.

5. On the national image of the church see Jan Shipps, "From Satyr to Saint: American Attitudes toward the Mormons, 1860–1960," (paper presented at the 1973 Annual Meeting of the Organization of American Historians).

6. Cook cited in William E. Smythe, "Utah as an Industrial Object-Lesson," *Atlantic Monthly* 78 (November 1896): 617; *Improvement Era*, April 1912: 555–59.

7. Julian Street, "The Mormon Capital," *Colliers* 54 (November 28, 1914): 32; Smoot Diary, August 15, 1915.

8. For the interconnections of the LDS leadership in politics, family life, and

business see D. Michael Quinn, "The Mormon Hierarchy, 1832–1932: An American Elite" (Ph.D. dissertation, Yale University, 1976).

9. Lund Journal, January 22, 1902; First Presidency to David K. Udall, October 15, 1904, Joseph F. Smith Letterbooks; JH, May 5, 1906, November 24, 1909; Richards Journal, July 14, 1910; Grant Diary, December 28, 1917, January 1, July 19, 29, August 7, September 13, 1924; Lund Journal, March 26, 1917.

10. Roberts, *Comprehensive History* (chapter 1, note 21, p. 319) 6:360; Grant Diary, November 10, 11, 1898; Wells Diary, November 14, 1898, January 3, 1899; Wendell P. Ashton, *Voice in the West: Biography of a Pioneer Newspaper* (New York: Duel, Sloan & Pearce, 1950), p. 249.

11. Lund Journal, May 13, 1903; Grant Diary, February 4, 9, 1924. On the competition of the two papers see O. N. Malmquist, *The First 100 Years: A History of the Salt Lake Tribune, 1871–1971* (Salt Lake City: Utah State Historical Society, 1971), p. 280.

12. Grant Diary, May 7, September 20, 1924, September 6, December 1, 1930; JH, April 14, 1923; Malmquist, *First 100 Years*, pp. 372–80.

13. Grant Diary, May 12, 1899; J. H. Smith Journal, January 4, 1900; *The Progressive*, February 7, 1914, and January and February 1914 passim; Street, "The Mormon Capital," p. 20.

14. Grant Diary, August 17, 1921, October 15, 1927.

15. Ibid., November 7, 1927, and passim.

16. Ibid., January 11, March 30, April 9, 12, May 1, October 4, 20, 31, 1928. For a general discussion of the history of the theater see George D. Pyper, *The Romance of an Old Playhouse*, rev. ed. (Salt Lake City: Deseret News Press, 1937).

17. Grant Diary, November 5, 1929.

18. Lund Journal, November 22, 1901; J. H. Smith Journal, November 22, 23, 1901; Leonard J. Arrington, *Beet Sugar in the West: A History of the Utah-Idaho Sugar Company, 1891–1966* (Seattle: University of Washington Press, 1966), pp. 71–72; JH, June 15, 1907.

19. Lund Journal, June 4, 26, 1903.

20. Joseph F. Smith to David Eccles, June 27, 1903, Joseph F. Smith Letterbooks.

21. Judson C. Welliver, "The Mormon Church and the Sugar Trust," *Hampton's Magazine* 24 (January 1910): 82–86; JH, May 19, 1909.

22. Lund Journal, April 8, 1910, June 19, 1911; Smoot Diary, June 14, 15, 19, 20, 21, 27, 29, 1911; J. H. Smith Journal, June 23, 1911.

23. Reed Smoot, "What Democratic Revision of the Tariff Really Means," *The Independent* 72 (March 14, 1912): 564.

24. Reed Smoot to Joseph F. Smith, February 8, 1909, cited in Merrill, "Reed Smoot" (chapter 1, note 23, p. 319), p. 152.

25. *Congressional Record*, 63rd Cong., 1st Sess, 1913, p. 2576; *The Progressive*, May 3, 10, 31, June 21, 1913; Sessions, *Mormon Democrat* (chapter 1, note 16, p. 318), p. 271.

26. Arrington, *Beet Sugar*, p. 80.

27. Ibid., pp. 79, 80, 82; Joseph F. Smith to Henry H. Rolapp, July 9, 1914, Joseph F. Smith Letterbooks; Lund Journal, April 16, 23, 1914; Smoot Diary, May 13, 14, 16, 1914; Nibley, "Reminiscences" (chapter 2, note 46, p. 323), p. 87.

28. Arrington, *Beet Sugar*, pp. 82–85, 90–93; Grant Diary, November 17, 1917.

29. Lund Journal, December 11, 1916, February 6, 1917, January 19, 1920; Joseph F. Smith to Charles W. Nibley, December 5, 1916, Joseph F. Smith Letterbooks; Grant Diary, January 15, 1920; J. R. Bachman, *The Story of the Amalgamated Sugar Company* (Caldwell, Idaho: Caxton Printers, 1962), passim.

30. Lund Journal, September 13, 1918; Charles W. Nibley, "Statement to the Stockholders of the Utah-Idaho Sugar Company," *New West Magazine* 11 (July 1920): 58–59; Smoot Diary, May 10, 11, 13, 18, 19, 21, 22, 1920; Nibley, "Reminiscences," p. 97.

31. Lund Journal, March 4, 9, 13, 1920.

32. Arrington, *Beet Sugar*, p. 96; Lund Journal, September 18, 24, 1918, August 19, 1919, January 2, May 18, December 28, and passim, 1920, August 16, September 11, 1917; Joseph F. Smith to Reed Smoot, June 23, 1917, cited in Clark, *Messages* (chapter 2, note 12, p. 321) 5:78.

33. Lund Journal, December 23, 1920; Arrington, *Beet Sugar*, p. 94.

34. Smoot Diary, May 11, October 8, 1920; Grant Diary, October 7, 1920; *Deseret News*, September 8, 1920.

35. Arrington, *Beet Sugar*, pp. 94, 98; Grant Diary, January 5, 10, 23, June 13, 14, 20, 21, July 7, 11, 14, August 8, 9, September 24, 29, 1921; Lund Journal, January 11, 1921.

36. Grant Diary, October 11, 18, and passim, 1921; Smoot Diary, June 21, October 18, 1921; *Salt Lake Tribune*, September 17, October 20, November 15, 1921; JH, October 20, 1921.

37. Grant Diary, October 18, 1921.

38. Ivins Journal, September 4, 1930; Arrington, *Beet Sugar*, p. 101; K. A. Moser, "The Beet-Sugar Industry and the Tariff with Special Reference to the Great Basin" (Master's thesis, Utah State University, 1933), pp. 10–11.

39. Grant Diary, January 1, September 14, 21, 1922; JH, April 7, 1922; Heber J. Grant to Antoine R. Ivins, August 31, 1922, FP, letters sent.

40. Grant Diary, March 10, 16, 21, 28, 1927; August 14, 15, 24, 1929.

41. Ibid., August 29, 30, 1929.

42. Smoot Diary, September 4, 1929; Grant Diary, September 4, 16, 17, 1929.

43. Ivins Journal, September 4, 1930; Grant Diary, September 23, October 18, 22, December 2, 3, 4, 6, 12, 15, 18, 24, 1930, January 3, 1931.

44. Arrington, *Beet Sugar*, pp. 123–32. The company recently closed its beet sugar operations in Utah and maintains operations only in the Pacific Northwest.

45. *The Progressive*, January 17, 1914; JH, November 17, 1920; *Salt Lake Tribune*, March 16, 20, 22, May 24, 1921; 42 U.S. *Statutes at Large* 9 (1921).

46. Grant Diary, May 2, 3, 1922; Smoot Diary, March 28, 1923; JH, August 9, 13, December 24, 1924.

47. Grant Diary, August 30, 1927, March 16, August 28, 1929, January 25, 1930; Smoot Diary, March 12, 1930; JH, March 13, 1930; Merrill, "Reed Smoot," pp. 184–85.

48. Moser, "Beet-Sugar Industry," p. i, for the antitariff comment; see also JH, January 31, 1930.

49. Arrington, *Great Basin Kingdom* (chapter 1, note 8, p. 318), pp. 391–93; Joseph F. Smith to Charles W. Nibley, December 4, 1899, and to W. B. Clarke, February 19, 1901, Joseph F. Smith Letterbooks; Smoot Proceedings 4:78–80, 245–52, 257–64; Lund Journal, June 9, 28, 1904; Grant Diary, January 21, 1927.

50. Smoot Diary, July 20–22, 1915, August 9, 12, September 2, 1918, March 20, June 7, 1923; Grant Diary, February 18, 1922, February 4, 1919; JH, June 7, 1923; Arrington, *Great Basin Kingdom*, p. 392; Lund Journal, May 18, 1905, March 27, October 12, 1918, February 5, 1919, March 10, October 22, 1920; Joseph F. Smith to Jeremiah E. Langford, Joseph Nelson, and Ashby Snow, December 13, 1906, Joseph F. Smith Letterbooks; Richards Journal, April 22, May 8, 27, 1925; John D. C. Gadd, "Saltair, Great Salt Lake's Most Famous Resort," *Utah Historical Quarterly* 36 (Summer 1968): 214–15.

51. Arrington, *Great Basin Kingdom*, pp. 394–99; Lund Journal, November 29, 1901, December 5, 1902. The company was the predecessor of Utah Power and Light Company.

52. Lund Journal, July 14, 17, 23, 1903; *Improvement Era*, February 1904, p. 316; Arrington, *Great Basin Kingdom*, p. 399.

53. JH, February 18, 1905.

54. Joseph F. Smith to Ben E. Rich, February 26, 1905, Joseph F. Smith Letterbooks; Lund Journal, March 21, August 4, 1905; JH, March 29, April 16, August 4, 1905.

55. Lund Journal, October 31, 1905; JH, May 16, 17, October 27, 1906; Arrington, *Great Basin Kingdom*, p. 408.

56. Grant Diary, August 10, 1927, July 15, 1928, January 21, 1931.

57. Lund Journal, February 7, 1905; JH, February 7, March 17, 1905; *Improvement Era*, July 1905, p. 717.

58. Grant Diary, August 11, 24, 1927, August 1927, passim.

59. Ibid., January 18, 23, March 26, April 7, June 2, July 6, 1928.

60. Ibid., May 22, 1922, March 30, 1923, November 16, 1928, December 31, 1930.

61. Grant Diary, April 19, 20, 1909; Lund Journal, April 19, 20, 1909; J. H. Smith Journal, April 20, 1909.

62. Daniel Bell, *The Coming of Post-Industrial Society: A Venture in Social Forecasting* (New York: Basic Books, 1973); John Naisbitt, *Megatrends: Ten New Directions Transforming Our Lives* (New York: Warner Books, 1982),

pp. 13–14. Naisbitt limits the term to information generation, but I believe it should include the expansion of a number of service industries.

Chapter 6: Administrative Modernization, 1900–18

1. This discussion is based on D. Michael Quinn, "The Evolution of the Presiding Quorums of the LDS Church," *Journal of Mormon History* 1 (1974): 21–37.

2. The best study of the office of a bishop is Dale Beecher, "The Office of Bishop," *Dialogue* 15 (Winter 1982): 103–15.

3. For a full discussion of this reorganization see William G. Hartley, "The Priesthood Reorganization of 1877: Brigham Young's Last Achievement," *BYU Studies* 20 (Fall 1979): 3–36, and Beecher, "Office of Bishop."

4. For a general discussion of these organizations see Allen and Leonard, *The Story of the Latter-day Saints* (chapter 1, note 1, p. 317), pp. 160–61, 336, 378–79, 422.

5. Wells Diary, April 6, 1900; Spahr, "America's Working People" (chapter 4, note 8, p. 329), p. 309.

6. Joseph F. Smith to Samuel E. Woolley, February 2, 1902, Joseph F. Smith Letterbooks; Talmage Journal, October 6, 1901; Joseph F. Smith to Anthony W. Ivins, February 6, 1900, Joseph F. Smith Letterbooks.

7. Clark, *Messages* (chapter 2, note 12, p. 321) 4:5; Talmage Journal, November 10, 1901.

8. Talmage Journal, December 8, 1911; for a discussion of administrative style see Thomas G. Alexander, "To Maintain Harmony: Adjusting to External and Internal Stress, 1890–1930," *Dialogue* 15 (Winter 1982): 44–58.

9. Young Journal, September 9, 1898, April 5, 8, May 4, July 17, 1900; Grant Diary, April 5, 1900.

10. Talmage Journal, October 17, November 10, 1901; Lund Journal, October 17, 24, 1901; J. H. Smith Journal, October 24, 1901. See tables 1, 2, 3, 4, and 5 in the Appendix for the administrative changes over the entire thirty-year period.

11. Grant Diary, April 5, 1900; J. H. Smith Journal, October 4, 1903; George A. Smith Journal, October 6, 1903.

12. Preston Nibley, *The Presidents of the Church* (Salt Lake City: Deseret Book, 1947), pp. 223–49.

13. Lund Journal, November 5, 6, 21, 25, 1901, March 6, 1902; Merrill Journal, February 27, 1902.

14. Lund Journal, passim; JH, December 22, 1909; Richards Journal, December 22, 30, 1909, January 30, 1913, October 2, 1913, February 17, 1916, and passim; Smoot Diary, July 6, 1910.

15. Young Journal, December 21, October 13, 1898.

16. Grant Diary, January 5, 1899; Lund Journal, December 5, 1901;

Joseph F. Smith to Nancy L. Richards, July 19, 1901, Joseph F. Smith Letterbooks; J. H. Smith Journal, December 12, 1901.

17. J. H. Smith Journal, October 13, 1899; Grant Diary, January 5, 1900; Richards Journal, May 22, 1906; Young Journal, September 20, 1901, March 22, 1899; Talmage Journal, May 31, 1899; Lund Journal, October 1, November 4, 26, 1901. For a general discussion of the salaries see Quinn, "The Mormon Hierarchy" (chapter 5, note 8, p. 331), pp. 127–30.

18. Lund Journal, November 14, 1901, January 29, 1902, July 10, 1903; John Henry Smith to L. W. Shurtliff, January 9, 1901, John Henry Smith Letterbooks, LDS Archives (hereinafter cited as J. H. Smith Letterbooks); Eckersley Journal, March 20, 1904.

19. JH, April 5, 1907; Grant Diary, April 2, 1908; J. H. Smith Journal, March 30, 1907, April 2, 1908; *Improvement Era*, February 1907, p. 316; Lund Journal, January 16, 1904.

20. Presiding Bishop, Annual Reports, 1908 and 1909, LDS Archives. (Hereinafter cited as PBO Report with date); Lund Journal, July 6, 1910.

21. Ibid., January 13, 1908, October 12, 1913, and passim; PBO Report, 1903; JH, May 1910.

22. Lund Journal, July 30, 1908; PBO Reports, 1909, 1913.

23. JH, December 4, 1902; Richards Journal, October 10, 1906; Grant Diary, 1898–1903 passim; Smoot Proceedings 3:8; First Council of the Seventy Minutes, November 9, 1899, LDS Archives.

24. Most of the following is based on Lund Journal, March 23, 24, 1901. The procedure was similar for other conferences; see Lund Journal, Grant Diary, and Richards Journal, passim.

25. See Richards Journal, October 18, 1908, for Beaver Stake.

26. Ibid., February 6, November 5, 1909, June 4, August 6, 1911, January 26, February 9, 1913, and passim.

27. Ibid., August 10, 1913.

28. Richards Journal, August 26, 31, 1908; Grant Diary, October 15, 1908; Smoot Proceedings 2:321–45, 59, 64–66; Lund Journal, October 25, 1899, February 15, 1900, May 15, 1901, March 25, 1902.

29. Lund Journal, April 7, 1908, and passim.

30. Richards Journal, May 21, 1911. Perhaps the best discussion of the operation of church courts in outlying areas is found in Mark P. Leone, *Roots of Modern Mormonism* (Cambridge, Mass.: Harvard University Press, 1979), chapter 5.

31. Lund Journal, August 16, 1916.

32. Clark, *Messages* 5:79; *Improvement Era*, November 1917, p. 9.

33. Ibid., April 1919, pp. 498–500.

34. Richards Journal, January 6, 1907, December 28, 1908; Grant Diary, October 1, 1907.

35. First Presidency to Nephi L. Morris, February 16, 1905, cited in Clark, *Messages* 4:100.

36. Grant Diary, December 7, 1916.

37. Ibid., December 4, 11, 1907; Lund Journal, December 4, 11, 1907; Joseph F. Smith to Charles W. Penrose, December 12, 1907, Joseph F. Smith Letterbooks.

38. Nibley, "Reminiscences" (chapter 2, note 46, p. 323), pp. 81, 83.

39. Ivins Journal, April 8, 1901; Clark, *Messages* 4:34, 46.

40. First Presidency, circular letter, January 1, 1910, Clark, *Messages* 4: 213–14.

41. Mormon D. Bird, "Personal History," in the author's possession; Allen and Leonard, *Story of the Latter-day Saints*, pp. 161–62; L. John Nuttall Diary, December 17, 21, 23, 1899, January 2, 1900, LDS Archives (hereinafter cited as Nuttall Diary).

42. Circular letter, September 12, 1901, cited in Clark, *Messages* 3:341; Lund Journal, January 22, 1904.

43. Clark, *Messages* 3:290; "Our Work," *Improvement Era*, March 1900, pp. 393–94; Lund Journal, March 13, 1902.

44. JH, April 19, 1900.

45. Lund Journal, August 6, 1899; Merrill Journal, April 23, 1900.

46. Grant Diary, September 20, 1901, October 19, 1899, and 1898–1903 passim; Lund Journal, May 18, 1902; Smoot Proceedings 1:778.

47. Lund Journal, November 15, 1902.

48. Richards Journal, September 26, 27, 1908.

49. Richards Journal, February 22, 1907.

50. JH, May 1910; *Improvement Era*, January 1910, p. 276.

51. For a discussion of the change in this basic orientation see Shipps, "In the Presence of the Past" (see chapter 4, note 33, p. 331), pp. 3–35.

52. FCS Minutes, March 14, October 10, and passim, 1900, December 4, 1901; Lund Journal, December 1, 1901.

53. FCS Minutes, October 1, 15, 1902. For a discussion of the later manifestations of this movement see William Hartley, "The Priesthood Reform Movement, 1908–1922," *BYU Studies* 13 (Winter 1973): 137–56. From the currently available evidence on the work of the seventies, it is clear that Hartley dates the origins of this movement too late.

54. FCS Minutes, September 30, 1903.

55. Richards Journal, January 30, May 31, 1907; First Presidency, circular letter, June 12, 1907, in Clark, *Messages* 4:157–59.

56. *Improvement Era*, December 1907, pp. 147–50, and September 1908, pp. 893–94; Grant Diary, June 10, 1908.

57. Grant Diary, December 17, 1908; Richards Journal, December 2, 22, 23, 1908.

58. First Council of Seventy to Quorums of Seventy, January 1912, cited in Clark, *Messages* 4:259.

59. *Improvement Era*, February 1912, pp. 377–78.

60. Talmage Journal, April 3, 1915.

61. Hartley, "The Priesthood Reorganization of 1877"; Lund Journal, August 9, 1906, October 6, 1903; Richards Journal, July 15, 1906.

62. Ivins Journal, October 8, 1906.

63. First Presidency to First Council of the Seventy, October 26, 1907, and idem, circular letter, November 6, 1907, in Clark, *Messages* 4:159–62.

64. Richards Journal, December 26, 1908; Grant Diary, November 30, 1908; J. H. Smith Journal, December 3, 1908; JH, November 29, 1908.

65. *Improvement Era*, March 1909, p. 397, April 1909, p. 498, and July 1909, p. 749; Grant Diary, March 20, 1909.

66. Lund Journal, October 19, 1909, January 20, 1910; Richards Journal, January 20, 1910.

67. Lund Journal, February 8, 1910; Richards Journal, February 8, 1910; Joseph F. Smith to David A. Smith, February 8, 1910, Joseph F. Smith Letterbooks.

68. Richards Journal, May 27, 1911, March 5, 1913; Lund Journal, June 10, 1913.

69. Lund Journal, August 13, 1913.

70. *Improvement Era*, November 1913, p. 61, and September 1915, p. 1024.

Chapter 7: New Directions in Church Administration, 1918–30

1. Lund Journal, November 17, 18, 19, 22, 1918.

2. The following is based on Grant Diary, July 3, 1918.

3. Lund Journal, November 21, 1918.

4. Ibid., November 23, 1918.

5. Ibid., May 25, June 1, 1919; JH, June 1, 1919.

6. Bryant S. Hinckley, *Heber J. Grant: Highlights in the Life of a Great Leader* (Salt Lake City: Deseret Book Co. 1951), chapters 3 and 4; Grant Diary, 1915–16 passim, February 20, 1917, July 3, September 28, December 1, 1915; Lund Journal, January 2, 1921.

7. Grant Diary, March 5, 6, 8, 10, 17, 1921; Richards Journal, March 10, 14, 1921. For all of the changes which took place see tables 1, 2, 3, 4, and 5 in the Appendix.

8. Grant Diary, May 16, 1925; Smoot Diary, June 4, 1925.

9. Talmage Journal, January 7, 1918; Lund Journal, November 27, 1918, January 13, 1919.

10. Lund Journal, November 27, December 29, 1918.

11. Grant Diary, January 28, 1919, April 25, September 20, 21, 1921, January 31, February 7, 1922; Smoot Diary, April 10, 1919; JH, February 8, 1922, November 26, 1923.

12. Grant Diary, 1927 passim.

13. Ibid., July 26, 1922.

14. Ibid., April 1, 1930.

15. On the acquisition of sites see Roberts, *Comprehensive History* (chapter 1, note 21, p. 319) 6:426–30, 525–26; Allen and Leonard, *Story of the Latter-day Saints* (chapter 1, note 1, p. 317), pp. 447–48, 510.

16. On architectural development see Allen D. Roberts, "Religious Architecture of the LDS Church: Influences and Changes Since 1847," *Utah His-*

torical Quarterly 43 (Summer 1975): 321–27; Peter L. Goss, "The Architectural History of Utah," ibid.: 223–39; and Paul L. Anderson, "The Early Twentieth Century Temples," *Dialogue* 14 (Spring 1981): 9–19. The statistical information on the amounts appropriated by the church comes from the Anthon H. Lund Journal and the Heber J. Grant Diary.

17. Grant Diary, February 26, March 15, 25, 31, June 9, 1908; Lund Journal, April 25, 1912; First Presidency to Nephi L. Morris, October 31, 1910, cited in Clark, *Messages* (chapter 2, note 12, p. 321) 4:218–19; JH, February 27, 1908.

18. On the development of standard plans see Martha Sonntag Bradley, "'The Church and Colonel Saunders': Mormon Standard Plan Architecture" (Master's thesis, Brigham Young University, 1981), pp. 31–50. See also Allen and Leonard, *Story of the Latter-day Saints*, pp. 509–10; Grant Diary, April 18, August 27, 1924.

19. First Presidency to Serge Ballif, November 19, 1921, FP, letters sent; and Heber J. Grant to Reed Smoot, August 26, 1922, ibid; Grant Diary, June 9, 1930, April 3, 1931; JH, December 29, 1930.

20. Grant Diary, December 19, 1919, January 20, 1921, June 1, 9, 1921; Smoot Diary, September 21, 1918, December 25, 1919; Quinn, "Mormon Hierarchy" (chapter 5, note 8, p. 331), pp. 127–30; Talmage Journal, July 13, 1916; John A. Widtsoe, *In a Sunlit Land: The Autobiography of John A. Widstoe* (Salt Lake City: Milton R. Hunter and G. Homer Durham, 1952), p. 161; Richards Journal, January 30, 1925.

21. Grant Diary, July 13, August 14, 1922, February 24, 1929.

22. Heber J. Grant to Nephi L. Morris, May 8, 1922, FP, letters sent; JH, February 3, April 25, 1923, May 26, 1930; Grant Diary, April 14, 1923, July 20, November 27, July 20, 1929.

Chapter 8: The Church Auxiliary Organizations

1. On this point see Thomas G. Alexander, "Between Revivalism and the Social Gospel: The Latter-day Saint Social Advisory Committee, 1916–1922," *BYU Studies* 23 (Winter 1983): 19–39. On the conflict over Fundamentalism in Protestantism see George M. Marsden, *Fundamentalism and American Culture* (see chapter 1, note 7, p. 318).

2. Church of Jesus Christ of Latter-day Saints, *Welfare Plan of the Church of Jesus Christ of Latter-day Saints: Handbook of Instructions* ([Salt Lake City]: Deseret News Press, 1969), pp. 1–2, 77–78, 88; idem., *General Handbook of Instructions* ([Salt Lake City]: First Presidency, 1968), p. 115 deals with collecting for disasters.

3. For a discussion of the movement in the progressive era for managerial efficiency see Samuel Haber, *Efficiency and Uplift: Scientific Management in the Progressive Era, 1890–1920* (Chicago: University of Chicago Press, 1964), and Samuel P. Hayes, *Conservation and the Gospel of Efficiency: The Progressive Conservation Movement, 1890–1920* (Cambridge: Harvard Uni-

versity Press, 1959). A discussion of other urban problems confronted by progressives will be found in John D. Buenker, *Urban Liberalism and Progressive Reform* (New York: Norton, 1978), and Joseph M. Hawes, *Children in Urban Society: Juvenile Delinquency in Nineteenth-Century America* (New York: Oxford University Press, 1971). For a discussion of one aspect of the moral reform movement, see James H. Timberlake, *Prohibition and the Progressive Movement, 1900–1920* (Cambridge: Harvard University Press, 1963).

4. On progressive influences in education see Lawrence A. Cremin, *The Transformation of the School: Progressivism in American Education, 1876–1957* (New York: Knopf, 1961). On other progressive points of view see Theodore Roosevelt, *The New Nationalism*, intro., William E. Leuchtenburg (Englewood Cliffs, N.J.: Prentice Hall, 1961); Woodrow Wilson, *The New Freedom*, intro., William E. Leuchtenburg (Englewood Cliffs, N.J.: Prentice Hall, 1961); and Betty Spears and Richard A. Swanson, *History of Sport and Physical Activity in the United States*, Elaine T. Smith, ed. (Dubuque, Iowa: William C. Brown, 1978), pp. 143–238.

5. Discussions of the controversy between progressives and conservatives in the progressive era will be found in Robert H. Wiebe, *Businessmen and Reform: A Study of the Progressive Movement* (Cambridge: Harvard University Press, 1962); Richard W. Leopold, *Elihu Root and the Conservative Tradition* (Boston: Little, Brown, 1954); and Paschal, *Mr. Justice Sutherland* (see chapter 2, note 43, p. 323).

6. *Handbook of the Relief Society of the Church of Jesus Christ of Latter-day Saints* (Salt Lake City: National Women's Relief Society, 1931), pp. 35, 40; Richard L. Jensen, "Forgotten Relief Societies, 1844–67," *Dialogue* 16 (Spring 1983): 105–25.

7. JH, September 28, 1905; for a full discussion of the grain storage program see Jessie L. Embry, "Relief Society Grain Storage Program, 1876–1940" (chapter 3, note 41, p. 326), pp. 6–7, chapter 4 and passim.

8. *Relief Society Handbook*, 1931, p. 42.

9. JH, May 20, 1905. For a general discussion of relief activity in the early twentieth century see Bruce D. Blumell, *Welfare Before Welfare: Twentieth Century LDS Church Charity Before the Great Depression* (Salt Lake City: Historical Department of the LDS Church, 1978).

10. JH, November 26, December 2, 1907, February 13, 1908, February 6, 1929, October 5, 1930.

11. *Relief Society Handbook*, 1931, pp. 56, 58; Lund Journal, May 29, 1901, September 8, 1902; Grant Diary, June 25, 1900.

12. *Relief Society Handbook*, 1931, pp. 56, 58; *Relief Society Magazine*, July 1914, p. 14; JH, June 26, 1920.

13. *Relief Society Handbook*, 1931, p. 59.

14. JH, April 4, 1922; Grant Diary, October 15, 1930; *Relief Society Handbook*, 1931, p. 64; Allen and Leonard, *Story of the Latter-day Saints* (chapter 1, note 1, p. 317), pp. 629–30.

15. *Relief Society Handbook*, 1931, p. 60.

16. Lund Journal, September 19, 1921; Andrew Jenson, *Church Chronology: A Record of Important Events Pertaining to the History of the Church of Jesus Christ of Latter-day Saints*, 2nd ed. (Salt Lake City: Deseret News, 1914), December 19, 1913; *Relief Society Magazine*, August 1916, p. 462, October 1926, pp. 517–18, January 1923, pp. 30–31, December 1926, pp. 630–33; JH, December 13, 1922.

17. *Relief Society Handbook*, 1931, p. 55; JH, April 21, 1927, October 4, 1928, January 27, 1923; Grant Diary, November 7, 1930, July 20, 1931.

18. *Relief Society Handbook*, 1931, p. 63; *Relief Society Magazine*, December 1923, pp. 623–24.

19. *Relief Society Handbook*, 1931, p. 64.

20. Clark, *Messages* (chapter 2, note 12, p. 321) 5:119; *Relief Society Handbook*, 1931, pp. 52–53; *Relief Society Magazine*, January 1923, pp. 12–13.

21. *Relief Society Handbook*, 1931, pp. 54–55; JH, June 27, 1919.

22. *Relief Society Handbook*, 1931, p. 55.

23. Desna Wallin Hansen, "The Development of the Women Suffrage Movement in Utah and Its Effect Upon Women's Participation in Politics, 1870–1920" (Unpublished seminar paper, Brigham Young University, 1968), pp. 2–13; Jean Bickmore White, "Woman's Place Is in the Constitution: The Struggle for Equal Rights in Utah in 1895," in Thomas G. Alexander, ed., *Essays on the American West, 1973–74* (Provo, Utah: Brigham Young University Press, 1975), pp. 81–104; Susa Young Gates, "A Message from a Woman of the Latter-day Saints to the Women in All the World," *Improvement Era*, April 1907, pp. 447–62; idem, "Utah Women in Politics," (n.p. [1913]), passim; *Deseret Weekly*, July 19, 1890; Theodore W. Curtis, "A Word for the Mormons," *Arena* 21 (June 1899): 722. For a general discussion of nineteenth-century Mormon women see Claudia L. Bushman, ed., *Mormon Sisters, Women in Early Utah* (Cambridge, Mass.: Emmeline Press, 1976).

24. JH, October 14, 1915, June 6, 1919; Lund Journal, May 9, 1916; and Smoot Diary, August 14, 1918, June 10, 1919.

25. Kate Carter, ed., *Treasures of Pioneer History*, 6 vols. (Salt Lake City: Daughters of Utah Pioneers, 1952–57) 1:42–44; JH, February 10, 1900; Gates, "Women in Utah Politics," p. 4; Jean Bickmore White, "Martha Hughes Cannon: Doctor, Wife, Legislator, Exile," in Vicki Burgess-Olson, ed., *Sister Saints* (Provo, Utah: Brigham Young University Press, 1978), pp. 383–97.

26. Mary W. Howard, "Women in Politics," *Improvement Era*, July 1914, pp. 865–68; Gates, "Utah Women in Politics," p. 10. For a biography see Leonard J. Arrington and Susan Arrington Madsen, *Sunbonnet Sisters: True Stories of Mormon Women and Frontier Life* (Salt Lake City, Utah: Bookcraft, 1984), pp. 141–49.

27. Melvin Erikson Thayne, "Smoot of Utah (United States Senator, 1903–1933)" (Master's thesis, Stanford University, 1950), p. 62; Lund Journal, January 16, 1919; *Improvement Era*, March 1915, pp. 379–87; JH, February 7, July 10, 1927.

28. *Relief Society Handbook*, 1931, pp. 42, 48, 49, 51.

29. Ibid., p. 51.

30. Ibid., p. 65.

31. *Relief Society Magazine*, March 1915, pp. 130–31, 140–41, December 1915, p. 528, October 1921, p. 578; JH, December 16, 1916.

32. Heber J. Grant to Dora Henderson, April 19, 1924, FP, letters sent.

33. Grant Diary, February 24, 27, 1928; *Relief Society Handbook*, 1931, pp. 54–55.

34. Roberts, *Comprehensive History* (chapter 1, note 21, p. 319) 5:478–79; Clark, *Messages* 3:303.

35. *Latter-day Saints Sunday School Treatise*, 2d ed. (Salt Lake City: Deseret Sunday School Union, 1898), pp. 9–11, 20; and *Proceedings of the First Sunday School Convention of the Church of Jesus Christ of Latter-day Saints, Monday, November 28, 1898* (n.p., ca 1898), p. 19; J. N. Washburn, "Ye Have Need that One Teach You," *The Instructor* 84 (June 1949): 269.

36. *Sunday School Treatise*, passim.

37. Nuttall Diary, 1899–1901, passim.

38. Spahr, "America's Working People" (see chapter 4, note 8, p. 329).

39. First Council of the Seventy Minutes, July 2, 1902.

40. First Presidency to Heber J. Grant, October 19, 1902, FP, letters sent; Lund Diary, January 24, 1904.

41. Clark, *Messages* 4:50; Lund Journal, February 19, 1903.

42. *Parent and Child: A Series of Essays and Lessons*, 3 vols. (Salt Lake City: Deseret Sunday School Union, 1908, 1909, 1915), 1:190–91.

43. Washburn, "Ye Have Need," p. 270; idem, "Capsule History of the Sunday School," *The Instructor* 84 (December 1949): 654.

44. Washburn, "Ye Have Need," p. 271.

45. Ibid., p. 270.

46. JH, December 28, 1927, December 17, 1927. It should be noted that these changes which took place in 1928 were part of a larger "Church Sunday School," or "Priesthood-Auxiliary" movement inaugurated at the behest of the Council of the Twelve. See Richard O. Cowan, "The Priesthood Auxiliary Movement, 1928–1938," *BYU Studies* 19 (Fall 1979): 109–10.

47. On the origins of the YMMIA see Allen and Leonard, *Story of the Latter-day Saints* (chapter 1, note 1, p. 317), p. 338. For an example of the sort of literary society that served as a forerunner of the MIA see Ronald W. Walker, "Growing Up in Early Utah: The Wasatch Literary Association, 1874–1878," *Sunstone* 6 (November/December 1981): 44–51. For a general history of the MIA see Scott Kenney, *The Mutual Improvement Associations: A Preliminary History, 1900–1950* (Salt Lake City: Historical Department of the Church of Jesus Christ of Latter-day Saints, 1976).

48. Allen and Leonard, *Story of the Latter-day Saints*, pp. 336–37, 460, 500.

49. *Improvement Era*, July 1900, p. 695, March 1904, pp. 289–92, July 1905, p. 709; First Council of the Seventy Minutes, June 4, 1902.

50. *Improvement Era*, June 1900, p. 632, July 1900, pp. 666–68, October 1904, pp. 152–53, November 1905, pp. 77–78, January 1905, pp. 235–36.

51. JH, October 17, 1901.

52. Joseph F. Smith, *Gospel Doctrine* (chapter 4, note 23, p. 330), pp. 488–89; *Improvement Era*, April 1908, pp. 476–78.

53. *Improvement Era*, August 1909, pp. 819–22, January 1909, p. 246; Grant Diary, December 2, 1908.

54. *Improvement Era*, September 1908, pp. 896–97, September 1909, p. 852, August 1911, p. 945; Richards Journal, August 30, 1912; Grant Diary, June 16, 1913.

55. *Improvement Era*, November 1917, p. 86; Lund Journal, March 14, 1918.

56. J. H. Smith Journal, September 13, 1911; Lund Journal, September 20, 1911; Smoot Journal, September 20, 1911.

57. *Improvement Era*, May 1911, p. 655, November 1911, pp. 89–90, September 1917, p. 1029.

58. *Improvement Era*, May 1913, p. 821, August 1912, pp. 954–55; Kenney, *Mutual Improvement Associations*, p. 25.

59. JH, April 1911 and September 2, 1911; *Improvement Era*, January 1912, p. 287, March 1912, pp. 254–61, January 1913, pp. 269–73, September 1913, pp. 1135–36, December 1913, p. 181.

60. JH, December 16, 1916, April 1921; Grant Diary, June 5, 1918.

61. *Improvement Era*, November 1916, p. 90.

62. Ibid., December 1922, pp. 207–9, April 1923, p. 495, June 1923, p. 724, July 1923, p. 931, March 1924, pp. 271–72; JH, May 13, 1926, February 19, 1930.

63. Kenney, *Mutual Improvement Associations*, p. 16; JH, April 17, 1915.

64. Kenney, *Mutual Improvement Associations*, p. 25.

65. Ibid., p. 17.

66. *Improvement Era*, November 1914, pp. 68–73; Grant Diary, May 27, 1916.

67. *Improvement Era*, July 1911, pp. 845–48, September 1914, pp. 1086–87, December 1920, p. 174, April 1915, p. 555; Richards Journal, December 13, 1911, November 18, 1914; Grant Diary, May 26, 1914.

68. Grant Diary, September 8, 1922; JH, April 9, 1923.

69. Ibid., February 19, 1927, June 7, 1929; Grant Diary, March 14, 1931.

70. For a general history of the Primary see Carol Cornwall Madsen and Susan Staker Oman, *Sisters and Little Saints: One Hundred Years of Primary* (Salt Lake City: Deseret Book, 1979). I have relied on this book for general information on the Primary organization.

71. Ibid., pp. 5–6, 9–11, 28–31, 50.

72. Ibid., p. 46.

73. Jill Mulvay Derr, "Sisters and Little Saints: One Hundred Years of Mormon Primaries," in Thomas G. Alexander, ed., *The Mormon People: Their*

Character and Traditions (Provo, Utah: Brigham Young University Press, 1980), p. 85.

74. Madsen and Oman, *Sisters and Little Saints*, p. 51.

75. Ibid., p. 47; Richards Journal, May 11, 1922; JH, May 11, 1922, April 5, 1924; Grant Diary, August 1, 1927, October 24, 1929.

76. Grant Diary, January 2, 1931; Madsen and Oman, *Sisters and Little Saints*, pp. 177–78.

77. For a general history of Religion Classes see D. Michael Quinn, "Utah's Educational Innovation: LDS Religion Classes, 1890–1929," *Utah Historical Quarterly* 43 (Fall 1975): 379–89.

78. JH, January 10, 1900, December 1, 1904.

79. Smoot Proceedings 2:106–111, 367, 370–71.

80. JH, January 16 and February 1905, March 29, 30, 1923, February 13, 24, 1924; Quinn, "Religion Classes," p. 388.

81. Grant Diary, March 26, 1908; Lund Journal, May 13, 1908, April 26, 1910, March 21, 1911.

82. See, for instance, Juanita Brooks, *Quicksand and Cactus: A Memoir of the Southern Mormon Frontier*, intro., Charles S. Peterson (Salt Lake City: Howe Brothers, 1982), pp. 164–68 and passim.

83. For a general treatment of the dance controversy in the nineteenth century see Davis Bitton, "'These Licentious Days': Dancing Among the Mormons," *Sunstone* 2 (Spring 1977): 16–27; Merrill, *Utah Pioneer and Apostle* (chapter 1, note 15, p. 318), p. 136.

84. First Presidency to Anthony W. Ivins, February 13, 1906, FP, letters sent; Ivins Journal, March 28, 1906; Grant Diary, October 6, 8, 1898, February 2, 1899, and January 31, 1900; Brooks, *Quicksand and Cactus*, pp. 164–68.

85. *The Progressive*, September 6, 1913; Lund Journal, November 29, 1913.

86. First Presidency to stake presidents, June 1923, Clark, *Messages* 5: 227–30.

87. JH, April 6, 1912, May 16, 1907; George A. Smith Journal, February 28, 1908.

88. Wells Diary, July 4, 1909; JH, August 30, 1911.

89. *Improvement Era*, August 1908, pp. 806–8, January 1913, pp. 262–63; Grant Diary, January 31, February 4, April 1, 1913; JH, June 3, 1907, January 1, 16, 1908, December 4, 1909, November 14, 1908; Clark, *Messages* 4:187–88.

90. This discussion is based on Alexander, "Between Revivalism and the Social Gospel."

91. See First Presidency to Stephen L Richards, June 26, 1922, in Grant Diary, June 26, 1922, for the full text of the letter.

92. Clark, *Messages* 5:216.

93. Grant Diary, September 29, 1927; Kenney, *Mutual Improvement Associations*, pp. 26–27; Cowan, "Priesthood-Auxiliary Movement," passim.

94. Grant Diary, February 16, 1929; Cowan, "Priesthood Auxiliary Movement," passim.

95. D. Michael Quinn, *J. Reuben Clark* (see notes to chapter 3, note 2, p. 324) pp. 260–269; Allen and Leonard, *Story of the Latter-day Saints*, p. 521.

Chapter 9: Definition of a Role for the Church Educational System

1. For a discussion of education in context see Allen and Leonard, *Story of the Latter-day Saints* (chapter 1, note 1, p. 317). A general treatment of the Latter-day Saints and education will be found in M. Lynn Bennion, *Mormonism and Education* ([Salt Lake City]: Department of Education of the LDS Church, 1939). A more recent account with a more thorough discussion of education outside the United States is Leon R. Hartshorn, "Mormon Education in the Bold Years" (Ed.D. dissertation, Stanford University, 1965). For educational development in the United States during the period see Cremin, *The Transformation of the School* (see notes to chapter 8, note 4, p. 340). On nineteenth-century Utah education see James R. Clark, "Church and State Relationships in Education in Utah" (Ed.D. dissertation, Utah State University, 1958).

2. On educational development in Utah see J. C. Moffitt, *The History of Public Education in Utah* (n.p.: privately printed, 1946); volume 1 of Ernest L. Wilkinson, *Brigham Young University: The First One Hundred Years*, 4 vols. (Provo, Utah: Brigham Young University Press, 1976); Ralph V. Chamberlin, *The University of Utah: A History of Its First Hundred Years* (Salt Lake City: University of Utah Press, 1960); and Joseph H. Jeppson, "The Secularization of the University of Utah to 1920" (Ph.D. dissertation, University of California-Berkeley, 1973).

3. On the secularization of the educational system see Stanley S. Ivins, "Free Schools Come to Utah," *Utah Historical Quarterly* 22 (October 1954): 321–42; and C. Merrill Hough, "Two School Systems in Conflict, 1867–1890," *Utah Historical Quarterly* 28 (April 1960): 113–28.

4. JH, September 6, 1900; Hartshorn, "Mormon Education in the Bold Years," pp. 28–29; Miller, "The Mormons: A Successful Cooperative Society" (chapter 4, note 8, p. 329), p. 2893; Lund Journal, August 22, 1901; First Presidency to Francis M. Lyman, December 22, 1902, in Clark, *Messages* (chapter 2, note 12, p. 321) 4:49.

5. Young Journal, September 26, 1900; Lund Journal, May 15, November 1, June 25, 1901, June 29, 1904, March 24, 1919; JH, July 22, 1919; *Improvement Era*, October 1919, pp. 1065–66; Grant Diary, July 16, 1919, January 27, 1922; Widtsoe, *In a Sunlit Land* (chapter 7, note 20, p. 339), p. 171.

6. Richards Journal, July 17, 18, 23, 1907.

7. Information on expenditures and enrollment comes from JH, June 16, 1910, December 16, 1916; Richards Journal, July 23, 1907; *Improvement Era*, August 1912, pp. 877–78; and Bennion, *Mormonism and Education*, pp. 200, 201. Some of Bennion's statistics seem low, perhaps because they do not include the colleges and universities.

8. *Improvement Era*, September 1908, pp. 825–33, August 1912, pp. 921–22, January 1910, pp. 240–43.

9. Elmer G. Peterson, "Training for Women: The Opening Vista of Greatest Opportunity," *Improvement Era*, July 1914, p. 849.

10. *Improvement Era*, January 1914, pp. 244–46.

11. Baker, "Vitality of Mormonism," p. 173, and Spahr, "America's Working People" (chapter 4, note 8, p. 329), p. 314. For a discussion of some of those brought to Utah see Wilkinson, *BYU* 2:368.

12. Spahr, "America's Working People," p. 314.

13. Ibid., p. 315.

14. Ely, "Economic Aspects of Mormonism" (chapter 4, note 8, p. 329), pp. 674–75.

15. Wain Sutton, ed., *Utah: A Centennial History*, 3 vols (New York: Lewis Historical Publishing Co., 1949), 2:1043.

16. Lund Journal, February 15, October 3, 1915; JH, October 4, 1915; Joseph F. Smith to Daniel Harrington, May 29, 1901, June 26, 1903, Joseph F. Smith Letterbooks; *Improvement Era*, November 1903, p. 56.

17. Grant Diary, April 29, 1921.

18. Clark, *Messages* 4:46, 59.

19. Merrill Journal, February 8, 13, 1900; Young Journal, April 17, June 8, 1900; Arnold K. Garr, "A History of Brigham Young College, Logan, Utah" (Master's thesis, Utah State University, 1973), p. 40.

20. Lund Journal, March 26, 1902, May 19, 31, 1909; JH, December 29, 1906, May 27, 1909; Wilkinson, *BYU* 1:396–98.

21. Merrill, *Utah Pioneer and Apostle* (chapter 1, note 15, p. 318), p. 152; Joseph F. Smith to Joseph R. Smith, February 5, 1900, Joseph F. Smith Letterbooks; Lund Journal, December 31, 1901.

22. Grant Diary, May 17, 29, August 3, 1900; J. H. Smith Journal, May 29, 1900.

23. Lund Journal, March 30, 1906.

24. Ibid., June 13, 1913, March 16, 1920.

25. JH, October 27, 1920, April 9, 1921, January 16, 1923, May 7, 1924.

26. Widtsoe, *In a Sunlit Land*, p. 171; Grant Diary, June 2, 1922.

27. Wilkinson, *BYU* 2:14.

28. Lund Journal, September 19, 30, 1903.

29. Joseph F. Smith to Joseph F. Smith, Jr., February 5, 1900, Joseph F. Smith Letterbooks; idem. to Benjamin J. Cluff, February 6, 1900, ibid; *Improvement Era*, May 1900, pp. 543–45.

30. Grant Diary, July 18, 1900.

31. Wilkinson, *BYU* 1:294–305; Grant Diary, July 18, 26, 1900.

32. Ivins Journal, August 1, 1900; *Improvement Era*, September 1900, p. 879; Grant Diary, August 9, 1900; Wilkinson, *BYU* 1:324.

33. Ibid. 1:326; Grant Diary, July 19, 1900.

34. Wilkinson, *BYU* 1:396–97.

35. Richards Journal, February 4, 1909; Garr, "History of BYC," p. 58.

36. Wilkinson, *BYU* 1:436–37; Richards Journal, April 27, 1911.

37. JH, January 17, 18, 1908, October 16, 1909; Wilkinson, *BYU* 1:408.

38. Lund Journal, September 22, 1914; Richards Journal, January 26, 1915; JH, July 11, 1919; Wilkinson, *BYU* 1:452–53.

39. Hartshorn, "Mormon Education," pp. 31, 35. The information on the source of Merrill's ideas was supplied by his daughter.

40. Lund Journal, March 26, 1916, April 17, 1918; Eckersley Journal, January 27, 1923; JH, September 8, 1924, December 25, 1927; Hartshorn, "Mormon Education," p. 35.

41. Hartshorn, "Mormon Education," p. 36; Grant Diary, February 27–28, June 12, 1928; Leonard J. Arrington, "The Founding of the L.D.S. Institutes of Religion," *Dialogue* 2 (Summer 1967): 140–43.

42. Grant Diary, January 13, 1931, February 16, 1929.

43. Grant Diary, August 25, 1924.

44. JH, May 24, 1927, April 24, 1926; Grant Diary, November 13, 1928, May 7, 31, 1924; Garr, "History of BYC," p. 75.

45. Grant Diary, February 14, March 29, 1929, February 7, December 3, 1930, February 16, 1931; JH, February 20, 1929.

46. JH, December 20, 1930; Grant Diary, January 13, 27, March 20, 1931; Allen and Leonard, *Story of the Latter-day Saints*, p. 504.

47. Wilkinson, *BYU* 2:47–153; JH, August 6, 1924; Grant Diary, September 17, 1924, May 27, 1927.

48. JH, August 19, 1928; Grant Diary, November 18, 1930.

49. Wilkinson, *BYU* 1:409–11.

50. Ibid.: 419.

51. Lund Journal, February 3, 1911; J. H. Smith Journal, February 3, 1911; Grant Diary, February 10–11, 1911; Richards Journal, February 10–11, 1911.

52. Lund Journal, February 20, 1911.

53. Lund Journal, March 3, 1911; Joseph F. Smith to Andrew K. Smith, February 9, 25, 1911, Joseph F. Smith Letterbooks; JH, March 12, 14, 15, 16, 1911.

54. Joseph F. Smith to George H. Brimhall, June 10, 1911, Joseph F. Smith Letterbooks; Lund Journal, March 31, 1911; *Improvement Era*, April 1911, pp. 548–51; JH, April 1911.

55. Ephraim Edward Ericksen, *The Psychological and Ethical Aspects of Mormon Group Life* (reprint ed., Salt Lake City: University of Utah Press, 1975), p. 65; Lund Journal, April 23, 1912. See also Richard Sherlock, "Campus in Crisis: Brigham Young University, 1911," *Sunstone* 4 (January-February 1979): 10–16.

56. Wilkinson, *BYU* 1:423–25, 428–29.

57. Wilkinson, *BYU* 1:512–14.

58. Jeppson, "The Secularization of the University of Utah to 1920," pp. 159–65; "Conditions at the University of Utah," *School and Society* 1 (March 27, 1915): 456; Lund Journal, February 20, 24, 26, March 16–18, 1915.

59. See *Outlook* 109:800; *Science* 41:637; *School and Society* 1:496, 630; *New Republic*, October 1915, pp. 274–75; *The Nation*, June 1915; *Sunset*,

May 1915, pp. 866–67, May 1916, p. 32; *Educational Review* 23 : 343, 49 : 537; *Current Opinion* 58 : 419, 59 : 111; *Literary Digest* 51 : 66.

60. "Conditions at the University of Utah," p. 456; JH, March 19, 1915; "The Eruption in Utah," *Sunset* 34 (May 5, 1915): 864–65; Jeppson, "Secularization of the University of Utah," pp. 165–68, 172.

61. Frank E. Holman, "The Policy of Repression, Suspicion, and Opportunism at the University of Utah," *School and Society* 1 (April 10, 1915): 515–21.

62. Joseph T. Kingsbury, "Discussion and Correspondence: Dean Holman's Criticism of the Administration of the University of Utah," *School and Society* 1 (May 22, 1915): 745–47.

63. Lund Journal, March 19, 1915.

64. Grant Diary, April 5, 1915.

65. Lund Journal, April 17, May 5, 1915; "Preliminary Summary of Findings of the Committee of Inquiry of the American Association of University Professors on Conditions at the University of Utah," *School and Society* 1 (June 12, 1915): 861–64.

66. Lund Journal, January 20, 24, February 7, 1916.

67. Lund Journal, January 18, 20, 1916.

68. "Discussion and Correspondence: Methods of the Board of Regents of the University of Utah," *School and Society* 3 (February 26, 1916): 314–16; Widtsoe, *In a Sunlit Land*, pp. 142–45. For a general history of the controversy see Chamberlin, *The University of Utah*, pp. 323–68.

69. Lund Journal, March 13, 1916; Widtsoe, *In a Sunlit Land*, p. 142.

70. On this point, compare Jeppson's discussion in "Secularization of the University of Utah," pp. 174–200, and Chamberlin's in *University of Utah*, pp. 335–37.

Chapter 10: Cooperation and Individualism in Mormon Society

1. A number of important sources exist on cultural developments. Perhaps the best introduction is in Richard D. Poll, Thomas G. Alexander, Eugene E. Campbell, and David E. Miller, eds., *Utah's History* (Provo, Utah: Brigham Young University Press, 1978), chapters 15, 16, 18, 31, 32, and 33. See also James L. Haseltine, *100 Years of Utah Painting* (Salt Lake City: Salt Lake Art Center, 1965); Franz K. Winkler, "Building in Salt Lake City," *Architectural Record* 22 (July 1907): 15–37; Rell G. Francis, *Cyrus E. Dallin: Let Justice Be Done* (Springville, Utah: Springville Art Museum, 1976); Eugene England, "The Dawning of a Brighter Day: Mormon Literature After 150 Years," in Alexander and Embry, eds., *After 150 Years* (see chapter 4, note 33, p. 331); Edward A. Geary, "The Poetics of Provincialism: Mormon Regional Fiction," *Dialogue* 11 (Summer 1978): 15–24.

2. For a discussion of these matters see Arrington, *Great Basin Kingdom*

57; First Presidency to Whom It May Concern, October 4, 1902, Joseph F. Smith Letterbooks; Lund Journal, October 10, June 16, 1902, March 2, 9, 1905; JH, March 2, 1905.

80. Grant Diary, November 14, 1907; Richards Journal, May 23, 1910. For a general treatment of the establishment of the Mormon settlements in Canada see Lawrence B. Lee, "The Mormons Come to Canada, 1887–1902," *Pacific Northwest Quarterly* 59 (January 1968): 11–22; Melvin G. Tagg, *A History of the Mormon Church in Canada* (Lethbridge, Canada: Lethbridge Herald, 1968) tends to be a listing of names of places and persons rather than an interpretive history.

81. On the establishment of the Mexican colonies see Blaine Carmon Hardy, "The Mormon Colonies in Northern Mexico, a History, 1885–1912" (Ph.D. dissertation, Wayne State University, 1963); for their later history see Thomas Cottam Romney, *The Mormon Colonies in Mexico* (Salt Lake City: Deseret Book, 1938).

82. Robert E. Quirk, *The Mexican Revolution and the Catholic Church, 1910–1929* (Bloomington: Indiana University Press, 1973), pp. 15–16; J. H. Smith Journal, June 26, 1899, June 17, October 22, 1901; First Presidency to Lorenzo E. Huish, October 10, 1899, FP, letters sent; JH, April 8, 1901.

83. J. H. Smith Journal, October 22, 1901; JH, January 11, 1905; Richards Journal, March 6, 1908; Ivins Journal, January 27, 1908.

84. JH, July 8, 9, 13, 1908, November 5, 1909.

85. Ibid., November 23, 28, December 2, 1910; Lund Journal, December 3, 5, 1910; and J. H. Smith Journal, December 5, 1910. For a discussion of the activities of Madero see Ramon Eduardo Ruiz, *The Great Rebellion, Mexico, 1905–1924* (New York: W. W. Norton, 1980), pp. 241–42; Ronald Atkin, *Revolution! Mexico, 1910–20* (New York: John Day, 1970), pp. 56, 63.

86. JH, December 17, 26, 1910, January 6, 1911; Ivins Journal, December 19, 1910, February 11, April 10, 1911.

87. Atkin, *Revolution*, p. 76; JH, February 6, 13, May 4, 6, July 8, 1912; Lund Journal; April 29, July 20, 22, 28, August 3, 1912.

88. Atkin, *Revolution*, p. 122.

89. JH, May 6, July 8, 1912; Lund Journal, July 28, August 3, 1912; Ivins Journal, July 20, 28, August 5, 14, 1912.

90. Lund Journal, August 12, October 4, 8, 1912; Smoot Diary, October 8, 1912.

91. JH, October 10, 1912.

92. Lund Journal, September 1, 8, 1912; Smoot Diary, March 12, 1913.

93. Lund Journal, April 23, 28, 1914; Robert E. Quirk, *An Affair of Honor: Woodrow Wilson and the Occupation of Veracruz* ([Lexington]: University of Kentucky Press, 1962); Ruiz, *The Great Rebellion*, p. 192.

94. Lund Journal, May 1, 1914.

95. JH, February 9, September 24, November 4, December 31, 1915; Lund Journal, March 10, 12, 14, 1916.

96. Joseph F. Smith to Reed Smoot, April 24, 1915, Joseph F. Smith Letterbooks; JH, May 1, 1916, January 27, February 19, March 22, June 26, September 8, 1917; Lund Journal, January 27, 1917.

97. Grant Diary, November 5, 1920, November 16, 1922; JH, February 15, June 11, 21, October 8, 1921, May 18, 1924.

98. Ibid., September 9, 1926; Quirk, *Mexican Revolution and Catholic Church*, pp. 10, 17, 96–97, 151–53, 167.

99. JH, February 22, 27, March 4, July 26, 28, August 21, 1926.

Chapter 11: The Church and Its Missions

1. On the British Mission see James B. Allen and Thomas G. Alexander, eds., *Manchester Mormons: The Journal of William Clayton, 1840 to 1842* (Salt Lake City: Peregrine Smith, 1974); and Stanley B. Kimball, *Heber C. Kimball: Mormon Patriarch and Pioneer* (Urbana: University of Illinois Press, 1981). On the population of Utah towns see May, "A Demographic Portrait of the Mormons, 1830–1980" (chapter 10, note 57, pp. 351–352), pp. 37–69.

2. First Council of the Seventy Minutes, February 22, 1899, January 3, 10, 1900; First Presidency to First Council of the Seventy, December 7, 1899, FP, letters sent; Joseph F. Smith to idem., December 27, 1899, cited in Clark, *Messages* (chapter 2, note 12, p. 321) 3:323; JH, January 6, 1900.

3. First Council of the Seventy Minutes, April 11, 25, 1900; Joseph F. Smith to bishops, March 2, 1912, in Clark, *Messages* 4:267–68.

4. First Council of the Seventy Minutes, March 21, 1900, March 27, April 18, 1901, August 20, 1902; First Presidency to stake presidents, August 5, 1904, in Clark, *Messages* 4:86–88.

5. Grant Diary, November 12, 1930.

6. *The Elder's Reference* (n.p.: Eastern States Mission, 1913); John H. Smith to Winslow Farr Smith, August 15, 1902, June 10, 1902, J. H. Smith Letterbooks; Francis M. Lyman, "Notes to be Referred to Daily by Missionaries," reprinted in Ben E. Rich, *Scrap Book of Mormon Literature* (Chicago: private printing, n.d.), p. 8.

7. JH, February 3, 1925; Grant Diary, September 29, 1927.

8. First Presidency, circular letters, August 22, 1900; Clark, *Messages* 3:327, March 15, 1913, ibid. 4:283, December 9, 1922, ibid. 5:221, September 20, 1926, ibid: 238; Grant Diary, November 27, 1920, March 19, 1927, November 12, 1930.

9. Joseph F. Smith to Hyrum M. Smith, November 7, 1912, Joseph F. Smith Letterbooks; Lund Journal, January 29, February 5, 1914; Richards Journal, January 28, 1914.

10. Joseph F. Smith to Samuel E. Woolley, December 7, 1899, Joseph F. Smith Letterbooks.

11. J. H. Smith Journal, October 4, 1900, August 22, 1901; Merrill Journal, October 2, 1901; Lund Journal, September 25, 1901.

12. George A. Smith Journal, October 10, 1904; Joseph F. Smith to Willard R. Smith, December 17, 1905, Joseph F. Smith Letterbooks.

13. Lund Journal, February 18, 1900, August 16, 1904; J. H. Smith Journal, December 11, 1902; Joseph F. Smith to Franklin R. Smith, December 27, 1908, June 20, 1909, Joseph F. Smith Letterbooks.

14. Brigham Young Journal, July 5, 1900; Joseph F. Smith to Joseph R. Smith, April 3, 1900, Joseph F. Smith Letterbooks.

15. Grant Diary, April 4, 1900; Richards Journal, Book 8, p. 190; Joseph F. Smith to Franklin R. Smith, February 19, 1910, Joseph F. Smith Letterbooks.

16. Richards Journal, November 20, 1906; JH, January 1, 1900, December 22, 1902, December 31, 1902; First Presidency to Francis M. Lyman, December 22, 1902, in Clark, *Messages* 4:50.

17. Richards Journal, January 29, March 30, 1909.

18. Deseret News, *1974 Church Almanac* (Salt Lake City: *Deseret News*, 1974), pp. 198–99.

19. Ibid., p. 206; JH, August 10, 1928, September 30, 1930.

20. Grant Diary, April 4, 1900.

21. Ibid., April 9, 1900.

22. Eugene L. Roberts, "The Missionary Problem," *Improvement Era*, June 1910, pp. 705–9.

23. Clark, *Messages* 5:109.

24. Grant Diary, January 21, 1924; JH, October 17, 1930; and Sessions, *Mormon Democrat* (chapter 1, note 16, p. 318), pp. 300–303.

25. Lund Journal, May 30, 1907; Richards Journal, May 31, 1907; J. H. Smith Journal, May 31, 1907; B. H. Roberts, *New Witness for God*, 2nd ed., 3 vols. (Salt Lake City: Deseret News Press, 1909–11) 2:116–19.

26. Ibid., vols. 2 and 3 passim.

27. Talmage Journal, September 20, 30, 1909; Richards Journal, September 27, 1909; Joseph F. Smith to German Ellsworth, June 29, 1910, Joseph F. Smith Letterbooks.

28. Pearl of Great Price, Joseph Smith Story; *Joseph Smith Tells His Own Story* (numerous editions).

29. Charles W. Penrose, "What 'Mormons' Believe: Epitome of the Doctrines of the Church of Jesus Christ of Latter-day Saints," in Rich, *Scrap Book*, pp. 29–38.

30. Charles W. Penrose, "Rays of Living Light," nos. 1–12 in ibid., pp. 202–43, 247–62.

31. Ben E. Rich, "A Friendly Discussion upon Religious Subjects," ibid, pp. 263–82.

32. R. M. Bryce Thomas, "My Reasons for Leaving the Church of England and Joining the Church of Jesus Christ of Latter-day Saints," ibid., pp. 468–79.

33. B. H. Roberts, "The Character of the Mormon People," ibid., pp. 173–90.

34. First Presidency to Samuel O. Bennion, ca. June 26, 1909, Joseph F. Smith Letterbooks.

35. Penrose, "Aim, Scope, and Message of the Mormon Church" (see chapter 4, note 8, p. 329); Deseret News, *1974 Church Almanac*, p. 206.

36. "The Life of a Mormon Girl," *Independent* 58 (February 23, 1905): 423–24.

37. JH, February 8, January 6, 1898, January 3, 1900.

38. Ibid., July 4, 1898, August 8, September 2, September 20, 1899, May 9, July 27, 1905, February 22, July 26, 1906.

39. Ibid., June 8, October 31, 1899, October 3, 1900.

40. JH, May 1928, November 7, 1930.

41. Ibid., January 7, September 26, 1898.

42. Ibid., October 24, 1899.

43. Ibid., June 23, 28, 1905, May 17, 1916, June 22, 1918; First Presidency to Francis M. Lyman, May 20, 1903, in Clark, *Messages* 4:54.

44. Grant Diary, April 12, 14, May 29, 1922; Heber J. Grant to George W. McCune, May 29, 1922, and to J. Reuben Clark, June 8, 1922, FP, letters sent.

45. Grant Diary, April 2, 1927.

46. JH, February 14, 1922, October 11, 27, 30, 1924, October 1, 4, November 24, 1928, August 19, 1929; Smoot Diary, August 30, 31, 1929.

47. Grant Diary, November 17, 19, 1928; Sessions, *Mormon Democrat*, pp. 288–89.

48. JH, January 23, October 29, 1898, October 3, 1899, September 21, 1900, May 17, 1902, September 29, 1906.

49. JH, November 2, 1899, February 13, 1900.

50. Ibid., July 31, 1900, January 24, 1910; First Council of the Seventy Minutes, February 4, 1903; Joseph F. Smith to Samuel E. Woolley, July 10, 1903, Joseph F. Smith Letterbooks.

51. JH, June 30, 1900, May 9, 1901.

52. Rulon S. Wells to First Council of the Seventy, July 13, 1898, in First Council of the Seventy Minutes, August 3, 1898.

53. JH, March 17, 1900; J. H. Smith Journal, April 16, 1903; Lund Journal, April 17, May 21, 1903; John Henry Smith to Winslow Farr Smith, June 3, 1903, J. H. Smith Letterbooks; First Presidency to Francis M. Lyman, May 20, 1903, in Clark, *Messages* 4:54.

54. Joseph F. Smith to Samuel E. Woolley, July 10, 1903, and to George C. Smith, August 24, 1905, Joseph F. Smith Letterbooks; JH, April 7, 1905.

55. JH, October 4, 1907, April 28, November 3, 1909, July 21, 1910; Smoot Diary, May 3, 1909.

56. Winifred Graham, *The Mormons: A Popular History from Earliest Times to the Present Day* (London: Hurst and Blackett, Ltd., 1913), pp. 199, 236.

57. Lund Journal, August 27, 1903; JH, January 19, 1905; First Presidency to Peter Mattson, May 11, 1905, in Clark, *Messages* 4:106; Andrew Jenson, *History of the Scandinavian Mission* (Salt Lake City: Deseret News Press, 1927), p. 407.

58. JH, June 9, November 15, 1900, January 14, 1905.

59. JH, March 3, 1900; Jenson, *Scandinavian Mission*, p. 377.

60. Hans P. Freece, *The Letters of an Apostate Mormon to His Son* (New York: Privately printed, 1908), pp. 13–17.

61. Lund Journal, September 19, 1911; Andrew Jenson, *Autobiography of Andrew Jenson* (Salt Lake City: Deseret News Press, 1938), pp. 480–81.

62. JH, September 25, 1911; Graham, *The Mormons*, p. 198; Jenson, *Scandinavian Mission*, pp. 458–59.

63. Graham, *The Mormons*, pp. 194–235; JH, July 15, 1908, November 18, 1907.

64. JH, February 2, 1899; see also January 14, 1898, and September 1, 1898.

65. Malcolm Thorp, "'The Mormon Peril': The Crusade Against the Saints in Britain, 1910–14," *Journal of Mormon History* 2 (1975): 69, 74–77, 83, 88; Joseph F. Smith to Charles W. Penrose, November 1, 1908, Joseph F. Smith Letterbooks; Richard L. Evans, *A Century of "Mormonism" in Great Britain* (Salt Lake City: Deseret News Press, 1937), pp. 209–11.

66. First Presidency to Editor, *London Times*, February 6, 1911, in Clark, *Messages* 4:221; JH, April 20, 29, 1911; Lund Journal, April 29, 1911.

67. JH, April 17, 1911, June 13, 1912.

68. Thorp, "Mormon Peril," pp. 82–83.

69. Ibid., pp. 85, 88; Joseph F. Smith to John P. Meakin, March 27, 1911, Joseph F. Smith Letterbooks.

70. JH, March 31, 1898, March 19, 1900, November 7, 1900, October 5, November 25, 1905, December 30, 1909, June 16, 1910, April 13, 1911, February 1, 1912.

71. JH, February 12, 1901; Grant Diary, February 14, June 18, 1901.

72. Ibid., August 12 to September 5, 1901, passim. William Rockwell Nelson's name is entered as William Rockwell Clarke in the diary.

73. Ibid., October 8, 9, 1901; JH, April 24, 1902.

74. Joseph F. Smith to Heber J. Grant, August 17, 1903, Joseph F. Smith Letterbooks; Nibley, *The Presidents of the Church*, 5th printing (Salt Lake City: Deseret Book, 1947), p. 306; JH, January 4, 1906.

75. *Improvement Era*, November 1914, pp. 74–75; Clark, *Messages* 5:78; JH, August 17, 1917; Deseret News, *1974 Church Almanac*, p. 198.

76. Richards Journal, June 15, November 19, December 5, 1916, March 1, 1918, September 1918, passim.

77. Ibid., January 10, 1918.

78. Richards Journal, May 7, 31, June 5, 6, 12, 1919; Smoot Diary, May 8, 1919.

79. JH, August 31, 1919; Smoot Diary, September 20, 25, 1919, June 15, 1920.

80. JH, May 3, 13, 1920; Smoot Diary, March 23, April 2, May 28, 1920.

81. JH, October 18, 1920; Smoot Diary, March 23, April 2, 1921; Heber J. Grant to Reed Smoot, August 24, September 14, 1921, in Clark, *Messages* 5:202, 204.

82. JH, January 28, February 23, March 8, June 18, 1922, June 26, 1924; Widstoe, *In a Sunlit Land* (chapter 7, note 20, p. 339), p. 186.

83. Grant Diary, November 4, 1922; Widtsoe, *In a Sunlit Land*, pp. 187–89.

84. Ibid., p. 189; Grant Diary, September 18, October 30, 1924; JH, November 23, 1924, July 10, 1926, May 27, 1927, September 21, 1930; First Presidency to Orson F. Whitney, April 28, 1926, FP, letters sent.

85. JH, March 17, May 31, 1927, September 20, 1928, May 10, 26, 1929; Smoot Diary, August 3, 1928.

86. Widtsoe, *In a Sunlit Land*, p. 189.

87. Melvin R. Ballard, ed., *Melvin J. Ballard: Crusader for Righteousness* (Salt Lake City: Bookcraft, 1966), pp. 75–84; *Improvement Era*, March 1926, p. 519.

88. JH, March 25, 1922, June 18, July 1, 1924.

89. First Presidency to Reed Smoot, February 28, 1923, in Clark, *Messages* 5:225; JH, October 14, 1924.

90. JH, June 12, 1924; Grant Diary, November 9, December 2, 1927; R. Lanier Britsch, "The Closing of the Early Japan Mission," *BYU Studies* 15 (Winter 1975): 171–90; J. Christopher Conkling, "Members Without a Church: Japanese Mormons in Japan, 1924–48," ibid.: 192–99.

91. Richards Journal, October 14, December 4, 1920; Grant Diary, November 9, 1920; Lund Journal, October 15, 1920; JH, February 19, December 25, 1921.

Chapter 12: Reshaping the Latter-day Saint Image

1. For a discussion of these matters see Larson, *The "Americanization" of Utah* (see chapter 1, note 5, p. 317), and Lyman, "The Mormon Quest for Utah Statehood" (see chapter 1, note 3, p. 317).

2. On Mormon pamphleteering in the nineteenth century see David J. Whittaker, "Early Mormon Pamphleteering" (Ph.D. dissertation, Brigham Young University, 1982).

3. This generalization is based on Shipps, "From Satyr to Saint" (see chapter 5, note 5, p. 331), adapted somewhat to impressionistic evidence cited below.

4. On developments during the 1890s see Lyman, "The Mormon Quest for Utah Statehood," especially chapters 3–7, and Larson, *The "Americanization" of Utah*, passim. On the parliament of religions see Davis Bitton, "B. H. Roberts at the World Parliament of Religions (1893)," *Sunstone* 7 (January-February 1982): 46–51.

5. Lund Journal, July 10, 1900.

6. First Council of the Seventy Minutes, August 7, 21, 1901, March 19, 26, April 2, June 11, 1902; Clark, *Messages* (chapter 2, note 12, p. 321) 4: 38–39; First Presidency to Nephi L. Morris, July 15, 1902, Morris Papers.

7. Lund Journal, July 10, 1900, July 22, 1903; First Council of the Seventy Minutes, June 10, 1903; Joseph F. Smith to Samuel W. Woolley, August 27, 1903, Joseph F. Smith Letterbooks; George A. Smith Journal, March 26, 1904; JH, August 25, 1906; *Relief Society Magazine*, November 1922, p. 559.

8. Jenson, *Church Chronology*, May 21, 1906.

9. JH, May 22, 1904, March 28, 1905, April 18, October 26, 27, 1906.

10. Bruce Kinney, "The Present Situation Among the Mormons," *Missionary Review of the World* 29 (August 1906): 616.

11. JH, February 20, 1900, September 8, 1905; Kinney, "Present Situation Among the Mormons," pp. 616–19.

12. JH, January 10, 1898, October 15, 1900, August 21, 23, 1901, April 18, May 21, 1902; James Biddle Halsey, "Mormonism As It Is Today," *The Era: A Monthly Magazine of Literature* 11 (June 1903): 518; J. M. Scanland, "The Mormon Power in America," *Gunton's Magazine* 18 (February 1900): 132; M. Katharine Bennett, "Letters to the Outlook: Mormonism," *Outlook* 82 (February 3, 1906): 278–79; Joseph F. McConkie, *True and Faithful: The Life Story of Joseph Fielding Smith* (Salt Lake City: Bookcraft, 1971), p. 30; *Improvement Era*, July 1903, pp. 618–19, July 1904, pp. 730–31; John D. Nutting, "Mormonism Today and Its Remedy," *Missionary Review of the World* 36 (April and May 1913): 355, 360. See also J. A. Livingston Smith, "Results of Missions Among the Mormons," ibid. 32 (November 1909): 851–52; Samuel E. Wishard, "Present-day Mormonism in Theory and Practice," ibid. 33 (November 1910): 807–15; JH, August 9, 1911, January 9, 10, February 3, 1912, January 9, 11, 1913, May 25, 1919. On the Reverend Mr. John Nutting and the Utah Gospel Mission see Stanley B. Kimball, "The Utah Gospel Mission, 1900–1950" *Utah Historical Quarterly* 44 (Spring 1976): 149–55.

13. I. Woodbridge Riley, *The Founder of Mormonism: A Psychological Study of Joseph Smith, Jr.* (New York: Dodd, Mead, 1902); William Alexander Linn, *The Story of the Mormons, from the Date of Their Origin to the Year 1901* (New York: Macmillan, 1902); Henry William Elson, *History of the United States of America* (New York: Macmillan, 1904); Joseph F. Smith to W. M. Threadgold, August 28, 1902, Joseph F. Smith Letterbooks; Lund Diary, October 6, 1903; JH, December 1906; John Quincy Adams, *The Birth of Mormonism* (Boston: Gorham Press, 1916), p. 84 and passim.

14. J. H. Smith Journal, September 13–14, 1911; Lund Journal, September 14, 1911; JH, September 21, October 27, 1911; Joseph F. Smith to Ben E. Rich, November 1, 1911, Joseph F. Smith Letterbooks; Talmage Journal, August 8, 1912. For a thorough treatment of the incident see Gary James Bergera, "'I'm Here for the Cash': Max Florence and the Great Mormon Temple," *Utah Historical Quarterly* 47 (Winter 1979): 54–63.

15. Smoot Diary, March 5, 1912; *Improvement Era*, February 1913, pp. 309–48; Franklin S. Spalding, *Joseph Smith, Jr., As a Translator: An Inquiry Conducted by Rt. Rev. F. S. Spalding, D. D., Bishop of Utah* (Salt Lake City: Arrow Press, 1912). Edward Meyer is probably Eduard Meyer (1855–1930). For pictures of the cuts see Facsimiles 1, 2, and 3 in Pearl of Great Price, "Book of Abraham."

16. Joseph F. Smith to Isaac Russell, February 2, 1913, Joseph F. Smith Letterbooks.

17. Lund Journal, April 12, 1913; Joseph F. Smith to Reed Smoot, January 31, 1913, to Isaac Russell, February 2, 1913, Joseph F. Smith Letterbooks; Grant Diary, January 15, 1913; *Current Literature* 54 (April 1913): 310–11.

18. *Improvement Era*, February 1913, pp. 309–48, March 1913, pp. 435–66, May 1913, pp. 691–704; Lund Journal, October 28, 1913. For recent scholarly treatment of the Book of Abraham see Richard P. Howard, "A Tentative Approach to the Book of Abraham," *Dialogue* 3 (Summer 1968): 92; Hugh Nibley, *The Message of the Joseph Smith Papyri: An Egyptian Endowment* (Salt Lake City: Deseret Book, 1975), pp. xiii, 1–3; Klaus Baer, "The Breathing Permit of Hor: A Translation of the Apparent Source of the Book of Abraham," *Dialogue* 3 (Autumn 1968): 109–34; Edward H. Ashment, "The Facsimiles of the Book of Abraham: A Reappraisal," *Sunstone* 4 (December 1979): 33–48; and Hugh Nibley, "The Facsimiles of the Book of Abraham: A Response," ibid: 49–51.

19. JH, December 10, 1910. For a detailed discussion of the episode see Michael S. Eldredge, "Silver Service for the Battleship Utah: A Naval Tradition under Governor Spry," *Utah Historical Quarterly* 46 (Summer 1978): 302–18.

20. Smoot Diary, April 5, May 4, 16, 17, June 14, 15, November 6, 1911.

21. JH, June 26, 1898, December 29, 1900, February 27, 1905; C. C. Goodwin, "The Truth about the Mormons," *Munsey's Magazine* 23 (June 1900): 324–25. See also *Improvement Era*, April 1909, pp. 503–4; JH, August 20, 1907, February 17, April 20, 27, 1911; Roberts, *Comprehensive History* (chapter 1, note 21, p. 319) 6:414–15.

22. LeRoy Armstrong, "Be Fair to Utah," *The Outlook* 89 (May 30, 1908): 269–70; Frederick Vining Fisher, "A Methodist Minister's View of Mormonism," ibid. 98 (July 29, 1911): 711–12; Dillon Wallace, "In the Land of Zion" (see chapter 10, note 54, p. 351); JH, October 17, 1908, November 23, 1911.

23. Lund Journal, September 16, June 20, 1902; Joseph F. Smith to Phebe Cousins, May 11, 1903, FP, letters sent.

24. First Council of the Seventy Minutes, September 7, 1898; *Improvement Era*, June 1900, p. 600; J. H. Smith Journal, May 27, 1899, April 18, November 20–24, 1900; Lund Journal, November 11, 1903; JH, September 4, 1908; Joseph F. Smith to C. Coulson Smith, August 12, 1909, Joseph F. Smith Letterbooks; J. H. Smith Journal, July 6, November 19–23, 1907, October 1–2, 1908; Smoot Diary, September 20, 1912; Lund Journal, November 13, 1913.

25. Halsey, "Mormonism as it is Today," 511; G. A. Irving, "Some Aspects of Mormonism," *The Outlook* 82 (January 1906): 32–35; *Improvement Era*, October 1903, p. 957.

26. JH, April 6, 1907; Lund Journal, March 25, 1907; Joseph F. Smith to William Glasmann, March 8, 1917, Joseph F. Smith Letterbooks.

27. Talmage Journal, January 4, April 5, 1907; Richards Journal, March 20–22, 1907; JH, April 5, 1907; Clark, *Messages* 4:142–55, reproduces the message.

28. Roberts, *Comprehensive History* 6:438, 440–41; JH, June 7–9, 1907; *Improvement Era*, July 1907, p. 724; B. H. Roberts, *Defense of the Faith and the Saints*, 2 vols. (Salt Lake City: Deseret News, 1907–12), 2:237–63.

29. Joseph F. Smith to Ben E. Rich, September 21, 1910, Joseph F. Smith Letterbooks; Lund Journal, October 18, 19, 20, 1910.

30. Smoot Diary, March 16, April 7, 8, 1911.

31. Clark, *Messages* 4:224–229; *Improvement Era*, June 1911, pp. 719–24.

32. Roberts, *Comprehensive History* 1:v–vi.

33. JH, June 30, 1910, July 12, 1912; Talmage Journal, February 4, 1913; Lund Journal, June 30, August 12, October 20–21, 1913; Smoot Diary, October 8, 1911.

34. Lund Journal, September 18, 1911; Talmage Journal, September 21, 22, 1911, August 8, 1912. Florence's was not the first example of visual attacks on the church. For a discussion of some of them in the form of cartoons see Davis Bitton and Gary L. Bunker, "Mischievous Puck and the Mormons, 1904–07," *BYU Studies* 18 (Summer 1978): 504–19; idem., "Double Jeopardy: Visual Images of Mormon Women to 1914," *Utah Historical Quarterly* 46 (Spring 1978): 184–202; and idem., *The Mormon Graphic Image, 1834–1914: Cartoons, Caricatures, and Illustrations* (Salt Lake City: University of Utah Press, 1983).

35. Mrs. George W. Coleman, "Recent Developments in Mormonism," *Missionary Review of the World* 41 (July 1918): 539; Talmage Journal, June 20, 1917; Lund Journal, August 4, 1917.

36. *Improvement Era*, March 1916, p. 464; Joseph F. Smith to J. C. Homans, February 18, 1916, Joseph F. Smith Letterbook; Clark, *Messages* 5:2–3; Lund Journal, April 15, 1915; Grant Diary, June 16, 17, 1921, May 19, 1924, May 1, 1927, October 11, 1930; JH, August 6, 1919, June 17, 1922, July 29, 1926; Smoot Diary, October 11, 1930.

37. JH, January 14, 1922, January 21, 1927; Grant Diary, November 21, 1924; Richards Journal, May 20, 1928.

38. Talmage Journal, April 15, 1915, December 29, 1916; Lund Journal, February 16, March 24, 1917; Grant Diary, October 16, 1917.

39. Talmage Journal, January 15, December 30, 1917.

40. "Mormonism as a Pioneer of the New Theology," *Current Opinion* 62 (March 1917): 198–99; Talmage Journal, January 3, 1918; Lund Journal, December 26, 1918; Clark, *Messages* 5:122; James E. Talmage, *The Vitality of Mormonism* (Boston: The Gorham Press, 1919).

41. Coleman, "Recent Developments," p. 539.

42. Smoot Diary, November 11, 1919; JH, November 12, 18–19, December 6, 1919.

43. Smoot Diary, April 14, 1919; JH, September 10, 1921.

44. Smoot Diary, July 23, 1915, August 3, 1920; JH, April 5, 1921.

45. Grant Diary, November 1, 1917; JH, January 9, 1919, April 6, 1920.

46. *Relief Society Magazine*, December 1915, p. 536; Donald C. Swain, "The Passage of the National Park Service Act of 1916," *Wisconsin Magazine of History* 50 (1966): 6; Grant Diary, June 18, 1919, September 11, 15, 21, 1920; and U.S. Senate, *Senate Report* 22, 66th Cong., 1st Sess.; Smoot Diary, June 18, 1919, September 11, 15, 1920; Thomas G. Alexander, "Reed Smoot and Conservation in the 1920s: Teapot Dome Revisited," *Utah Historical Quarterly* 45 (Fall 1977): 352–68.

47. Talmage Journal, March 24, 1921; Grant Diary, May 3, 1921.

48. Franklin S. Harris and Newbern I. Butt, *The Fruits of Mormonism* (New York: Macmillan, 1925), pp. iii, 6–15, 18–29, 37–41, 43–68.

49. Grant Diary, March 2–5, 1929.

50. JH, January 17, 1899, January 8, 1900, June 30, July 1, October 2, 5, 1905; Lund Journal, September 16, 1902, August 23, 1903, February 9, 1904; George A. Smith Journal, February 9, 17, 1904, and passim; Joseph F. Smith to Edward A. Smith, February 12, 1904, Joseph F. Smith Letterbooks.

51. JH, August 31, 1928, July 15, 1929; Grant Diary, February 18, 1929.

Chapter 13: The Adoption of a New Interpretation of the Word of Wisdom

1. On the temperance and prohibition movements see Joseph R. Gusfield, *Symbolic Crusade: Status Politics and the American Temperance Movement* (Urbana: University of Illinois Press, 1963); Timberlake, *Prohibition and the Progressive Movement* (chapter 8, note 3, p. 339); Norman H. Clark, *Deliver Us from Evil: An Interpretation of American Prohibition* (New York: Norton, 1976).

2. The most complete treatment of the Word of Wisdom is Paul H. Peterson, "An Historical Analysis of the Word of Wisdom" (M.S. thesis, Brigham Young University, 1972). On the origins see ibid., pp. 6–16, 19–20. See also W. J. Rorabaugh, *The Alcoholic Republic: An American Tradition* (New York: Oxford University Press, 1979). Some question exists as to the development of the text of the Word of Wisdom, now Section 89 of the Doctrine and Covenants. Verses 1 through 4 were italicized and unnumbered and presented as an introduction to what was Section 80 of the first edition (1835).

3. Peterson, "Word of Wisdom," passim.

4. Peterson, "Word of Wisdom," pp. 55–79; Robert J. McCue, "Did the Word of Wisdom Become a Commandment in 1851?" *Dialogue* 14 (Autumn 1981): 66–77; Leonard J. Arrington, "An Economic Interpretation of the Word of Wisdom," *BYU Studies* 1 (Winter 1959): 47. Some of those making statements remembering Brigham Young's declaration that the Word of Wisdom was commandment included John Taylor in 1853 and Joseph F. Smith in 1909. It seems quite clear, however, that the principle was not generally regarded in the same way as today—that is, as essential for holding responsible positions in the church or for participating in temple ordinances.

5. Heber J. Grant Diary, May 5, June 30, 1898, LDS Church Archives; JH, May 5, 1898. See George D. Watt, et al., eds., *Journal of Discourses*, 26 vols. (Liverpool, 1855–85), 12:27ff.

6. Lund Journal, January 9, August 31, September 2, 1900, July 10, 1901; Emmeline B. Wells Journal, September 8, 1900, February 4, 1902, February 19, 1903, Special Collections, Brigham Young University Library; George Albert Smith Journal, March 10, 1905, Smith Family Papers, Western Americana Collection, University of Utah Library.

7. Young Journal, January 9, July 9 and 11, 1901; Grant Diary, July 11, 1901; Lorenzo Snow to Ephraim Caffall, March 18, 1901, FP, letters sent.

8. Grant Diary, June 30, 1898, August 17, 1900, July 11, 1901.

9. *Improvement Era*, May, 1902, p. 559, July, 1902, p. 731; Lund Journal, June 26, 1902; First Presidency to C. R. Hakes, August 1, 1902, to John W. Hess, October 31, 1902, to H. S. Allen, November 1, 1902, FP, letters sent.

10. First Presidency to L.B. Felt, December 13, 1905, ibid; J. H. Smith Journal, July 5, 1906; G. A. Smith Journal, August 5, September 2, 1905; George F. Richards Journal, May 27, June 2, June 16, 1906, LDS Archives.

11. Gusfield, *Symbolic Crusade*, pp. 31–34, 36, 56, 71, 83, 87, 100–103.

12. This interpretation is a summary of Dyer's "Adoption of Prohibition" (chapter 2, note 57, p. 323), and Jan Shipps, "Utah Comes of Age Politically: A Study of the State's Politics in the Early Years of the Twentieth Century," (chapter 2, note 57, p. 324). See also Brent G. Thompson, "Utah's Struggle for Prohibition, 1908–1917" (Master's thesis, University of Utah, 1979).

13. Dyer, "Adoption of Prohibition," p. 2; John R. Winder to Reed Smoot, December 9, 1907, in Clark, *Messages* (chapter 2, note 12, p. 321) 4 : 163.

14. Edward H. Anderson, "Events and Comments," *Improvement Era*, January 1908, pp. 234–36; Lund Journal, January 3, 1908; Grant Diary, January 5, 1908.

15. Ibid., and March 18, 21, 25, 1908.

16. Dyer, "Adoption of Prohibition," pp. 14–19.

17. Ibid., pp. 10–11, 43–44; Lund Journal, January 23, 26, 27, 1909; J. H. Smith Journal, January 26, 1909.

18. Joseph F. Smith to C. Elmo Cluff, December 28, 1915, Joseph F. Smith Letterbooks; *Improvement Era*, March 16, 1916, p. 461, April 1917, pp. 555–58, November 1917, pp. 11, 64, March 1919, pp. 371–80; *Relief Society Magazine*, February 1918, pp. 146, 160, April 1919, pp. 238–39, September 1919, pp. 527, 593.

19. George F. Richards Journal, March 26, 1921. Information on the temple recommend book from K. Heybron Adams, formerly of the LDS Archives.

20. LDS Church, *Handbook of Instructions*, No. 14, 1928 (n.p., 1928), p. 11; Idem. *Handbook of Instructions*, No. 15, 1934 (n.p., 1933), p. 10.

21. John S. H. Smith, "Cigarette Prohibition in Utah, 1921–23," *Utah Historical Quarterly* 41 (Autumn 1973): 358–372.

22. *Improvement Era*, March 1923, p. 472, September 1923, p. 1041, November 1923, p. 145, April 1926, p. 713, November 1927, pp. 5–19, December 1927, p. 109.

23. Grant Diary, January 21, 1927; JH, March 26, 27, 29, November 24, 1929; *Relief Society Magazine*, May 1929, p. 245.

24. JH, January 29, April 9, June 8, 1930; *Improvement Era*, August 1930, pp. 659–60.

25. Richards Journal, November 1, 1922; Grant Diary, November 1, 1922, October 23, 29, 30, 1930; Talmage Journal, November 1, 1922; Reed Smoot Diary, November 1, 1922, March 29, 1923, October 30, 1930.

26. Grant Diary, January 5, 10, 14, 1928.

27. Ibid., October 27, November 17, 1930, July 17, August 3, 1931.

28. JH, October 3, December 1, 1929, June 9, November 28, 1930; Journal of Anthony W. Ivins, Utah State Historical Society, Notes for 1931; John Kearnes, "Utah, Sexton of Prohibition," *Utah Historical Quarterly* 47 (Winter 1979): 17–18.

29. *Improvement Era*, March 1917, pp. 432–35.

30. Grant Diary, October 15, November 11, 12, and 16, 1924; First Presidency Letter of May 6, 1971, Edgemont South Stake Letter Files.

31. [John A. Widtsoe], *The Word of Wisdom* (British Mission, 1930); Grant Diary, November 23, 1930.

32. Roy W. Doxey, *The Word of Wisdom Today* (Salt Lake City: Deseret Book Company, 1975), pp. 13–14.

33. Some of the statements and reminiscences are cited in Doxey, *Word of Wisdom Today*, pp. 10–13, and in John A. Widtsoe and Leah D. Widtsoe, *The Word of Wisdom: A Modern Interpretation* (Salt Lake City: Deseret Book Company, 1937), p. 28. Here I am speaking of specific revelations rather than the type of revelation mentioned later in this article. I would differentiate between what might be termed instant revelations and revelations derived from long and prayerful consideration of a particular problem under the inspiration of the Holy Spirit.

34. On this point see Rorabaugh, *The Alcoholic Republic*, and Paul E. Johnson, *A Shopkeeper's Millennium: Society and Revivals in Rochester, New York, 1815–1837* (New York: Hill and Wang, 1978).

35. On this point compare Gusfield, *Symbolic Crusade*, with Clark, *Deliver Us from Evil*.

36. Allen and Leonard, *The Story of the Latter-day Saints* (see chapter 1, note 1, p. 317), pp. 213–214; Leonard J. Arrington, Feramorz Y. Fox, and Dean L. May, *Building the City of God* (chapter 10, note 2, p. 348), pp. 341–348; Thomas G. Alexander, "The Reconstruction of Mormon Doctrine: From Joseph Smith to Progressive Theology," *Sunstone* 5 (July-August 1980), pp. 24–33.

Chapter 14: Definition and Explication of Church Doctrine

1. On the persistence of and challenge to the Baconian ideal in late nineteenth- and early twentieth-century Protestantism see Marsden, *Fundamentalism and American Culture* (see chapter 1, note 7, p. 318), pp. 55–62. The passages interpreted literally are particularly 2 Nephi 2:22 and Alma 12:23 in the Book of Mormon.

2. On the Antinomian controversy see Emery Battis, *Saints and Sectaries: Anne Hutchinson and the Antinomian Controversy in the Massachusetts Bay Colony* (Chapel Hill: University of North Carolina Press, 1962). On the Holiness movement see Timothy L. Smith, *Called Unto Holiness: The Story of the Nazarenes: The Formative Years* (Kansas City, Mo.: Nazarene Publishing House, 1962).

3. Talmage Journal, January 21, 1883, March 15, May 4, 1884, March 14, 1898, September 13, 1899; *Improvement Era*, February 1900, p. 256.

4. Widtsoe, *In a Sunlit Land* (chapter 7, note 20, p. 339), pp. 66–67; Idem., *Joseph Smith as Scientist: A Contribution to Mormon Philosophy* (Salt Lake City: General Board of the YMMIA, 1908).

5. Ibid., p. 1.

6. Ibid., pp. 11, 17, 19–29.

7. Ibid., pp. 35–37. In the Kirtland Temple members experienced direct contact with God and beings from his presence as well as the change of their physical surroundings.

8. Ibid., pp. 57–60, 104–6, 113.

9. Ibid., pp. 109–13.

10. *Improvement Era*, April 1909, pp. 489–94, March 1909, pp. 505–9.

11. Ibid., pp. 391, 393.

12. Richards Journal, September 27, 1909; Talmage Journal, September 27, 30, 1909; J. H. Smith Journal, September 27, 1909; Lund Journal, October 14, 15, 20, 1909.

13. *Improvement Era*, November 1909, pp. 75–81.

14. Roberts, *New Witness for God* (chapter 10, note 5, p. 349) 1 : 422, 435; 2 : chapter 1 passim.

15. *Improvement Era*, September 1914, pp. 1040, 1043–45.

16. Lund Journal, September 22, 1914.

17. Ibid., January 16, 1915.

18. John A. Widtsoe, *Rational Theology as Taught by the Church of Jesus Christ of Latter-day Saints* (Salt Lake City: General Priesthood Committee, 1915), pp. iii, 3, 10, 20–22.

19. Ibid., pp. 45–46.

20. Ibid.

21. Ibid., pp. 46–48; see 2 Nephi 2 : 22–23.

22. Widtsoe, *Rational Theology*, pp. 26–27, 61–62, 64, 146.

23. Lund Journal, December 7, 11, 1914.

24. Talmage Journal, September 14, 1914.

25. Ibid., April 19, 1915; Lund Journal, May 4, 6, 1915; Grant Diary, May 18, 20, June 8, 10, 1915; Richards Journal, June 15, 24, 1915; James E. Talmage, *Jesus the Christ: A Study of the Messiah and His Mission According to Holy Scriptures Both Ancient and Modern* (Salt Lake City: Deseret News, 1915). On the writing of the volume see John R. Talmage, *The Talmage Story: Life of James E. Talmage, Educator, Scientist, Apostle* (Salt Lake City: Bookcraft, 1972), pp. 176–87.

26. Richards Journal, June 19, 1916; Clark, *Messages* 5 : 23–24.

27. Lund Journal, January 21, 1915. Pratt had asserted that "a law of nature has never been broken. And it is an absolute impossiblity that such law ever should be broken." He had also written: "In the former resurrection those raised left the earth and ascended, or were translated far on high, with the risen Jesus to the glorified mansions of his Father, or to some planetary system already redeemed and glorified. The reasons for thus leaving the earth are ob-

vious. Our planet was still in its rudimental state, and therefore subject to the rule of sin and death. It was necessary that it should continue thus, until the full time of redemption should arrive; it was, therefore, entirely unfitted for the residence of immortal man." Both passages were deleted. Parley P. Pratt, *Key to the Science of Theology*, 5th ed. (Liverpool: John Henry Smith, 1853), pp. 104, 139, and 7th ed. (Salt Lake City: Deseret News, 1915), p. 97.

28. Ibid., 5th ed., pp. 39–41, 46, 100–102; 7th ed., pp. 48, 92–94, 100.

29. Doctrine and Covenants, 1883 ed.

30. Ibid., pp. 54–55; Talmage Journal, January 3, 1918.

31. Ibid., March 11, 1921; Richards Journal, March 11, July 19, 1921; Grant Diary, August 20, 1921.

32. Clark, *Messages* (chapter 2, note 12, p. 321) 5:102–6; Doctrine and Covenants (1981 ed.), Section 138.

33. Lund Journal, October 31, 1918.

34. For a discussion of the Fundamentalist-Modernist controversy see Marsden, *Fundamentalism and American Culture* (chapter 1, note 7, p. 318), and Paul A. Carter, *The Spiritual Crisis of the Gilded Age* (Dekalb: Northern Illinois University Press, 1971). For the impact of evolutionary thought in the LDS community during the early twentieth century see Duane E. Jeffrey, "Seers, Savants, and Evolution: The Uncomfortable Interface," *Dialogue* 9 (Autumn-Winter 1973): 41–75, and Richard Sherlock, "A Turbulent Spectrum: Mormon Reactions to the Darwinist Legacy," *Journal of Mormon History* 5 (1978): 33–59.

35. Charles W. Penrose to Joseph W. McMurrin, October 31, 1922, FP, letters sent.

36. Grant Diary, June 22, 1922; First Presidency to William Jennings Bryan, June 24, 1922, FP, letters sent; *Relief Society Magazine*, August 1924, pp. 393–94.

37. Frederick J. Pack, *Science and Belief in God* (Salt Lake City: Deseret News Press, 1924), pp. 212–15, 220–21.

38. Ibid., pp. 206–7, 221.

39. Ibid., pp. 8–9, 11–13, 178, 182.

40. Ibid., pp. 116–125.

41. John A. Widtsoe, *In Search of Truth: Comments on the Gospel and Modern Thought* (Salt Lake City: Deseret Book Co., 1930), passim.

42. JH, July 18, 1925; "Mormon View of Evolution," September 1925, cited in Clark, *Messages* 5:243–44.

43. Richards Journal, July 29–30, 1925; *Improvement Era*, October 1925, pp. 1109–31. For a discussion of the Scopes trial see Marsden, *Fundamentalism and American Culture*, pp. 184–88, 212–14.

44. *Improvement Era*, October 1928, p. 886, October 1930, pp. 804–5.

45. Grant Diary, April 8, 1927; Truman G. Madsen, "The Meaning of Christ—The Truth, the Way, the Life: An Analysis of B. H. Roberts' Unpublished Masterwork," *BYU Studies* 15 (Spring 1975); 260 and passim; and idem., *Defender of the Faith* (chapter 1, note 26, p. 319), pp. 338–45.

46. Jeffrey, "Seers, Savants, and Evolution," p. 56.

47. Joseph Fielding Smith, "Faith Leads to a Fulness of Truth and Righteousness," *Utah Genealogical and Historical Magazine* 30 (October 1930): 145–58.

48. Grant Diary, May 22, 1930, January 16, 1931.

49. Ibid., January 25, 1931. See also Madsen, *Defender of the Faith*, p. 345.

50. Jeffrey, "Seers, Savants, and Evolution," pp. 64–65, 74–75; Grant Diary, February 25, March 30, 1931; James E. Talmage, *The Earth and Man: Address Delivered in the Tabernacle, Salt Lake City, Utah, Sunday, August 9, 1931* (Salt Lake City: Church of Jesus Christ of Latter-day Saints, 1931).

51. Grant Diary, August 16, 1931.

52. JH, May 29, September 15, 1900; *Improvement Era*, October 1900, pp. 939–41, 914–18; Lorenzo Snow to Isaac Riddle, October 23, 1900, FP, letters sent; Whitaker Journal, November 7, 1900; Talmage Journal, October 7, 1900, March 3, 1901; Grant Diary, March 3, 1901; Clark, *Messages* 3:333; Ivins Journal, April 8, 1901; Young Journal, January 1, 1900.

53. JH, December 18, 1926. See also conference talks of general authorities.

54. Smoot Proceedings 3:25; *Improvement Era*, April 1901, p. 466. For the nineteenth-century view on the authority of the priesthood see Klaus J. Hansen, *Quest for Empire: The Political Kingdom of God and the Council of Fifty in Mormon History* ([East Lansing]: Michigan State University Press, 1967) p. 36.

55. Grant Diary, October 8, 1898, January 19, 1899; Lund Journal, January 19, 1899, January 27, 1902; George Reynolds to Henry C. Jordan, March 15, 1899, and to W. G. Sears, October 1, 1900, Lorenzo Snow to James John Abbot, June 19, 1901, First Presidency to Andrew Kimball, July 14, 1902, First Presidency to Hyrum Ricks, May 16, 1903, FP, letters sent; Joseph F. Smith to Joseph E. Robinson, August 12, 1901, Joseph F. Smith Letterbooks; JH, August 2, 1900; Penrose, "Aim, Scope, and Methods of the Mormon Church" (chapter 4, note 8, p. 329), p. 607.

56. Lund Journal, January 9, 1900, September 14, 1903; Leonard J. Arrington, "Economy in the Modern Era," in Ricks and Cooley, *History of a Valley*, p. 205.

57. First Presidency to Fred Tadje, October 18, 1929, cited in Clark, *Messages* 5:268; First Presidency Message, September 1, 1924, ibid. 5:235; JH, August 4, 1924, December 18, 1926; Grant Diary, February 18, 1929.

58. Joseph Smith, *History of the Church of Jesus Christ of Latter-day Saints*, 6 vols. (Salt Lake City: Deseret News, 1902–1912), 1:297; Gordon Irving, "The Law of Adoption: One Phase of the Development of the Mormon Concept of Salvation, 1830–1900," *BYU Studies* 14 (Spring 1974): 291–314; Smith, *History of the Church* 5:167–68; Linda King Newell, "A Gift Given: A Gift Taken: Washing, Anointing, and Blessing the Sick Among Mormon Women," *Sunstone* 6 (September-October 1981): 16–25.

59. Merrill Journal, June 12, 1900; Grant Diary, March 10, 1903; Lund Journal, February 14, 1905, September 19, 1913.

60. Ibid., November 19, 1912.

61. Lund Journal, February 12, 1915, May 21, 1918.

62. Richards Journal, December 14, 1922; First Presidency to George F. Richards, December 15, 1922, circular letter, January 18, 1923, in Clark, *Messages* 5:224; First Presidency to B. H. Roberts, June 2, 1924, FP, letters sent.

63. Newell, "A Gift Given," pp. 16–18; Wells Diary, January 24, February 5, 20, 1903, October 31, 1904.

64. Joseph F. Smith to John D. Chase, August 13, 1901, Joseph F. Smith Letterbooks; First Presidency to J. T. Lesueur, January 20, 1906, and to William A. Hyde, October 3, 1905, FP, letters sent.

65. Clark, *Messages* 4:312–17; Lund Journal, February 4, 1911, December 30, 1918; Wells Diary, June 24, 1909.

66. Claudia L. Bushman, *Mormon Sisters* (see chapter 8, note 23, p. 341), p. 17; First Presidency to A. W. Horsley, December 29, 1922, and to President Charles, November 6, 1923, FP, letters sent.

67. At the time of organizing the Relief Society in 1842, Joseph Smith "gave a lecture on the Priesthood, showing how the sisters would come in possession of the privileges, blessings and gifts of the Priesthood, and that the signs should follow them, such as healing the sick, casting out devils, &c." In the summary of the talk, Joseph is reported to have spoken "of delivering the keys of the Priesthood to the Church, and said that the faithful members of the Relief Society should receive them in connection with their husbands." Smith, *History of the Church* 4:602, 604; see also Newell, "A Gift Given," pp. 17, 20; D. Michael Quinn, "Response," *Sunstone* 6 (September-October 1981): 26–27.

68. *Improvement Era*, March 1907, p. 395, June 1910, pp. 735–38, August 1910, pp. 936–37, September 1911, p. 1032, May 1913, p. 827; Lund Journal, June 13, 1908, August 18, 1915.

69. Bushman, *Mormon Sisters*, pp. 7–8 and passim; *Improvement Era*, January 1900, pp. 172–73, December 1904, pp. 109–11; Eckersley Journal, May 16, 1900, January 31, 1901; George A. Smith Journal, August 6, 1905; Smith, *Gospel Doctrine*, p. 251; Nuttall Diary, August 7, 1899; Wells Journal, February 25, 1900, July 26, 1903; JH, October 25, 1900; Lund Journal, February 1, 1903, June 13, 1908.

70. Kenney, "Mutual Improvement Associations" (chapter 8, note 47, p. 342), p. 12; Eckersley Journal, June 14, 1919; Wells Diary, passim; Lund Journal, February 13, 1917.

71. First Presidency to Heber Q. Hale, March 28, 1923, FP, letters sent.

72. Grant Diary, January 4, 1898; Lund Journal, January 7, 1900. For the nineteenth-century situation see Kimball, *Heber C. Kimball* (see chapter 11, note 1, p. 354), pp. 61–63, 113–14, 248–49; Bushman, *Mormon Sisters*, pp. 3, 6, 11.

73. Grant Diary, January 9, April 3, 1900.

74. *Improvement Era*, November 1905, pp. 55–56.

75. Grant Diary, January 8, 1916, August 2, 1929; Smoot Diary, April 8, 1916; Ballard, *Melvin J. Ballard* (see chapter 11, note 87, p. 358), p. 66.

76. Joseph F. Smith to Joseph J. Porter, February 11, 1902, Joseph F. Smith Letterbooks.

77. Grant Diary, August 8, 9, 1928, May 14, 1930.

78. Kuhn, *The Structure of Scientific Revolutions* (see chapter 1, note 35, p. 320), pp. 56, 59, 64–65, chapters 7 through 10. Victor W. Turner, *The Ritual Process: Structure and Anti-Structure* (Chicago: Aldine, 1969), chapter 3.

79. Lund Journal, December 23, 1917; Widtsoe, *Rational Theology*, p. 157; Pack, *Science and Belief in God*, pp. 28–30, 33.

80. Lund Journal, December 8, 1914.

81. Whitaker Journal, January 27, 1918.

82. Allen and Leonard, *Story of the Latter-day Saints* (chapter 1, note 1, p. 317), pp. 424–25, 480.

83. JH, January 1910; Lund Journal, November 18, 1909.

84. Richards Journal, May 18, 20–21, 1922; JH, March 1924, September 17, 1929, December 23, 1930.

85. Lund Journal, February 4, 1911; Richards Journal, February 13, 1913; Joseph F. Smith to William W. Burton, December 9, 1910, Joseph F. Smith Letterbooks.

86. *Improvement Era*, May 1923, p. 652; Richards Journal, April 17, 1922, October 24, 1922, January 13, April 6, November 1, 1923, January 17, 1924, December 10, 1926, April 20, 1928.

87. Grant Diary, March 10, 1927, and 1927 passim; Smoot Proceedings 3:184.

88. Richards Journal, April 2, 1926.

89. Ibid., September 10, 28, 1926; Smoot Diary, September 11, 29, 1926.

90. Richards Journal, January 3, February 20, 1907, December 14, 1909, September 11, 1914, April 23, 1925; Grant Diary, July 17, 1920.

91. Richards Journal, April 14, 16, 19, 1923, July 12, 1924.

92. JH, January 25, 1915; First Presidency circular letter in Clark, *Messages* 5:110; Lund Journal, July 2, September 25, 1919, October 14, 1920; Richards Journal, April 7, 8, 12, June 25, 1921, April 14, 16, 19, 1923, July 12, 1924.

93. Richards Journal, January 27, May 31, 1922.

94. Ibid., October 11, 1922, April 5, 1923.

95. Ibid., April 14, May 17, 1923.

96. First Presidency, circular letter, June 14, 1923, FP, letters sent.

97. Richards Journal, April 12, June 25, 1921.

98. Ibid., November 15, December 10, 27–28, 1921.

99. Ibid., June 3, July 7, August 21, 1922, April 14, 16, 19, 1923, July 12, 1924; Grant Diary, July 21, 30, 1922.

100. Richards Journal, December 9, 1926, January 25, 1927.

101. First Council of the Seventy Minutes, October 24, 1900.

102. Lorenzo Snow to Edward Koyle, Jr., December 19, 1900, FP, letters sent; Grant Diary, April 12, 1900; JH, June 10, 1900; Lund Journal, April 15, 1902; *Improvement Era*, February 1903, pp. 303–8; Richards Journal, February 8, 1907.

103. Richards Journal, February 8, 1907; Joseph F. Smith to Elias A. Smith, Jr., July 21, 1913, Joseph F. Smith Letterbooks; *Improvement Era*, November 1923, p. 180; JH, June 2, 1924; Helen Z. Papanikolas, "Toil and Rage in a New Land: The Greek Immigrants in Utah," *Utah Historical Quarterly* 38 (Spring 1970): 181; idem, ed., *The Peoples of Utah* (Salt Lake City: Utah State Historical Society, 1976), p. 323. For a general history of the KKK in Utah see Gerlach, *Blazing Crosses in Zion* (chapter 3, note 67, p. 327).

104. First Council of the Seventy Minutes, May 27, July 15, 1903; Lund Journal, May 23, 1903; Talmage Journal, January 13, 21, 22, 24, 1921; Richards Journal, January 21–24, 26, 1921. For further information on these and other matters see B. H. Roberts, "Book of Mormon Difficulties: A Study," and "A Book of Mormon Study," B. H. Roberts to Richard R. Lyman, October 24, 1927, in B. H. Roberts, *Studies of the Book of Mormon*, ed. Brigham D. Madsen (Urbana: University of Illinois Press, 1985). Roberts was particularly concerned that the "brethren" consider the problems addressed in his studies, especially in regard to their impact on the youth of the church and casual inquirers (Roberts, *Studies of the Book of Mormon*, p. 79). See also Truman G. Madsen, "B. H. Roberts and the Book of Mormon," *BYU Studies* 19 (Summer 1979): 427–45, and George D. Smith, "'Is There Any Way to Escape These Difficulties?': The Book of Mormon Studies of B. H. Roberts," *Dialogue* 17, no. 2 (Summer 1984): 94–111. For an attempt to deal with some of the problems see John L. Sorenson, *An Ancient American Setting for the Book of Mormon* (Salt Lake City: Deseret Book, 1985).

105. Richards Journal, March 18, April 13, October 12, 1920; Lund Journal, May 26, April 15, July 3, 28, 1902; Grant Diary, November 9, 1920, *Relief Society Magazine*, February 1921, pp. 96–97; *Improvement Era*, February 1921, pp. 53–55; Clark, *Messages* 5:186; Talmage, *The Talmage Story*, pp. 192–93.

106. For a preliminary discussion of this idea see Shipps, "In the Presence of the Past" (chapter 4, note 33, p. 331), pp. 3–35.

Index

Note on the Author

THOMAS G. ALEXANDER is professor of history and director of the Charles Redd Center for Western Studies at Brigham Young University. His previous publications include *A Dependent Commonwealth: Utah's Economy from Statehood to the Great Depression* (with Leonard J. Arrington and Dean L. May), *A Clash of Interests: Interior Department and Mountain West, 1863–96*; and *Mormons and Gentiles: A History of Salt Lake City* (with James B. Allen).